The BODY HEALER PROTOCOL

Heal Your Body and Transform Your Life with High Vibrational Living

Irini Dieringer

Published by Wolfwood Press
1425 Broadway, Suite 206666
Seattle, WA 98122

copyright@wolfwoodpress.com

Published in the United States of America

First edition published 2017

Library of Congress Control Number is available upon request.

Paperback (Color) ISBN: 978-0-9993140-0-5
Paperback (B/W) ISBN: 978-0-9993140-2-9
eBook ISBN: 978-0-9993140-1-2

Cover Art by Eden Graphics

Editorial by Sharon Honeycutt

Interior Design by Laura Reynolds

Energy Illustrations by Irini Vazanellis

DISCLAIMER

This publication is designed to provide accurate and authoritative information in regard to the subject matter covered, and this book should by no means be considered a substitute for qualified medical professional advice. It is sold with the understanding that the publisher and author are not engaged in rendering medical services. The publisher and the author make no representations or warranties with respect to the completeness of the contents of this work. The health advice presented in this book is intended only as an informative resource guide to help you make informed decisions; it is not meant to replace the advice of a physician or to serve as a guide to any self-treatment. The author and publisher expressly disclaim responsibility for any adverse effects arising from the use or application of the information contained herein. The fact that an organization or website is referred to in this work as a citation and/or a potential source of further information does not mean that the author or the publisher endorses the information that the organization or website may provide or recommendations it may make, nor does the cited organization endorse affiliation of any sort to this publication. Also, readers should be aware that due to the ever-changing information from the web, Internet websites and URLs listed in this work may have changed or been removed.

All trademarks or names referenced in this book are the property of their respective owners, and the publisher and author are not associated with any product or vendor mentioned.

ACKNOWLEDGMENTS

I'd like to start by humbly acknowledging the spiritual guidance that led me to the path of high vibrational living. The constant flow of information and inspiration has served as my driving force, enriching my world beyond measure and opening me up to a deeper and more profound respect and appreciation for all life.

I'm incredibly lucky and honored to be surround by an amazing family who have unconditionally loved, supported, and encouraged me on my mission to share what I have learned with the world. Thank you so much for always being there for me.

A very special thanks to my wonderful husband for his endless patience and understanding on my literary journey.

I'm very grateful to the pioneers, such as Dr. Richard Gerber, Dr. Raymond Rife, Deepak Chopra, John and Ocean Robbins, Bruce Tainio, Jane Roberts, and many others who helped pave the foundation for a new era of awakening we are only just beginning to enter.

A big thank you to all the people who were instrumental in bringing this book together. The lovely layout of my book reflects the creativity of Laura Reynolds who developed a theme with subtle beauty. Laura, I hope the pleasure of the final result far outweighs the pain it caused you! A big thanks to Fran at Eden Graphics for bringing her artistic vision to the beautiful cover design and creating such a striking energy visual. Sharon Honeycutt, my wonderful editor, thank you for helping me transform a muddled mess of grammatical errors into a polished manuscript – it was a very humbling experience.

Last, but not least, to the pets and animals whose presence have enriched my life beyond measure and helped me want to make this world a better place for all living things, I'm eternally grateful for your companionship along my journey.

To all my readers ready to walk the path of power and live the high vibrational life,
I dedicate this book to you.

PREFACE

Dear Friends and Readers,

Welcome to the world of high vibrational living! I'm honored that I get to introduce you to the world of high vibrations and share this journey of discovery with you.

I'd like to spend a few minutes explaining what high vibrational living is and showing you how it is a whole new way to transform your entire life by harnessing the power of energy. I ask only that you make a small commitment of just 1 month to my program. If you will do that, I promise that you will never turn back.

Lighter & Brighter

Over the past few years, the term "energy" has popped up in many different catchphrases. You may have heard of "energy frequency" or "life force energy." How about "high vibrational foods" or "energy medicine"?

Prior to learning about high vibrational living, when we wanted to make changes in our lives, we looked at the circumstances we didn't like and took physical action with the goal of successfully making these changes. Sound familiar? This approach, however, does not deal with the fundamental root cause that lies at the bottom of any imbalance we're experiencing, whether that imbalance is with our body—being overweight, suffering from a chronic disease, or feeling depressed; or with our lives—being in debt, working in a job we don't enjoy, or being in an unfulfilling or unhappy relationship. Sometimes, we may feel a sense of discontentment and disconnection, yet we don't know why. In short, we're experiencing an imbalance that expresses itself in some form as unhappiness or dissatisfaction.

When it comes to trying to make our lives better, we habitually try to change the *effect* without changing the *cause*. What if I told you that the root cause of *any* imbalance can be reduced to two simple words? And what if I told you that you can restore your body and your mind to a state of balance—and all the circumstances in your life to a state of happiness and contentment—at any moment in time using the power of these two words?

A Different Perception

Energy Frequency: Everything that exists can be reduced to these two simple words. Science may have taught us that every object has its own vibrational frequency, but the world of quantum physics has expanded this knowledge to take us into a new era. We now know that everything that exists possesses a vibrational frequency, be it a physical object (such as an apple, a table, our physical body) or a nonphysical object (a thought-form, an emotion, a feeling).

The frequency that radiates out from our body is the cumulative result of the thoughts we think, the foods we eat, and the lifestyle choices we make.

Our frequency can attract higher vibrational people, events, objects, and circumstances that are the stuff dreams are made of, or it can attract just the opposite—debt, ill health, unhappy situations, and depression. By raising our vibrational frequency, we can immediately begin attracting different things into our lives that also resonate at these higher frequencies. Let me take you by the hand and show you how to do just that.

In the coming years, high vibrational living will become a household phrase as more and more people embrace the fundamental truth that they have the power to change everything in their lives by actively learning how to change their vibrational frequency. Disease will no longer exist as we will have risen above the frequencies that generate these diseases. Depression will transform into contentment, and debt into wealth. Poverty is the result of poverty consciousness, and it will be a part of the world we leave behind.

In short, we are embarking on a path where we evolve far beyond where we are now, as the power of high vibrational living propels us into a whole new world of discovery.

This journey begins by recognizing that almost everything you have been told about dieting, health, happiness, and longevity is unreliable and will yield marginal results at best. These old paradigms encompass a tunnel-vision approach if they do not address energy frequency, which is the foundation—the root cause—of the imbalance we are trying to address.

A Bit about Me

Since my early teens, I have been immersed in a relentless pursuit for the meaning of life. I soaked up every book I could find on philosophy, metaphysics, mind/body medicine, and the energetics of the human body. I became deeply absorbed in quantum physics at the same time I began discovering the interconnected nature of all things. This knowledge began to form a key to finding answers to questions I had about creation and existence that had evaded me.

My qualifications don't just come from my studies, a degree, or some other piece of paper. What helps me effectively guide you on this journey and identify with you is that I've been where you are now. You'll get the benefit of learning from someone who has personal experience, someone who's been to hell and back when it comes to their body.

I've weighed 210 pounds (being just over 5 foot), living the life of eating Jack in the Box for breakfast, McDonald's for lunch, and an endless variety of fried foods and frozen meals for dinner. My staple foods were Twix, Toblerone, Peanut M&Ms, and double Western bacon cheeseburgers from Carl's Jr. I've lived through acne that was so bad, I hated leaving the house. I've had cellulite that was so awful, I wouldn't be caught dead in shorts or a bathing suit. I've experienced depression and anxiety that was so intense, I'd pray that when I went to sleep at night, I'd not wake up the next morning. I've suffered insomnia that was so chronic, I'd go for over a week at a time with no sleep, which led to an addiction to Ambien. I also suffered from terrible restless leg syndrome and all sorts of gastrointestinal issues.

When it comes to diets and dietary philosophies, I've lived through so many I lost count long ago. Diet pills and supplements? Well, you could start a supplement megastore with what I've used!

I have also felt completely powerless, immersed in debt and working dead-end jobs that could barely provide enough to enable me to make my rent payment and pay for basic utilities, never mind food and gas. Embracing my power to recognize that I am the master of my destiny and that I could manifest whatever I wanted was not a part of my reality.

Really ... I've been there.

At the end of it all, I discovered that being slim wasn't about following any diet, and being healthy wasn't about popping pills or placing blind faith in doctors and a healthcare system that has directly contributed to today's healthcare epidemic. Feeling happy and fulfilled and successful wasn't about believing that I was destined for mediocrity, while other people were destined for all the great stuff I was being denied, nor was it about blaming others for my lot in life or wallowing in my own pity party. It was all about understanding that every single life experience I was having was a result of my state of mind, my environment, and the diet and lifestyle choices *that either raised or lowered my vibrational state.*

When it comes to healing from disease, my experience has taught me that high vibrational energy and high vibrational foods are the most powerful "drugs" on earth.

The transformation of my body and my life began with the transformation of my mind. It all came down to energy and vibration—what energy is, how it impacts us, and how we can work with it and direct it. I quickly realized that the only obstacle to an amazing life was me. I simply lacked an understanding of the nature of reality and the role energy plays, and when I finally figured that out ... well, there was no stopping me from claiming the destiny of MY choice!

I began as an ordinary girl investigating extraordinary things and came full circle to the realization that we are all extraordinary beings.

Today at 46, I'm in better shape than I have ever been in my life. I'm a healthy, vibrant 131 pounds with no health issues and flawless bloodwork at my annual physicals. I live in a beautiful home with more than enough money to be very comfortable. I am blessed to be surrounded by my incredible family of the human, furry, and scaly kind. Debt and poverty consciousness are no longer part of my reality because I released them a long time ago.

My Goal

I have no desire to convince anyone of anything. I don't have a religion or philosophy or a diet to promote. My goal is to simply help you break free from the illusion that you're less than capable of easily achieving everything you've ever wanted in life, and to help you awaken and understand how powerful you really are. I will help you release the social conditioning, outdated beliefs, and limiting perceptions that bind you to a life of limits and lack, disease and distress.

Once you experience a higher vibrational state, you'll no longer need to follow the "diet of the moment" or "guru of the day" to search for the answers because you'll understand that you possess all you need to have whatever you want. The words "diet" and "illness" will no longer be part of your vocabulary, and your health will experience a quantum leap forward. The words "debt" and "struggle" will lose their power, and all you want to achieve will flow to you effortlessly. How? Because your vibrational frequency dictates whether these things come to you or whether they don't.

You are about to embark on the path toward achieving success, living a happy and healthy life, healing your body, and transforming yourself into the limitless being you were born to be.

Are you ready? Well then, let's get started!

Irini Dieringer
Castle Rock, Colorado
November 1, 2017

TABLE OF CONTENTS

PART III: LIVE, THRIVE, EVOLVE!

INTRODUCTION

This book is going to introduce you to a whole new way of life, forever changing your perception of the world and your place in it. You'll experience a higher level of consciousness that will reveal to you the limitless nature of your existence and your infinite potential to be, do, and have whatever you choose.

Whatever you came here to find, I promise that not only will you find the answers to your questions, but you'll also discover so much more! Let's take a quick look at what the Body Healer Protocol has in store for you.

Your body will transform

Disease will become a thing of the past as you learn how to rebuild your health, bulletproof your immune system, and transform chronic disease into radiant health. Your weight will normalize, and the niggling aches and pains will fade away. Your entire digestive tract will be healed, freeing you from common complaints, such as gas, heartburn, indigestion, postnasal drip, constipation, and diarrhea. You'll move from medication-dependent to medication-free and see why age is not synonymous with sickness. In short, you'll experience a level of health you've never encountered before.

You will ...

Speed up your metabolism naturally
Lose weight quickly and easily—no diets
Heal your body from disease
Bulletproof your immune system
Make healthy and highly nutritious food choices
Detoxify your body with high vibrational foods
Prepare simple, quick meals
Eliminate cellulite and tighten loose skin
Slow down the aging process

When it comes to weight loss, the Body Healer Protocol is the fastest, healthiest, and most effective approach to not only getting rid of all the excess pounds, but also keeping them off. There are no diet foods filled with synthetic chemicals, refined ingredients, pesticides, or GMOs. No tape measures, scales, calories, or calculations. No more meal plans following rigid low-carb, high-protein, or low-fat guidelines. Why? Because these are part of the problem, not the solution. They are a tunnel-vision approach to weight loss, and they are not in the best interest of your weight OR your long-term health.

Your mind will transform

The biggest change you'll experience is that you'll feel inexplicably happy just to be alive. Knowing that you can achieve anything you want and that *you* are your *only* limit permanently frees you from stress and anxiety. Depression melts away as you enter a state of inner calm and contentment. Your intuition skyrockets as you become in tune with the world around you, and you'll experience levels of consciousness and creativity that will change your life forever.

You will ...

Sharpen your mind and memory
Dissolve stress
Heal from depression
Eliminate antidepressants and sleep aids
Develop extrasensory abilities

Your life will transform

As you strip away your limiting thoughts and perceptions, all things become possible. You begin to realize your potential to become the limitless person you were born to be. In the MIND section of the protocol, you'll learn how to master the power of energy to manifest your goals and create the life of your dreams. Because debt can only exist in poverty consciousness, your money worries become a thing of the past.

Step-by-step instructions will take you by the hand and show you how to:

- ***Discover*** your passion and unlock your potential
- ***Change*** your life by changing your mind
- ***Remove*** obstacles and limitations to your success
- ***Turn*** dreams and goals into accomplishments
- ***Discover*** the 7 golden rules to creating the life you want
- ***Get empowered***, get motivated, and GET going!

The Body Healer Protocol is the most powerful protocol on this planet when it comes to achieving a state of vibrant health and longevity. It's a 100 percent natural, noninvasive approach designed to quickly cleanse the body at a cellular level, remove accumulated toxins, and resolve physical, emotional, and psychological imbalances.

How is it possible that a protocol can do all this? How can a protocol fix everything in your life and bring you back into a state of perfect balance?

It's all about high vibrational living.

It's about learning how to raise the vibrational frequency of your body to a healthy range through the power of high vibrational living. We do this by following the Body Healer Protocol.

Let me take you by the hand and show you how to experience a mind/body transformation that will change your world forever!

BEFORE WE DIG IN

Before we get started, let's talk about what to expect and how to follow the program. As you read through each section, take all the time you need to absorb the information. Give yourself permission to open up and experience a new way of looking at both yourself and the world around you.

Important! Follow the Order of the Program

Because this program builds upon itself and is meant to be experienced in a specific sequence, I'm asking you not to randomly view pages or sections until you've completed the entire program. This way, you'll gain the most benefit and learn all the important elements you need to know.

Homework Assignments

Each homework assignment is very important, so please make sure you complete them. As you work through these assignments and progress through each section, you'll begin to seriously reevaluate not only what you've considered to be healthy choices when it comes to the food you eat and your lifestyle habits, but also the very nature of your existence and the role you play in consciously creating your day-to-day reality.

You'll begin to think more expansively as you embrace the concept that you are a powerful creator. You move from powerless to empowered and explode through limiting thoughts and actions. A fundamental change in your mind-set becomes the driving force that propels you from a state of disease to a state of health.

Can't You Just Give Me a Quick Summary of What to Do?

Sorry, but there's no such thing as a "quick summary" when it comes to losing weight, getting healthy, and learning the principles of high vibrational living. Why am I not simply telling you what to do, what to eat, and what lifestyle changes to make without explaining why? Because in order to make these changes permanent and to fully grasp the consequences that can come from not integrating these changes into your life, you need a solid understanding of *why* they're important.

It is very important you take the time to learn the "why's."

You need to understand the critical role that energy and vibrational frequencies play in your health and evolution, and how your eating habits and lifestyle choices affect both your state of mind and the health of your body. Without this understanding, you would find it difficult to grasp the true cause of imbalance. It would never fully hit home, and the "summary" would be meaningless.

When something makes sense, it clicks, and you experience a mind-shift. When something hits a nerve and illuminates that lightbulb in your head, when you have a moment of true understanding, that's when real change takes place.

When something is right and you know it, you can feel it. It resonates with you on a deeper, more meaningful level because you're tapping into a fundamental truth to who you really are. You suddenly know you're on the right path and that you've made the right decisions because you *feel* it deep in your gut, not because of this protocol, your doctor, your parents, your spouse, your neighbors, your friends, or a health guru on the Internet. This is the moment the transformation begins.

So, no, I can't give you a summary, but I can promise you this: The Body Healer Protocol is not complicated. In fact, it's very simple! All the concepts are easy to learn and just as easy to integrate into your life.

Prepare for Change

There's no doubt about it: a natural approach to living and healing from disease is a radical departure from the more traditional, medicated way of thinking, just as eating natural, healthy foods is radically different from eating the foods that make up the standard American diet.

Always embrace your starting point, wherever it is. If you have farther to go than the next person, that simply means you'll experience a more dramatic transformation. Let this be a powerful motivating force! Restoring your entire being to a state of vibrant health is a process, not a single event. Results won't happen overnight, but change begins immediately and results will follow quickly.

Any diet or healthcare program that promises you overnight success; any "cure" based on supplements, powders, or pills; or any concoction that promises a magical transformation is selling you fool's gold. By the time you've finished this protocol, you'll be supremely confident and secure in your knowledge of how to rebalance your body so that you'll never fall victim to these fads again.

Getting Centered

If you've received a disease diagnosis such as cancer, heart disease, or diabetes, you may be in a state of shock or panic. You may feel lost, helpless, and overwhelmed by fear. If this describes how you feel, the first thing we're going to do is get centered. For the next few minutes, stop and take a breather. You don't experience this type of shock to your system every day, but you also don't get to decide to reclaim your power to make some very big changes—changes that turn the tables and immediately begin restoring your body to health—every day either.

> "Out of clutter, simplicity is the trademark of genius."
>
> Robin S. Sharma

If you've taken too many trips on the diet merry-go-round and feel resigned to throwing in the towel and being overweight for the rest of your life, then you can breathe one great big sigh of relief because you've reached your destination. Excess weight is a health condition that involves the breakdown of various systems within the body. We don't treat it by "going on a diet." Instead, we restore the organs and systems to a state of health using a whole-body approach. The end result is that the body heals on all levels, with the natural side effect of achieving your perfect weight. It simply "happens."

If knowing what to do suddenly feels too complicated, understand that it's not. If taking action seems too difficult, understand that it will be much easier than you think, because once you commit to the protocol and take the first step, you'll be well on your way.

The very first step involves accepting and anticipating that changing your health means changing your life, and fully embracing that change.

The Energy of Change

When it comes to making big changes in our lives, we must first recognize and honor the process of transitioning from where we are to where we're headed. That transition can be uncomfortable. When we energetically set changes in motion, it's perfectly normal to experience instability and to feel uneasy as we release our attachment to the old and begin opening ourselves up to the new. This is a time for reevaluation, for making big changes to diet and lifestyle habits, for challenging our beliefs and the foundations they're built on, and for letting go of what no longer serves our greater growth.

The arrival of any health condition is a sign that our body has become imbalanced and that, in order to heal, change is inevitable. If we continue as we are, it's highly likely that our health will continue to decline. The energy of change can sometimes appear as destructive because by its very nature it's transformational. It involves changing habits that have been ingrained for a long time, changing the way we think, and embracing a new and much more expansive mind-set. We must begin deconstructing the beliefs that imprison us into believing that health is beyond our control and that our only options are highly invasive treatments and a medicated approach to living. Our insecurities and fears will crumble in the face of this enlightenment.

> "It takes courage to grow up & become who you really are."
>
> E. E. Cummings

We often feel resistance when we begin to let go of the familiar because it's all we know. We're used to it, it's comfortable and predictable, yet it's also what brought us to our current state today. We often feel fearful of anything that takes us out of our comfort zone, and swift and unexpected change (which often seems to arrive from nowhere) challenges our sense of security.

Regardless, in order for you to take control of your health and heal yourself of any health condition, you must be prepared to make some big changes. When we release our need to cling to outdated beliefs that tell us we have little control over our health and what will become of us, we set the wheels of change in motion. In no time, we are propelled into a new emotional and psychological space with the courage to push forward into unchartered territory. Not only does the light at the end of the tunnel become brighter, but the tunnel itself begins to disintegrate.

The Highs & Lows

Tough times will happen ... guaranteed! You're human, not superhuman—yet. You'll be incredibly proud of your progress in the protocol, and you'll feel fantastic about how well you've committed to new diet and lifestyle habits, and even though you've faithfully integrated the energetics of a completely different mind-set ... you'll experience a setback. Whether it's something as small as eating food that you know is harmful to your health or the emotional trauma of an upsetting medical test result that spirals you into panic, setbacks happen to all of us.

Remember ... *healing is a process, and it will take time.* When you have a setback, don't let it sap your motivation or make you feel that you've somehow failed. You haven't. Just get yourself right back on track as soon as possible because a setback is never a reason or an excuse to give up. It was just a moment where you veered off the path and then quickly stepped right back to where you should be. If everybody who experienced a setback gave up, heaven knows where we'd be in our state of evolution.

Always keep this in mind:

The present moment is always your point of power.

Because you've been hard at work cleaning up and detoxifying your body, it will bounce back quickly from any setbacks.

Once you begin to incorporate the principles of high vibrational living into your life, your body will naturally begin to function at a higher frequency. You'll no longer need any guru, website, or book (including this one) to tell you what's high vibrational and what's not, because you'll instinctively know. You'll sense it. You'll be fully empowered to no longer need anyone or anything for external validation.

The Root Cause of Disease

Let's launch into our first section and learn all about the root cause of disease (humans and pets alike). We'll begin by exploring the fascinating world of light, energy, and vibration, and we'll discover how it holds the golden key to health, wealth, and happiness.

Are you ready? Great! Then let's get started ...

PART I

THE FOUNDATION

THE ROOT CAUSE OF DISEASE

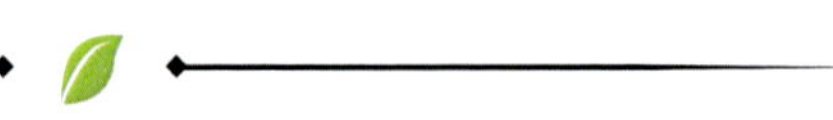

IT'S ALL ABOUT ENERGY & VIBRATION

Even though our physical senses fool us into thinking objects are solid, they aren't. Everything around us is made up of energy vibrating at different frequencies. Everything that exists, each object (including our body), is a whirling mass of intelligent, responsive, vibrating energy.

Not only does our body have its own vibrational frequency, but so does each of our organs. Every illness also vibrates at a given frequency, as does every food, such as a fruit, vegetable, nut, seed, and grain.

The energy that radiates out from our physical bodies interacts with other energies around us, and our surroundings, the quality of the food we eat, the air we breathe, the water we drink, and the thoughts we think affect that energy. It's constantly changing, depending on the thoughts and emotions we experience at any given moment in time, as well as the thoughts, emotions, and energy of others in our home and work environments.

This energy is the fuel that continuously recreates not only our bodies, but also the life that we experience based on our thoughts and intentions. Although we can't see this energy with our physical eyes, it does exist. Using special types of photography and equipment, we can actually see and measure this energy.

Not only are we composed of energy, but our bodies are also very effective transmitters and receivers of energy. Our thoughts play an important role in our energetic state; because they're created from energy, the higher the quality of our thoughts, the higher the vibration they generate. The lower the quality of our thoughts, the lower the vibration they generate. When we think and speak, we send out ripples of energy, affecting life all around us. Our state of mind, whether positive or negative, exerts a powerful effect on the vibrational state of our body.

Fear-based energies, such as anxiety, stress, anger, doubt, envy, criticism, and hate, are low vibrational in nature and can create havoc within our energy system. They can cause sluggish energy flow or energy blockages, or they can overstimulate energy in areas of the body. Similarly, love-based emotions, such as love, kindness, gratitude, peace, and generosity, are high vibrational in nature and assist in raising the overall vibration of our bodies.

Whether it's unhealthy diet and lifestyle choices, environmental factors, or negative (fear-based) thoughts that consistently fill our minds, all of these things have one thing in common: they lower the vibrational frequency of the body to the point that it becomes receptive to disease.

Our Blueprint

The energy that forms our physical body does so based on an energetic pattern called a blueprint, which determines how energy is ultimately expressed in our physical form. Each person possesses a unique blueprint, and as we evolve and become more enlightened beings, this blueprint evolves and changes how our physical body looks and functions.

Using the analogy of a computer, sometimes our blueprint produces corrupt data (unhealthy cells and tissues); however, our blueprint also contains the original set of instructions to replace corrupt data with uncorrupt data (healthy cells and tissues). So once we raise the vibrational frequency of our body, the blueprint automatically begins to replicate healthy cells again.

Because we're evolving, our blueprint is different from our ancestors'. It has slowly evolved to enable us to access higher vibrational frequencies, abilities, states of consciousness, and in turn, a "lighter" version of our physical body. This is why strictly following our ancestors' diets isn't the answer nor is it in our best interest when it comes to our health and longevity today.

Evolving beyond Disease

To evolve beyond a life of all imbalance (disease, weight problems, stress, depression, and fear-based emotions), you need to:

1. Learn how to raise the frequency of your body through the food you eat and the lifestyle habits you adopt, and
2. Learn how the frequencies of surrounding energies impact you.

With this knowledge, you can free yourself from the illusion that you're powerless when it comes to transforming both your life and your health. This protocol will teach you how your food, your state of mind, the way you breathe, and the type of basic physical activity you choose are major components to restoring your blueprint expression to full radiance.

Before we get into how we quickly and efficiently cultivate a state of health, let's spend a few minutes talking more about our body's frequency and the frequency of disease.

VIBRATIONAL FREQUENCIES OF THE BODY

During his agricultural work, Bruce Tainio of Tainio Technology invented a machine called the BT3 Frequency Monitoring System that contains a highly sensitive sensor that measures bioelectrical frequencies. This system can also measure human vibrational frequencies by taking readings of various parts of the body and averaging those numbers together. This machine is currently used in the agricultural industry and is considered 100 percent accurate.

Studies conducted in 1992 by Tainio Technology showed that when a person's frequency drops below the optimal healthy range, the immune system becomes compromised, which reinforced findings of earlier researchers (more on these findings below).

The daytime frequency of a healthy human body vibrates at an average of 62–78 MHz. Below are the frequency ranges for various parts of the body:

72–90 MHz – the brain

72–78 MHz – the human body from neck up

60–68 MHz – the human body from neck down

62–68 MHz – the thyroid and parathyroid glands

65–68 MHz – the thymus gland

67–70 MHz – the heart

58–65 MHz – the lungs

55–60 MHz – the liver

60–80 MHz – the pancreas

Even more interesting, however, was the discovery that a different frequency is associated with each disease, and that when our body's frequency drops, we become more susceptible to these diseases. Human cells can start to change (mutate) when their frequency drops below a frequency of 62 MHz.

58 MHz – the frequency receptive to colds or the flu

55 MHz – the frequency receptive to candida overgrowth

52 MHz – the frequency receptive to pneumonia/Epstein-Barr

42 MHz – the frequency receptive to cancer

20 MHz – the frequency when death begins

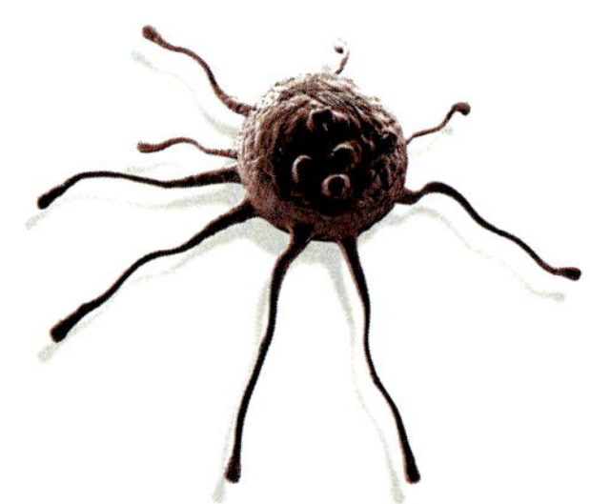

Vibrational Frequencies of Essential Oils

Working with Gary Young, a naturopathic doctor[1] Tainio also measured the frequencies of various therapeutic-grade essential oils and found some interesting results:

320 MHz – Rose (Rosa damascena)

118 MHz – Lavender (Lavendul angustifolia)

105 MHz – Myrrh (Commiphora myrrha)

105 MHz – Blue Chamomile (Matricaria recutita)

98 MHz – Juniper (Juniperus osteosperma)

96 MHz – Sandalwood (Santalum album)

85 MHz – Angelica (Angelica archangelica)

78 MHz – Peppermint (Mentha piperita)

56 MHz – Galbanum (Ferula gummosa)

52 MHz – Basil (Ocimum basilicum)

What is a MHz?

MHz is an abbreviation for megahertz. The MHz number is a measurement of how fast molecules vibrate (known as their "frequency").

1 hertz	=	1 cycle per second (CPS)
1 kilohertz	=	1,000 CPS
1 megahertz	=	1 million CPS
1 gigahertz	=	1 billion CPS
1 terahertz	=	1 trillion CPS

What about the Frequency of Our Environment?

Let's take a look at the different things that affect our vibrational frequency.

- Every single type of food we eat contains its own vibrational frequency, some much higher than others. Fresh, organic, sun-ripened fruits and vegetables resonate at a much higher frequency than heavily processed, refined foods and canned foods, which essentially resonate close to or at 0 MHz (more on this later). What happens when we continually eat foods that vibrate at a lower frequency than our bodies? We begin to automatically resonate to these lower frequencies, opening the door to disease.
- Our thoughts and feelings have a measurable vibrational frequency. A negative mental attitude can lower a person's frequency by 10–12 MHz, whereas a positive mental attitude can raise it by the same amount or more.
- Chronic stress causes a big dip in our vibrational state. Most of us experience stressful situations and emotional challenges on a daily basis; after all, we're only human. But for many people, stress becomes chronic and long-term, and it's this type of stress that damages the body.

- Environmental pollutants, such as those in the air we breathe and the water we drink, lower our body's frequency. Chemical contaminants in municipal water are especially damaging because we drink and bathe in this water every day.
- Because we use them daily and in large quantities, artificial and denatured chemicals and ingredients in personal-care products, such as lotions, toothpaste, shampoos, conditioners, and cosmetics have a very detrimental impact on our body's frequency.
- All the electrical devices in our home (and office)—lights, televisions, radios, phones, cell phones, microwaves, appliances, and computers—emit electromagnetic frequencies that are chaotic. No, you don't have to give them up, but be mindful that they can and do affect the human energy field. The healthier your body is and the better you care for it with appropriate food and lifestyle choices, the less your electrical devices will negatively affect you.

Living a high vibrational lifestyle can help us raise our body's vibration to the point that it naturally begins to resonate at a higher frequency and can no longer be a breeding ground for sickness.

In further studies, Tainio and Young also discovered frequency changes within the body when different substances were introduced. For example, simply holding a cup of coffee caused a frequency drop of 7 MHz, while drinking the coffee caused a frequency drop of 14 MHz. When essential oils were then introduced, the frequency loss was regained within a matter of seconds, but without the essential oils, it took 3 days to recover the frequency drop.

Being aware of the different things that impact us at a vibrational level can help us begin to take steps to reduce our exposure to those that can lower our body's vibration and to increase the things that raise our vibrational level. In doing so, we close the door to sicknesses and diseases that resonate at lower frequencies.

Lower frequencies cause physical degenerative changes to the body. Higher frequencies stimulate not only health restoration, but also intuitive, extrasensory, and transformative responses within the body that are spiritual in nature.

The study of energy frequencies shows us that natural foods and healthy lifestyle habits heal us and that unhealthy foods and lifestyle habits harm us. If the majority of our diet doesn't contribute to raising our frequency above 60, then we have a problem.

Diseased states thrive only in a low frequency environment, not in a high vibrational body. By changing our vibrational state, we can prevent the future development of symptoms and illnesses—ranging from the common cold to cancer—before they occur.

Cancer Cured

Doctor and scientist Royal R. Rife, MD (1888–1971) developed a machine called a "frequency generator" in the late 1920s that applied specific frequency currents to the body. He discovered that not only does every cell, tissue, and organ resonate at its own frequency, but that every disease also has a specific frequency, as Tainio later discovered.

Dr. Rife demonstrated that using specific frequencies, he could destroy a cancer cell or a virus. He also found that certain frequencies could prevent the development of disease, whereas others could neutralize it. Substances with higher frequencies destroyed diseases of a lower frequency.

In the 1930s, Dr. Rife successfully treated 1,000 patients who were diagnosed with incurable cancer, and he was honored with 14 awards and an honorary doctorate. Pharmaceutical companies tried unsuccessfully to buy out his research and equipment. His office was subsequently raided, his research paperwork stolen, and the machine that cured the "incurable" cancer patients was destroyed.

Fortunately, before his property was destroyed, the University of Southern California appointed a special medical research committee to bring terminal cancer patients from Pasadena County Hospital to Dr. Rife's clinic in San Diego, California, for treatment. The research team included both pathologists and doctors to examine all patients ninety days after the treatment.

The committee concluded that a staggering 86.5 percent of patients were completely cured.

Treatment was adjusted for the remaining 13.5 percent of the patients, and they responded within the following four weeks. The total recovery rate was 100 percent, a boast no pharmaceutical company or cancer treatment center on earth can make. Rife had effectively developed a 100 percent–effective cure for many forms of cancer.

"Using specific frequencies, cancer cells or a virus can be destroyed. Certain frequencies can prevent development of disease, whereas others can neutralize it."

Dr. Royal R. Rife

Why isn't the general public aware of this? Why is this technology not in use today? Treating cancer is a multibillion-dollar business, and there's no profit for the pharmaceutical giants who produce chemotherapy drugs if cancer is cured. The National Institutes of Health (NIH) estimated the overall cost of cancer to be over $200 billion. Making cancer go away is not in Big Pharma's best interest.

Similar Findings

- Robert O. Becker, MD, author of the best seller The Body Electric, tells us that the human body has an electrical frequency, and that a person's health can be determined by the frequency of their body.
- In the early 1980s, Swedish radiologist Bjorn Nordenstrom discovered that by putting an electrode inside a cancer tumor and running a milliamp of DC current through that electrode, the growth of the tumor can be stopped and dissolved.
- Nikola Tesla (1856–1943), an American inventor and pioneer in the field of electrical technology, stated that if we could eliminate certain outside frequencies that interfered in our bodies, we would have greater resistance toward disease.
- Richard Gerber, MD, author of the best seller Vibrational Medicine, stated that administering therapeutic doses of frequency-specific subtle energy in the form of vibrational medicines is one of the best ways to change dysfunctional patterns in our energy bodies.
- Albert Szent-Gyorgyi, Nobel Laureate in Medicine (1937), stated, "In every culture and in every medical tradition before ours, healing was accomplished by moving energy."

The Hippocrates Health Institute

The Hippocrates Health Institute also conducted research into the electrical frequencies of various types of food and the effect that electrical charges have on the frequency of healthy cells. Together with the photographic research conducted at UCLA in the mid-seventies, which measured the energy level in different foods, they created a list of these foods from the highest to the lowest in energy content.

Foods highest on the list are those exposed to the most sunlight, or "life-force energy," because their cellular structure can capture and maintain far greater amounts of energy from the sun. Dr. Brian Clement, director of the institute, rates the life-force energy of food based on the radiance they contain and emit, and he gives a star rating based on their radiance. The greater the star rating, the greater the nutritional value and electrical frequency of that food.

Findings included the following:

- Ripe, organic, unprocessed fruits, vegetables, algae, sprouts, and edible flowers are highest on the list, with their dehydrated counterparts falling to the bottom of the list.
- Cooked vegetables are neutral. They neither contain nor emit energy.
- Meat and dairy were found not only to emit no energy, but to absorb energy from the body when consumed, depleting energy reserves.

Details regarding these foods and the amount of energy they emit can be found in Dr. Clements' book, *Hippocrates Life Force*.[2]

When Hippocrates set up his clinic over 2,000 years ago, one of his criteria was for the clinic to be built on a stream where watercress could grow. Watercress is a high vibrational plant that grows in water and is high in vitamin C, antioxidants, and water content. It naturally helps clear the body of infections and cleanses the kidneys and urinary tract.

Before we dig into the protocol and learn how to take practical steps to create major change in our lives, let's spend a few minutes talking about how we get sick and how we heal. We'll also dispel the common myth that we're doomed to become a victim of our genes. We most certainly aren't!

HOW WE GET SICK, HOW WE GET HEALTHY

Contrary to popular belief, genetics plays a very small part in our sickness and health. Scientists have discovered that genetics account for less than 5 percent of health issues that run in families. Our environment plays a far greater role in what becomes of us.

You are NOT a victim of your genes.

The reason we often develop the same diseases and conditions as our parents isn't because of our genes; it's because we follow in their diet and environmental footsteps.

The following four factors determine our genetic expression—which of our genes are switched on, and which lay dormant:

1. Our eating habits
2. Our lifestyle habits
3. The thoughts we think and the beliefs we adopt
4. The environmental toxins we expose our bodies to

The belief system we adopt and the thoughts we think are the two most important players here. Our thoughts are very powerful energy generators that determine the quality of our life and our health.

- One of the largest cancer research centers in the world has concluded that the primary cause of cancer is not genetic. Even if cancer runs in your family, this by no means indicates you'll also suffer from the disease. The human body is naturally highly resistant to cancer, and cancer is genetically recessive, not dominant.[1]
- Only 5 percent of all cancer cases can be attributed to genetic defects, whereas the remaining 95 percent are rooted in the patient's environment and lifestyle.[2]
- The World Health Organization states that the primary determinants of most cancers are lifestyle factors, dietary and exercise habits, environment carcinogens, and infectious agents, rather than inherited genetic factors.[3]
- Recent research in psychology, genetics, and neuroscience have shown that environmental conditions are much more powerful than genetic influences in determining intelligence. Social psychologist Richard analyzed a large number of such studies, which revealed that the environment influences not just IQ as measured by standardized tests, but also actual achievement.[4]

"The primary determinants of most cancers are lifestyle factors such as tobacco, dietary & exercise habits, environmental carcinogens, and infectious agents, not inherited genetic factors."

World Health Org. (WHO)

This knowledge puts us in a very powerful position because it means we have a lot of control over our health and well-being.

How We Get Sick

People often have no idea how their health problems started or how to fix the problem. They're unaware that diet and lifestyle choices are both the causes and contributing factors to most diseases in the Western world, which means they don't know what changes to make to heal themselves. They're also unaware that these choices, good or bad, are the direct result of the energy behind the thoughts they think and beliefs they hold to be true. **It is this energy that causes them to make either healthy or unhealthy choices.**

Before we talk about the concept of how the energy of our thoughts and beliefs helps shape the health of our bodies, let's first talk about what physical events occur to create sickness.

At the most basic level, all diseases are caused by toxins that have built up within the body to the point that the body begins to degrade. The bloodstream, cells, tissues, organs, and systems of the body become slowly saturated with the overload of toxic elements, and disease sets in. As a health condition deteriorates, the weaker organs and systems begin to break down first, including the joints and arteries.

Let's take a look at how chronic conditions develop:

STEP 1: The body becomes depleted

The body becomes depleted from the steady influx of various pollutants. These pollutants can come from chemicals, pesticides, and heavy metals in processed and refined food; chemicals in the air we breathe and the water we drink; chemicals in personal-care products and household/garden chemicals; chronic stress; and various other sources. The body can no longer conduct "internal housecleaning" because it's overloaded with the continual inflow of new toxins. It reaches a point where the incoming toxins are building quicker than they can be eliminated, and because it doesn't have the necessary resources to repair itself, the body begins to feel tired and run down.

STEP 2: Toxic buildup continues

The toxic buildup continues, and the body experiences a state of internal inflammation. General bodily symptoms, especially gastrointestinal problems, begin to develop, and we try to fix them with over-the-counter medicines (ibuprofen, Tylenol, Tums, fiber supplements, etc.). We're not sure why we don't feel our best; we just know that we don't feel great. We ignore symptoms and write off aches, headaches, and digestive problems such as heartburn, constipation, gas, indigestion, or diarrhea as typical, age-related, or as unimportant. This is a mistake. These symptoms are very important. They're the "early warning sign" messengers alerting us to a problem. Taking over-the-counter and prescription medications soon becomes part of the problem, not the solution.

STEP 3: Inflammation builds

The inflammation within the body continues, and we experience actual pain. A doctor classifies the disease and prescribes standard medications to help treat it. If the lifestyle factors that created the condition in the first place aren't addressed, the medication acts as a Band-Aid, temporarily helping as the condition continues to deteriorate. Often, medications create secondary health issues (especially when taken for an extended period of time), which may not become apparent until later, and some medications directly contribute to the development of bone-related diseases, gastrointestinal disorders, and cancers.

STEP 4: Chronic inflammation

At this point, the inflammation has become chronic, and the body's systems become sluggish. Tumors often begin to develop and may or may not be discovered. Medications progress to other more invasive or aggressive medications that have a long list of dangerous side effects, and surgery often follows. The body experiences significant physical pain and emotional distress. Tissues, organs, and systems no longer function normally, and cells may succumb to irreversible or seriously debilitating conditions, such as cancer and autoimmune diseases.

Sources of Imbalance

A healthy body radiates vitality. Not only does it have more than enough energy to fully function, but it can also repair itself and create a reserve of energy to protect against disease. The body continually repairs us and compensates for our habits that wear it down. It's very resilient!

However, when the body lacks the nutrients it needs from the right diet, or when it becomes chronically stressed or worn down by depleting lifestyle habits, that's when it slowly becomes overloaded with a buildup of toxic waste. Instead of spending its time repairing the body, it's continually "fire-fighting" as it tries to eliminate the constant intake of new toxins.

It's no secret that Americans are getting sicker and fatter and hopelessly dependent on medications. They suffer higher rates of chronic disease, cancer, autoimmune conditions, and obesity than any other country in the world. American children are also the most chronically sick and disabled.

Let's take a look at the factors responsible for this dismal picture:

Outside sources of imbalances (there are quite a few)

- Pesticides and herbicides in our foods, household, and garden products
- Artificial chemicals in our food (there are over 10,000)
- Genetically modified foods
- Factory-farmed meats and fish
- Irradiated foods
- Microwaved foods
- Consistent high-temperature cooking/charred foods
- Contaminated water (municipal water often contains many contaminants)
- Contaminated air (especially within city areas)
- Environmental, commercial, and industrial pollutants
- Medications and supplements
- Stimulants (caffeine, energy drinks, recreational/prescription drugs)
- Alcohol, nicotine, and drugs

On any given day, the average American dinner plate contains not just one, but an assortment of these offenders. The typical American diet is the unhealthiest and most denatured food on the planet, consisting primarily of junk that is toxic to the body.

The industrialization and chemicalization of our food chain (as well as our environment) is the single-biggest cause of the disease epidemic we're experiencing.

Inside sources of imbalances

- Stress
- Fatigue
- Metabolic waste (a natural by-product of metabolism)

If we remove the elements from our body that cause it to break down, it no longer has to focus its attention on trying to eliminate new toxins. Instead, it can focus on repairing, detoxifying, and healing it of any diseased condition.

When it comes to restoring balance to the body and curing an illness, we do it by:

1. Understanding how we get sick, and removing the cause(s)
2. Understanding how we get healthy, and providing the body the tools it needs to heal

Once we do that, the body's innate intelligence does the rest.

How We Get Healthy

Just as most plants in the natural world require sunshine, healthy soil, clean air, and water to grow to their potential, the body must be nurtured with the essentials so that it can flourish. If we deprive our body of what it needs for basic health, then its vibrational state lowers and it gravitates toward ill health and disease.

Whether you have heart disease, diabetes, arthritis, varicose veins, cancer, cellulite, or thyroid disease, the answer is always the same, and it isn't complicated. Always begin by replacing unhealthy food and lifestyle habits with healthy, high vibrational ones, and by changing the way you think. This is the only way to the absolute best quality of health and life you can possibly achieve. Healing is a process accomplished by the body, and only the body, and it's only possible when you provide it with the right tools. In addition, your health potential depends on how quickly you make these changes.

Whether or not a health condition is reversible depends on how far the disease has progressed within the body. The good news is that the body has a remarkable resilience and capacity to heal itself. Many physical degenerations and "irreparable damage" can be reversed with diet and lifestyle changes and by adopting a different mind-set. Having given their body what it needs and left it to its own devices, many people have seen very serious, and even terminal, illnesses resolve naturally—sometimes quickly, sometimes slowly.

Many doctors tell their patients that their chronic conditions aren't curable and tie them to medications for life, or they tell them that their condition requires invasive tests and surgeries. Thousands of patients have proved them wrong and not only reversed their condition naturally, but also fully restored themselves back to health with no more need for medications.

> **"When it comes to disease, the answer is always the same. It isn't complicated. Begin by replacing unhealthy food & lifestyle habits with healthy, high vibrational ones, & change the way you think."**
>
> Irini Dieringer
> The Body Healer

If you have been diagnosed with a very serious or terminal condition, remember this: *no matter what your situation or what illness you're suffering from,* never, ever underestimate the capacity of your body to heal itself. It's incredibly resourceful, and its natural expression is to always gravitate toward health.

There may be times when irreversible damage or deformity (such as a severed limb) limits our capacity to recover. In such cases, we can only do our best to maximize our healing potential. But when it comes to chronic and terminal disease, there have been countless cases where illnesses have been tagged as "terminal" only to have the patient not only survive, but fully recover.

If you have cancer, regardless of what primary factors caused your cancer, research now clearly indicates that the progression of the disease isn't dependent on only the type of cancer itself. No matter what the type of cancer, it's the body's internal environment, especially the health of the immune system, which plays the most significant role in influencing whether the disease progresses or regresses. If you're a cancer survivor, recurrence is dramatically reduced in patients who take specific steps to strengthen their immune system—something that happens automatically when you raise your vibrational frequency.

THE VIBRATIONS OF HEALTH

If you're suffering from a health condition, your healing potential is determined by:

1. How quickly you integrate high vibrational foods and lifestyle habits
2. How quickly you remove diet and lifestyle factors that contribute to sickness
3. The amount of toxins already in your body
4. The depletion of energy in your body
5. Past injuries resulting in irreversible damage

Things that are low vibrational in nature will not only deplete the body, but will also cause us to energetically attract low vibrational foods, lifestyle habits, and addictions. These things, in turn, lower our vibrational state, and we end up in a vicious circle. Remember:

Our healing potential is based on our body's frequency.

Diet and nutrition are only one piece of a much larger puzzle; we need far more than just a nutritious diet to be healthy and high vibrational. Our body's essential needs are physical, emotional, spiritual, and physiological—needs that we can only meet when we understand how the type and quality of our thoughts affect our entire being.

The thoughts we think on a daily basis dramatically impact our frequency. Positive thoughts generate energy that's higher in frequency than negative or fear-based thoughts, so changing the way we think can set in motion important changes on an energy level. When we think high vibrational thoughts, we suddenly and automatically attract healthier environments and healthier relationships. We instinctively adopt healthier habits that heal us as we elevate to higher vibrational frequencies, which not only propels us into a state of health, but also helps us access abilities and skills we never knew we had. We'll talk about this in much more detail later on in the protocol.

Health Is a Personal Responsibility

When we look for instant gratification from pain or discomfort, we nearly always reach for pills and prescriptions and forget to ask the important question:

"What created my condition?"

If we make the effort to answer that question, we may not only heal ourselves, we may also come to understand the cause of the condition, which will help us remove it. Unfortunately, because it's easier to relieve ourselves of the responsibility of addressing the root cause of our problem, we often choose to pop medications and/or supplements. After all, this is exactly what most medical doctors tell us to do, so who are we to disagree with them?

Who are we? We are the ones who suffer the consequences.

A medicated approach to your health will never work. If you take any medications, you should always be working to decrease and eliminate them (whenever possible) rather than relying on them.

If you continue on the same path that created your health issue(s), and if you keep treating symptoms with a variety of drugs and supplements, your chances of remaining the same (or getting worse) are high. The fact is, becoming reliant on medications helps pave the road to future chronic disease. The only way to become healthy is to make healthy foods, thoughts, and habits a part of your daily life.

Educate yourself! Don't medicate yourself!

Each of us is personally responsible for our own health. That responsibility doesn't lie with someone else, and it doesn't mean we put blind faith in a doctor that recommends medications, or traditional nutritionists and dietitians trained to make dietary recommendations based on the same government food pyramids that helped create the current health crisis.

If these very well-intentioned individuals haven't expanded their education into a more natural, holistic direction, then the negative health impacts of genetically modified foods, irradiated foods, microwaved foods, nonorganic produce (and the serious health conditions conclusively linked to food pesticides), and the dangers of eating factory-farmed meat are completely lost on them.

Luckily, more and more people are questioning traditional dietary advice, and in response, the natural health movement is one of the fastest-growing industries today.

Changing your life isn't easy, but the reward is priceless. Though it may feel like a roller coaster at times, embracing your natural ability—your birthright—to both improve your health and change your entire life's experience is an exciting, worthwhile journey.

You are PURE POTENTIAL.

Many of us are surrounded by friends and family who are overweight, over-stressed, depressed, and immersed in the standard American diet that helped create the chronic disease epidemic today. We owe it not only to ourselves, but also to those we love to be a shining example of what we can all accomplish.

Before we leave the subject of medications, let's be absolutely certain we understand *the illusion of medications*.

WHY DRUGS DON'T CURE

Living in the golden age of pharmaceutical giants (more commonly known as "Big Pharma") and their multimillion-dollar advertising campaigns, Westerners have become deeply entrenched in a medicated approach to health. The average senior citizen takes at least 13 different types of medications throughout any given 12-month period, and they're usually unaware that most of these medications carry serious warnings/side effects that often create secondary health conditions.

Common side effects from very common drugs include cancer, suicidal thoughts, addictive behavior, low libido, raising or lowering of blood pressure, weight gain, insomnia, blood clots, diarrhea, constipation, and a host of other gastrointestinal disorders that contribute to leaky gut. Yet we quickly pop these pills, blindly trusting that our doctors would never prescribe something that could be potentially dangerous to us. Unfortunately, they do. Every day.

CANCER – DIABETES – HEART DISEASE – OBESITY

The biggest killer diseases suffered in the US are largely preventable through our diet and lifestyle choices. Consider obesity. It's an easily preventable condition, yet in every US state, the current obesity rate is above 20 percent, in 41 states it's at least 25 percent, and in 13 states it's over 30 percent.

Even though the World Health Organization states that cancer is a disease of both environment and lifestyle factors, neither the government nor the medical system promotes any public education or guidance on natural and noninvasive methods of disease prevention. Even though adopting healthy dietary habits is a method of disease prevention that would save billions of dollars each year, the government turns a blind eye to it and encourages a medicated approach to life while subsidizing unhealthy food.

In the face of corporate greed, the government succumbs to pressure from the powerful food and pharmaceutical lobbyists. Should the American public get healthy, these mega-corporations stand to be the biggest losers—to the tune of tens of billions of dollars each year. In a win-win for the food and pharmaceutical giants, the junk-food market provides the food, which in turn contributes to the chronic diseases, which in turn keeps the thriving pharmaceutical companies in business and keeps America a medicated nation.

A Medicated Approach to Life

As a medicated nation, we Americans pop over-the-counter and prescription pills for everything, often when we don't need to. We medicate ourselves for depression, to sleep better, for indigestion, for headaches. We medicate ourselves to suppress chronic inflammation (instead of getting to the root cause of the problem), and our doctors even medicate us *before* we get sick because we have a "risk factor." Before a child is born, it's been medicated via the prescription and nonprescription drugs taken by mom. A medicated approach to life is the most health-depleting way to live. Not only that, but adverse drug reactions (ADRs) are one of the leading causes of death each year in the US.

Over-tested, Overtreated, Overmedicated!

We are over-tested, overtreated, and overmedicated. Americans spend more money on medications and healthcare than Japan, France, Italy, Spain, the United Kingdom, Australia, New Zealand, Canada, Mexico, Brazil, and Argentina combined, and yet we are much sicker. We have a healthcare system that encourages unnecessary procedures, surgeries, and medications, rather than one that encourages patients to follow natural solutions, such as dietary changes, exercise, and stress reduction.

Consider these facts:

> **"Both prescription narcotics & heroin are two of the most lethal drugs available."**
>
> U. S. Justice Department

- An estimated 30 percent of all medical procedures, medications, and tests may be completely unnecessary, which is even more significant when considering the cost of medical care runs into the tens of billions each year.[1]
- A statistical study of hospital deaths in the US conducted at the University of Toronto revealed that pharmaceutical drugs kill more people every year than are killed in traffic accidents.
- American doctors operate on wrong body parts as often as 40 times per week.[1]
- A staggering 210,000 deaths per year are associated with preventable harm in hospitals. Given search-capability limitations and the incompleteness of medical records, the true number of premature deaths associated with preventable harm to patients was estimated at more than 400,000 per year[2] Some estimate that the number of deaths due to medical error is the equivalent of if a jumbo jet crashed every day, and 3 times the number killed each year in US traffic accidents.
- During a 12-month study, more than 2 million Americans who were hospitalized suffered serious adverse drug reactions (ADRs). Of these, over 100,000 died as a result. The researchers concluded that ADRs are now the fourth-leading cause of death in the US after heart disease, cancer, and stroke.

- In 2012, the American Board of Internal Medicine Foundation reported on the most overused tests and treatments that provide limited or zero benefit to the patient (or caused more harm than good), warning doctors against using 45 tests, procedures, and treatments. The 2013 report added yet another 90 tests and treatments to the list.

The quality of healthcare in the US is so poor that in a recent comparison of 13 countries, the US ranked twelfth—second from the bottom—behind Japan, Sweden, Canada, France, Australia, Spain, Finland, the Netherlands, the UK, Denmark, and Belgium.[3]

The American medical system is reactive medicine that truly shines in treating trauma and emergencies, such as a broken bone or an allergic reaction. Saving the life of a burn victim or starting a stopped heart are other great examples of where we're very lucky to have traditional medicine. But when it comes to treating diseases, successful healing requires a whole-body approach that comes from addressing many different factors. Understanding the interconnected nature of diet, physical activity, our state of mind, our lifestyle choices, and the health of our body is not part of the medical-training curriculum.

Conventional medicine treats symptoms, not causes, with little focus on root cause and prevention.

Instead, it focuses on treating symptoms with either drugs, surgeries, or procedures. We are conditioned to swallow a potion or pop a pill at the first sign of any ache or pain. Because the problem's root cause is rarely addressed, many patients suffer continued poor health, cancer relapses, and end up medicated for life. In the end, all they have to show for it is failing health and debt from medical bills.

Disease in Aging Is NOT Natural

Traditional medicine also teaches us to expect disease as a natural part of the aging process, but disease is *not* a natural part of aging—far from it! In many examples of long-lived cultures, residents live to a ripe old age and suffer none of the degenerative conditions associated with old age that result from modern Western diet and lifestyle habits.

What's Wrong with Medications?

Can drugs be lifesavers? Absolutely! In fact, they save lives every day. They have an important place in medical emergencies, surgeries, procedures, and to manage debilitating pain. We should be very grateful for them. But that doesn't change the fact that 95 percent of the time, their use is unnecessary.

Pharmaceutical drugs and supplements are a double-edged sword. They can make us feel better—temporarily. They may reduce our anxiety, help us sleep, and relieve our pain, but they do not truly fix the problem.

At best, drugs provide pain relief, typically by masking and suppressing symptoms such as inflammation and by artificially stimulating or suppressing the body. The relief from pain that we get from taking painkillers over an extended period of time often comes at the expense of other bodily systems—especially our kidneys—that are adversely affected by the foreign chemicals in those medications.

At their worst, drugs create new diseases in our body, can cost large sums of money, can be highly addictive, can cause alarming physical and psychological changes, and their side effects cause hundreds of thousands of deaths per year. Drugs should be used as a very last resort and definitely not as a "go-to" for common conditions like colds, gastrointestinal discomforts such as gas or constipation, sore muscles, and general aches and pains.

Some drugs, such as prescription narcotics, are highly addictive and create drug dependencies.

By their very nature, pharmaceutical drugs are damaging; they are powerful chemicals with powerful side effects that damage the body and throw our vibrational state into chaos. No doctor can guarantee you won't experience harmful side effects from the drugs they prescribe, simply because they have no idea whether you will or you won't. Every prescription comes with documentation on the side effects that you may or may not suffer. Many patients have no idea that the potential drug side effects (such as cancer) are far more dangerous than the condition the drug is meant to treat.

The Old Paradigm

The use of pharmaceutical drugs (both prescription and nonprescription) is part of the old paradigm of the "modern medicine" system of healing. There will come a time when they will no longer be used as they are today and will only be necessary for emergency trauma, such as a cortisone shot for a bee sting, pain relief for severe trauma, surgeries, or life-saving interventions after an accident. Because the new paradigm raises the vibrational frequency of the body to a level where it's no longer receptive to disease or imbalance, the need for any type of medication will become drastically reduced.

While you slowly migrate yourself to a new state of being, you may need medication as part of your reality. As your health and your energetic quotient increase, your need for medication will automatically decrease. Work with your doctor on a schedule where, as you see improvement, this improvement correlates with a slow and steady lowering of your medication until you no longer need it.

If your doctor tells you that you'll need that medication for life and isn't open to the prospect of you healing yourself naturally, then consider firing your doctor and getting a new one with a more natural and holistic approach. I've lost count of the number of people who have had chronic health conditions such as diabetes, cancer, and heart disease who—once they made key lifestyle changes and ate a diet rich in high vibrational foods—went on to beat their illness and be free of any need for medications. This was in direct opposition to their doctors who told them they would either (1) be on medication for life, or (2) have a shortened life expectancy.

We can try to take the easy way out and eliminate our symptoms with drugs, but in doing so, we harm our bodies. Not only do we say goodbye to high vibrational living, but we also increase the likelihood of future sickness because we've failed to address the root cause. On the surface it may seem far easier to relieve ourselves of the work and self-discovery involved. But a medicated life will never work because drugs may eliminate symptoms, but they absolutely do not create health.

Risk Factors

Some doctors promote drugs for risk factors, advocating pill-popping to prevent a problem that doesn't currently exist for fear that it "might" appear in the future. In this situation, a patient may be perfectly healthy, but because they "may" become sick based on family history, they're treated unnecessarily with medications, despite having no physical condition at all. As we've seen, genes play a very small role in whether or not we develop the same diseases as our parents or other family members.

Instead of doctors educating patients on prevention, they treat them as though the disease is inevitable. Pharmaceutical companies encourage doctors to do this because "pre-diabetes" and "pre-heart disease" drugs are big moneymakers.

A Word About Our Children

When it comes to the new generation, the statistics are even worse. Raised with poor eating habits and fed highly processed and chemicalized junk foods, chronic disease is now commonplace in both children and adolescents.

Our kids are overfed and undernourished. Fries, burgers, hot dogs, pizza, donuts, cookies, sugary drinks, high-fat and high-sugar milk products, and frozen meals are the diet staples of millions of American children. At the current disease rate, they stand to live a shortened lifespan when compared to their parents.

The new generation growing up in the US is being unaffectionately labeled as "Generation Rx," since the average child takes at least one prescription medication and artificial multivitamin supplement.

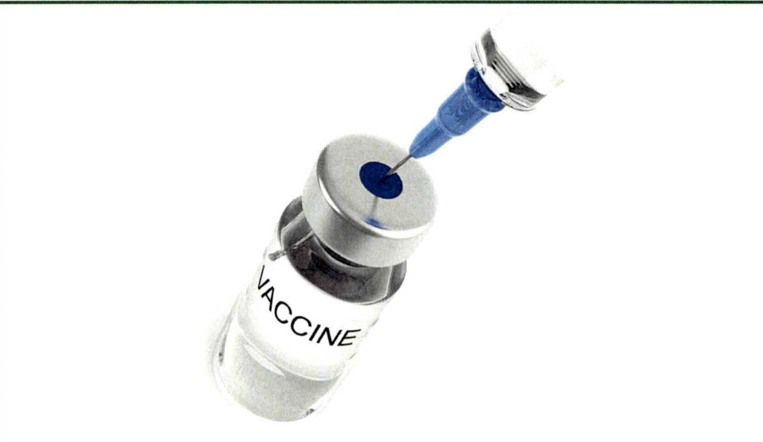

OVER-VACCINATED

35 years ago, 7 vaccines were given to infants and children. Today, children who follow the US schedule recommended by the Centers for Disease Control and Prevention (CDC) receive a whopping 69 doses of 16 vaccines by the time they've reached 6 years old, the highest amount given in any country, making US children the most over-vaccinated in the world. As if 16 vaccinations isn't enough, the pharmaceutical giants have 145 new vaccines in development and want to make them all mandatory. Billions in profit are riding on them.

A child's immune system continues to develop and strengthen long after birth. Because of this, other countries strongly disagree with the US vaccination schedule when it comes to infants under 2 years of age, believing it is not strong enough to withstand such an overload without health consequences.

US children are also the most chronically ill and disabled, suffering far more childhood illnesses than other children worldwide.

- One-third of children and adolescents ages 6-19 are considered overweight or obese.
- 1 in 100 are diagnosed with autism, while 11 million are diagnosed with ADHD.

- Childhood cancers are now the leading cause of death in children.
- Asthma cases are steadily rising at an unprecedented rate.
- 1 in 6 kids are now diagnosed with a behavioral, developmental, or neurological disorder.

Not only are children overmedicated with pharmaceutical drugs, they are also fed daily supplements containing artificial chemicals. A child eating a healthy diet should never need supplements (especially multivitamins). Supplements should be given for a diagnosed deficiency and then stopped once the child is no longer deficient. The most common reason for nutritional deficiencies is an unhealthy diet.

If you're pregnant or have children, this protocol will teach you how to raise your children on healthy foods that will set them firmly on the path of health and longevity.

And Let's Not Forget Our Pets

"Dogs in this country now suffer from as many cancers as people do, if not more."

Matthew Breen
Genomics, CCMTR

Just as the average American is getting fatter and sicker, so too are the pets they own—and for the same reasons. A dog's genetics are close to 90 percent similar to ours, and there is a direct link between our pets' health and the quality of their diet and environment. If they live in our homes, breathe the same air, walk on the same pesticide-ridden grass we do, drink the same municipal water, and eat similar types of highly processed pet foods (the ingredients may differ, but the processing and denaturing is the same), then it stands to reason they'll suffer the same diseases we do.

Processed pet food is as bad for our pets' health as processed human food is for ours, and their skyrocketing rates of chronic disease mirror ours as both food chains become heavily industrialized and contaminated.

Pet medications have their side effects, just as human medications do. Common flea and tick medications cause both severe and subtle reactions in thousands of pets each year, and some ingredients are linked to cancer, allergies, and asthma. Product labels warn that they should not touch human skin (but are considered "fine" to place on a pet's skin.)

CANCER Cancer now affects a staggering 1 in 3 dogs. Almost 50 percent of all dogs over the age of 10 will develop cancer.

HEART DISEASE 10 percent of dogs suffer from heart disease.

DIABETES 1 in 60 dogs are diagnosed with diabetes.

OBESITY An estimated 54 percent of dogs and cats in the US (93 million) are overweight or obese.

Just as these diseases are largely preventable in us humans by simply making some key diet and lifestyle changes, we can also prevent them from developing in our pets by making the same changes for them.

WHAT ABOUT SUPPLEMENTS?

At some time or another, we've all fallen for the idea that we need to take supplements. Highly persuasive marketing campaigns and outrageous claims, most of which have no studies to back them (other than those done by the manufacturers themselves), pique our interest. We can't help it—it's only a few bucks anyway, and what do we have to lose if they don't work!

The vast majority of people who take supplements take them every day, month after month, year after year, with nothing to quantify whether they do any good. Many just assume they need to take a daily supplement in case of a dietary deficiency instead of addressing their diet.

So let's talk about some very important reasons why you should ditch the supplements:

- Almost all supplements in the marketplace are synthetically-made products, and the majority are manufactured in China. We'll discuss in more detail why both foods and supplements from China should be avoided later in the protocol.
- Nutrients that have been isolated and sold in supplement form impact the physical body much differently than the nutrients found in the original whole food where they work synergistically with thousands of other components in that food.
- Taking them for fear that we "may" be deficient if we don't—even though there's nothing wrong with us—is a bad reason to take a supplement.
- Just as with medications, supplements and herbal products can artificially stimulate the body, suppress bodily symptoms, and cause unwanted side effects. In larger quantities, they quickly become very unhealthy.
- Several popular supplements deplete or reduce the absorption of other nutrients in the body, creating a deficiency where none existed in the first place.
- Some of the most common synthetic supplements on the marketplace (and in most multivitamins), including vitamin A and folic acid, have been conclusively linked to serious health conditions. Others, such as calcium supplements from popular manufacturers, are not only poorly absorbed, but are often found to contain contaminants, such as lead, in amounts that pose a health concern.
- The money you spend on supplements could be spent on other things that are much better for you. Some supplements are very expensive, and most people take several types. The costs add up quickly.

With all of this said, there is a more important reason why, in most cases, you should ditch supplements: Your health is the direct result of the quality of your diet and your state of mind. You are ultimately the one in control of the health of each and every cell in your body. Given that, the only purpose taking a supplement can possibly serve is as a distraction and a Band-Aid.

Supplements Have Their Place (Albeit a Very Small One)

While you work to restore balance in your body, supplements can be a wonderful (and temporary) friend in your journey. For long-standing, chronic health conditions such as cancer, specific natural supplements can assist in your recovery and are definitely preferred over toxic pharmaceutical drugs. But once balance has been restored and your condition has healed, and once your diet is healthy, you should have little need for supplements. There are a few exceptions to this rule, which we'll talk about later in the protocol. We'll also go over the difference between synthetic vs. whole-food-based supplements and how to make the best purchasing choices.

If you're taking the average synthetic multivitamin as a substitute for eating a healthy diet, you're doing your body more harm than good. Supplements are a poor and distant second to fresh, healthy food choices, and unless they're raw whole-food supplements, they have no measurable energy frequency.

HOMEWORK

Let's take a break for a few minutes to do a small homework exercise. All you need is pen and paper (or a smartphone or tablet):

Non-Prescribed Supplements

Make a list of any supplements you take and ask yourself the following questions:

- Why am I taking this supplement? Do I have a deficiency?
- Do I understand each ingredient on the label, and how will each affect my body?
- Does the label state the ingredients are extracted from whole-food sources? If not, they are likely synthetic.

Prescribed Supplements

If a doctor, dietitian, or nutritionist recommended a supplement, was it based on the results of a blood test that showed you were deficient or on a general recommendation? Were you educated on what dietary changes to make to resolve this deficiency or simply told to take the supplement? If it was prescribed for a chronic disease, were you given information about the studies that conclusively show this supplement will help your condition?

Medications

Make a list of any medications you're taking and why you're taking them. Ask yourself the following questions:

- Do you feel they can be eliminated or reduced with diet and/or lifestyle changes?
- Did your doctor prescribe diet and/or lifestyle changes before prescribing pills?
- What action would you take if the medication was no longer available for your condition?

Over-the-Counter (OTC) Drugs

When taking OTCs, do you look for natural solutions first and use the OTC drugs only as a last resort? If you take OTC drugs habitually (e.g., for gastrointestinal issues), have you actively looked for ways to address the problem so that you can avoid using these drugs again in the future?

Health Is a Whole-Body Approach

Now that we have talked about why a medicated approach to sickness is not in the best interest of your health and well-being, let's talk about why a whole-body approach is always the best one.

Most diseases are nutritionally controllable.

We've known for a while that disease is caused by a breakdown of the immune system; now we know about all the different things that contribute to that breakdown. Eliminating disease begins with taking action to strengthen our immune system because this is a critical piece of the health puzzle. When we strengthen our immune system, we automatically begin to strengthen the organs and tissues of the body and cleanse our entire system at the cellular level because our immune system is intimately linked to *every* bodily function. The immune system is not a "piece of the body" or an "object" inside the body. It exists throughout our entire organism and can be nourished at the highest level only by diet and lifestyle choices and thoughts that are high vibrational in nature.

When it comes to either health or disease, the key players are our environment, our state of mind, what we put into our mouths, and what we put onto our skins (children and pets included). The cleaner and healthier our diet and environment, the healthier our bodies and the bodies of our children and pets are.

It all starts with learning how to make the right choices and then taking swift action on those choices. The Body Healer Protocol will take you by the hand and help you do just that.

Our Built-In Early Warning Systems

We've learned that disease cannot thrive in a body that resonates at a higher frequency than the disease itself. When we're aware of the different things that affect us at a vibrational level, we can begin to take steps to reduce our exposure to the things that lower our frequency (and attract diseased states), and we can increase the things that raise it.

Let's spend a few minutes talking about two early warning systems we all have that help clue us in that something isn't quite right:

1. Our gastrointestinal (digestive) system
2. Chronic inflammation

THE GASTROINTESTINAL SYSTEM

DIGESTION & ELIMINATION

When it comes to understanding our health, a critical piece of the puzzle is the health of our digestive system (known as the gastrointestinal system, or GI tract).

The most important factor in determining our general health is how well our GI tract functions. GI problems are often the first sign the body is in distress.

The many pieces of our digestive system are responsible for taking in food and breaking it down from large food molecules into tiny nutrients that the body then absorbs. These nutrients (including water and electrolytes) pass through the intestinal wall and into blood or lymph to nourish our bodies. The GI tract is also responsible for the quality and quantity of the waste we excrete after we've absorbed all the nutrients in our food.

When any part of this system becomes imbalanced, we experience common issues such as gas, constipation, diarrhea, and acid reflux that become chronic. Left unchecked, these early warning signs can lay the foundation for more serious conditions such as irritable bowel syndrome (IBS), leaky gut, autoimmune diseases, and intestinal/colon cancers. Unfortunately, early warning signs are often ignored and waved off as insignificant.

Let's spend a few minutes looking at the different things that can affect our ability to digest food and eliminate waste.

Healthy Digestion = Good Health

In the world of natural healthcare (such as naturopathic medicine, traditional Chinese medicine, or Ayurveda), two of the first questions you'll always be asked are "How is your digestion?" and "How are your bowel movements?" The answers to these questions are very important because when problems begin to occur within our digestive cycle, they can progress into chronic conditions or diseases.

A healthy digestive system is the foundation of good health, so the kinds and quality of food and water you put into your body are extremely important. High-quality nutrition is essential for the continual building of healthy cells and tissues throughout the body. Your level of stress also determines how efficiently the body can absorb nutrients and eliminate waste matter.

The reason we see so many different symptoms of health problems within the digestive and elimination cycles is that digestion is a massively complex process that involves several systems of the body:

- The endocrine system, which secretes hormones necessary for the absorption of nutrients
- The nervous system, which sends signals that control our hunger level, the passage of food through our body, etc.
- The cardiovascular system, which transports nutrients to cells via the blood supply
- The lymphatic and urinary systems, which eliminate waste

HOW WE DIGEST & ELIMINATE

The digestive tract of an adult is about 30 feet long and runs all the way from the mouth to the anus. It has many different parts to it and involves several organs.

It should take less than 12 hours from the time you swallow a piece of food to the time you excrete it, but the types of foods eaten today in the heavy combinations we eat them often extends this time to 24-72 hours. This time frame depends on a few different factors:

- The quality of food eaten
- How much is eaten (a large meal slows down emptying)
- How different foods are combined in one meal
- Physical activity
- Our stress level (stress in all forms slows down movement)
- Aggression and anger, which speed up movement
- Medications we're taking
- Illnesses or infections we may be experiencing

A piece of fruit eaten alone, for example, is easily and quickly digested in 30-90 minutes, but when eaten after a meal of steak and potatoes, the transit time can easily extend to 24 hours or more.

Stress can wreak havoc on our digestive system, reducing both blood flow and the contraction of digestive muscles, decreasing the secretion of enzymes needed to absorb nutrients in food, and increasing the secretion of stomach acid. The colon can also give us either diarrhea or constipation during stress.

The longer food sits in our stomach, the more it begins to putrefy and ferment, which in turn causes most of the common digestive complaints we experience, such as gas and indigestion.

The large intestine also houses an entire ecosystem of microflora (300–500 species of bacteria) that are crucial to healthy digestion. Antibiotics, toxins, medications, unhealthy foods, etc. can kill this very important microflora that helps us digest our food, in turn causing waste to sit in our colon longer. The longer it sits, the more toxic to the body it becomes, setting the stage for IBS and colon diseases. If we aren't having regular, daily bowel movements, we're increasing our toxicity.

Digestive Disorders

The one thing many digestive disorders have in common is that once we clean up our diet and make key lifestyle changes, such as reducing our stress level, these disorders resolve on their own without any medical intervention or need for medications. On the contrary, some medications contribute to and exacerbate many digestive disorders, while others do nothing to help us solve the problem.

Antacids are simply Band-Aids. They have no part in fixing the problem that made us swallow them in the first place.Symptoms stemming from digestive disorders can be as vague as feeling tired to difficulty focusing on a task, and as obvious as diarrhea, constipation, and tummy pains.

Other complaints directly related to digestive disorders include the following:

- Skin conditions (acne, rashes)
- Mood disorders
- Compromised immunity
- Food allergies and sensitivities
- Nutritional deficiencies
- Gallstones
- Celiac disease
- Toxification
- Leaky gut syndrome
- Liver and kidney disorders
- Parasites
- Yeast infections
- Destruction of gut microflora (the effect of antibiotics)
- Gastritis and ulcers
- Indigestion
- Candida
- Acid reflux/GERD
- Constipation
- Diarrhea
- IBS
- IBD
- Diverticulosis

If you're having digestive issues, before you reach out for a prescription medication or OTC antacid, love your body enough to get down to the root cause of the problem by first addressing any diet and/or lifestyle habits that are likely the culprit.

Introductions, please!

When it comes to the health of our GI tract, there are some very important guys that play critical roles in the digestion, absorption, and elimination of all our food. Let's go meet the wonderful inhabitants of our gut!

BACTERIA & GUT MICROFLORA

The bacteria in our gut play a very important role not only in digestion, but also in other aspects of our health and well-being. They contribute to immunity, are involved in the synthesis of vitamins, ferment complex indigestible carbohydrates, and protect the body from harmful bacteria and other bad guys that produce toxins.

It's impossible to achieve vibrant health if your gut microflora is out of balance.

Scientists have identified over 400 species of microflora in our gut, which translates to trillions and trillions of bacteria in the average intestinal tract. In fact, we have about ten times as many bacterial cells in the body as human cells! Each time we eat a meal, this intestinal microflora acts as a digestive powerhouse, helping to break food down into nutrients the body can use.

Staying healthy depends on the constant "balancing act" between good vs. bad bacteria in our digestive system. Because our intestinal microflora is a type of good bacteria and has a beneficial effect on our health, they are called probiotics (pro-life), as opposed to antibiotics (antilife).

Certain types of intestinal microflora appear to play an important role when it comes to health conditions. They may also be contributing factors that help explain why some people develop obesity and diabetes and others do not (all other conditions being similar). Researchers are exploring how bacteria that naturally reside in the gut of people and animals can provide a missing link in helping to prevent and treat these and other conditions.

How Our Intestinal Flora Becomes Imbalanced

A single course of antibiotics is sufficient to wipe out our entire gut microflora, and when our balance of healthy bacteria is disrupted, secondary health issues can be triggered. Let's take a look at some common things that can destroy this delicate balance:

- **Medical Treatments (chemotherapy, radiotherapy, colonoscopies)**
  Chemotherapy and radiotherapy kill good bacteria just as they kill cancerous cells because these treatments can't discriminate between the two, so they wipe both out at the same time. This is the reason many cancer patients suffer from very uncomfortable gastrointestinal problems.

- **Antibiotics & Antibacterial Medications**
  Antibiotics and antibacterial drugs can play an important, life-saving role; unfortunately, these drugs are widely and indiscriminately overprescribed. One prescription is often sufficient to wipe out the entire bacterial population of the gut, resulting in a favorable environment for bad bacteria that can then be very difficult to drive out.

Because of the overuse of antibiotics, stronger strains of superbugs now exist that can enter the body and are resistant to both medications and the beneficial bacteria in the body. Antibiotic resistance is now recognized as a serious problem in the healthcare industry, and there is a growing list of bacterial infections that no longer respond to traditional antibiotics.

- **Antibiotic Residue in Meat & Dairy**
  Over 95 percent of the meat sold in the US is called "factory-farmed" meat, meaning the animals are raised in confined feedlots, and 80 percent of antibiotics manufactured in the US are used in factory-farmed meat and dairy. This is often due to both the unsanitary living conditions and the cruel and inhumane conditions animals are kept in that require antibiotics to prevent infections.

  Large doses of antibiotics are fed to these crowded, confined animals, which then transfer to our food supply and affect our health. In addition, they are excreted in animal manure, and environmental testing has found varying quantities of medicated additives in our waterways. These antibiotics not only contribute to the destruction of our microflora, but also lead to antibiotic resistance. If you eat meat that isn't organic or pasture-raised, then you're eating factory-farmed meat.

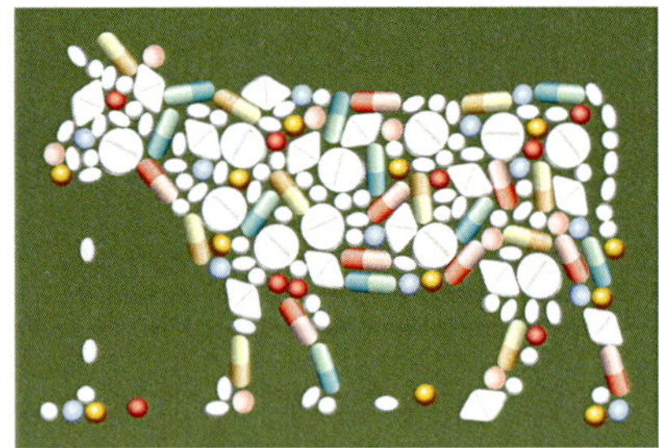

- **Heavy Metals**
  Mercury, lead, arsenic, cadmium, nickel, silver, and other metals are extremely toxic, even in trace amounts. The contamination sources vary from industrial pollutants and commonly used household chemicals, to supplements and herbal formulas.

- **Environmental & Industrial Pollutants**
  These types of pollutants, such as those found in household and garden chemicals, industrial work environments, and our air and water supplies are especially dangerous. A significant portion of toxic chemicals are also found in everyday personal-care products, such as toothpaste, deodorants, shampoos, conditioners, soaps, lotions, and cosmetics.

- **Excessive Dietary Fiber**
  For certain medical conditions and after certain medical procedures, doctors often recommend fiber to replace bacteria and form stools, but excessive fiber taken in supplement form causes fermentation. The by-products of this fermentation destroy beneficial bacteria in the same way acids and alcohols are routinely used to sterilize surgical instruments—they burst bacterial membranes on contact.

  As the fermentation destroys bacteria, we need more and more fiber to form stools. If we suddenly stop the fiber supplements and no longer have the beneficial bacteria we need, constipation sets in as soon as the large intestine clears itself of the remaining bulk. If we then take laxatives, the diarrhea literally washes out even more of the beneficial bacteria from our gut, and we get caught up in this cycle.

  Instead of eating fiber-rich foods, many people rush to the store and take fiber supplements en masse to either firm up stools or stimulate a bowel movement, and they end up being forced to take these supplements on a regular basis. Not only is this artificial overstimulation unhealthy, but excessive supplemental fiber can cause hemorrhoids, diverticulosis, IBS, and colon cancer.

  If you need more fiber, ALWAYS increase your fiber intake by eating more fiber-rich whole foods, such as vegetables, fruits, and sprouted grains, rather than taking any supplements to artificially stimulate your bowels.

- **Excessive Acidity (diet, medications, stress)**
  An acidic diet, medications, or lifestyle factors such as stress can cause our body to become overly acidic.

An imbalance of our intestinal microflora can also cause us to wake up during the night feeling extremely hot, similar to extended hot flashes. The heat produced by harmful organisms can also inflame and dry the intestines, causing constipation.

Microflora imbalances can also lead to the development of a variety of commonly known bad guys, including yeast (candida albicans), klebsiella, proteus, helicobacter pylori, giardia, pseudomonas, citrobacter, and cryptosporidia, among others.

Signs of an Unhealthy Gut

There are some obvious telltale signs that our intestinal microflora is out of whack. Any one of these signs may also indicate other health conditions, and a comprehensive digestive stool analysis (CDSA) at a medical lab can help make this determination:

Constipation & diarrhea: With constipation, there is too little bacteria to loosen up the formed feces and keep them moist because, unlike other stool components, bacterial cells retain moisture. With diarrhea, bacteria are literally being washed out of the gut.

Skin conditions: Including acne and rashes.

Yeast buildup: This occurs in the vagina or mouth (oral/vaginal thrush) and on the skin and is very common when taking antibiotics. Without gut microflora, yeast multiplies without competition. Yeast can cause us to experience too much gas, causing extreme discomfort and stomach distention.

Chronic/frequent infections: These types of infections, especially respiratory infections such as bronchitis, asthma, postnasal drip, sinus congestion, and allergies, usually appear after a routine respiratory infection treated with antibiotics, which in turn wipes out the gut microflora.

Blood-clotting problems & easy bruising: This can also indicate a deficiency of vitamin K (a by-product of bacterial metabolism) or vitamin C. Anticlotting medications such as aspirin, ibuprofen, naproxen (NSAIDs), warfarin, and others may also contribute to the destruction of gut microflora.

Neurological problems: Vitamin B_{12} is essential for normal nervous system functioning, and our B_{12} levels can be affected by gut microflora imbalance. Numbness and tingling of the hands and feet, paleness, shortness of breath, chronic fatigue, a sore mouth and tongue, and mental confusion are the most common symptoms of a vitamin B_{12} deficiency. A high-quality B_{12} supplement is the only way to quickly treat and reverse these symptoms. Because a B_{12} deficiency is now commonplace, we'll talk about this vitamin in more detail later in the protocol.

Now that we understand why gut bacteria is necessary for healthy digestion, let's take a leap into something we may not know very much about. It's time to learn what enzymes are and why they're an important piece of the health puzzle.

THE ALL-IMPORTANT ENZYMES

When we think about food and nutrition, a few things come to mind: What kind of food should I eat? What should I avoid? How much protein and carbohydrates and fat do I need? Do I need vitamin and mineral supplements?

The word "enzymes" never enters the picture, even though we need enzymes—especially food enzymes—not only to digest and metabolize all the food we eat, but for life itself. They're needed for every chemical reaction that occurs in the body.

Eating, breathing, moving, and thinking all require enzymes. When we bleed, our blood can't coagulate without the assistance of enzymes. No vitamin, mineral, or hormone can do any of its work without enzymes. The cells, tissues, and organs in our bodies all function because of the presence of metabolic enzymes. These enzymes convert the food we eat into nutrients that our body can use. It doesn't matter what nutrients you give your body; without enzymes, they're useless.

In short, all life—whether it be plant, animal, or human—requires the presence of enzymes to sustain that life. They're a precious asset and determine how effectively our bodies can maintain a high state of health and fight disease. When the body heals itself, it's the body's metabolic enzymes that are involved in the "curing." No other mechanism can produce the cure to any illness.

What Are Enzymes

An enzyme is a tiny chemical that performs a specific job. Some enzymes do specific things at specific temperatures, some do these things with or without oxygen, and some with or without water. There are thousands of different enzymes in our body continually being used and eliminated through our urine, sweat, and feces.

Let's take a look at the 3 types of enzymes and discuss why food enzymes are so important for our health. We'll also look at what happens to our body when we eat enzyme-poor foods.

Types of Enzymes

There are 3 categories of enzymes:

1. **Metabolic Enzymes**
   Metabolic enzymes run our bodies. Every organ and tissue has its own metabolic enzymes that perform specific jobs. Hundreds of these metabolic enzymes are necessary to carry out the work of the body, to repair damage and decay, and to heal us from disease.

2. **Food Enzymes**
   Food enzymes are present in raw and lightly cooked whole foods, as well as raw supplements, and they help our bodies predigest the food we eat. For example, when we eat an apple, the enzymes in the apple help our bodies to very efficiently break down and digest that apple.

   Food enzymes also help our own digestive enzymes break down food. To function properly, food enzymes should be eaten as part of a whole food (rather than in supplement form) because they function synergistically with other nutrients in that food (e.g., vitamins, minerals, and antioxidants).

"The DNA itself is lifeless. What gives the cell its life & personality is enzymes. They govern all bodily processes. The malfunction of even one enzyme can be fatal. Nothing in nature is so vital & tangible in our life, yet so poorly understood."

Dr. Arthur Kornberg
Nobel Prize, Genetics

3. **Digestive Enzymes**

   The body produces digestive enzymes, which help break down the food we eat:

   - Protease is an enzyme that digests protein.
   - Amylase is an enzyme that digests carbohydrates.
   - Lipase is an enzyme that digests fat.

   Our saliva contains a high concentration of amylase, whereas the stomach contains protease. The pancreas produces all three enzymes to help us digest food, as well as many other types of digestive enzymes.

Why Food Enzymes Are So Important

Raw foods such as fruits, vegetables, nuts, seeds, and raw (unpasteurized) dairy naturally contain a large amount of food enzymes. The type of enzyme a food contains is dependent on the nutrients that food contains. For example:

- Fatty foods such as nuts, seeds, and dairy contain higher amounts of the enzyme lipase to help us digest the fat content.
- Lean, raw meats contain large amounts of protease in the form of cathepsin to help us digest the protein.
- Carbohydrate foods contain higher concentrations of amylase and less of the lipase and protease to help us digest the carbohydrates.
- Many fruits and vegetables contain large quantities of the enzyme cellulase, which is needed to help us break down the plant fibers.

Nature has supplied fresh, raw foods with all the necessary food enzymes to help us digest these foods. Food enzymes also convert certain phytochemicals into their active forms within our body. For example:

Myrosinase

Found in cruciferous vegetables such as Brussels sprouts, cauliflower, kale, collard greens, bok choy, broccoli, cabbage, turnip, daikon, and radishes, myrosinase contains glucosinolates, which are converted into isothiocyanates that are important in inducing phase II enzymes (critical anticancer agents).

Alliinase

Found in allium vegetables such as onions, garlic, leeks, scallions/spring onions, and chives, alliinase contains alliin, which is converted to allicin. Allicin has antimicrobial, antithrombotic, antiarthritic, anticancer, and lipid-lowering capabilities. This is why garlic is commonly used as a therapeutic agent.

What Happens When We Eat Enzyme-Poor Foods?

Our body's organs, especially the pancreas, produce enzymes to digest food and to supply our organs with the enzymes that they need, but they weren't built to be the sole provider of enzymes to help us digest food—this is primarily the job of food enzymes. It's very important to get fresh enzymes from the food in our diet because our pancreas and other enzyme-making organs wear down when they're overworked. More importantly, these organs need to focus on producing enzymes that assist in normal metabolism and internal housekeeping. They are responsible for:

- Rejuvenation of cells
- Growth
- Elimination of daily toxins from the food we eat, water we drink, air we breathe, and the chemicals in household cleaners and personal-care products we come into contact with

- Strengthening our immune system

In a healthy body, the production of enzymes for digestion should be minimal. But when we eat the standard diet filled with processed foods and artificial ingredients, not only do we create a toxic load that overtaxes the body, but these foods are completely devoid of food enzymes. The pancreas now must divert its energy toward producing food enzymes to digest this food, instead of producing enzymes to eliminate the new inflow of toxins and to conduct general internal housekeeping.

Over time, eating a diet devoid of food enzymes contributes to the depletion of all the body's organs and systems and builds a foundation ripe for chronic disease—all without our knowledge or realization that it's happening. The pancreas especially feels this burden. Let's explore this in more detail.

HOW ENZYME DEPLETION AFFECTS HEALTH

Enzymes & Our Organs

The food we eat affects the size and weight of our organs. A diet lacking food enzymes forces the pancreas to work harder to create these missing enzymes, which then enlarges the pancreas.

For better or worse, the quality of the food we eat directly impacts the health of every organ and tissue in the body. Clinical research has shown over and over again that poor nutrition and enzyme depletion significantly affect the weight of important glands such as the pituitary, testicles, ovaries, pancreas, adrenals, and thyroid, as well as other organs.

- Published organ-weight studies show that during experimentation, both the size and weight of the pancreas changes depending on the type of diet eaten. When food in the diet lacked food enzymes, the pancreas was forced to produce more of its own enzymes and became enlarged.[1]
- Scientists discovered that the pancreas of laboratory-fed mice was 2.5 times heavier than that of wild mice (pancreas weight % of 0.84 compared to 0.32). When returned to their enzyme-rich raw diet, their pancreas returned to normal size.
- In comparing the pancreas of rats eating a raw natural diet vs. rats eating a cooked diet, the pancreas of the rats on the raw-food diet were one-third the size of the pancreas of cooked-food rats where the enzymes had been destroyed. The study concluded that the pancreas enlargement was due to the additional work required by the pancreas to process the enzymes that were now deficient in the food.[2]
- When white rats were fed a diet containing 80 percent sugar (enzyme-free), a marked difference was reported in the size and weight of all principal organs and glands.[3]

An important note is that wild mice are typically disease-free. When laboratory mice are dissected at the end of their life span, however, a shocking number of human degenerative diseases are present after eating a heat-treated laboratory diet devoid of food enzymes.

Heat-treated and refined foods caused the most drastic changes in the size and appearance of the pituitary gland and pancreas.

When animals were fed diets with restricted enzymes, damage in the pituitary was similar to (and sometimes identical to) that found in humans who eat conventional food with a greatly reduced amount of food enzymes.

Let's take a look at how a lack of food enzymes not only causes the pancreas to enlarge, but also decreases brain size, can contribute to obesity, and triggers premature aging.

Enzyme Depletion & the Pancreas

In an average adult, the pancreas weighs approximately 3 ounces. When we eat food that contains no food enzymes to help our bodies digest our food, the pancreas must then produce its own enzymes to do the job instead. It sends out messages to the body to look for metabolic enzymes it can turn into digestive enzymes, a process that means the body must now function on fewer metabolic enzymes (the guys who are busy running our bodies and doing continual house-cleaning and toxic-waste removal).

When the pancreas is forced to do more work, it enlarges (just as any muscle does when we exercise it repeatedly), except the pancreas doesn't need this type of exercise. It wasn't built to do this job.

Enzyme Depletion & Brain Weight

In looking at brain weight as a percentage of body weight, the brains of wild meadow mice are nearly twice as heavy as those of tame laboratory mice. When animals become domesticated, we typically change their food and reduce or remove raw foods, which changes their nutrition. When rats are given a processed laboratory diet, body weight goes up, and brain weight goes down. In lab mice, such brain weight changes can happen in as little as one month.

When non-domesticated creatures give up their food and eat the processed diets we give them, research has shown that their brains lose weight and they become much more susceptible to the same types of diseases we humans suffer. As a side note, obesity also accompanies these changes.

Enzyme Depletion & Obesity

Overactive or underactive glands can affect body weight, and certain foods over-activate the glands—namely the pancreas and pituitary—that control obesity.

The quality of calories in the food we eat is far more important than the number of them. Raw calories in whole foods (even raw nuts when eaten in small quantities—especially almonds and walnuts) are relatively non-stimulating to the glands and tend to stabilize weight.

Tests on the abdominal fat of 11 extra heavyweights (ranging from 280 to 430 pounds, with an average of 340 pounds) discovered a deficiency of the enzyme lipase in their fat deposits, the same enzyme that helps the body to digest and metabolize fat.[(4)] A conclusion reached was that obesity and abnormal cholesterol deposits are significantly increased by eating fats deficient in lipase. Lipase is found in raw, fatty foods (both plant-based and animal-based).

This is why traditional cultures, such as the Eskimos, that ate a very high-fat animal-based diet ate those foods raw. They were preserving this important enzyme to help the fats digest in their bodies. Multiple long-term scientific studies show that these cultures suffered none of the cardiovascular and cholesterol disorders that are now epidemic in our Western industrialized food chain, even though their fat intake was much higher.

Illness can also be a sign that our enzyme levels are depleted. Any illness or inability to recover from illness as fast as we usually do can indicate an issue with enzyme production, or enzymes that aren't functioning properly.

Enzyme Depletion & Aging

Enzyme depletion and aging go hand in hand. Every person is born with a supply of enzymatic energy from birth, and this potential can either be used wisely or wasted quickly. This supply is finite, and the faster we use up our enzymes, the more prematurely we age. Preserving enzymes is important business! How does the body's enzyme supply become depleted? By forcing it to produce food enzymes unnecessarily.

IMPORTANT! If we don't include plenty of fresh, whole foods in their raw or lightly cooked form in our diet, we are missing out on the food enzymes that help us digest the nutrients in the food. Our body's organs are then forced to create these missing enzymes.

Over time, these overworked organs become less able to keep up with the daily jobs of internal cleansing, rejuvenation of cells, elimination of toxins, and strengthening of our immune system. The result? Premature aging. When nature designed the human body, it wasn't designed for refined or processed foods or for a diet heavy in cooked foods. The human body naturally thrives on a diet high in fresh, live foods full of food enzymes. These are the foods that should form the majority of our diet.

What Happens to Enzymes as We Age

Substantial research shows us that enzyme activity becomes increasingly weaker as we grow older. The more we eat foods that contain food enzymes earlier in life, the higher our enzyme potential will be as we age. The higher our enzyme potential, the more we postpone the effects of old age. Conversely, eating a diet low in enzyme content does the exact opposite: we use up our enzyme potential faster and age sooner.

Spending more enzymes than we conserve is an enzyme-depleting way to live.

Remember: If food enzymes do some of the work as they're supposed to, then fewer digestive enzymes are needed from the body and our enzyme potential wears out at a much slower rate. Let's look at what the studies show:

- The presence of enzymes in the saliva of young adults is 30 times stronger than in persons over 69 years of age.[5]
- In testing 1,200 urine specimens for the starch-digesting enzyme amylase, it averaged twice as much in young people as compared to elderly people. Less food eaten also resulted in fewer digestive enzymes required.[6]
- The enzyme amylase is much weaker in older men than in younger men. Results concluded that the enzyme deficiency in the older group was due to the exhaustion in the cells of the pancreas.[7]
- Production of the enzyme catalase decreases with old age in potato beetles, fireflies, and adult grasshoppers.[8]
- Production of the enzyme lipase, the fat-digesting enzyme, was found to be reduced in older rats as compared to adult rats in their prime.[9]
- In testing the digestive enzyme levels of pepsin and trypsin in individuals ranging from 12-96 years, in the older group, both enzymes were found to be decreased to one-quarter of the strength. Amylase in saliva was also found to be markedly decreased. The amylase and lipase in the pancreatic juice was slightly decreased.[10]

REMEMBER …
The more we eat enzyme-depleted foods, the sooner we age.

No matter what you do in life, you can't change the fact that you'll always be using up enzymes, simply because you're alive and breathing. However, you can control the rate at which you use them by making the right food and lifestyle choices, and by not doing things that deplete and destroy them. Eating enzyme-rich foods enables the body to focus more on producing metabolic enzymes, helping to regenerate our bodies. When our metabolic enzyme potential is exhausted, the end of life is triggered.

HOW WE DEPLETE OR DESTROY ENZYMES

We move toward enzyme bankruptcy silently, with or without symptoms. As we divert enzyme production away from what our organs and tissues need and toward digesting food instead, we achieve a shortened lifespan, poor organ health, premature aging, and illness.

It's Beginning to Sound Familiar

We do several things to our food that contribute to the damage or destruction of food enzymes:

- **Eating Processed & Refined Food**
  These foods have been stripped of the food enzymes naturally present in unprocessed, fresh foods. Food manufacturers often use various enzymes in the production of their foods, but all of these enzymes are destroyed by the cooking process either before they reach the consumer or when consumer cooks the food further.

- **Drugs & Alcohol**
  Recreational drugs, prescription drugs, nonprescription drugs, and alcohol all negatively affect our enzyme supply.

- **Food Irradiation & Microwaves**
  Irradiating and microwaving both damage food by breaking up molecules and creating free radicals, destroying enzymes and other essential vitamins, including vitamins A, C, E, K, the B vitamins, amino acids, and fatty acids.

- **Taking Starch or Protein Blockers (weight-loss pills)**
  Some people try to lose weight by eating starch or protein inhibitors (in the form of pills, capsules, or liquids), which are special enzyme inhibitors that prevent the body from digesting starches or proteins. Unfortunately, the pancreas sees the enzymes are missing and is then forced to secrete large quantities of enzymes to try to digest the food instead. These enzymes are then passed out of the body.

  In a study, trypsin (protein) inhibitors fed to rats and chickens in their food enlarged the pancreas and greatly increased enzyme secretion by the pancreas. These secretions were then wasted and excreted from the body.

- **Frequent Snacking**
  Snacking also wastes enzymes. A research study compared two groups of rats, one restricted to eating once a day, compared to another group snacking and frequently eating. The lifespan of the frequent snackers was shorter by 17 percent (688 days compared to 587 days). Far fewer enzymes were produced in mice fed only once a day. They also had lower body weight and more enzymes present in their tissues, which is why these animals lived longer. Enzymes were produced multiple times each day by the constant snackers, which likely contributed to their shortened lifespan.(1)

  There is nothing healthy about frequent snacking. It wastes not only enzymes but also energy as the body uses a tremendous amount of energy to digest food. Biologists estimate that the body spends over 50 percent of its energy on the digestion and elimination of food. Frequent snacking is an unhealthy habit that robs your body of energy—energy normally focused on other important metabolic processes.

  Several diets out there now recommend eating as often as 6 times a day. If your diet recommends frequent meals and snacks, ditch it! Your digestive system was never meant to function in overdrive, and all this does is deplete your energy. If you need to snack between meals, it's because you're not eating enough of the right foods (high in nutrition) at those meals. Adjust the quality and quantity of your food, and nix the snacking.

- **High-Temperature Cooking**
  Cooking over 118° F for a prolonged period begins to destroy food enzymes. Most enzymes that help to convert nutrients from our food into nutrients our body can use are destroyed between 118° F and 160° F because they're very heat-sensitive.

  Whether broiling or boiling, baking or stewing, frying or roasting, the act of cooking destroys enzymes. Generally speaking, if water is too hot to touch, it will likely damage enzymes in food. Let's talk about this a little more.

Cooking Food Isn't the Problem

If humans have been cooking for such a long time and they're still going strong, how can cooking be so detrimental? Let's take a look:

It's not that cooking is detrimental: Previously, the majority of our diet came from raw foods, such as salads, veggies, nuts, fruits, and unpasteurized dairy, as well as fermented foods. Cooked foods formed a *much smaller* portion of the foods we ate. High-temperature cooking is far more common now than it ever was in traditional cultures.

It's not simply that we eat a lot of cooked foods: Before the food even reaches us, before we cook it, it's seriously damaged. Whereas 50 years ago, food was naturally organic, today it's laced with pesticides. Animals are pumped with antibiotics, hormones, and steroids and fed an unnatural diet of genetically modified soy and corn. Most of the food in the supermarket is processed, filled with chemicals and additives (some of which are banned in other parts of the world, such as Europe, because they are carcinogenic, disrupt hormones, or for other negative health impacts).

Our cooking methods are also to blame: Charring foods and frying them in hydrogenated oils create new chemical compounds that have been conclusively linked to cancer.

We can offset these negatives when we balance eating lightly cooked foods with plenty of fresh, raw foods. Unfortunately, in the typical Western diet, healthy foods and salads often end up as garnishments or the smallest part of the meal.

Pasteurized Dairy Depletes Our Enzymes

Pasteurization heats milk to a temperature that causes the milk to undergo significant changes and destroys beneficial bacteria, nutrients, and enzymes, including ingredients that are natural protectors of the milk and that help our bodies predigest it. This is why some people are unable to properly digest pasteurized milk and yet have no problem digesting raw milk.

Enzymes from a mother's breast milk contain dozens of food enzymes, especially lipase, to assist newborn infants in digesting the milk. Studies have shown it also contains a significant number of bacteria. Does this mean we should be pasteurizing breast milk too? Of course not! Breast milk is raw because it needs to be raw to provide both the enzymes and immunity factors necessary to be considered a complete food for nursing.

When a baby sucks pasteurized milk from a bottle, the pasteurization has destroyed nutrients and enzymes that help a baby predigest proteins in the milk. Take a look at the differences between breast milk, raw milk, pasteurized milk, and pasteurized infant formulas. The significant difference in beneficial components present speak for themselves:

Component	Breast Milk	Raw Milk	Pasteurized Milk	UHT Milk	Infant Formula
B-lymphocytes	active	active	inactive	inactive	inactive
Macrophages	active	active	inactive	inactive	inactive
Neutrophils	active	active	inactive	inactive	inactive
Lymphocytes	active	active	inactive	inactive	inactive
IgA/IgG Antibodies	active	active	inactive	inactive	inactive
B_{12} Binding Protein	active	active	inactive	inactive	inactive
Bifidus Factor	active	active	inactive	inactive	inactive
Medium Chain FAs	active	active	reduced	reduced	reduced
Fibro nectin	active	active	inactive	inactive	inactive
Gamma Interferon	active	active	inactive	inactive	inactive
Lactoferrin	active	active	reduced	inactive	inactive
Lysozyme	active	active	active	inactive	inactive
Mucin A Oigosaccharides	active	active	reduced	reduced	inactive
Hormones / Growth Factors	active	active	reduced	reduced	inactive

Source: "Randomized controlled milk trial," *The Lancet*

When we eat a diet rich in natural and unpasteurized foods, the enzymes found in these foods help us properly digest the nutrients. Incidentally, the biggest and most serious milk recalls in the dairy industry have been of pasteurized milk, *not* unpasteurized milk.

How Heat Affects Proteins

Amino acids, the building blocks of protein, begin to deteriorate at 118° F and most are destroyed at 160° F. When we eat this damaged protein, it creates inflammation in the body. The next time you cook a piece of meat and get excited about the amount of protein you're eating, think again. The protein has been significantly degraded, which is why it's important not to cook meat for extended periods at high temperatures or to overcook or char it.

In contrast, there are many veggies, sprouted grains, and superfoods that don't need cooking and that contain over 18 amino acids (including all essential ones) that can benefit us – far more than what is contained in meat after it has been cooked.

But What about the Eskimos?

Traditional Eskimos ate huge quantities of meat, but it was raw. Long-term studies were conducted on Eskimos who ate several pounds of raw animal fat per day. Not only was there an absence of obesity, but the studies found clean arteries and a *complete lack of heart disease.*

Traditional/primitive cultures understood that raw and fermented foods (versus a predominance of cooked and pasteurized foods, the latter of which didn't even exist) were the key to vitality and freedom from degenerative disease.

Raw fat contains the enzyme lipase, which is found in all raw foods containing animal or vegetable fat. Animal flesh and organs also contain an enzyme called cathepsin within the meat itself, which helps us digest the protein in meat. When an animal eats prey for food, it also inherits the cathepsin inside that prey's belly.

In case you're wondering, no, I'm definitely not advocating eating raw meat! I'm simply illustrating the importance of food enzymes in our diet and how they contribute to our health.

Lipase used to be present in olive oil, back when it was thick and opaque, but when factories began refining it and producing clearer versions, the commercial production destroyed the lipase content.

The easiest way to separate fat from the lipase that helps us digest that fat is to destroy it using high-temperature cooking, which is why we should only purchase oils labeled as cold-pressed and unrefined.

Most primitive cultures weren't vegetarians, nor were they vegans (although some were semi-vegetarians). On the contrary, most ate large quantities of meat, fish, and/or dairy and yet were robust and strong, free of most of today's diseases. Although this is considered a healthy diet, it is not a high vibrational diet, which is now necessary for us as a species to not only evolve beyond disease, but also embrace our unlimited potential as humans on this earth.

Inflammation

Now that we've learned all about how we digest and absorb nutrients, and about the importance of gut microflora and enzymes, let's learn about an often misunderstood but very important warning sign our body gives us when something isn't quite right.

INFLAMMATION

Understanding Inflammation

Inflammation is the natural response our body gives us in defense of injuries, infections, and internal stresses. There are two different types of inflammation:

1. **Acute Inflammation**
   Acute inflammation comes on very quickly and produces an immediate reaction in response to physical injuries (e.g., pulling a muscle, fracturing or breaking a bone) and infections (caused by viruses, bacteria, parasites, or a fungus). Bug bites and bee stings are great examples of things that can cause an instant inflammatory reaction.

   The immune system sends key nutrients to the damaged area by increasing the blood flow, which in turn creates the swelling, heat/redness, and pain, normally localized to the area of the body that's inflamed.

   Inflammation is an essential part of the healing process. Sometimes a cortisone shot or antihistamine medication can save our lives in the event of an overwhelming inflammatory response, such as from an allergy to a bee sting. These are great examples of where traditional medicine shines in cases of trauma and medical emergencies.

2. **Chronic Inflammation**
   A hot topic in the world of diet and nutrition today is chronic inflammation, which is an internal inflammation that builds up over a period of time in response to an unhealthy diet and/or stress. Instead of responding only to an injury and healing us (as with acute inflammation), the immune system is in a continual fire-fighting mode.

Several different things can cause chronic inflammation. Let's see if they sound familiar:

- Inflammatory foods and foods that cause allergies/sensitivities
- Emotional stress
- Physical stress/overexertion
- Obesity—visceral fat cells (the deep fat around our organs) secrete inflammatory molecules that can cause low-grade inflammation and insulin resistance.[1]
- Smoking
- Imbalanced hormone levels
- Environmental and household contaminants (household cleaners, pesticides, air fresheners, adhesives, plastics, etc.)
- Chemicals in personal-care products (soaps, cosmetics, shampoos and conditioners, lotions, sunscreens, toothpaste, mouthwash, deodorants, etc.)

Sleep disorders, such as general insomnia, sleep apnea, and narcolepsy, can also cause chronic inflammation, especially if we're overweight.[2][3]

Often it's not one specific thing that causes chronic inflammation, and what causes inflammation in one person may not in another. It depends on our health and the strength of our immune system. Unfortunately, when the body is fed an unhealthy diet or suffers prolonged stress, not only does this contribute to inflammation, but we're also depriving our body of the foods it needs that naturally heal and eliminate that inflammation. It's a double whammy!

It's the chronic inflammation that concerns us, and it's the type we address in this protocol.

Why Chronic Inflammation Is Dangerous

The problem with chronic low-level inflammation is that, like stress, it silently and seriously damages our health. We're completely unaware of it. It can go undetected for a long period of time and not be discovered until it's caused enough cellular destruction to produce the symptoms of a disease.

When the immune system is in a continual reactive mode, it never "shuts off." There is a continual cycle of destruction and healing. This constant overproduction of immune cells damages our body and creates free radicals. Homocysteine levels also become raised (a risk factor for heart disease). Without realizing it, we set the stage for disease.

Chronic inflammation can be very dangerous. The number of diseases and autoimmune conditions linked to chronic inflammation is staggering:

- Heart disease
- Cancer
- Diabetes
- Depression
- Chronic kidney disease
- Osteoporosis
- Arthritis
- Weight gain
- Gastrointestinal disorders (IBS, GERD, Crohn's disease, ulcerative colitis, pancreatitis)
- Alzheimer's disease[4][5]
- Premature aging and a shortened lifespan

Eliminating Inflammation

Even though inflammation can lay the foundation for disease, inflammation itself is not a disease. It's a health condition almost always caused by diet and lifestyle choices. When it comes to addressing inflammation, there are two approaches we can take:

Natural – Using natural anti-inflammatories (such as from foods, whole-food supplements, and changing lifestyle habits).

Conventional – Using anti-inflammatory and/or immunosuppressant drugs.

The Body Healer Protocol uses a natural approach to reducing inflammation. The great news is that reducing and eliminating chronic inflammation isn't complicated! It's something you can begin right now, and your body will respond rapidly. We'll hit inflammation from 6 different angles, which together form the 6 points of the protocol.

1. **FOOD:** We remove foods that cause inflammation and replace them with foods that are naturally detoxifying and anti-inflammatory. When necessary, we supplement our diet with whole-food anti-inflammatory supplements that help us reduce inflammation.
2. **BREATH:** We learn how to breathe correctly, more fully oxygenating our body. The more oxygenated we become, the more vitalized we become. Waste is more efficiently removed from our body, and we lower our inflammation.
3. **MOVEMENT:** We increase our activity and stimulate the flow of lymph, helping the body to detoxify by more efficiently eliminating toxins and other waste.
4. **ENVIRONMENT:** We eliminate personal-care products and household cleaners containing toxic chemicals that contribute to inflammation.
5. **ENERGY:** We learn how to work directly with high vibrational energy, drawing it into our body. This naturally reduces and eliminates inflammation.
6. **MIND:** We use the power behind our thoughts and intentions to help reduce inflammation. The mind has an incredibly powerful effect on the biological functions of the body.

The Conventional Approach to Treating Chronic Inflammation

Conventional doctors often treat inflammation with anti-inflammatory drugs. When it comes to chronic inflammation, this medicated suppression is a Band-Aid approach that fails to address the root cause of the inflammation. Some commonly used non-steroidal anti-inflammatory drugs (e.g., Advil and Motrin) can cause harm when taken over an extended period of time to relieve inflammation. They're associated with increased intestinal permeability (creating gaps in the intestinal wall that allow infections and toxins to pass through it). It can then take months for the intestinal wall to heal after the medication has bee stopped.[(6)(7)]

Let's first take a look at the dangers of taking synthetic anti-inflammatories or immunosuppressants, and then talk about the steps you can take to support yourself and protect your health if you need to use them.

ANTI-INFLAMMATORY & IMMUNOSUPPRESANT DRUGS

Natural medicine views inflammation very differently compared to traditional medicine, which aims to suppress it with drugs. The immune system produces inflammation for a reason, and artificially suppressing it doesn't address why the inflammation exists. Immunosuppressant drugs also suppress the immune system, severely compromising its ability to both heal the body and protect it against other conditions and diseases.

A traditional doctor will rarely advise an anti-inflammatory diet and a reduction in medications. Their number-one goal is to quickly reduce inflammation to offer their patient relief, and medication is the quickest route.

In all fairness to doctors, their expertise doesn't lie with diet, nutrition, and lifestyle changes as methods to prevent disease and reduce inflammation. Doctors are limited to using the tools in their toolbox, and they focus on trying to reduce symptoms (including pain) with drugs, even though these drugs (especially anticancer drugs) both suppress and cause damage to the immune system. They also have very serious side effects when taken long-term.

Doctors can only do the best they can with the training they have. Fortunately, many doctors are beginning to recognize the serious deficiencies of our healthcare system and do the best they can to function within it. This includes expanding their education to integrate more natural and noninvasive methods of healthcare into their practice.

Cold or Flu? Avoid Over-the-Counter Drugs That Suppress Inflammation

When we suffer from the common cold or the flu, our body produces a fever to help us both get rid of the illness and feel better sooner. Taking common over-the-counter drugs, such as aspirin, ibuprofen, or acetaminophen (Tylenol) can be counterproductive as they suppress the body's own ability to produce the antibodies that kill the offending pathogens. Vioxx and Celebrex are two examples of prescription anti-inflammatories. What happens when we take them? It takes the body longer to combat the cold and increases our chances of getting a secondary infection.

Common anti-inflammatory drugs not only cause serious and unseen internal side effects, they have also killed thousands of people. Natural anti-inflammatories, however, are not only very beneficial but also lack the side effects of drugs.

Immunosuppressant Drugs Damage Our Immune System

Most people take the list of potential side effects on prescription drug labels far too lightly. Immunosuppressant drugs taken for extended periods of time can cause organ damage and may later create secondary conditions worse than the original illness for which the drugs were prescribed.

When immunosuppressant drugs are taken for a chronic disease, they have the side effect of impairing the immune system and its ability to fight other diseases and infections. Chemotherapy treatments for cancer are an example of medications that not only attack cancer cells, but also other healthy cells, including those found in the bone marrow and other parts of the immune system. This is why the recurrence rate on some cancers is high (breast cancer has a 15-20 percent recurrence rate within 10 years of treatment). If the disease comes out of remission, the body is much less able to defend itself the second time around, and the recurrence is often fatal.

Sometimes, anti-inflammatory and immunosuppressant drugs not only fail to help us, but they can also cause gradual health deterioration. With nothing left in their toolbox, traditional doctors aren't able to offer anything better than a "limited timeline."

How to Protect Yourself While on These Drugs

Anti-inflammatory and immunosuppressant drugs should be used with extreme caution, and only along with other important healing elements, such as diet, exercise, removal of stress, and natural therapies. When a disease enters remission, these elements will strengthen the body immeasurably to not only heal, but also prevent any future disease recurrence.

If you choose to take immunosuppressant drugs, it's very important that you also:

- Spend time learning about and understanding the root cause of your condition; this protocol is designed to help you do just that.

- Understand that, by their very nature, these drugs compromise the immune system. Make sure you thoroughly understand the side effects.
- Do your very best to provide your body with the tools it needs to self-heal while taking the medication. Following this protocol should be right at the very top of the list.

If you're taking any anti-inflammatory medications, as your condition improves through diet and lifestyle changes, work under your doctor's supervision to slowly and steadily reduce the medication until it's no longer needed. If your doctor isn't open to working with you, consider working with an integrative doctor with a more natural approach who specializes in working with chronic disease. These doctors understand the critical links between diet, stress, and health and will always recommend a cleansing, detoxifying diet while decreasing medication when the time is right.

With this approach, not only is inflammation reduced, but the immune system is no longer suppressed by synthetic medications.

IMPORTANT!

Drugs such as prednisone may be part of the treatment your doctor recommends when fighting a serious condition such as cancer. Even though your goal should be to eliminate medications as soon as possible, it's very important NOT to suddenly stop taking these drugs without your doctor's consent. While on this protocol, work very closely under your doctor's guidance to slowly, but steadily, reduce these drugs as your health improves. If you continue to reduce the medication and pain returns, increase the dosage to the level where pain is easily tolerable while continuing with the protocol.

REMEMBER:

Immunosuppressant drugs work by artificially suppressing inflammation and our immune system. By providing the body with the tools it needs to heal (the right diet and lifestyle habits) and removing the things that cause it harm, we can drastically increase our body's ability to naturally heal itself.

Time to Take Action – Let's Get Started!

We've talked about the basics of energy and about old and new paradigms. We've also talked about what causes the body to get sick and what it needs to become healthy. We now also understand how our digestive system provides us with important clues when something isn't quite right. It's now time to return to the 6 points of the protocol we talked about earlier and begin to take action on each one.

Let's get started with diet and detoxification!

PART II
THE PROTOCOL

DIET & DETOXIFICATION

THE VIBRATION OF FOODS

Food has a powerful effect on the body's ability to both prevent and heal disease. What we put in our mouths is very important to our overall state of health, and one of the biggest threats is the manipulation of our food chain with chemicalized food. On any given day, the ingredients in the average American meal consists of an assortment of:

Foods that contain...

- Heavy metals
- Hormones, antibiotics, and steroids
- Trans fats
- Food dyes
- Genetically modified ingredients
- Artificial colors and flavors
- Artificial sweeteners
- Synthetic vitamins/foods
- Excitotoxins (addictive ingredients)

as well as foods that are prepared by...

- Highly processing and refining it
- Microwaving it
- Irradiating it
- Pasteurizing it
- Canning it
- Spraying it with pesticides
- Using artificial preservatives
- Cooking it at high temperatures

Foods absorb vital nutrients from the soil in which they grow. Unfortunately, these nutrients are significantly depleted by soil contaminants, such as pesticides, as well as by how the food is prepared, resulting in nutritionally and vibrationally dead food. To make matters worse, refined and synthetic foods contain excitotoxins—ingredients that cause you to become addicted to those foods and crave more of them. Most people are addicted to the toxic standard American diet and are committing a slow suicide with food.

Our bodies are not designed for this onslaught, and as time goes by, we both overwhelm it and deprive it of critical nutritional needs. Degenerative diseases naturally follow.

Why High Vibrational Foods Are Important

High vibrational foods are lighter and less dense and are high in water content. Foods with the highest vibration measured are the ones exposed to the sun and that absorb the most sunlight; they are literally filled with "liquid light."

These high vibrational foods are ripe, organic raw fruits and leafy green vegetables. Not only do they contain the highest concentration of oxygen and light energy, but these living foods are also naturally hydrating to the body. If you juiced them, most would give you a lot of juice because they contain so much water!

Coincidentally, acupuncture is used to stimulate the flow of oxygen throughout areas of the body that are depleted of oxygen.

Healthy High Vibrational Foods

What foods are high vibrational in nature? Let's take a look:

- Sunlight (sunlight is a very important nourishing "food" for the body)
- Fresh, clean water, free from industrial contaminants common in municipal water
- Ripe, raw organic fruits, especially fruit juices
- Ripe, raw organic vegetables, especially leafy greens and reds
- Sea vegetables
- Raw sweeteners (raw honey; fresh stevia leaf; fresh, raw sugar-cane juice)
- Sprouts (sunflower, alfalfa, clover, mung beans, cress, broccoli...)

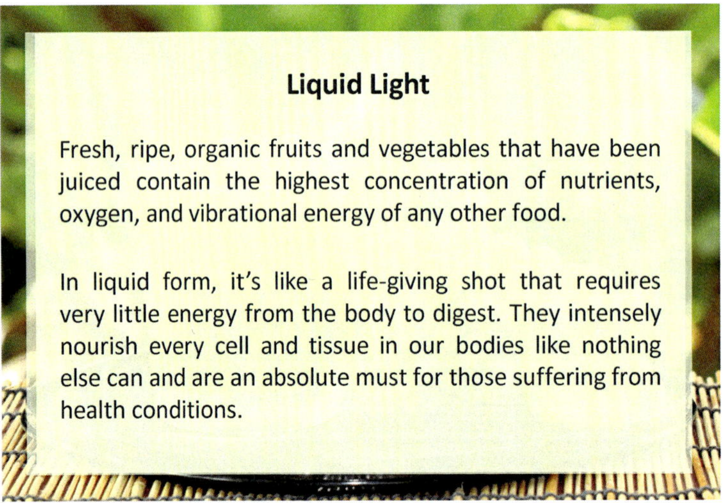

Liquid Light

Fresh, ripe, organic fruits and vegetables that have been juiced contain the highest concentration of nutrients, oxygen, and vibrational energy of any other food.

In liquid form, it's like a life-giving shot that requires very little energy from the body to digest. They intensely nourish every cell and tissue in our bodies like nothing else can and are an absolute must for those suffering from health conditions.

Healthy Medium Vibrational Foods

These are produce foods altered by simple preparation methods:

- Lightly cooked vegetables
- Freeze-dried and dehydrated (dried) fruits and vegetables

Generally speaking, lower vibrational foods are heavier and denser and contain much less water. When water content is removed from foods that are naturally high in water content, there is a significant measurable drop in their frequency.

Low Vibrational Foods

There are two types of low vibrational foods:

1. The type that's compatible with the human energy field and provides us with important nutrients, and
2. The type that isn't compatible and that damages the human energy field; these are the refined and denatured foods that form the bulk of the industrialized Western food chain.

Just because something is denser and lower vibrational doesn't mean it's unhealthy for you. It does, however, mean that it vibrates at a slower rate, and if you eat a lot of it in your diet, you will too. If you enjoy these foods, they should form a small quantity of your diet.

Let's take a look at the different types of low vibrational foods and make sure we permanently etch them in our memory.

COMPATIBLE Lower vibrational foods	INCOMPATIBLE Lower vibrational foods
Organic root vegetables, light-med cooked or raw (e.g., beets, potatoes, turnips, parsnips).	Heavily processed, overcooked, or genetically modified root vegetables.
Organic, high-fat fruits and vegetables (e.g., olives, avocados, coconuts, plantains).	Processed or refined high-fat fruits and vegetables; refined coconut products.
Organic, raw nuts or seeds, soaked before eaten to increase their digestibility; raw nut butters (e.g., peanut, cashew, almond).	Roasted nuts or seeds, or any nut or seed that is not labeled as raw; processed nut butters.
Chocolate high in cacao (70% or more) with no unnatural ingredients; consider exploring raw chocolate brands.	Processed chocolate products (which usually contain artificial chemicals and/or pasteurized dairy).
Organic, unpasteurized (raw) or fermented dairy products (cheese, milk, butter, yogurt, infant formula); raw cheese is now available in every major supermarket chain in the refrigerated natural-food section. Some natural-food markets carry an extensive selection of specialty raw goat, cow, and sheep's milk cheese. Make sure the dairy comes from pasture-raised animals.	Pasteurized dairy products (cheese, milk, butter, yogurt, infant formula), which are often highly processed and contain other unwanted ingredients.
Wild-caught fish; organic, pasture-raised, grass-fed meats that are raised on their natural diet.	Factory-farmed meat or fish, fed an unnatural diet of genetically modified corn and/or soy.
Organic sprouted or fermented seeds and grains (e.g., sprouted quinoa); eat in small quantities; see below regarding gluten.	Flour; cooked, non-sprouted grains; heavily processed grains.

Unrefined (cold-pressed or expeller-pressed), organic nut and fruit oils; examples include avocado, walnut, olive, coconut, palm, flax seed, macadamia, and pecan.	**Refined oils, genetically modified oils, hydrogenated oils (common ones include vegetable oil, soybean, canola, corn, sunflower, safflower, cottonseed, grape seed oil); most commercial oils are now genetically modified unless they state otherwise.**
Organic wine.	**Nonorganic wine; hard liquor.**
Eggs from pasture-raised or grass-fed organic birds.	**Eggs from factory-farmed chickens, fed an unnatural diet of genetically modified corn and/or soy.**

Lower Vibrational "Foods" That Cause Serious Damage

When you eat incompatible lower vibrational foods, they create chaotic patterns of energy within the body and disrupt the body's ability to harmoniously vibrate at high levels. The following foods, however, are not only incompatible, many of them slowly but surely destroy the body at a cellular level.

If you look carefully at the list below and think about the products on the shelves at the average grocery store, you'll realize that these items form the bulk of what fills the aisles. Not only are many devoid of nutrients (or filled with synthetic chemicals), but some shouldn't be classified as food at all.

- Refined foods (including refined grains, sugar, and salt); these include most breads, pastas, cookies, pastries, potato chips, candy, and many frozen and canned foods.
- Deep or heavily fried foods; foods that have been cooked at high temperatures, blackened, or charred
- Standard canned and bottled drinks (sodas, fruit drinks, pasteurized drinks)
- Food that has been sprayed with pesticides
- Food that contains artificial/synthetic ingredients (chemicals, colors, preservatives, flavors, any ingredient on the list that is not a natural food)
- Food that contains artificial stimulants (e.g., taurine or caffeine found in energy drinks, energy bars, and energy supplements)
- Nicotine and drugs (pharmaceutical, over-the-counter, and recreational)
- Supplements (most sold in stores are artificial, lab-made supplements)
- Diet foods (including diet bars, diet drinks, and diet supplements, as well as highly processed protein powders)

Corn & Soy: The Worst Offenders

Corn and soy are two of the absolute worst offenders in the processed-food world today. Not only is processed soy "sludge" a main ingredient in hundreds of diet, vegan, and vegetarian foods, but derivatives of both corn and soy are now found in over 95 percent of processed foods as "hidden" ingredients.

Unless it's organic, nearly all corn and soy in the US is genetically modified.

The next time you look at the ingredient list of a packaged food, you'll most likely discover at least one of these items:

Processed Soy Derivatives

Nearly all soy derivatives come from genetically modified soy, and include:

- ingredients with the word "soy"
- soy flour
- lecithin
- hydrolyzed vegetable protein
- soy protein isolate
- protein concentrate
- textured vegetable protein (TVP)
- vegetable oil (fully, or partially hydrogenated)
- soybean oil
- plant sterols
- soy sauce
- soybean oil
- guar gum

The *only* soy that should ever be eaten is soy that hasn't been genetically modified in the form of organic soybeans (edamame), organic fermented soy, or unpasteurized soy sauce (Nama Shoyu).

Processed Corn Derivatives

Nearly all corn derivatives come from genetically modified corn, and include:

- ingredients with the word "corn"
- citric acid, any citrate ingredient
- ferrous gluconate
- cellulose
- corn starch / meal / flour
- corn syrup
- high-fructose corn syrup
- corn oil
- monosodium glutamate (MSG)
- dextrin, maltodextrin, dextrose, polydextrose, glucose, maltitol, maltose, mannitol, ethanol
- saccharin
- hydrolyzed vegetable protein

The *only* corn ingredient that should ever be eaten is fresh, organic sweet corn.

SOY TODAY – NOT A HEALTHY FOOD

Today's soy is nothing like the healthy food eaten by traditionally by eastern cultures. Soy products no longer undergo the lengthy fermentation process to render them more digestible and reduce the levels of isoflavones (a type of phytoestrogen). In Asia, traditional soy was also eaten in *very small amounts* that Americans today would consider a condiment (up to 2 tablespoons/day).

Soy is now a highly processed, genetically modified, dead food that is found in countless processed foods, shakes, milks, coffees, and snacks. You may think that a "skinny soy latte" is a healthy choice, but think again. It's not, no matter what savvy advertising tells you.

Soy consumption has exploded in the American diet as food manufacturers have rushed to capitalize on the sale of soy-based products. Cleverly deceptive marketing techniques cover food packages with false health claims and pictures of healthy, active people enjoying soy products. The term "heart healthy" is slapped on many of them, even though the American Heart Association has stated that soy does NOT lower cholesterol, nor does it prevent heart disease. Exploiting soy for profit is big business. The food industry has spent millions to convince consumers that soy products are part of the new, healthy food revolution by blazing ridiculous health claims. Many vegetarian and vegan foods, pet foods, and farmed animal foods contain very large amounts of processed soy.

Many people assume that because soy products appear all over their local health food store, it must be a health food. Today's processed soy is not a healthy food. Nor does it magically cure disease. It's shocking that some health professional still recommend it in the diet.

The concern over the serious health dangers of soy are so significant that the following foreign governments and multiple agencies worldwide have issued warnings against it:

- Israeli Health Ministry
- British Dietetic Association
- British Committee on Toxicity of Chemicals in Food
- French Agency for Food
- German Institute of Risk Assessment
- Australian & New Zealand Food Agency

Soy & Infants

Infants fed soy formula are at the highest risk of experiencing health issues.[1][2][3] Kaaya Daniel, author of "*The Whole Soy Story: The Dark Side of America's Favorite Health Food*" states "It's the only thing they are eating, they are very small, and at a key stage developmentally." Daniel explains how the estrogens in soy affects the hormonal development of these children, and will affect their growing brains, reproductive systems, and thyroid development. Vegan mothers may significantly affect the health of their baby by drinking soy milk and eating soy-based products during pregnancy and lactation, due to the estrogen content found in soy.

The Israeli Health Ministry warned that:

- Babies should not drink soy formula
- Children should eat soy no more than once/day to a maximum of 3 times per week
- Adults should exercise caution due to increased risk of breast cancer and adverse effects on fertility

These recommendations were based on the conclusions reached by a committee of nutritionists, oncologists, pediatricians, and other specialists who spent more than 1 year examining the evidence. They concluded that the estrogen-like plant hormones in soy can cause adverse effects on the human body.[4]

Soy & the Thyroid

The toxins and plant estrogens in soybeans were powerful enough to disrupt menstrual cycles in women, as well as appear to damage the thyroid due to naturally occurring isoflavones.[5]

Soy & Cognitive Decline, Alzheimer's & Dementia

A recent study on Japanese Americans living in Hawaii found a significant statistical relationship between two or more servings of tofu a week and accelerated brain aging.[6] Those participants who consumed

> tofu in mid-life had lower cognitive function in late life and a greater incidence of Alzheimer's disease and dementia. It was also noted that those who ate a lot of tofu looked five years older by the time they reached 75 or 80.[7]

Despite what the food industry has done to soy today, eating good old-fashioned organic soybeans and/or fermented soy in small quantities can be healthy.

Eating Fatty Foods

When transitioning away from processed foods (which are naturally dense) and incorporating healthier foods and more fruits and veggies in our diet, one of the first things we often do is replace these processed foods with other dense, heavy foods out of habit. What are these foods?

Well, they are some of the yummiest foods on the planet!

- Avocados and guacamole-based dips
- Olives, olive dips
- Nuts and seeds
- Nut/seed-based butters, dips, and pates
- Nut milks (especially almond and coconut milk—avoid all processed soy milk)
- Nut and seed loafs and crackers
- Unprocessed and raw desserts and cookies
- Unrefined, cold-pressed oils (coconut oil, flax-seed oil, avocado oil, olive oil)

THE HIGH-FAT PITFALL

Many people—especially vegetarians, vegans, and raw foodists (newbies and long-term followers alike)—succumb to this pitfall when adopting a healthy diet. As these high-fat ingredients quickly become daily staples, we eat them in very large quantities, filling up on mass amounts of fat from healthy fat sources (often in excess of 50 percent of our diet and usually closer to the 75 percent mark). Most people are completely unaware of just how easy it is to transform a healthy meal into a very high-fat meal, and they convince themselves that just because their ingredients are healthy, their meal is healthy too.

Let's take a close look at two great examples of what seem like healthy, light, meals and see how easily we can drastically skew the fat ratio lower the vibrational energy in these meals.

FRUIT & NUT SMOOTHIE

Here is a very basic smoothie recipe, similar to what my clients tell me they make. Some have larger quantities of the high-fat ingredients. They also often drink them together with other high-fat foods, such as yogurt:

- 1 cup almond milk
- 1 tablespoon flax seeds
- 1 cup mixed berries
- 1 tablespoon coconut oil

This smoothie averages a whopping 51 percent fat, and it translates to a very "heavy" smoothie that takes much longer for the body to digest.

Now, let's make a couple key changes:

- 1 cup coconut water
- 1 cup pineapple
- 1 cup berries
- 1 bunch spinach

The fat ratio now plummets all the way to 2 percent. What a tremendous difference! We now have a healthy, high vibrational smoothie that digests quickly and easily.

SALAD

The Salad: A simple salad with an array of veggies, such as tomatoes, mixed greens, cucumber, sweet corn, spring onions, carrots, bell peppers, mushrooms, celery, and various fruits starts off being naturally very low in fat (under 7 percent).

Add a tablespoon of seeds or crushed nuts here, a tablespoon of oil there, and a big hunk of avocado (it's common for all three to be added in larger amounts), and you suddenly arrive at more than 80 percent fat. These "harmless sprinklings" shift the fat scale dramatically.

The Dressing: Don't forget the salad dressing! Popular, healthy oil-based dressings (some of which are blended with nuts or avocados) often top 70 percent fat, easily taking a lovely, light, healthy salad and transforming it into a dense, high-fat meal that takes far longer (and much more energy) to digest.

It's easy to make your own delicious, healthy salad dressings with just a few common ingredients, for example:

Lemon juice | mustard | minced garlic or ginger | miso paste | apple cider vinegar | brown rice vinegar | balsamic vinegar | sea salt | black pepper | your favorite herbs | nutritional yeast (for a cheesy flavor) | cayenne pepper (to add some spice) | natural sweetener (e.g., coconut sugar, maple syrup)

It's not that we need to remove the fat because healthy fats are very important in our diet, but rather we need to pay attention to the amount we use. Adding only one-third of an avocado to this salad is more than enough healthy fat to complete the meal.

When I talk to people about their daily meals, they often begin by excitedly telling me how healthy their diet is—how low-fat their meals are and how proud they are of their stock of healthy ingredients. However, when we begin to break down the ingredients and discover the fat content, they're genuinely shocked. Vegetarians and vegans who constantly struggle with weight loss have looked at me in utter dismay and confusion when we sat own and calculated their average daily fat intake to be over 70 percent.

Are these fats much better than processed and cooked fats? Absolutely! But too much fat is just that—too much fat. When we engage in high-fat eating, we're not doing our body any favors. Because fats are dense and heavy, they place a strain on our digestive system and take longer for our bodies to digest, which is an energy-depleting and low vibrational way to live. Contrary to the misinformation quoted in other diets, fat is not the primary fuel source for the body. High-quality carbohydrates are the primary fuel source for the body (and the only fuel source for the brain). More on this later.

1. **Always aim to get your fats from whole foods instead of liquid oils**

   Liquid oils are not health foods! These are products that have been extracted from their original whole-food source and are now a 100 percent fractionated fat product from which all other nutrients have been stripped.

   Whole foods high in healthy fats include avocados, durian fruit, olives, nuts, and seeds. Their nutrients are meant to be digested as a whole. Similar to supplements, the fat is no longer the same healthy nutrient after it's been isolated and extracted, and the enzymes present that help us properly digest the fats have been removed.

   Liquid oils should be consumed in only very small quantities. They should always be organic and unrefined/cold-pressed, and they should come from whole-food sources (olive oil, avocado oil, flax-seed oil, coconut oil, pistachio oil, etc.).

2. **If your goal is to lose weight, eat these foods, but in small quantities**

   For example, eat 1-2 ounces of nuts each day, or have half a medium avocado chopped into a salad or with a meal. Perhaps a slice or two of raw cheese.

   Avocados are high in fat but not as dense, so they can be used more liberally. They can be blended to create a variety of dips and desserts, as well as eaten in a veggie sandwich or chopped up in a salad.

The Saturated-Fat Myth

When it comes to eating healthy fats, some of the best and most nutritious foods are the ones from nature that may also be high in saturated fat.

Diets of traditional cultures were very high in saturated fats from natural sources, including plants (coconut oil), animals (organ meats), unpasteurized dairy (butter, cheese), fish (including fish eggs), eggs, nuts, and seeds. In these cultures, today's chronic diseases didn't exist. The people were virtually free of heart disease, and high cholesterol was never an issue in traditional cultures that consumed large amounts of eggs and butter.

> "Traditional cultures ate large quantities of saturated fats from both plant & animal sources, yet were free of the heart disease & other chronic health conditions of today."
>
> Weston A. Price Foundation

But they weren't consuming the unhealthy eggs and dairy of today's food chain. Food studies have conclusively shown that healthy saturated fats aren't the culprit. It's what we've done to these fats that has created the problem.

Most doctors don't understand that the contributing factors to heart disease come from:

- The saturated fats from our heavily processed and refined food chain
- The pasteurization of our dairy, which is then not properly digested by the body
- Contributing factors to chronic disease from eating factory-farmed meat
- Our sedentary lifestyle
- Our high level of stress

Feel free to enjoy your saturated fats from healthy, whole-food sources in small quantities.

Freeze-Dried & Dehydrated (Dried) Fruits

Dried fruits are great for a sweet tooth and for treats, including figs, dates, apricots, and other fruits that have been sun-dried. Look carefully at the ingredient list, however, to make sure they haven't been dried with oil, sugar, or other ingredients. Look for unsulfured and unsweetened dried fruits. Blending dried fruits, especially dates, into smoothies or a small quantity of fresh nut milk tastes heavenly! They also make wonderful additions when blended in home-made salad dressings!

Although dehydrated foods are no longer considered "whole foods" because the water has been removed, their nutrients are still intact, and they're healthy, nutritious foods. Because the water has been removed, they have a dehydrating effect on the body. They're dense, lower vibrational foods that should be eaten in small quantities.

Grains & Legumes

When it comes to grains and legumes, always aim for organic and sprouted, which are found in every health-food store and some supermarkets and can be purchased cooked or raw. Focus only on the non-glutinous "ancient" grains, preferably sprouted (quinoa, chia, millet, oats, amaranth, teff, buckwheat, and sorghum). There are several brands of sprouted grain breads and crackers on the market such as **Food for Life** (the makers of the Ezekiel bread line) and **Alvarado Street Bakery**. Popular sprouted legumes include chickpeas, lentils, and mung beans.

Sprouted Grains vs. Non-Sprouted Grains

Let's take a look at the difference:

- When compared to their non-sprouted counterpart, sprouted grains are minimally processed and contain a much higher concentration of important nutrients and micronutrients, such as antioxidants and vitamins.
- Sprouted grains also contain higher amounts of protein and smaller amounts of starch (and come in lower on the glycemic index).

When we take a raw grain and sprout it, it becomes more easily digestible because sprouting breaks down the enzyme inhibitors (such as phytic acid) that bind to nutrients and prevent our body from absorbing them. These nutrients include magnesium, calcium, copper, iron, and zinc. After sprouting, our body is then able to absorb these minerals.

Sprouted grains can be eaten cooked or raw. Cooking increases the digestibility of grains, but it also lowers the nutritional content of heat-sensitive nutrients.

Some of the most nutritious foods on this earth include quinoa, buckwheat, and amaranth. Considered "pseudo-grains" (quinoa and buckwheat are seeds), these foods rarely cause any gastrointestinal distress. They do not contain any gluten and are high in protein and rich in minerals.

Because grains are very heavy foods, either eat them alone, or enjoy them with vegetables and salads that are on the lighter side (as opposed to heavy, starchy veggies such as potatoes). If you enjoy grains, consider them a small part of your diet because they are low vibrational in nature. Grains are also linked to an accumulation of visceral (belly) fat, especially during middle age and hormonal changes associated with menopause.

What about Gluten?

Gluten has become a serious problem for thousands of people, and this number is rising steadily. The ancient grains of our ancestors have now been genetically modified, hybridized, soaked with highly toxic pesticides, and then heavily refined before they come anywhere near our plate.

Although gluten does not agree with some people, gluten itself is often not the culprit; it's what the agricultural industry has done to the gluten that's created the epidemic. This is also why we should never put the grains in our mouths—unless they are (1) organic, (2) non-GMO, and (3) sprouted.

Grains and legumes are unique in that they contain both starches and proteins, which make them more difficult to digest (you'll see why a little later in this section).

For these reasons, I always recommend eliminating *all* grains and legumes completely for 1 full month. Then, reintroduce non-glutinous ancient grains only while monitoring any reaction the body experiences. A significant amount of people are surprised to discover an unwanted reaction from their body when they reintroduce grains, even ancient grains (usually in the form of bloating or abdominal discomfort, or acne). If your body gives you a thumbs down, then it is in your best interest to walk away from it.

If your goal is to lose weight, eat grains and legumes in very small quantities or not at all. Once your body weight has normalized, try reintroducing them and see how your body responds. You will likely experience some type of digestive discomfort. Because grains and legumes are considered "heavy" foods, limiting them in your diet is in your best interest regardless of your weight.

Flour

Flours are finely ground grains, nuts, seeds, legumes, or vegetables. Even though many flours are high in nutrients, the manufacturing process used to refine these flours can remove most of this nutrition. Flours are also very dense foods and rank low on the vibrational scale. Aim to transition them out of your diet completely, except for rare occasions.

Raw Sprouts

Sprouts are some of the most nutritious foods on this earth. In fact, they're considered superfoods because of the density of their nutrients. You can buy raw sprouts from the produce section of the supermarket, with a greater selection usually available at natural grocery stores.

The most popular sprouts include:

Adzuki beans | alfalfa | arugula | broccoli | clover | cress | fenugreek | garbanzo beans | lentils | mung beans | sunflower | wheat berries | mustard | radish

You can also buy seed packets from the store and sprout them yourself. Sprouting kits are inexpensive and are available online and in natural grocery stores.

Your Goal

When it comes to high vibrational living, your goal is to gravitate toward lighter foods that are higher in water content.

THE MAJORITY OF YOUR DIET (OVER 75%)

Fruits / vegetables
High in water content, lighter, easy to digest

THE MINORITY OF YOUR DIET (UNDER 25%)

Legumes / grains / nuts / seeds / animal products
Low in water content, denser, more difficult to digest
(with a small quantity of high-quality fatty foods)

The Intuitive Side of Food

When it comes to knowing which foods we need, our bodies will intuitively begin to gravitate toward foods that contain the nutrients it needs once we clean out the garbage. In addition, many natural foods also communicate to us which parts of our body they benefit the most if we pay close attention to their shape, color, and texture. Sound intriguing? Let's take a closer look.

FOOD & ENERGY

We now know that different types of food vibrate at different frequencies—some much higher than others. Fresh, ripe fruits and vegetables resonate at a much higher frequency than cooked, processed, and canned foods, which are much lower on the vibrational scale.

What happens when we continually eat large quantities of foods that vibrate at a lower frequency than our bodies? We begin to "entrain" (synchronize) to these lower frequencies and open the door to diseases that also vibrate at these lower frequencies.

QUICK REFRESHER ON ENTRAINMENT

Entrainment is very important because it is the key to understanding how our food, our environment, our thoughts, and the thoughts of others affect our health and well-being.

We "entrain" to rhythms around us all the time, even though we're unaware of it. This means that our internal rhythm speeds up or slows down to match stronger, more consistent rhythms around us, and if we live in chaotic or high-stress environments, we begin to synchronize with this chaotic energy.

If we consistently fill our bodies with low vibrational foods, we lower the overall vibrational rate of our body to match this lower frequency.

One of the most important (and simplest!) ways we can bring about dramatic health change is through the foods we eat.

When we consistently eat a diet of high vibrational foods, we begin to re-create our body a little differently because the "source material" is of a much higher quality. This means that every single cell we create that forms every tissue, organ, and piece of bone becomes recalibrated to a higher frequency. As a result, a level of healing infuses our entire being.

The vitalizing power of high vibrational foods has stood the test of time. These foods contain essential nutrients our bodies need to thrive, and they've restored many people from terminal diseases back to a state of radiant health.

Food & Intuition

Intuitively, our body already knows what foods it needs. A continual communication occurs on a molecular level that guides the body in how to function. The foods we eat have specific physical and energetic properties that communicate with our bodies because of a synergy that exists between us and the natural world.

Over time, we've stopped listening to our body's signals and become desensitized to its voice. But once we clear out the junk and return to a healthy diet that sustains us, and once we free ourselves of refined and processed foods filled with chemicals, pesticides, antibiotics, hormones, GMOs, irradiated food, and other unhealthy items, we reset the body's sensitivity. We then naturally begin to crave what we truly need, and the cravings for "real food" will be strong. If we then try to return to our previous unhealthy habits, our body will very quickly respond with a thumbs-down, giving us unpleasant symptoms to alert us that something's wrong.

The Doctrine of Signatures

When we become mindful of the food we eat on a regular basis, and if we really begin to pay attention to the shape, texture, and color of that food, some very interesting facts come to light.

The "Doctrine of Signatures" is a philosophy recognizing that the shape and structure of a plant reveals a signature—a resemblance to the organ or part of the body that it nutritionally benefits.

Paracelsus (1493–1541) was a Swiss-German physician, botanist, and alchemist who established the role of chemistry in medicine. He developed the concepts behind the doctrine, which then went on to become an important part of natural medicine in the Middle Ages. It was used by herbalists as well as Christian and Muslim folk healers.

> **"Medicine does not consist of compounding pills & plasters; it deals with the very processes of life, which must first be understood before they may be guided."**
>
> Paracelsus
> Swiss-German Physician

Let's take a look at a few examples from the doctrine:

Walnuts

When a walnut shell is cracked open, it reveals a nut that looks like a tiny version of the human brain. Walnuts are high in brain nutrients, such as essential fatty acids, that are beneficial to brain health.

Carrots

When you slice a carrot crosswise, the pattern resembles the pupil and iris of a human eye. We know that the beta-carotene in carrots is important to our eye health.

Tomatoes

Tomatoes are red and contain chambers, just like the human heart. Tomatoes are rich in the antioxidants that help protect the heart from disease.

Citrus Fruits

When sliced crosswise, citrus fruits look just like female mammary glands. They play a role in breast health and the movement of lymph in and out of the breasts.

Peanuts

In their shells, peanuts look similar to male testicles. They have a significant effect on the testicles and sexual libido (arginine, the main component of Viagra, comes from peanuts).

Grapes

Grapes hanging in a cluster are shaped like the human heart. Grapes contain phytochemicals, such as resveratrol, flavonoids, and quercetin, that are heart- and blood-vitalizing nutrients.

How We Damage Foods

An interesting fact about us humans is that we can take perfectly healthy food and destroy it completely by what we do with it before it gets anywhere near our mouths! Let's take a look at how the methods used to prep food before we buy it, as well as what we do to it ourselves before chowing down, damage the food we eat.

HOW WE DAMAGE FOOD

Today's food preparation and preserving methods drastically alter the energy of our food. They can take a naturally high vibrational food and effectively reduce the measurable energy frequency to close to zero.

For example, a fresh, ripe, organic apple can resonate as high as 80 MHz, but if you take that same apple and cook it, refine it, or can it, you reduce that measurable rate all the way down to single digits. Apples, corn, and soy are great examples of inherently healthy whole foods that have been broken down and so highly processed that all health-giving properties are completely destroyed beyond recognition.

Food prep methods that lower the energy of food (and may reduce it to zero) and destroy its nutritional content include:

REFINING IT

Refining food strips foods of nutrients. This is due to:

- Refining methods
- Adding artificial chemicals, such as flavors and colors
- Adding artificial fillers, preservatives, and sweeteners
- Adding synthetic vitamins during "enriching" or "fortifying"
- Adding excitotoxins (highly addictive food chemicals)

CANNING IT

Many cans and plastics containing food and drinks are made with bisphenol A (BPA) and other chemicals. BPA is an estrogen-like chemical has been linked to a variety of health problems, including infertility, reproductive damage, metabolic disorders, and neurobehavioral disorders.[1]

Storing food in cans significantly lowers its measurable vibration, sometimes transforming it into a completely dead food, depending on the level of processing and refining.

IRRADIATING IT

Food irradiation is a method of preserving food that exposes it to radiation in the form of gamma rays, X-rays, or electron beams. It reduces nutrients in food, destroys beneficial bacteria, and produces toxic and carcinogenic by-products. It also masks unsanitary food practices in the agricultural industry.

MICROWAVING IT

Microwaving is another form of food irradiation. In studies, microwaving was found to significantly destroy antioxidant value and to seriously diminish other nutrients.[2] [3] Multiple studies by German, Russian, and American research facilities confirmed that not only does microwaving food destroy important nutrients and cause others to be less bioavailable, microwaved food also has a detrimental effect on our blood chemistry and various bodily systems.

Microwaving also destroys the nutrients in breast milk and baby formula, creating neurotoxic by-products and fostering the growth of bacteria.[4] [5] It destroys the digestive enzymes that help babies efficiently digest the milk protein[6] and can cause chronic constipation in children.[7]

GENETICALLY MODIFYING IT

The problem with genetically modified food is twofold:

- Genetically modified foods contain mutated proteins that studies have shown cause organ damage, reproductive harm, and early death in rodents and other animals. Several important studies have been conducted outside the US that mirror each other in these findings. This is why GMOs must be labeled in over 70 countries worldwide (unfortunately, not in the US).
- Genetically modified foods have a devastating impact on our environment as they require massive quantities of pesticide usage and chemicals to survive.

The Environmental Protection Agency (EPA) labels GMO corn as a pesticide because it has been engineered to produce its own internal insecticide. This corn is found in thousands of processed food items.

COOKING IT AT HIGH TEMPERATURES

Once the temperature of food reaches 118° to 120° F, some of the nutrients and enzymes begin to degrade, with almost all food enzymes destroyed at 160° F. (We talked about enzymes earlier in the protocol.)

Cooking food at high temperatures has been conclusively proven to create carcinogenic chemicals, such as polycyclic aromatic hydrocarbons (PAHs) and advanced glycation end-products (AGEs), especially when we broil, char, or deep fry it.

PASTEURIZING IT

Pasteurized foods include dairy (pasteurized cheese, milk, butter, yogurt, and infant formula), fruit drinks, and others.

Always avoid pasteurized food products. The pasteurization process:

- Causes serious damage to both nutrients and enzymes and denatures the protein content.
- Destroys the bioactive components that not only help us digest the milk proteins, but also help a baby develop a strong immunity for life; a detailed study found that babies fed pasteurized milk vs. breast milk suffered double the sicknesses,[8] with another study confirming a link between pasteurized dairy to an increase in childhood allergies, seasonal asthma, current wheeze, hay fever, rhinitis symptoms, and atopic sensitization.[9]
- Renders the calcium in milk unusable by the body; this unabsorbed calcium is then stored in the soft tissues of the body, causing calcification. Osteoporosis and bone-related diseases are highest in Western countries that drink the most pasteurized dairy products.[10] The Harvard Nurses' Health Study (following 78,000 nurses for over 12 years) showed no protective effect of increased milk consumption on fracture risk. **On the contrary, it found that those who drank 2 or more glasses of milk per day have twice the risk of hip fracture than those who drank a glass a week or less.[11]** There are several other large-scale studies showing that high calcium intakes double the risk of hip fracture.[12] [13]

- In animal studies, in a comparison between feeding raw milk vs. pasteurized milk, those fed pasteurized milk showed poor growth, muscle stiffness, emaciation, and weakness, and they suffered death within 1 year. Autopsies revealed atrophied muscles streaked with calcification and calcium deposits under skin, in joints, in the heart, and in other organs.(14) (15)

There is nothing healthy about eating any pasteurized milk product.

PESTICIDES IN OUR FOOD & ENVIRONMENT

Eating foods sprayed with pesticides and spraying these pesticides in our yards and gardens are some of the most seriously damaging things we can do to our bodies.

In infants, children, and pets, they are especially dangerous. Studies have conclusively linked pesticides to cancer, Parkinson's disease, fetal death, nervous-system damage, stunted growth, non-Hodgkin's lymphoma, autism, and ADHD.

Using pesticides and herbicides in our homes and gardens:

- Increases the risk of childhood leukemia 7-fold(16)
- Increases the likelihood of brain cancer and soft-tissue sarcoma in children(17)
- With 4 or more yearly lawn applications, doubles the risk of canine lymphoma in dogs(18)
- Increases fetal death rates when exposure occurs during weeks 3 to 8 of pregnancy(19)
- Increases the risk of having a child with autism(20)
- Is associated with cognitive decline(21)
- Can increase the likelihood of Parkinson's 2.5 fold.(22)

HOW ABOUT FREEZING FOOD?

Freezing fresh, whole foods isn't the best thing we can do to them, and it does measurably lower their vibration; however, it doesn't damage our health, and many nutrients do survive the freezing process. When it comes to having our favorite foods year-round that can only be found seasonally, freezing is very handy. Our family loves to add cranberries to smoothies and veggie juices, but fresh cranberries are only available in the fall/early winter where we live. Storing organic cranberries in the freezer is the next best thing.

Feel free to include some frozen whole foods, but make them a small part of your diet, and definitely avoid any diet that consists of eating frozen meals.

Step by Step

We now understand the basics of high vs. low vibrational foods and have a solid foundation when it comes to understanding food, frequency, and disease, it's time to get practical and take action on what we've learned.

LET'S GET PRACTICAL

In this section, we'll talk about:

1. Which foods to eat, and which to avoid
2. How to mix 'n' match foods for maximum energy
3. The question of organics
4. A rainbow of textures and flavors
5. Beginning the day light
6. Portion sizes
7. Getting rid of the garbage
8. Shopping "high vibrational" style
9. Transitioning
10. The kickstart detoxification

At the end of this section, we'll also talk about specific modifications to make for candidiasis, diabetes, and cancer.

Here's a quick refresher on the foods we'll transition out of our diet and the new ones that will take their place. But don't worry! We won't remove all the old foods overnight. Instead, we'll remove them at a pace you can manage, and we'll talk about how to transition from where you are to where you need to be.

THE "IN" CROWD

THE BEST

These are the foods that will form the bulk of your diet. We begin by increasing them, while decreasing other foods we want to move away from:

- Fresh, clean water that's free of industrial contaminants found in tap water
- Ripe, raw, organic fruits
- Ripe, raw, organic vegetables, especially leafy greens
- Raw sweeteners (raw honey, fresh stevia leaf, dates, coconut sugar)
- Sprouts (alfalfa, clover, mung beans, cress, broccoli, sunflower...)
- Sea veggies

Liquid Light

Aim to make fresh fruit juices or smoothies a permanent part of your day. They're incredibly dense in nutrients and have the highest oxygen content and vibrational energy of any food or drink you can have. Your only investments will be a juicer, blender, and chopping knife.

THE NEXT BEST

Feel free to include these liberally:

- Lightly cooked high-water-content vegetables
- Cooked starchy vegetables (e.g., potatoes, yams, root veggies)
- Frozen, freeze-dried, and dehydrated fruits and vegetables

IN SMALLER QUANTITIES

The following foods are fine in small quantities. Your first goal is to decrease them to 25 percent of your diet (a quarter of your plate), and then reduce them further from there. The more of them you eat, the energetically "heavier" you'll be; the less of them you eat, the energetically "lighter" you'll be.

- High-fat fruits and vegetables (e.g., olives, avocados, coconut flesh)
- Raw nuts and seeds (soak 6+ hours before eating to increase digestibility and then refrigerate)
- Desserts made from whole-food natural products (e.g., coconut, cacao, unrefined oils, nuts, seeds, raw chocolate, unpasteurized dairy)
- Unpasteurized or fermented dairy (e.g., cheese, milk, butter, yogurt, kefir)
- Wild-caught fish
- Organic meat and eggs from pasture-raised animals
- Sprouted or fermented ancient grains (raw and cooked)
- Legumes
- Cold-pressed or expeller-pressed organic nut and fruit oils (e.g., avocado, walnut, olive, coconut, flax seed, walnut, macadamia nut, pecan)
- Wine (organic)

Let's talk about these foods in a bit more detail.

Healthy Animal Products (meat, fish, eggs, and dairy)

Only buy meat, poultry, and eggs that are organic and are from animals that have been pasture-raised. This helps ensure that these animals haven't been subjected to the cruel and inhumane conditions in American factory farms, and that they don't contain antibiotics, growth hormones, and other unwanted, unhealthy chemicals.

Fish should be wild-caught and not factory-farmed, and if possible, tested for mercury levels. Several health-food stores that sell fresh seafood have some of the fish they sell tested for mercury content. Ask at the fish counter.

Dairy

Animal-based milks include goat's milk, sheep's milk, and cow's milk. As we discussed earlier, never drink pasteurized milk products as they are some of the unhealthiest and most mucus-forming foods on the planet. It's especially unhealthy to feed pasteurized milk to a newborn (second to soy milk) as studies show pasteurized dairy significantly increases the number of infections infants experience.

When we eat inflammatory foods such as pasteurized dairy, our nasal tissues produce mucus to neutralize and excrete the irritants and/or toxins causing the inflammation. Foods that increase mucus production are foods to avoid.

Raw cheese is available in many grocery stores. Even though a wider selection of raw cheese will be available at health-food stores, these days, common supermarket chains sell the Alta Dena and Organic Valley brands of pasture-raised raw cheddar and goat's milk cheese. Other raw dairy products, such as milk and yogurt, are legal in several states throughout the US where they can be found in grocery stores and local farms. In other states, their sale is illegal.

Oil & Vinegar

Oils

We touched on this earlier, but here's a reminder to please keep your liquid-oil purchases to an absolute minimum (unless you use them for massages, of course!). They've been extracted from their whole-food form and stripped of all nutrients to leave behind a product that's 100 percent fat—a product that's low vibrational in nature. Instead, choose to get your healthy fats directly from the foods they were extracted from.

When you do buy liquid oils, keep the following 4 points in mind:

- Buy only unrefined, cold-pressed oils
- Buy only nut, seed, or fruit oils
- Make sure the oil is labeled as non-GMO
- Completely avoid "vegetable oil," which is an unhealthy product

Good oil choices include avocado oil, almond oil, coconut oil, flax-seed oil, olive oil, grapeseed oil, sunflower oil, and walnut oil.

Vinegars

There are many popular vinegars that we can use for different things, ranging from house cleaning, to personal-care products, herbicides (20 percent horticultural vinegar), and for use in our foods. Food-grade vinegars include:

- Apple-cider vinegar (always buy raw and unfiltered)
- Balsamic vinegar (including specialty fruit balsamics)
- Coconut vinegar
- Malt vinegar
- Raisin vinegar
- Rice vinegar
- Ume plum vinegar
- Wine vinegar

Some vinegars are infused with herbs, flowers, and spices to give them an extra-special flavor. When it comes to buying vinegar, pay close attention to the ingredient list and watch out for anything sneaky! Plan to use vinegar in small quantities as even though it's not an unhealthy food, it's not a fresh, whole, naturally high vibrational food either. It can also affect the body's ability to digest food it's eaten with.

Spices & Condiments

Spices

Because most spices last us for a while and are inexpensive, it's worth investing in organic spices, especially considering that many are now imported from China. (For organic spices, look at the label to make sure it isn't sourced in China where USDA inspections on organic produce are almost nonexistent.) Make sure your spices contain whole-food ingredients and haven't been mixed with anything else.

When it comes to salt, buy only unrefined natural sea salt, and use it only in very small quantities. There's more than enough sodium in natural foods to provide the body with what it needs.

There are many types of natural salts to choose from, ranging from basic to specialty salts.

Condiments

Condiments may seem innocent, but they're notorious for containing all sorts of unhealthy ingredients that food manufacturers sneak in. Watch out for the undesirables such as sugar, salt, and "natural flavors," which shouldn't be on the list.

Let's take a look at two very common condiments and compare healthy vs. unhealthy ingredients:

MUSTARD

Vinegar, water, mustard seed, spices
vs.
Sugar, soy lecithin, xanthan gum, natural coloring*

KETCHUP

Tomato puree, vinegar, mustard, sea salt, onion, spices
vs.
Corn syrup, sugar, salt, tomatoes, flavoring, coloring*

*The only time "natural coloring" is acceptable is if the label specifically states that the coloring is from a whole food (e.g., annatto or paprika)

Desserts

Let's face it, whether it's a piece of cheesecake or a piece of chocolate, most of us love our desserts.

It goes without saying that if you feel like a dessert, gravitate first toward fruits and dried fruits. But if you need that extra-special something, aim to choose only healthy desserts that contain healthy ingredients.

Health-food stores are now full of incredibly tasty tarts, bars, and cakes made from only healthy ingredients such as coconut oil, vanilla bean, almonds, sea salt, nuts, fruit, and cacao. Hail Merry is a great example of a dessert manufacturer who makes healthy tarts and macaroons to die for, created only from natural ingredients.

Sherbets, freezer pops, and other frozen items that contain only fruit, unpasteurized dairy, or other natural ingredients are just fine, but always avoid soy desserts completely. We'll talk about soy in more detail below.

Chocolate

For chocolate lovers, choose dark chocolate with a high cacao content (70 percent or more) and watch out for added sugar, soy derivatives, and other unhealthy ingredients. Due to the rapidly growing health-food movement, a great selection of healthy chocolates is now available.

Follow these tips for buying chocolate that is both awesome *and* good for you!

- Choose high cacao content (70 percent or more).
- Choose organic to avoid pesticides. If possible, choose a raw brand. This means the nutrients haven't been destroyed by processing and high cooking temperatures. Two raw brands include Go Raw and Righteously Raw.
- Read the ingredient list *very* carefully.

Let's take a look at common ingredients in chocolate and see what gets a thumbs-up vs. a thumbs-down.

Thumbs Up	Thumbs Down
• Cacao butter	• Soy lecithin
• Cacao powder	• Natural or artificial colors*
• Cacao nibs	• Natural or artificial flavors
• Sea salt	• Sugar
• Carob	• Corn starch
• Nuts	• Corn syrup
• Honey	• High-fructose corn syrup
• Nut/fruit/seed oils (e.g., coconut)	• Vegetable fat
• Vanilla bean	• Hydrogenated oils
• Herbs	
• Botanicals (e.g., lavender)	
• Essential oils	

* Unless it specifically states the color or flavor comes from a whole-food item.

Keep in mind what you already know: Most dessert items are very dense foods that are low on the vibrational scale. Keep them to a minimum and aim to steadily reduce them in your diet.

Other Healthy Foods

Let's talk about a few other healthy ingredients that are perfectly fine to buy, but which should be eaten in only small quantities:

Sweeteners

Purchase natural sweeteners only. The naturally occurring sugars in whole-food carbohydrates—not the ones in processed foods or the ones artificially created in the lab—are sugars the body was built to digest.

Baking Ingredients

This includes arrowroot, baking soda, baking powder, and other similar ingredients. Transition flour out of your diet because, as we know, the original grains, nuts, seeds, veggies, and legumes in the flour have undergone a manufacturing process that strips away many of the original nutrients in these foods. Flour is also a very heavy, dead food. Keep your flour purchases to a minimum, and while you transition away from them, use only unbleached, unrefined, whole-grain flour.

Drinks & Plant-Based Milks

When you increase the fruit and vegetable content of your diet, you'll find you need to drink much less because these are naturally nourishing and hydrating foods.

When you do reach for a drink, choose:

- Fresh mineral or spring water, or filtered water
- Organic, herbal teas
- Carbonated products containing natural ingredients (e.g., squeezed lemon or lime—*not* "natural flavors")
- Fresh-squeezed veggie or fruit juices
- Wine, preferably organic and enjoyed in small quantities

If you're like me and plain-old water just doesn't quite cut it, feel free to make it more exciting. Add citrus fruits, such as lemon, lime, or oranges slices. I often keep a big pitcher in the refrigerator with a mixture of all three. Sometimes I simply add some rosewater and chia seeds to my water—whatever I can do to make it more exciting!

Plant-based milks include almond milk, coconut milk, oat milk, and rice milk. Most are heavily processed and contain many unwanted ingredients. Unless you can make or buy pure nut milks without any extra ingredients (commonly found in natural grocery stores), avoid them completely. If you do drink them, enjoy them in small quantities as they are a heavy, lower vibrational food.

Let's take a look at the ingredients in a healthy almond milk vs. a very popular brand on the market:

Malk
Almonds, filtered water, sea salt

vs.

Very Popular Almond Milk Brand
Almond milk (filtered water, almonds), natural flavor, sea salt, ocust bean gum, sunflower lecithin, gellan gum. Vitamins and minerals: calcium carbonate, vitamin E acetate, zinc gluconate, vitamin A palmitate, riboflavin (B_2), vitamin B_{12}, vitamin D_2

Wow, what a big difference between the two! Also, the vitamins and minerals in the second example are synthetically derived.

As we learned earlier, avoid soy milk and all processed soy products completely.

ON THEIR WAY OUT

When it comes to shopping for food, sometimes we need a bit of guidance when it comes to understanding how to recognize unhealthy choices that are cleverly disguised as health foods. Knowing the difference between healthy vs. harmful is especially important when it comes to serious health conditions.

Buying fresh produce, nuts, seeds, and oils is much simpler than buying packaged foods that often contain many mixed ingredients. Manufacturers purposely make it very difficult for us to distinguish a healthy ingredient from an unhealthy ingredient.

Not anymore!

Unhealthy Foods

Not only do these foods not belong in a healthy diet, they are also either toxic or create toxic by-products. Most of them contain a variety of the following different types of food chemicals:

- Buffers / artificial preservatives / neutralizers / moisture-content controls / flavorings / colorings / bleaching agents / maturing agents / psychological-activity controls / stabilizers / processing aids

Let's take a look at what some of these chemicals look like on food labels:

- Hydrogenated or partially hydrogenated oils
- Natural flavors (unless specifically stated to be from a natural food)
- Artificial colors (e.g., red 40, yellow 6, blue 1)
- Sugar
- Salt (except unrefined sea salt)
- Sugar alcohols (e.g., erythritol, glucitol/sorbitol, glycerol/glycerin, isomalt, lactitol, maltitol, mannitol, sorbitol, xylitol)
- Added vitamins (artificial nutrients present in many "enriched" or "fortified" foods)
- Artificial stimulants (e.g., taurine or caffeine found in energy drinks, energy bars, and energy supplements)
- Artificial sweeteners [e.g., saccharin (Sweet'n Low), sucralose (Splenda), acesulfame K (Sunett), neotame (NutraSweet)].
- The word "corn" unless it indicates fresh, non-GMO sweet corn
- The word "soy" unless it indicates whole soybeans that are non-GMO, or unpasteurized soy sauce (Nama Shoyu)
- Any other chemicals you don't recognize

Other foods to avoid include:

- Factory-farmed animal products (meat, fish, eggs, dairy); if it doesn't say "wild-caught," "free-range," or "pasture-raised," avoid it.
- Diet foods (including diet bars, diet drinks, and diet supplements—all dead foods)
- Microwave foods
- Pasteurized foods
- Irradiated foods
- Genetically modified foods (GMOs); look for the "Non-GMO Project Verified" stamp. Also, organic foods are not genetically modified.

Do most of these products sound natural? No, they don't. The true nature of these foods and their ingredients is hopefully very obvious to you by now, and the repetition is helping to hammer home why it's important to eliminate them. The general public has no idea how unhealthy most supermarket foods are (or that they contain food chemicals banned in other countries where clinical studies have shown them to be dangerous and/or cancer-promoting).

As a general rule, if you don't know exactly what an ingredient is, don't put it in your mouth. The same goes for personal-care products and your skin, which we'll look at in more detail later in the "Environment" section of the protocol.

Unhealthy Drinks

When it comes to drinks, there are so many on the market to avoid:

- Sodas
- Pasteurized milk and fruit drinks
- Soft drinks (including iced teas with sugar and artificial ingredients)
- Nonorganic wines and hard liquor
- Stimulant drinks and sodas

Supplements

Supplements have become some of the most abused and unnecessary products on the planet. Most are synthetic and have a detrimental impact on the body. Some of the most commonly purchased daily multivitamins contain synthetic ingredients that are detrimental to our health.

If you're eating a healthy diet high in organic produce, your need for supplements should be close to zero. Unless you're recovering from a health issue where a deficiency has been confirmed, nix them entirely from your diet.

There are a couple exceptions to this rule, which we'll discuss in much more detail later in the "Using Supplements" section.

Stimulants & Addictions

Addictions come in all forms. Many people don't realize they're addicted to processed and refined junk food. These foods contain substances called "excitotoxins," chemicals used by food manufacturers that cause us to crave more of them. Other common addictions include:

- Caffeine
- Energy drinks, bars, and supplements
- Nicotine
- Alcohol
- Prescription and nonprescription drugs
- Recreational drugs

Stimulants artificially stimulate the body, and some are milder than others. Caffeine uses mechanisms similar to those that amphetamines, cocaine, and heroin use to stimulate the body, but on a much milder level. The end result is an artificial, forced stimulation of the metabolic and other systems of the body.

If you can't function properly in the morning without your coffee fix and have to rely on caffeine to feel energized or mentally alert, you have an addiction. It's also a warning sign. If your goal is to have a healthy body and raise its vibration to heal and prevent future disease, you need to address your unhealthy addictions.

The only way to get high vibrations is to get high on life, not stimulants.

MIX 'N' MATCH FOODS

We use a significant amount of energy in the digestion, absorption, and elimination of the foods we eat. Depending on which foods we eat together in any given meal, our digestion can be rapid and have an energizing effect on our body, or it can be very slow and have a de-energizing effect.

The concept of which foods should and should not be eaten together has been around for decades, but we can thank Harvey and Marilyn Diamond and their best-selling book *Food for Life* for bringing the subject to the spotlight.

How We Digest Our Food

When we mix certain foods together in a meal, it affects how that food is digested. To understand why mixing some types of food together creates a sluggish digestion (a big energy drainer), we need to have a very basic understanding of how we digest proteins, fats, and carbohydrates.

"It's not what we eat, but what we digest & assimilate that adds to our health."

Herbert M. Shelton, ND
Doctor, Author

When we eat food, we begin by chewing it, which mixes the food with saliva and begins the digestive process. Our taste buds send impulses to the brain to signal whether a protein, carbohydrate, fat, or a combination is being eaten. We then secrete digestive enzymes at various intervals throughout the digestive process to help us digest that food:

Proteins
Proteins need proteolytic enzymes (proteases) to break down the protein into amino acids. A highly acidic environment is needed for these to be effective. Protease enzymes include pepsin, trypsin, chymotrypsin, bromelain, and papain.

Fats
These need an enzyme called lipase to break down fatty foods into fatty acids. A neutral environment is need for lipase to be effective, and it's destroyed in high acidity.

Carbohydrates
These need amylase enzymes to convert starches to glucose. A neutral to slightly alkaline environment is needed for amylase enzymes to be effective, and they're destroyed in high acidity. Amylase enzymes include lactase, diastase, sucrase, maltase, invertase, and glucoamylase.

In the stomach, hydrochloric acid and more digestive enzymes are secreted. The concentration of the acid and the type(s) of enzymes produced in the stomach depend on the type(s) of food we have eaten.

Different Foods Digest at Different Rates

Depending on what we eat, certain foods digest much more quickly than others. When eaten alone:

- Fresh fruits digest very quickly, in 15-45 minutes.
- Juiced vegetables and fruits digest in 15-45 minutes.
- Vegetables (non-starchy/non-dense) digest in 1-2 hours.
- Vegetables (starchy/dense) digest in 2-3 hours.
- Animal proteins (meat, poultry, fish, dairy) digest in 4-6+ hours.
- Grains, beans, and lentils are more difficult to digest because they contain both starch and protein and can take 5-6 hours or more.

The types and combinations of foods we eat should pass easily through the body. When we eat one food type at a time, or eat food of similar types, the food will always digest the most efficiently and quickly.

Here's Where the Problem Comes in

Starches need a more alkaline environment to digest in the body, but proteins need a highly acidic medium. When we try to digest both at the same time, the body produces two different types of digestive enzymes that tend to neutralize each other (mixing an acid with an alkali has a neutralizing effect). More and more digestive juices are produced in an attempt to try to digest both food types, sometimes greatly increasing the length of time digestion takes.

The more energy required to digest the food, the less energy is available for the body, and the more tired, heavy, and bloated we feel.

Anyone for Indigestion, Gas, or Bloating?

When you eat something that digests very quickly (e.g., an orange, which takes approximately 30 minutes to digest) after a meal of rice and chicken (which can take anywhere from 8-16 hours or more to digest when eaten together), then the fruit remains in the digestive tract for much longer than it should. It begins to ferment, producing gas, indigestion, bloating, and other internal discomfort. Let's take it one step farther: If we had that chicken and rice for lunch, and then follow it up with another similar meal several hours later for dinner, do you see how the digestive system could quickly become very bogged down?

Depending on which foods are eaten together and how often we eat, a food that should take 1-2 hours to digest can take all the way up to 24 hours or more, depending on the ingredients. This is why we feel like taking a nap or feel drained of energy after a big dinner or a multi-course meal at a restaurant—we've overtaxed our entire gastrointestinal system. Nap time!

When food stays in our digestive tract longer than it should, it begins to rot and produce toxic by-products:

Fermentation
Carbohydrates ferment when not digested in a timely manner, producing unwanted by-products such as carbon dioxide, acetic acid, lactic acid, and alcohol.

Putrefaction
Proteins putrefy when not digested in a timely manner, producing unwanted by-products such as ptomaines and leukomaines.

The longer your meal stays inside you, the more toxic the waste becomes. Fermentation and putrefaction are primary causes of digestive disorders such as gas, constipation, diarrhea, indigestion, and stinky stools. If ignored, these conditions progress to more serious problems such as IBS. Indigestion (gastritis) is so common in Americans today that it's now considered both "normal" and "accepted" to take Tums, Rolaids, Alka-Seltzer, and anti-gas meds. Billions of dollars are spent annually on antacids and other products for conditions resulting from unhealthy eating practices.

Indigestion isn't normal, nor is it healthy.

Digestive-related diseases are rising at an alarming rate, as are the number of prescription and over-the-counter temporary fixes. Rather than remove the cause of indigestion or bloating or gas, many people see drugs as the simpler solution. However, adding drugs simply compounds the problem, giving the body more unwanted, unnatural substances to remove.

Not only does our body spend a considerable amount of energy digesting complex, heavy food combinations (along with food chemicals and other unwanted ingredients), it now has to remove the foreign substances in medications for digestion, too. Is it any wonder our body succumbs to chronic health conditions?

Most diseases begin with a breakdown of the gastrointestinal system. This is why healthy digestion and elimination of waste is very important.

If Nature Mixes Food Types, Why Shouldn't We?

Nature herself offers us many foods that contain a mixture of proteins, fats, and carbohydrates. In fact, almost all natural foods are starch-protein combinations. Protein is also present in almost everything we eat, but in most foods there is such a small amount of it that we ignore it when in combinations.

Nature often packages protein and fat together in foods (e.g., nuts, seeds, meats, and dairy). Beans and lentils are examples of foods that are considered carbohydrates, but they're high in protein too. Beans contain 25 percent protein and 50 percent carbohydrates (which is why many people experience bloating and gas after eating beans). Dairy is another example of a protein that also contains a significant amount of fat.

Notice that even though these foods are healthy, they're also all classed as "heavy" foods—denser in nature, lower in water content, and lower on the vibrational scale. They're complex and take longer to digest when eaten alone, never mind when they're eaten with other food types.

TIP #1: Start with healthy

Properly mixing and matching foods and high vibrational living are more about eating a healthy diet and tuning in to how your body reacts after eating single foods as well as different combinations of foods. It's not about following a rigid food-combining chart. As we just mentioned, nature herself provides foods that combine proteins, fats, and carbohydrates. The truth is that if you're eating a diet composed primarily of high vibrational foods, and if you've cut out all the undesirables, then you'll experience a quantum leap in health and in your emotional, physical, and psychological well-being.

TIP #2: Then move on to high vibrational

As your diet becomes healthier and you include more and more high vibrational foods and you feel ready to take the next step on the high vibrational ladder, that's the right time to more strictly adhere to which foods mix best together. At that point, you'll eat denser and more complex food combos occasionally and in smaller quantities with low-starch vegetables that are high in water content.

In a moment, we'll talk about a simple approach to mixing and matching foods that you can easily incorporate into your meals.

Other Things That Affect Our Digestion

Aside from what foods to eat together, other things can affect (sometimes severely) our ability to digest food. These include:

- Stress
- Overeating
- Chronic health conditions
- Added salt
- Coffee
- Alcohol
- Drugs
- Vinegar

How to Mix 'n' Match Food

There are 5 types of foods we consider when deciding which mix best together:

Fruits
Eat fruit and fruit juices alone or with salad veggies that are high in water content, and wait at least 30 minutes before eating other food.

Vegetables
Eat with proteins *or* starches *or* fats.

Starchy Carbohydrates & Vegetables
Eat with all vegetables, and wait 4-6 hours before eating other food.

Fats
Eat with low-starch vegetables or fatty fruits (e.g., olives and avocados), and wait 4-6 hours before eating other food.

Proteins
Eat with low-starch vegetables, and wait 4-6 hours before eating other food.

A Word About Fruits

The reason we eat fruits alone is that they digest very quickly in the body when they're eaten alone. However, if we eat fruits with other types of foods, they'll be held up in our stomach while the rest of the food is being digested. The sugars in the fruit then begin to ferment, creating indigestion and other stomach issues.

Melons are digested especially quickly compared to other fruits, decomposing very quickly in the stomach if they're held up. Often, people who complain that melons and other fruits give them indigestion suffer because they eat these fruits either with or after other foods. If you've experienced this, try eating fruit alone, or before eating other foods, and see the difference you experience.

Fruits can, however, be mixed with veggies that are very high in water content, such as tomatoes, cucumbers, jicama, or leafy greens. Chopped-up strawberries and cucumbers, with a squeezed lemon and an orange wedge, make a wonderfully refreshing dish! Lemons and limes can be combined with different food types because we eat them in such small quantities.

A Word About Veggies

There are two types of vegetables:

- The non/low-starch kind such as celery, cucumber, lettuce, zucchini, cauliflower, and greens. These vegetables are very high in water content and digest quickly.
- The dense, starchy kind such as potatoes, yams, root vegetables, and winter squash. They're low in water content and take longer for the body to break down and digest. They're considered "starchy carbohydrates."

A Word About Milk Products

Drink milk alone and unpasteurized or not at all. Milk is the perfect food for infants, which is why mammals produce it to nurture their young. The nutritional content is also specific and appropriate only for babies of the same species (e.g., a cow's milk for a calf, a human mother's milk for a human infant; both milk nutrients are not the same). Infants secrete an enzyme called rennin to digest milk proteins. After infancy, our body no longer needs rennin, and this secretion is greatly reduced.[1] [2]

Milk is also a gastric insulator, meaning that when it enters the stomach, it turns into curds that coat and insulate our stomach, impairing the digestion of other foods until the milk has been digested.

Let's Make It Simple

"All things in moderation, including moderation."

Socrates

At first glance, this may sound pretty challenging! After all, it makes many favorite dishes a no-no (meat and potatoes, cheese sandwich, chicken and rice, macaroni and cheese, spaghetti and meatballs). Any sandwich that isn't a salad/avocado sandwich wouldn't make the list either.

For most people, worrying about which foods to mix with what is simply too rigid and unrealistic (not to mention, miserable). It can also make eating out at restaurants a daunting experience. Being healthy may be the goal, but keeping things simple is what makes it realistic.

The key to success is to begin by using moderation when it comes to approaching which foods we should eat together. The healthier you become, the more you'll naturally begin gravitating toward healthy combinations because of how they make you feel. By beginning to include just a couple simple changes into your eating habits at a pace you can manage, you not only make it so much simpler, but you also make a big difference in your health and your energy.

Let's take a look at some helpful tips to ease us into this new mind-set:

1. Begin simplifying your meals by reducing the number of foods to 2-3 at any given meal.
2. Choose one meal a day where you eat only one type of food (e.g., a variety of fruits for breakfast or salad veggies for lunch).
3. Choose one meal a day where you properly combine your foods.
4. Also called a "mono meal," choose one meal every other day where you eat only one specific type of fruit or vegetable to fullness (e.g., a big plate of ripe watermelon, or oranges, or cucumbers, or apples, or zucchini).

Now, that doesn't sound too difficult, does it?

Once you begin to include "lighter" eating choices, they'll become a habit, and you'll naturally gravitate toward healthy food combos. Don't worry if you find it a little confusing at first, and if you mix foods in questionable combos. You'll soon get the hang of it, and the more you follow the principles, the better you'll feel, and the more energized your body will become.

Light & Bright vs. Dull & Heavy

You'll start to experience a difference within your body when you start to mix foods in a way that allows for quick, efficient digestion. You'll be shocked by just how much lighter, more energized, and less sluggish you feel. Tuning in to how your body feels after eating different types of food together is the best way to understand how different combos can greatly affect your digestion and your energy level.

Avoid the dull approach:

Mixing Different Types of Heavy Foods That Don't Digest Well Together
The food sits in your digestive tract far longer than it should and needs much more energy to fully digest. Complex and heavy mixtures of food will always cause us to feel sluggish and uncomfortable.

Eating Too Many Meals & Snacks - Grazing!
Forcing your digestive system to work 24/7 and to devote its entire day to digesting meal after snack after meal after snack is a very energy-depleting way to live. The digestive system isn't meant to be in overdrive all day every day. Eating high vibrational meals 3 times each day, with small snacks of fruits or very quickly digestible foods, frees the body from this energy-draining approach to eating. It's important to avoid spending the day grazing. We need to allow our digestive system a rest between meals.

Any diet that recommends multiple meals and snacks throughout the day is a diet that lacks enough of the right nutrients at each meal to sustain our body for the right period of time.

REMEMBER!

When we efficiently digest food, our body is then able to divert much more energy toward removing toxic buildup, rebuilding tissue, healing the body from disease, general internal house cleaning, and building an energy reserve. This is a very important key to our health and to living a high vibrational lifestyle.

Healthy, high vibrational foods give us the greatest bang for the buck because not only do they digest very quickly, but they also flood us with energy instead of depleting energy for digestion.

Fresh vegetable and fruit juices top the list because they digest very quickly and deliver the maximum energy to our bodies, yet take very little energy to digest.

Let's Talk about Pesticides

Now it's time to move on to the next practical step and talk about the big difference between eating organic foods as compared to non-organic foods.

THE QUESTION OF ORGANICS

One of the most common questions people ask me is whether there's a big difference between organic and nonorganic food, and if so, to what degree.

There's a very big difference between foods that have been sprayed with pesticides and foods that haven't. Not only are organic foods more nutrient dense and flavorful, but much more importantly, foods that have been sprayed with pesticides have been conclusively linked to multiple types of cancers and other serious health conditions.

Many health studies have proven the devastating impact of pesticides in the food we eat. Some of these studies show such serious damage to our health that once people learn about them, they can't fathom how today's chemical pesticides can be a part of our food chain. Even in very small amounts, pesticides can damage developing brain cells, with infants and pets being especially susceptible to their effects.

Not surprisingly, foods sprayed with pesticides emit a much lower vibrational frequency than foods that are pesticide-free. Healthy, high vibrational foods can be reduced all the way down to zero on the vibrational scale, depending on the amount of pesticides used.

Let's explore 6 important reasons to choose organic produce whenever possible:

#1: Pesticides Are Slow, Steady Killers

Common sense tells us that eating food covered with pesticides can't be good for us; after all, pesticides by their very definition are killers. But many people don't realize just how toxic they are.

Testing by various organizations such as the **Environmental Working Group** has shown that foods grown and sprayed with pesticides carry residue of these poisons within their physical composition. Regularly eating foods containing these particles over time damages the cellular integrity of the body, and increases the likelihood of developing serious neurological conditions and chronic diseases such as cancer.

"The risk of canine malignant lymphoma increases 2-fold with 4 or more applications of 2, 4-D each year, a popular ingredient in many lawn & garden pesticides."

Journal of the National Cancer Institute

Pesticides Are a Path to Disease

Because the damage to our bodies from eating and drinking pesticides can take years to produce a cumulative effect in the body, it's easy to ignore their potential to harm us. Organic food may be the more expensive choice, but when it comes to your health, you can end up saving thousands in healthcare. You also can't put a price on the stress caused by sickness.

The average ear of corn grown in the US contains 3 different insecticides. This corn is the backbone of the new "chemicalized" US food system. It's used in farm-animal feed, in corn syrup, and in thousands of processed human and pet food products.

The reality is that if you care about your health, you can't afford *not* to begin incorporating organic produce into your purchases. The health benefits of a diet rich in organic fruits, vegetables, nuts, seeds, and legumes far outweigh eating a diet of processed and pesticide-ridden food. When it comes to high vibrational living, it's a must.

FOR CANCER PATIENTS

If you've been diagnosed with cancer, you should include as much pesticide-free food as possible in your diet. This is one of the most overlooked yet serious factors when it comes to healing from cancer.

Children & Pets at Serious Risk

Earlier, we talked about how both pets and children are especially at risk from pesticides in the environment and in their food. Infants, children, puppies, and kittens grow at such a rapid rate. Their vital organs, bone structure, and muscles are developing, and they're highly susceptible to toxins in these foods. Pound for pound, they drink 2.5 times more water and eat 3-4 times more food.

Let's take a look at the types of illnesses conclusively linked to pesticides in various health studies:

Adults & Young Adults	Infants, Children & Pets
• Neurological disorders • Cancer - non-Hodgkin's lymphoma[1][2] - breast - brain[1][10] - prostate[1] - large intestine[1] - neuroblastoma[10] • Cognitive decline[3] • Parkinson's disease[4][13]	• Developmental delays • ADHD • Growth & development[5] • Childhood leukemia[6][10] • Soft tissue sarcoma[6] • Canine malignant lymphoma[7] • Fetal death[8] • Neuroblastoma[9] • Autism spectrum disorders[11] • Neurological disorders[12]

Even in small amounts, pesticides can harm developing brain cells. They have no place in our food chain and should never be fed to an infant during the first two years of their life. Aim to provide only organic foods during this time.

During pregnancy, the unborn fetus is also at risk. Exposed to pesticides in the womb, the risks of neuro-developmental disorders, especially autism, increase.

The good news is studies have shown that, within days of switching schoolchildren's diets from conventional food to organic fruits and vegetables, many pesticide metabolites become undetectable in urine and are cleared from a child's body. This isn't only because of the pesticide-free food, but also because fruits and veggies are nutrient dense and help the body quickly heal from and purge these toxins.

#2: Organic Food Contains More Nutrients

Organic produce is grown in soils that haven't been depleted by the continual use of damaging chemicals. Studies have shown that organically grown foods contain more vitamins, minerals, enzymes, and other micronutrients than those harvested from largescale, nonorganic farms using chemical treatments.

One of the most powerful ways to experience the vital goodness and energetic nature of natural food is to eat it in its whole, organic form.

"Household & garden pesticide use increases childhood leukemia risk as much as 7-fold. Kids also suffer higher rates of brain cancer and soft tissue sarcoma."

Journal of the National Cancer Institute

- Research shows that organic produce contains 50–60 percent higher levels of cancer-fighting antioxidants than nonorganic fruits and veggies. Organic ketchup alone has double the antioxidants of conventional ketchup. Organically grown tomatoes contain higher levels of beneficial flavonoids (antioxidants associated with a range of health benefits).[14]
- A research team analyzed the levels of two beneficial flavonoid-type antioxidants, quercetin and kaempferol, in dried tomatoes. They found that tomatoes grown using organic methods contained 79 percent more quercetin and 97 percent more kaempferol, as compared to tomatoes grown by conventional methods.[15]

- Organic crops contain a much higher number of certain antioxidants (vitamin C, polyphenols, and flavonoids) and minerals. They also contain lower levels of nitrates and heavy-metal contamination as compared to conventional crops.[16]
- Studies show that antioxidant and protein content is of a higher quality in organic crops as compared to conventional crops.[17]

#3: Organic Farming Protects the Land

Organic crops are rotated each year to allow the soil to retain its nutrients between growing cycles. Animal grazing is also rotated to allow grasses to recover and replenish with the seasons. The soils are composted with broken-down plant matter, and some farmers, similar to when wine growers harvest grapes, plant seeds according to biodynamic farming practices (e.g., during specific moon phases). In short, organic farmers work to co-create with nature and respect the natural environment.

In contrast, large-scale farming methods rely on chemicals to produce food. These chemicals destroy healthy soil bacteria and ecosystems, depleting the soil of essential minerals and nutrients necessary for growing healthy produce.

A natural ecosystem creates its own process to self-regulate growth. Farming methods in existence for over 5,000 years use time-tested principles that govern the sustainability of their systems, yet biotech companies (pesticide manufacturers and producers of GMOs) look at these systems as primitive and peasant-like.

Organic farming cuts out the use of dangerous pesticides and herbicides, protects our groundwater and our wildlife, and promotes soil fertility. Even though crop yields tend to be lower on organic farms, they also tend to be the same as or more financially successful than conventional farms because the overhead is lower (no need to buy synthetic pesticides and fertilizers, pay royalties for buying GMO seeds, or buy expensive farming equipment for pesticide spraying).

The Worms Have It

Microorganisms in the soil are very important for the growth of plants. Earthworms plays an important part in enriching the soil. When they eat the soil, these worms produce enzymes and also help to loosen the soil, allowing water and air fuller access. Soil rich in worm casts and enzyme-rich manure helps produce healthy plants. The reason manure is a fantastic fertilizer is that it contains urine, feces, and straw, which are naturally powerful fertilizers.

In comparison, synthetic fertilizers and poisonous pesticides lower the vitality of growing plants and destroy this natural ecosystem. They kill the microscopic creatures that are a critical part of the life cycle of healthy, enzyme-filled nutrients.

Plants grown in depleted, unhealthy soils are not only unhealthy and lower in nutrition, but unhealthy soil automatically attracts far more pests (resulting in more pesticide use).

#4: Cruel & Inhumane Practices

In the US, over 95 percent of the meat sold in stores and served at restaurants is called "factory-farmed" meat. Not only is eating factory-farmed meat harmful to your health, but the treatment of animals on factory farms is intolerably cruel.

The factory-farming practices in the US are banned in places such as Europe and Australia, as they are considered inhumane.

Are We Really This Uncivilized?

Far from the pretty pictures of happy cows grazing in green pastures that we find on labels, factory-farmed animals are cramped into tiny spaces and physically and sexually abused, with confined dairy cows viewed as "milking machines." Chickens are kept in cages and areas so small their wings snap, or with so many in a barn that movement is severely impacted (considered "cage free"). Thousands of cows and pigs never make it to the slaughterhouse because they die from filthy living conditions and abusive treatment, hence the daily antibiotics they are fed.

Whistle-blowers and investigators have risked their lives to film animals being kicked, stabbed, horrifically abused, and beaten to death in these huge facilities on a regular basis. These whistle-blowers are heavily penalized and threatened for exposing such acts, and in some states, the Ag-Gag Bill has made whistle-blowing illegal. In these states, workers aren't allowed to discuss the cruelty they witness at factory farms. The shameful Ag-Gag Bill protects the milk and meat industries by preventing the reporting of the cruel, illegal treatment of animals.

Always choose organic, pasture-raised meat and dairy.
If you buy (or eat at restaurants) factory-farmed meat that isn't organic or pasture-raised, you indirectly contribute to animal cruelty and abuse on a mass scale.

#5: Washing Produce Does Not Remove Pesticides

If you think washing your fruits and veggies removes the pesticides, think again. Today's pesticides and herbicides are created to withstand farming irrigation so that the pesticides don't wash away when the farmers water the plants. Rinsing and scrubbing produce in your sink doesn't remove this residue. The pesticides are absorbed by the root system of the plant and distributed throughout the entire organism, so no amount of washing will remove them.

The average conventionally grown apple has 20-30 artificial chemicals on its skin, even after it's been washed. A 2006 USDA test found 81 percent of potatoes tested still contained pesticides, even after being both washed *and* peeled. According to the Environmental Working Group, the pesticide content of the potato is one of the highest of 43 different fruits and vegetables tested.

The EPA officially labels GMO corn as a pesticide because it produces its own internal insecticide.

Some GMOs (e.g., BT corn, the most commonly produced genetically modified corn in the US) are engineered to produce their own internal insecticide. This "pesticide corn" is used in farm-animal feed, corn syrup, high-fructose corn syrup, and thousands of processed human and pet food products.

Using White Vinegar

How can you avoid pesticidal residue on your produce? Buy organic. But if you do buy conventional produce, keep a spray bottle handy, fill it with white vinegar, and spray it on produce to neutralize any pesticides on the skin. This won't remove pesticides within the food, but it will help neutralize them on the surface.

It's not necessary to buy expensive fruit and vegetable sprays. Spraying plain white vinegar will do the job just as well!

#6: They Are More Flavorful

Organic foods are often much more flavorful than their nonorganic counterparts, in part because their size isn't artificially and unnaturally increased. The difference is clear when trying a simple experiment of growing your own organic strawberries (or other fruit) and comparing their taste with the taste of their conventional counterpart from the supermarket. They'll be so much sweeter!

Going Organic

Making the switch to 100 percent organic is tough for many families who choose not to pay higher prices, or who don't want give up their favorite foods that are nonorganic. Many of us can't afford to buy all organic fruits and vegetables all the time. It's expensive!

Let's talk about 4 money-saving tips to help make the switch to organic:

1. Be strategic with your organic purchases. Some fruits and veggies contain much higher amounts of pesticides than others. For example, broccoli, asparagus, and onions have lower levels of chemicals than strawberries, apples, and cherries. Choose organic produce for the worst offenders and nonorganic for the ones that contain fewer pesticides.

   The Environmental Working Group developed a list of the "dirty dozen" and "clean 15," which is updated regularly and helps us choose nonorganic produce with the least amount of pesticides. View the Dirty Dozen vs. Clean 15 list at **www.ewg.org/foodnews**.
2. Buy organic produce that's on sale. Sometimes, organic produce can be the same price, if not cheaper, than conventional produce.
3. Check out the local farmers' markets (and actual farms) for your produce, and especially for eggs from pasture-raised chickens and for raw cheese and dairy products. These products are often cheaper than the ones in the store. If you need help finding local growers and organic markets, check out Local Harvest (**www.localharvest.org**), or ask around at nearby natural health-food stores.
4. Buy organic, pasture-raised meats close to expiration (when on sale) and cook them immediately. They're often cheaper than their nonorganic counterparts.

Recognizing Organic Produce in Stores

In supermarket chains and health-food stores, one way to recognize organic products is by how clearly the store arranges their food. Many stores now contain a natural-food section where they keep their organic and GMO-free food. When it comes to fresh produce, take a look at the product PLU code (short for "price look-up code"), which is on either a sticker or a label wrapped around the produce:

Unfortunately, no federal mandate in the US requires that food be labeled as GMOs. Many Americans say they would avoid GMOs if they were labeled, so many seed companies don't want gardeners to know which of their seeds are genetically modified.

If you live in the US, the only way you can be sure you aren't eating GMOs is to purchase organic. (This is a nonissue in the 60+ other countries that are legally required to label their products as GMOs.)

Organic Foods & Heavy Metals

Currently, the USDA organic standards place no limits on heavy-metal contamination in certified organic foods. This means that organic products can contain various heavy metals, including mercury, lead, cadmium, arsenic, and aluminum. There's also no limit on the contamination of PCBs, BPAs, and other synthetic chemicals that are allowed in certified organic foods and supplements.

We may not have control over these contaminants, but the cleaner our body, the more quickly and efficiently our organs and systems will remove these incoming toxins and the less damage they'll do.

Organic Food from China

"FDA inspections are a mere 2.3% of the total of all imported food products from China."

Democrats on the House Appropriations Committee

Unfortunately, produce from China can bear the USDA organic seal, but this seal is highly questionable considering the current food-safety standards in China. Organic Chinese farms are rarely inspected by US organic certifiers to enforce compliance with the USDA organic food and agriculture standards.

At this time, the terms "organic" and "China" don't belong in the same sentence.

A Rainbow of Textures & Flavors

Let's move on to the 4th practical step and talk about just how exciting healthy, natural foods really are!

A RAINBOW OF TEXTURES & FLAVORS

Foods from nature can be incredibly rich and flavorful, with a wonderful array of textures. Think of the sweet, tart taste of a piece of pineapple, or the deep, rich flavor of pure maple syrup. How about the crisp, cool crunch of a cucumber, or the juicy splash of sweetness in a ripe, crunchy slice of watermelon?

An endless variety of spices from all over the world adds a whole new dimension to just how flavorful natural foods can be, as can combining sweet foods with foods that contain much less sugar.

We often try to mask the healthy foods we eat with condiments that aren't so healthy instead of using natural "food condiments" to enhance their unique flavor and texture. Natural foods cover the entire spectrum of favors, including:

Sweet: Raw honey, pure maple syrup, dried figs and apricots, dates, stevia leaf

Cheesy: Nutritional yeast, raw cheeses

Salty: Seaweed, sea vegetables, sea salt

Tangy: Dash of balsamic vinaigrette, lemon juice, lime juice, fermented foods, tamarind

Astringent: Pomegranates, persimmons, parsley

Spicy: Black pepper, chili peppers (cayenne, jalapeño, serrano, habanero), Indian spices, Cajun spices

Filling Flavors: Avocados, olives, nuts, seeds, nut/seed butters, yams, sweet potatoes, butternut squash

Adding Treats: A glass of wine or mead with dark chocolate slices or slices of raw cheese

Exciting flavors are all there in either food or spice form. We just need to get a bit creative, such as mixing and matching to create tastes we enjoy. With little effort, we can make a tantalizing variety of dishes, dips, and dressings.

With this in mind, one of the best things you can do for yourself is to learn how to make your own dips and sauces. When I say "learn," I mean very simple recipes that take just a few minutes and include only a few ingredients. You can whip them up in less than 5 minutes and give an amazing burst of flavor to veggies and salads you would otherwise consider quite bland and tasteless.

Experiment using different ingredients to create your own flavors. Aim to use foods that have the highest vibrational frequency.

Dips & Dressings

When it comes to recipes, there are many different recipe books are available containing a wonderful variety of whole-food, healthy dips and dressings. Here is a selection of several of my favorite that are easy and quick to make, and that will help you get creative when it comes to making your own combos.

Feel free to adjust them as needed, adding and subtracting to your heart's content. I often add Herbs de Provence to my dips (a mixture of herbs from Provence, France: oregano, thyme, rosemary, marjoram, savory). Experiment to see which herbs you like best:

AVOCADO-BASED DIPS

Satiate your appetite with the creamy, filling taste of fresh avocados:

Mayocado

- 2 ripe avocados
- Pinch sea salt
- 2 tablespoons lemon juice
- 1/4 cup crushed cashews (or favorite nut of your choice!)
- 1 tablespoon parsley
- 1 large garlic clove, finely chopped or minced
- Water to your preferred consistency

Blend or mix well with a fork.

Spinach Avocado

- 1 medium avocado
- 1 well-chopped small onion
- 2 cups well-chopped spinach or kale
- 1 tablespoon lemon juice
- 1/2 to 1 teaspoon sea salt
- Cracked pepper to taste

Mix well with a fork.

NUT-BASED DIPS

For a more filling dip, try these (they're high in fat, so use sparingly):

Hazelnut Vinaigrette

- 1/4 cup crushed or well-chopped hazelnuts
- 1 tablespoon balsamic vinegar
- 1 tablespoon olive oil
- 3 garlic cloves, chopped
- Sea salt to taste

Mix well with a fork.

Poppin' Pine Nut Dressing

- 6 oz. chopped broccoli, cauliflower, and red bell pepper
- 3 oz. water
- 1 oz. pine nuts
- Sea salt to taste

Blend well in blender or food processor.

FRUIT-BASED DIPS

Tantalize your taste buds with fruity and tangy sauces that give blander veggies a burst of flavor:

Balsamic Fig Dip

- 6 oz. figs
- Balsamic vinaigrette to taste

Blend well in blender or food processor.

Homemade Jam

- 8 oz. of your favorite fruit, soaked in water for 8-10 hours
- 7 oz. water
- Small amount of raw honey

Blend well, adding more water or fruit as preferred.

VEGGIE-BASED DIPS

Veggie dips are versatile, can be seasoned and spiced, and are brimming with vitalizing nutrients:

Spicy Veggie Dip

- 2 zucchinis, well chopped
- 3 scallions, well chopped
- 1/2 cup raw tahini
- 2 tablespoons olive oil
- 3 garlic cloves, finely chopped
- 1/8 teaspoon cayenne pepper

Blend or mix well.

Olive Tapenade

- 6 oz. tomatoes
- 2 oz. olives, pitted and well chopped
- 2 garlic cloves, finely chopped

Mix well with a fork.

TOMATO SALAD/SAUCE

This tomato salad is a staple in our household. We mix it with chopped veggies for a larger salad, have it with our main meal, or mix it with kelp noodles (nutritious, crunchy sea noodles—they have no flavor of their own and so take on the flavor of whatever sauce is mixed with them ... no seaweed taste whatsoever!).

- 6 oz. cherry tomatoes, halved, then quartered
- 2 chopped scallions
- 1/4 cup sweet corn (optional)
- 1/2 chopped avocado (optional)
- 2 large garlic cloves, finely chopped
- 1/4 cup chopped cilantro
- 1 tablespoon olive oil (optional)
- Sea salt, cracked pepper, and oregano to taste
- Several loosely chopped basil leaves

Mix well with a fork.

Recipes

For a great selection of healthy salads, appetizers, dips, entrees, and desserts, head over to the Body Healer recipes (**www.thebodyhealer.com/recipes**). Our recipe section offers some fun, creative ways to serve dishes brimming with highly nutritious, high vibrational foods.

You'll also find some great ideas for making irresistible water-based drinks bursting with the flavor of citrus and fruits!

Let's move on and talk about the best way to start our day when it comes to healthy, high vibrational eating.

BEGINNING THE DAY LIGHT

Always begin the day with light, energizing foods (if you want to feel energized). A heavy, low vibrational breakfast of dense foods can significantly reduce your energy levels.

The more energy you have, the higher your healing potential

Many people peter out by midafternoon because their breakfast and lunch have bogged down their digestive system. The types of foods they ate or the combinations in which they ate them caused much of their energy drain.

To avoid this, aim for choices such as:

- A selection of fresh, chopped fruits
- A selection of crunchy salad veggies
- A fruit smoothie with various greens
- A veggie juice

While you're transitioning, enjoy sprouted grain bread with veggies (e.g., lettuce, tomato, cucumber, and avocado sandwich). Remember to wait 30 minutes after eating any fruit.

From a high vibrational standpoint, the habit of eating a mixture of fried bacon or sausage or ham + eggs + toast or fried hash browns, as well as other heavy breakfast foods, such as pancakes, waffles, pasteurized butter, and processed jelly is as energy-depleting as we can get. Eating this way is just about the worst way we can begin our day or treat our body.

Once you walk away from these choices in favor of lighter, healthier foods, I promise you that the difference in your health, in how you feel, and in how efficient your digestion becomes will prevent you from ever wanting to return to this way of eating again.

Candidiasis, Diabetes, & Cancer

If you are suffering from candidiasis, diabetes, or cancer, we'll talk about some modifications to make later in this section.

Eat Light to Heavy

With every meal you eat, including breakfast, always eat the food on your plate "light to heavy," and eat it slowly. This means you should eat the fruit first, followed by the salad next, followed by the cooked veggies, and then followed by heavier starches or proteins. Eat at a slow pace to make sure the lighter foods that take the least amount of time to digest are less likely to be held up by the heavier foods.

The concept of wolfing food down on a 10-minute break or, worse still, gulping it down at a stop sign or red light, reduces the efficiency of our digestive system. Europeans shake their heads at us in pity when they see how quickly we eat. The French routinely take 2-3 hours to sit, relax, and enjoy their meals. They talk about their day, laughing and enjoying each other's company. The rushed pace of American eating is unfathomable to them!

How Much?

Now that we know the best way to begin our day, let's move on to the next practical step and talk about portion sizes.

PORTION SIZES

Although we don't have to measure out portion sizes, we need to be mindful of not overeating dense foods (starchy veggies, grains, animal products) and high-fat items (nuts, seeds, oils, avocados, olives). These should be eaten in small quantities.

The great news is that our diet is very high in fruits and vegetables that are high in water content, and these foods come in a big variety and can be eaten in unlimited quantities. They're also very filling because of their water content.

For portion sizes, use the following guidelines:

Food	Quantity
Raw fruit	Unlimited, but eat dried fruits in small quantities (small handful each day).
Raw veggies (non-starchy)	Unlimited.
Cooked veggies	Unlimited (non-starchy). Limit starchy veggies to 1 cup/day.
Raw sprouted grains	1 cup/day. Omit if eating cooked sprouted grains or legumes.
Cooked sprouted grains or legumes (beans, peas, lentils)	1 cup/day. Omit if eating raw sprouted grains.
Raw nuts & seeds	Small handful each day (1-2 oz.). Omit if eating high-fat plant food.
High-fat plant food	Small quantities (e.g., 1/2 medium avocado each day). Omit if eating nuts or seeds.
Animal food (meat, fish, eggs, dairy)	2-3 oz. a maximum of 2-3 times/week: – Pasture-raised meat (free-range) – Unpasteurized (raw) dairy – Pasture-raised eggs (free-range) – Wild-caught fish

Slow Down

One of the biggest reasons we overeat is we eat our food so quickly. We often feel full when we eat less, but we never give our body time to register it is full.

From the moment we begin eating, it takes approximately 20 minutes before the brain begins to signal we feel full, and that is plenty of time to eat too much if we eat too fast.

As you eat each type of food on your plate, slow it down. Chew your food well, and get into the habit of putting your fork down every few mouthfuls. When we take at least 20-30 minutes to finish a meal, we significantly reduce our chance of overeating, which means we'll be much less likely to focus on dessert! On the other hand, make sure you eat enough to feel satisfied, or you'll be more likely to snack shortly after.

If you feel full and there's still food on your plate, clear your plate away quickly to avoid eating leftovers simply because they're sitting in front of you.

Are You Really Hungry?

Sometimes, we eat out of habit. Our watch says we need to eat, whether we're hungry or not. If lunchtime comes around and you're not yet hungry, then don't eat! If you wake up in the morning and don't feel hungry for breakfast, then pass on it or have a small piece of fruit.

There are times when our digestive system calls out for a rest. It may still be digesting food from an earlier meal or from the evening before, or it may be purging toxins. We can see this in the animal world: when a dog or cat has an upset stomach, they won't eat, or they'll eat grass to help purge and normalize their system. Honor your body's request for a food rest, and instead, provide it with plenty of fresh water or fruit/vegetable juices.

Hunger vs. Habit

We should always wait until our body genuinely signals a need for food before we put anything into our mouth. There's a big difference between real hunger and eating out of habit, and the more in tune we are with our body, the more we'll be able to tell the difference between hunger and habit.

A great little test to tell the difference is to ask yourself what you feel like eating. Is it something healthy? If not, mentally substitute that desire for something healthy. Do you still "feel" hungry? True hunger will never say no to healthy foods full of nutrients.

Always Eat Lighter Foods First

As we just discussed, when you eat a meal, always eat the light and less dense foods first, followed by the heavier foods. After eating the lighter foods, put down your fork, and wait a few minutes before eating the heavier foods.

Out with the Old, in with the New!

Before we fill our fridge and kitchen cabinets with healthy, high vibrational foods, we need to make space for them by clearing out all the junk that no longer serves the beautiful body of light (and health!) we're creating. Get ready to roll up your sleeves—it's time to take out the garbage!

GETTING RID OF THE GARBAGE

Before we merrily trot off to the store to stock up on healthy foods, we have to first make room for it by cleaning out the garbage. For some foods, the parting may be easy, and for others, bittersweet.

Investing in being healthy and happy and vibrant is the most amazing gift you can give to yourself. This is a turning point: you're making a conscious decision to walk away from the old, unhealthy foods and lifestyle habits in favor of healthy, high vibrational foods and lifestyle habits that heal your body and restore you to a state of balance.

Don't Make It a Secret

Tell Your Family

It's important to tell your spouse (or significant other) and your immediate family that things are changing. You've made a new commitment to healthy living, and they're more than welcome to join you. Explain that the standard American diet no longer serves your beautiful body and has no place in your kitchen.

If you have family members that aren't ready, willing, or able to move to a different eating lifestyle, then make compromises you can all be happy with. His-and-her cabinets are ideal; your spouse can store food you want to avoid (such as cookies, crackers, and refined foods) in their cabinet, and you can store nuts, seeds, healthy desserts and treats, dried fruits, and other items in yours. Respectfully ask that any junk food always be kept in cabinets and out of your view.

Family Members & Food

Are you worried about a family member with unhealthy eating habits?

When it comes to influencing other people's lifestyle and eating habits, you're at your most powerful when you set a living example. The proof will be in the changes that people see in you. If and when they ask for more information, willingly share your knowledge. Never force-feed (no pun intended!) what you know down someone else's throat. Let them respond and react to the positive changes they see in you.

For family members who are curious and want to know more, share both what you know and the positive changes you're experiencing. If they want to change their eating habits along with you, that's great! Every time you prepare a meal for them, celebrate that you're helping make a difference in their health (and their life).

Children & Food

If you have young children, it's a different matter. You're in control of their diet; as well as providing only healthy foods, help your children understand which foods are good for them, and which foods will hurt them. Have fun getting creative with healthy foods and how you prepare them. Even the way you arrange them on a plate can help make them more fun and exciting! How about lining food up on a plate to make it look like a caterpillar, or arranging it into different shapes like a pyramid or circle?

We have a responsibility not to feed our children unhealthy foods—especially not junk food—ever. Young children are sponges and often mimic what they see. By setting the very best example you can, and at the same time *educating* your children about why some foods are better than others, you'll make an imprint. Blending greens or a veggie juice with a fruit smoothie is a simple way to entice children to eat foods that aren't so exciting to them.

But educating doesn't mean being rigid and dogmatic. It means speaking with honesty and understanding, patiently teaching them that some foods heal and some foods harm. Speaking from your heart about how amazing healthy food can be is a language that children intuitively understand.

Tell Friends & Relatives

Kindly explain to all friends and relatives who visit you that your home is now a healthy one. If they'd like to bring treats, ask that they please focus on healthy treats (barring a good bottle of wine!). Also let them know that the meals you prepare will now be made with only healthy, nutritious ingredients. Asking for the support of those around you (and letting people know how important their support is to you), will often arouse their interest and excitement.

Some people will look forward to healthier meals and ask for tips on how to prepare healthier meals for themselves and their families. Others may wave off your new eating approach in the beginning, but after they see the visually amazing impact healthy living has on your appearance, your mood, and your state of mind, their curiosity will get the better of them.

Some people will show no interest, which is just fine. As long as they respect your decision and don't try to sabotage or thwart it, it's important to also respect their choice.

Grab Those Boxes!

You'll need several strong, sturdy boxes for all the items you're getting rid of. Make this fresh, new start a fun experience! Consider including your friends and family—that way, you can affirm your new lifestyle with those you love. They may happily relieve you of your whole stash, such as cookies and candy and canned goods, which is another incentive for them to help!

Whichever way you do it, turn the music up or put a great movie on in the background, and enjoy every minute of this purge. It's a whole new beginning!

Are you ready to make the most important investment you'll ever make when it comes to your body and your health?

Great! Then let's have fun and go at it!

Ditch It

Look at every single packaged item in your refrigerator, freezer, and cupboards (that includes secret hiding places!) and get rid of anything that contains refined foods and chemicals you don't recognize as whole foods. This includes:

- Refined ingredients (chemicals, coloring, flavoring, anything hydrogenated, anything bleached or enriched)
- Refined corn or soy (we talked about common corn and soy ingredients earlier)
- Refined oils (keep only organic "cold-pressed" or "unrefined")
- Canned goods (look for glass-jar versions instead, or if you must buy canned food, make sure it's labeled as BPA-free)
- Factory-farmed meat, fish, and eggs (only "free-range" or "pasture-raised")
- Condiments with chemicals (only whole-food ingredients, spices, and vinegars; especially watch out for pickles and relishes that often contain food coloring to give them that strange greenish-yellow glow! These colorings are toxic and carry warning labels in countries other than the US.)
- Pasteurized dairy (milk, cheese, butter)
- GMOs (if not organic, look for the non-GMO project seal on any packaged foods)

The Cookbooks

When it comes to your cookbooks, fill your shelves with recipe books that focus on healthy, whole-food ingredients. Traditional Middle Eastern, Mediterranean, and African cookbooks offer ethnic recipes that have a wide variety of healthy, tasty, flavorful recipes.

Expand your cookbook shelf to include recipe books on subjects such as juicing, smoothies, and raw-food dishes. Most contain easy-to-make recipes. If you enjoy gourmet cooking, a big selection of healthy gourmet cookbooks are now available. One of my favorite is from a raw-food chef with a thriving LA restaurant; the recipes are rather complex, but the dishes are truly delectable and far surpass many gourmet-cooked dishes when it comes to flavor and taste.

Remove all cookbooks focused on unhealthy ingredients such as sugar, flour, and refined grains. They aren't in the best interest of your new, healthy body and will create nostalgia for past eating habits while you develop new ones.

Substituting Healthy Baking Ingredients

If you have dessert cookbooks with recipes you love, but that are loaded with flour, sugar, and butter, look for ways you can transform these recipes into a healthier version using ingredients such as coconut oil, maple sugar, and honey. Keep in mind that these recipes are very dense and often very high in fat. They aren't in the best interest of your health, so aim to make them as healthy as possible while keeping them to a minimum in your diet.

Let's take a look at some ingredient substitutions:

- If a recipe calls for sugar, always avoid processed white sugar. Substitute with healthier sugars instead, such as coconut sugar, maple/date sugar, or sucanat (sugar cane natural).
- If a recipe calls for flour, pass on bleached white flour; look for whole-grain or grain-free flours instead (e.g., coconut flour, garbanzo bean flour, almond flour, etc.). They will change the flavor and texture of the recipe, so you may need to experiment.
- If a recipe calls for butter, check out the ingredient list on the butter; many contain chemicals you don't want in your body. Choose pasture-raised ghee if available (clarified butter), which is lactose-free and much lower in fat.

Speaking of butter, let's compare two popular butters on the market. Do *not* make the mistake of choosing the butter with fewer calories! It's about quality, not calories. It's about healthy ingredients vs. chemicals and processed oils that cause disease. What many dieters fail to understand is that these chemicals contribute to ill-health because the body is unable to properly metabolize them. Non-dairy and vegan spreads are often the worst offenders in terms of unhealthy ingredients and genetically modified soybeans.

Take a look at the ingredient difference between two very popular butters:

Organic Valley Pasture-Raised Butter

Certified organic butter, salt

vs.

Popular Spread

Natural oil blend (soybean, palm fruit, extra virgin olive, fish, flaxseed and canola oils), water, contains 2% or less of whey (from milk), salt, natural and artificial flavor, sorbitan ester of vegetable fatty acids and mono diglycerides of vegetable fatty acids (emulsifiers), soy lecithin, DL-A-Tocopheryl acetate (vitamin E), vitamin A palmitate, vitamin D, vitamin B6, vitamin B12, lactic acid, beta-carotene color, and potassium sorbate, TBHQ and calcium disodium EDTA (to preserve freshness)

Wow, what a difference! Which one would you rather use?

The Kitchen Tools

I highly recommend some kitchen tools that are not only inexpensive, but if you start with quality items and take good care of them, they'll last for many years. These tools will help you prepare food easier and faster, and give you a much greater variety when preparing healthy food dishes.

The Essentials

- Blender
- Food processor
- Juicer
- Large cutting board
- Good set of knives
- Assorted measuring cups and spoons

Optional

- Spiralizer
- Dehydrator
- Sprouting jars

Blender/Food Processor

These are used to blend fruits and veggies into smoothies, and also to make purees. Some make nut butters, and some also act as a food processor to shred, pulverize, grind, and chop. The Vitamix is a popular, high-end blender with a powerful high-speed motor. Although it's on the pricey side, it's a solid unit backed by a lifetime warranty. After 6 years of daily use, I finally burned out a motor; it was replaced quickly with no questions asked.

Many other good-quality blenders are more affordably priced, some coming as part of a "set" containing a blender and food processor (with different-sized chopping containers). A great example is the Ninja, which has a blender as well as a food processor for chopping or pureeing food. They make several different products, including the Ninja Master Prep Professional for under $100 (my favorite) that has different-sized containers for food processing.

These and many other blenders are available online and in stores. Kitchen stores offer a great variety; however, I've found the prices much cheaper online. Check out the reviews to see customer feedback before making your purchase.

Juicer

Three types of juicers are on the market, ranging from $40 all the way up to over $250, depending on their ability to extract juice from greens such as wheat grass. There's no reason to break the bank over a juicer, and paying more doesn't necessarily mean it's the best product for you.

1. Basic Centrifugal Juicers
   This is the most common type. They do the job quickly and efficiently and have a wide spout to push veggies and fruits into. Less chopping up means quicker juicing!

2. Masticating (Cold-Press) Juicers
   These are able to extract more juice and fiber, and some can grind nuts to make nut milk. Juicing is a much slower process, but the yield is a little greater than from a centrifugal juicer.

3. Wheat-Grass Juicers
   These are made exclusively for extracting juice from wheat grass and leafy greens.

For those of you who don't like to spend all your time juicing (like me!), a basic juicer is all you need. You may take a small hit on the amount of juice extracted, but it's small, and juicing is much quicker. I've used several juicers, and the expensive ones aren't always the best. My most recent Hamilton Beach

Wide Mouth Juicer was only $60 and has been a workhorse for 4 years. It also has a wide spout, which means I don't have to spend my time chopping up veggies into small pieces. The Breville Juice Fountain Plus is more expensive, but also a good, solid unit. With both juicers, I can chop, juice, and clean up in under 5 minutes - can't get much better than that!

Chopping Board & Knives

A basic chopping board and a high quality, sharp knife is a must to slice and dice veggies, fruits, and herbs. A good knife will easily slice through denser produce such as beets, winter squash, pineapples, and potatoes.

Complete knife sets can be priced very reasonably and come with a variety of different types of knifes.

Spiralizer

Spiralizers are so much fun, and they're also easy to use and inexpensive (under $40 from Amazon)! This cool gadget "spiralizes" food such as zucchini, beets, jicama, and carrots for yummy veggie-based pastas. Mix with a home-made tomato or pesto sauce and you can create a much healthier and lighter alternative to heavy grain-based pastas.

Time to Go Shopping

Okay, now that we've cleared out the garbage, let's go shopping! Bring the following shopping list with you. Don't worry—nothing about the list will deprive you or leave you feeling hungry.

We'll be shopping for foods that are either fresh or have been very minimally processed. Finding these foods is easy because when most of your food is fresh from the produce department, you won't have to worry about reading complicated ingredient lists on prepackaged foods.

Grab your wallet and head for the door. It's time to go shopping ... high vibrational style!

SHOPPING "HIGH VIBRATIONAL STYLE"!

Most major grocery-store chains have a natural and organic food section. Make these the main focus for your food shopping. If you have access to a natural health-food store, such as Sprouts, Natural Grocers, Earth Fare, or Whole Foods, check out their selection and compare prices. I often shop at Natural Grocers, which sells only 100 percent organic produce, and their produce is often cheaper than their organic counterpart at our local big grocery store.

You'll find a much better selection for some items in a natural grocery store. Not only that, but certain healthier foods can only be found in these stores. Examples include raw nuts; raw nut butters (many health-food stores have a grinder for you to grind your own nut butters); organic, cold-pressed nut and seed oils (e.g., avocado oil or walnut oil); Nama Shoyu (unpasteurized soy sauce); healthy snacks; and certain organic vegetables and herbs. Because some of these items are only eaten in small quantities, they can last a while, which helps offset any extra cost. Purchasing items online can save you money too.

Let's get down to business and take a look at our shopping list. When it comes to fruits and veggies, remember to choose organic where possible—especially for those very high in pesticide residue. Save your nonorganic food choices for foods that test low in pesticides. Check out the Environmental Working Group's Dirty 12 & Clean 15 at **www.ewg.org/foodnews** for the latest updates.

– FRESH FRUITS –

Feel free to choose from the many wonderful choices available—especially those high in water content and antioxidants, such as citrus fruits, melons, apples, grapes, cherries, and berries.

– FRESH VEGETABLES –

Focus on salad veggies and the leafy greens, such as kale, lettuces, spinach, Swiss chard, cilantro, parsley, tomatoes, cucumber, jicama, zucchini, and collard greens. Focus less on the heavier, starchy veggies, such as potatoes, yams, winter squash, and beets (unless you're juicing them). As with fruits, always choose organic wherever possible.

Onions, leeks, and garlic are used extensively in both Ayurvedic and Oriental medicine. The allicin compound in the onion family is antimicrobial, antithrombotic, antiarthritic, and anticancer. Garlic also adds a wonderful flavor to meals and dips.

– SPROUTED ANCIENT GRAINS & LEGUMES –

Sprouted grains are found in every health-food store and some supermarkets. Focus only on the non-glutinous ancient grains (quinoa, chia, millet, oats, amaranth, teff, buckwheat, and sorghum). Popular sprouted legumes include chickpeas, lentils, and mung beans.

– RAW DAIRY –

Even though a wider selection of raw cheese will be available at health-food stores, most grocery stores now sell the Alta Dena and Organic Valley brand of raw cheddar and goat-milk cheese. Most major supermarket chains now have a great variety of unpasteurized cheese in their specialty cheese section. Ask at the counter for help finding "raw" or "unpasteurized" cheese, or look on the cheese label.

In some US states, such as Arizona, California, Connecticut, Idaho, Massachusetts, Nevada, New Hampshire, New Mexico, Pennsylvania, South Carolina, and Washington, raw dairy is legally available in stores, whereas in other states it isn't.

– LIQUID OILS –

Use sparingly, and buy only organic and unrefined/cold-pressed nut or seed oils (this ensures they are non-GMO). Popular examples include olive oil, avocado oil, coconut oil, and flax-seed oil. Many other specialty oils are also available, such as walnut oil, hemp-seed oil, pistachio oil, hazelnut oil, truffle oil, pecan oil, and macadamia oil.

– MEAT, FISH, & EGGS –

Buy only meat and eggs that are labeled as organic and are only from animals who have been pasture-raised. This ensures that not only have the animals been raised humanely and in their natural environment, but also that the foods don't contain antibiotics, growth hormones, and other medicated additives. Pasture-raised foods are also much higher in nutrient value.

Fish should be wild-caught, and if possible, tested for mercury levels. Avoid or severely limit your intake of fish known to contain higher levels of heavy metals (tuna, shark, or swordfish).

– SPICES & CONDIMENTS –

Purchase only unrefined sea salt and use sparingly. An amazing variety of gourmet natural salts is available. When purchasing condiments, read the ingredient list very carefully. Only natural ingredients such as tomatoes, apple cider vinegar, pepper, sea salt, and other herbs and spices should be listed ... nothing else.

– SWEETENERS –

Purchase only natural sweeteners—the more unrefined, the better. These include:

- Raw honey
- Coconut sugar
- Date sugar
- Unrefined maple syrup and maple sugar
- Whole-leaf stevia
- Blackstrap molasses
- Rapadura
- Sucanat (sugar cane natural)

Unlike sweeteners such as honey and date sugar, agave syrup undergoes heavy processing to create the syrup. There are much better natural sweeteners to choose from.

– VINEGARS –

Read the ingredient list carefully for hidden ingredients. Great choices include:

- Apple cider vinegar (always buy raw and unfiltered)
- Balsamic vinegar
- Red or white wine vinegar
- Ume plum vinegar

- FLOUR -

Flours are finely ground grains, nuts, seeds, vegetables, or legumes. Flour and products containing flour are transitional foods, and the goal is to wean them from your diet completely. They should form an extremely small part of your shopping list and be eaten rarely. Always choose unbleached and unrefined flour.

- FROZEN & PACKAGED FOODS -

These should also form a very small part of your diet. If you buy any packaged or frozen foods, read the ingredient lists very carefully, and make sure that every single ingredient on that list is a natural whole food.

What are examples of whole foods? Apples, tomatoes, onions, celery, garlic, spices, lentils, quinoa, herbs, etc. What isn't a whole food? Any chemical, vitamin (which is usually synthetic), coloring, flavoring, or other artificial or unpronounceable ingredient that isn't a whole food! If in any doubt, ditch it.

Shopping Tips

The most important shopping tip is that for any item you buy that's not from the produce section, read every single item on the ingredient list very carefully. If an ingredient is questionable, then put it right back on the shelf.

1. Wherever possible, always choose organic.
2. Always select fresh, whole foods over canned, packaged, or frozen foods. Try to avoid canned foods, but if you do buy them, make sure they're listed as BPA-free. Eat canned foods only in very small quantities.
3. Avoid any "natural coloring" or "natural flavoring" unless the label specifically states it's from a vegetable or fruit (e.g., coloring from paprika). A "natural flavor" is far from natural and can contain up to fifty different chemicals per flavor.
4. Refined sugar, corn, soy, and their derivatives are present in almost every refined food and frozen meal. Be especially careful to watch out for these unhealthy, genetically modified offenders that register as zero on the vibrational scale.
5. NON GMO Project VERIFIED Avoid purchasing genetically modified foods. In the US, the only way you can make sure the food you buy isn't genetically modified is to look for the non-GMO project seal on the label. Many brands are committed to non-GMOs and use this seal.

Organic foods aren't genetically modified; however, if you don't see the non-GMO project seal, check to see if it contains any nonorganic ingredients.

You'll quickly discover that the easiest way to make shopping a simple, uncomplicated experience is to focus on fresh foods and limit (as much as possible) your purchases of any packaged food items.

Sound Strict?

Yes, and for a very good reason! This is a wake-up call. We're eliminating foods that should never be in our food chain. These are chemicalized and industrialized foods that we've assumed are safe, and that millions worldwide eat at every meal. But they aren't healthy or safe. The foods we're eliminating are not only very low on the vibrational scale, but they also destroy our health at a cellular level. In short, they're a root cause of disease.

This is the only path to take when it comes to high vibrational health and a life free from disease. I care very much about your health and want you to care about and nurture the beautiful body you live in! There's no good reason to continue eating unhealthy foods. After you cut them out and reap the many benefits, I promise you won't regret it.

LET'S TALK ABOUT TRANSITIONING

Honoring the time your body needs to adjust to not only a new way of eating, but a new approach to living, is very important. Be patient and give your body the time it needs to adapt.

The bigger the change, the easier you must be on yourself, so it's always best to change habits at a pace you can manage. Your chances of success are far greater when you transition at a manageable pace, and your chances of falling off the wagon are far higher if you try to move quicker than your mind and body are ready for. Perceptions don't change overnight, nor do habits or addictions, but they will change quickly.

If you've lived on processed food, canned food, and frozen meals for many years and decide to eat a diet full of high vibrational food with a zero-tolerance policy for indiscretions, then in the beginning, the journey will be more challenging. Unless you're suffering from a chronic disease, this isn't a time for militancy or an "all-or-nothing" mindset. Instead, keep your eyes focused on the end result, and honor the time it will take you to adjust to new foods and new eating habits. The good news is that if you're committed, change will happen quickly, and these new eating habits will soon become a way of life.

Helpful High Vibrations

The sooner you begin a high vibrational diet, the sooner your body will naturally begin to function at higher vibrational frequencies. It happens automatically. These new frequencies will have a subtle yet profound effect on every part of your life; they'll cause you to gravitate toward what's healthy and away from what isn't. Soon, you won't need "willpower" because you'll lose interest in foods that are unhealthy and low vibrational because of how they make you feel.

Pace Yourself

Every person is unique. How fast you progress is dependent on where your starting point is and how much work you have to do. Radical change requires a very high level of discipline that's easier for some people than for others.

If you've always eaten the standard American diet of processed foods and you suddenly decide to become a vegetarian or vegan overnight, you may or may not have the level of discipline required for such a sudden, drastic change. Your body may rebel and fight you every step of the way. Transitioning at a manageable pace is a much better approach.

One by One

If you experience difficulties, avoid cutting back on too much all at once. For example, cutting out all refined foods is a massive undertaking; it's the biggest challenge most people face. Trying to do that while giving up caffeine, and cooked grains, and long-time favorite desserts, and cutting back on meat and dairy ... that's all simply too much. Nixing one habit at a time is a much easier approach, and making changes on a weekly basis makes it a doable goal.

Begin by choosing one item to remove from your life for a period of 1-2 weeks, and let your body (and mind) adapt to that adjustment. While it's natural for change to be challenging and for you to have a few slip-ups, if it seems downright impossible and you find yourself cheating at every turn, then reevaluate and make some adjustments.

Instead of completely eliminating the food, begin by cutting back on it, and decrease the amount you eat on a slow but steady basis. Meanwhile, begin cutting out the next item on the list. Always keep your focus on where you're headed and keep moving forward.

Some unhealthy food choices or habits may not be an issue for you. For example, you may not be much of a coffee drinker, or you may not smoke or drink sodas. Fantastic! You get to cross these things off the list before you even begin!

IMPORTANT! For Those with a Chronic Disease

If you suffer from a chronic disease such as cancer, heart disease, diabetes, or an autoimmune disorder, changing your diet as quickly as possible is the key to a faster recovery. Be extra firm with yourself about your commitment and about how ready you are to walk away from your condition and restore your body to health. If you fall off the wagon, don't stress; just get right back on track.

Take Heart in the 30-Day Rule

It only takes between 21-30 days for new habits to kick in and for unhealthy addictions and destructive habits to lose their power.

When you give up addictive foods, the first few days are always tough, but cravings and urges will pass much sooner than you think! Long-standing habits rarely change overnight, which is why short-term diets never lead to lasting results. If you want to achieve success, you have to allow time for the foundation of healthy eating and lifestyle choices to take hold, and understanding the 30-day rule keeps the light at the end of the tunnel always in your view.

By the time you reach the 30-day mark, several things have happened:

1. **Addictive, Destructive Habits Have Weakened**
   You've taken steps to replace old habits with new ones, and the body is now beginning to adapt to these new habits.

2. **Your Body's Sensitivity Is Reset**
   For example, if you're a heavy soda drinker or fill your iced teas with sugar, you've become very accustomed to sugary drinks. But if you completely omit *all* sugary drinks from your diet for 30 days and then suddenly drink a soda, it'll taste sickly sweet—like drinking liquid sugar. Similarly, if you omit all added salt from your diet for 30 days and then eat a bag of salted potato chips or nuts, they'll suddenly taste far too salty and you'll be shocked at how you respond to them.

   After you eliminate processed food for 30 days, if you begin eating it again, your body will likely produce a swift reaction to it, often in the form of digestive issues. Common signs include tummy discomfort, constipation, mucus (in the back of your throat), diarrhea, acne, a general sense of fatigue, or other symptoms.

3. **Proof Positive**
   You'll see 100 percent, definitive proof of the benefits of your new food choices in both the way you feel and the way you look, and that becomes a powerful driving factor.

It'll quickly become clear that unhealthy foods just aren't worth it because of how you feel after eating them, or you may (very occasionally) choose to have them (or a healthier version of them) and then spend the next day or two flooding your body with high vibrational foods to help it snap right back. A healthy body will quickly bounce back from occasional foods on the no-no list, and from temporary, short-lived stress.

Transitional Foods

We eat transitional foods to get us from where we are now to a healthy, higher vibrational state. They may not be the best foods we could eat, but they're also far from the worst. Use these foods to help you transition from lower vibrational foods to higher ones as they can help ease you into much healthier eating habits.

Transitional:	Work toward:
Nuts and seeds (e.g., roasted), 1-2 oz. max each day	Raw nuts and seeds, 1-2 oz. max each day *And on toward:* Uncooked, sprouted or fermented grains
Cooked, unrefined grains	Cooked, sprouted grains
Organic chocolate (no junk ingredients!)	Raw chocolate (several brands are on the market)
High-quality organic coffee, caffeinated teas	Water with lemon/lime, coconut water, freshly juiced fruits and veggies
Whole-grain pasta	Spiralized veggies (great with a simple homemade tomato sauce)
Sandwiches made with sprouted grain/corn breads and tortillas*	Sandwiches made with leafy greens or fruit/veggie wraps**
Using oil for salad dressings	Using lemon or lime juice, and whole-food-based dressings
Red or white wine	Organic red or white wine
Frozen whole-food fruits and veggies	Fresh whole-food fruits and veggies (where possible)
Raw/unpasteurized soy sauce (e.g., Nama Shoyu)	Coconut aminos*** (tastes and looks similar to soy sauce)
Meat, fish, and eggs, 2-3 oz., maximum of 3-4 times/week	Meat, fish, and eggs 2-3 oz., maximum of 2 times/week or less
Properly combine 1 meal each day	Properly combine 2 meals, then every meal each day

* Fresh corn is usually classified as a vegetable, and dried corn (including popcorn) is classed as a grain. Fresh, raw, non GMO sweet corn is always the preferred method of eating corn.

** Several different types of fruit or veggie wraps are on the market, some made with raw ingredients. My favorites are Blue Mountain Organics basil wraps and Pure Wraps paleo coconut wraps. They're the perfect size, and unlike some raw wraps, they don't break or fall apart when wrapped around food.

*** Coconut aminos looks and tastes just like soy sauce, but this tasty product is made from the sap of coconut blossoms. It doesn't taste like coconut. Not only does it contain vitamins and minerals, but it also has 17 naturally occurring amino acids. It's neutral on the pH scale and has a glycemic index of 35. The Coconut Secret brand is the most popular and can be purchased online and in most health-food stores.

Transitioning Tips

Use these tips to help you transition to healthier, higher vibrational eating habits. They're time-tested and invaluable in helping you overcome transitional challenges:

Focus Your Attention on What's in Front of You, Not Behind You: Where the mind goes, energy flows, so don't send it flowing toward memories and foods from the past. Focus forward. Soon, not only will you grow to love the foods you'll be eating, but your body will literally *crave* them for their nutrients.

My most favorite breakfast in the world used to be bacon and eggs with toast dripping in butter ... it was to die for. Now, I fill up on a veggie juice, a large selection of fruits, or a fruit and kale smoothie, and I wouldn't have it any other way.

Crowd out the Bad with the Good: This is a fantastic tip to help get rid of bad foods without feeling deprived, and it's very simple: If you feel an urge to have an unhealthy food, begin first by (1) eating and filling up on a healthy food, (2) drinking at least 6-8 oz. of fresh water, and (3) waiting 20 minutes. If you then still want the unhealthy food, then eat it; you'll find yourself eating much less of it.

Let's take a look at two examples of crowding out:

1. If you eat donuts or bagels with cream cheese for breakfast, don't deprive yourself. But *before* you choose to eat them, (1) eat 2 bananas and 1 orange (or 3 large pieces of other fruit of your choice), (2) drink at least 8 oz. of fresh water, and (3) wait 20 minutes. After that, by all means, begin chomping down on the donut or bagel if you still feel like it ... but slowly. You'll likely be feeling full, so you may change your mind. Or you may choose to have a few bites—perhaps half—and then throw away the rest. You may even choose to eat all of it, and if that's the case, next time, increase the amount of the healthy food you eat beforehand.
2. If you're having whole-grain pasta or rice, prepare it with lots of veggies and a large salad. Then, make sure you eat the salad first, and then eat the veggies. Eat them slowly in a relaxed manner. At least 20 minutes later, begin the pasta.

With this approach, you aren't causing your body to rebel because it feels deprived. In fact, you're doing the opposite: you're giving yourself permission to have what you want. This magical tip dilutes any rebellion your mind may be searching for! Always eat light and healthy first and in large quantities, and heavy and less healthy last. Increase the lighter and healthier to the point that you reach fullness. After all, a stomach can hold only so much, and it will simply not be able to handle all the heavier stuff too!

Focus on the Flavors You Like & Maximize Them: When we eat a diet high in living foods, we have a tremendous amount of variety. If there's something you can't stand, such as beets or root veggies, then don't eat them! If there's something high vibrational you love, then eat more of it.

Everyone's an individual with different taste sensibilities, and you must individualize this way of eating for yourself. Choose what works for you and eat what you enjoy!

Sneak in Less-Loved Foods with Your Favorites: When it comes to nutrients and goodness, some foods are powerhouses, yet they may not tantalize your taste buds. Kale, spinach, and Swiss chard are three great examples that, by themselves, may not make you want to jump up and down in joy and wolf them down in excitement—but there's a sneaky way to include them in your diet ... a fruit smoothie!

If you create a fruit smoothie with just a few ingredients and add a bunch of these nutrient-dense greens, all you'll taste is the fruits. The greens will also tone down the sweetness of some very sweet fruits. For diabetics, focus on fruits that cause lower spikes in sugar, including kiwis, pomegranates, apricots, cherries, berries, grapefruit, and plums.

Every morning our family has a veggie juice or a fruit smoothie. It's a staple in my day, and the leafy greens are a very important part. In the beginning, I admit to forcing myself to have the veggie juice. I rationalized that even though I didn't like it very much, it was good for me. It took about 2-3 weeks before I woke up in the morning and actually "felt" my body begin to subtly crave that juice. And it wasn't just the nutrients in the juice it was craving ... it was the taste of the juice. I'm not sure how I realized the difference, but intuitively, I just did. Now I can't do without it! I'll share my favorite juice and smoothie recipe later in this section.

Occupy Yourself: If you're the type of person who lives to eat, rather than eats to live, then you focus your life around food. You often think about your next meal (and the meal after that). Now is the time to break that habit because there's much more to life than food.

If you occupy yourself with other things, then you can't be thinking about food, so plan to keep yourself busy. Substitute those food thoughts with other thoughts, such as your work and your personal life, taking up a hobby, house projects, gardening (perhaps planting seeds for your favorite foods and herbs in the garden), getting involved in a good book, or keeping yourself busy in general.

Always Eat S. L. O. W. L. Y.: As we know, it takes around 20 minutes before the brain begins to signal feelings of fullness, and that's plenty of time to eat too much if we eat too fast. We could often feel full and satisfied on less, but we eat so quickly that we eat more than we should and end up feeling needlessly stuffed.

Avoid Grazing & Snacking: If you tend to continually graze or snack, recognize that it's not in the best interest of your digestive system, your energy level, and your vibrational state.

The "3 meals and 2-3 snacks" philosophy of some diets keeps your digestive system overloaded. Instead, make sure you're supplying your body with enough of the right type of foods at each meal to sustain you.

If this is a habit you need to break:

- Make sure that you have enough to eat at each meal.
- Begin by slowly increasing the amount of time between each meal.
- Snack only on fruit or veggies as they digest the quickest.
- If weight loss is part of your goal, save part of your meal as a snack.
- Always snack on "mono" items (one whole-food item, rather than several).

Be Prepared with Your Food Choices: A saying that rings true, especially when it comes to changing your eating habits, is this: "Failure to prepare is to prepare to fail."

Plan what you'll eat and when, and have it available. If your schedule is busy, then take 30 minutes every 2-3 days to quickly prepare food. Slice, dice, and chop different fruits and veggies or other foods, and have them ready to grab. Make several dips (such as a homemade salsa or guacamole), and cook a batch of sprouted grains or legumes, such as quinoa or lentils.

If you're a sandwich addict (and I am!), then have some sprouted grain bread or wraps on hand and begin to occasionally swap them out for large kale or collard green leaves.

If You Love an Unhealthy Food, Don't Have It Around: If you love an unhealthy food, make sure you have no access to it. By keeping it out of sight, you help to keep it out of mind.

Make Healthy Substitutions for Unhealthy Foods: When it comes to unhealthy foods we love, let's take a look at some great healthy substitutions we can make. These are wonderful not only for ourselves, but also for our children:

- Peanut butter vs. raw peanut or almond butter
- Pasteurized cheese vs. raw goat, sheep, or cow's milk cheese
- Candy bars vs. dried fruits
- Cookies vs. bananas and honey or fruit
- Soda vs. coconut water or fresh fruit juices
- Processed jam vs. jam made from blended fruit, honey, and water
- Milkshake vs. raw nut milkshake blended with fruit
- Refined chocolate vs. carob chips or high-cacao chocolate with healthy ingredients

Never Beat Yourself Up If You Goof Up: Goofing up is inevitable! If you eat something unhealthy, let it go and get yourself right back on track. If you're sincere about changing your life and are committed to the end result, the indiscretions will become fewer and fewer. You can't expect to be a superhuman (yet!). You're going to make mistakes.

When you learned how to ride a bike, did you figure it out the first time you sat on the seat? When you learned how to drive a car, were you an expert the first time you sat behind the wheel? When you take tests, do you always get 100 percent? Of course not! Then why would you be so hard on yourself now?

Make High Vibrational Mono-Meals a Part of Your Life: One of the absolute best things you can do for your digestive system is to include high vibrational mono-meals in your diet on a regular basis—and you have a huge variety to choose from. Great examples include a big plate of ripe watermelon, or a bowl of cherry tomatoes, cherries, or strawberries. It could also be cucumbers sliced lengthwise and sprinkled with a little sea salt, cracked pepper, and lemon juice.

Pick your favorite high vibrational food and eat it to your heart's content. Don't limit the quantity; eat it slowly and eat it to fullness.

Okay, moving on .... It's time to talk about detoxification and why high vibrational living naturally cleanses and detoxifies your body 24/7.

DETOXIFYING THE BODY

The energetic blueprint of our body is designed to radiate vibrant health, to be free from pain, and to naturally detoxify and repair itself as necessary. When we provide it with nutritious food, a healthy lifestyle, and a positive state of mind, our body has an innate knowledge of how to repair itself at its own pace.

If our body hasn't been damaged irreversibly, it will always aim to restore itself to health. The only thing we need to do is stop interfering.

Health conditions (especially digestive disorders) and disease are the accumulation of waste that's built up and settled throughout the fluids, tissues, and organs of the body. We didn't create the body we now have overnight. It's the sum total of every action we've taken, all the food we've eaten, what we've exposed our body to, and every thought we've ever had (which we'll talk about in much more detail in the "Mind" section of the protocol.

As we learned earlier, we absorb toxins throughout our body from both external sources (toxins in our food and environment) and internal sources (the ones we produce). The average person is in a constant state of detoxifying and re-toxifying as we go about our daily business. Even if our lifestyle is healthy and our diet is perfect, and even if we're positive, happy, optimistic creatures, our body creates its own metabolic waste simply as a result of cellular metabolism. A healthy liver and kidneys easily remove these new toxins.

What Is a "Detox" (or "Cleanse")

Living and eating in harmony with the natural world results in the body detoxifying and normalizing all its processes.

Also known as a cleanse, the term "detox" has become a big buzzword in the health world. In a broad sense, it means to eat specific foods (and/or take supplements) for a specific time period to help the body detoxify itself of accumulated waste.

When we clean up our act, switch to healthy foods, and stop taking in more toxins, our body gets a chance to play catch-up and clean house. As our body cleanses itself, toxins are released into the bloodstream for disposal through our elimination organs, such as the liver, kidneys, skin, and lungs. These workhorses are continually removing toxic waste from our body in a process called detoxification. Even though our mind plays the most important role in the quality of our health, the way our body physically begins healing itself from disease is through this detoxification process.

If you're now wondering what the difference is between a healthy diet and a detox, there is none. In reality, detoxification simply means to give the body what it needs while subtracting the things that harm it, which should already be our natural state of being every day. On a healthy diet, we automatically detoxify as this biological action is a part of who we are. There's no need to pay for "seasonal cleanses" or "do a detox."

We'll be kick-starting our new eating habits with a stricter version of the protocol, which I call a "power detox," for two reasons:

1. We want to give our bodies a wake-up call that big change is coming and that we're ready to get started.
2. When we undergo the right type of detox (foods high in water content that are very easy to digest), we give our gastrointestinal tract a rest while at the same time flooding it with the most powerful nutrients available. This frees up a substantial amount of energy the body can now use to begin purging waste and healing damaged tissue and health conditions.

Detox to Retox to Detox

Some detox diets involve eating specific foods, while others are based on taking a variety of supplements, herbs, and powdered drinks. Some are based on drinking only juices, and others may be a combination of all these choices. Many detoxes are marketed as a "spring cleanse" or "summer detox" or "weight-loss cleanse," and some are branded with exciting, eye-catching names. Some are reasonably priced, and some are ridiculously expensive.

Many people detoxify when they do a cleanse (if they do it properly) and then quickly return to their old eating habits ... re-toxifying their body. Every few months they repeat the cycle. Detox to retox to detox to retox isn't a healthy approach to detoxification. A cleanse isn't something to do "every spring" or "every summer" or for a weekend a month. Nor is it something you should ever need to pay for. You'll never have to pay money for a detox or cleanse again after this program because you'll be "detox-smart"! The only thing you'll need to buy is the food you eat.

If you regularly sign up for detox programs or are considering signing up for one, then consider this a great time to get off the detox bandwagon for good. The very definition of high vibrational living is eating a diet that naturally cleanses and detoxifies your body every moment of the day: 24/7, 365 days a year. Once you're on the right track, detoxification is simply a part of healthy living and a part of who you are.

BEGINNING YOUR DETOX

The faster we remove the toxic-waste buildup from our body, the cleaner we become, and the more efficient our body's organs and systems become. This waste doesn't include just the toxins we've collected from the chemicals in our food, air, and water, but it also includes the excess weight we carry.

If we're seriously ready to take a quantum leap in our health and well-being, then we need to get busy accelerating detoxifying the waste we now carry by kick-starting the process. This is especially important if you suffer from any health condition, as waste accumulation creates the foundation for disease.

We can fast-track our detoxification two different ways: with juicing, or with fruits and vegetables for 2 weeks. Either one is just fine. Raw, organic fruit and vegetable juices are a fantastic, very powerful way to heal the body. Combined with enough rest and sleep, there's no better way to heal the body and get "vibrationally high."

– OPTION 1 –

FRUIT & VEGGIE JUICING & SMOOTHIES

The only equipment you'll need is a juicer, a blender, a sharp knife, and a cutting board. Fruits and veggies should always be freshly juiced, never pasteurized as with commercial fruit juices. Select a wide variety of fruits and veggies, especially ones of bright, beautiful colors that are high in antioxidants (which we'll talk about in the next section). Drink at least 10 oz. 4-5 times each day, or whenever you feel hungry.

Experiment with different combinations in your drinks, or check out the many juicing books on the market that offer some great recipes.

Because juices are quickly digested by our body, we should always use organic produce where possible, especially during detoxification when we want to avoid drinking any pesticides.

Be especially mindful of ginger and garlic and where it comes from, as the majority is now imported from China.

Here are my two favorite recipes that are a staple in our household. One is our own homemade version of a V8, and the other is a fruit smoothie to die for! Both are easy to make and yummy to drink. Feel free to change the ingredients in them as you like, and drink as much as you like.

Home-made V8

- Carrots (2 large)
- Cucumber (1/2)
- Celery (3 stalks)
- Beets (1 med)
- Kale (1/2 bunch)
- Tomato (2 med)
- Lemon (1 whole, w/skin)
- Ginger (1-inch chunk)

Tropical Fruity

- Pineapple (2 chopped slices)
- Banana (1 med)
- Coconut water (8-10 oz.)
- Kale/chard/spinach (1/2 bunch+)
- Berries (large handful, your choice)

For veggie juices, here are some helpful tips to get started:

- Always add a whole lemon to help balance the earthy taste. It makes a big difference! I find it hard to drink veggie juices without adding a lemon.
- If the juice still tastes too "earthy," add a Granny Smith apple. The tart sweetness makes a big difference in the way a veggie drink tastes.
- Adding cranberries can also balance out an earthy taste with tart sweetness.
- Juicing a hunk of ginger and/or garlic can flavor and spice up juices beautifully!
- Carrots and sweet potatoes juiced and then mixed with pumpkin-pie spices (premixed from the store or purchased separately) make a fantastic "dessert" drink and taste just like pumpkin pie!

Except for lettuce, many greens (such as spinach and kale) don't juice very well. For these, make your juice, add the juice along with the greens to your blender, then blend well. This way you benefit from having the *entire* greens.

Creating a veggie juice (such as carrot, celery, and yams) and then adding it to the blender with more fruits and veggies is a great way to create new combinations. An exciting splash of flavor can be created by adding fresh mint, cilantro, or citrus juices.

IMPORTANT! Adding onions, scallions, leeks, or kohlrabi to your veggie juices can make them taste downright awful and destroy the entire juice! I don't recommend adding them to any juices simply because they taste terrible in liquid form. This doesn't include garlic, which is a healthy addition that can give a nice shot of "spice" to any raw drink.

– OPTION 2 –

FRUITS & VEGGIES

Similar to juicing, this detox method focuses on the juices and smoothies above, as well as solid fruits and veggies. Remember to eat fruits separately from dense vegetables to increase your body's ability to digest them both.

Fruits should always be eaten raw, and vegetables can be lightly cooked if necessary, but aim to include many raw salad veggies and leafy greens in salads.

If you're treating candidiasis, diabetes, or cancer, there are a few tweaks to make, which we'll talk about a little farther on in this section.

These alkalizing detoxes helps normalize the glycemic load and are naturally anti-inflammatory. They also rich in fiber, antioxidants, and phytochemicals. A significant number of people have completely cured their heart disease and diabetes on plant-based diets. Not only have they reversed their diabetes, but some have gone from insulin-dependent to no insulin in under a month.

In Gabriel Cousens' "There Is a Cure for Diabetes" program, a 1-week, green-juice fast followed by organic raw foods is consumed. Cousens reported that most type 2 diabetes participants are able to discontinue medications and insulin and achieve normalized blood sugar. Type 1 participants were reported to dramatically reduce, and in some cases discontinue, insulin use.[1]

If You're a Newbie

If you're new to fruits and veggies and they aren't a big part of your regular diet, then choose the second fast-track option. This is plenty challenging, and it's the approach I recommend to almost every client—even the health-conscious ones. Why? Because it's easier! Many of us miss chewing and crunching foods if we can only drink them.

If Your Diet Is Already Healthy

If you already incorporate a large amount of fruits and veggies in your diet, and if you already juice your own juices and smoothies on a regular basis, then begin with the first option. You can also do 1-week Option #1 *followed by* 1-week Option #2. This is a wonderful way to infuse your body with the maximum energy potential available from fresh, living foods.

What about Enemas & Colonics?

I often get asked the question: Do I have to do enemas, have a colonic, or take herbal supplements to cleanse my colon? No—absolutely not. Can they help? Depending on who you go to for the treatment, the type of colonic, and which herbs you take, they may help, but they aren't necessary. The caveat is for certain cancer treatment protocols that use specific types of colon cleansing to stimulate toxin removal from the liver and bloodstream. These enemas are an integral part of treatments done at specific intervals and under supervision.

If you're following one of the options above, not only are you providing yourself with the highest-quality nutrition on earth at a cellular level, but your body will automatically begin relieving itself of the waste not only in your colon, but from your entire system.

When the "colonic craze" began, several detox programs emerged claiming that colonics are necessary for a proper cleanse. I completely disagree. I've never found this to be the case, and I've never had reason to recommend them to my clients. I don't consider them to be a very natural approach to detoxification. Inserting an object into your rectum and manually filling your colon with water to expel waste is not a necessary way to purge.

As your body becomes cleaner, and as you incorporate more high vibrational foods, you'll notice that your body naturally eliminates waste on a regular schedule and in large quantities without being forced by vigorous, uncomfortable purging methods. A well-functioning digestive system should never require a colonic.

Colonics vs. Enemas

Both colonics and enemas involve inserting an object into the rectum that's connected to a water source, which then pushes water into the colon. An enema cleans the lower part of the colon and requires a single infusion of water, whereas a colonic focuses on clearing the entire length of the colon and involves multiple infusions of water to do the job. Sometimes, multiple colonics are required over several appointments, depending on the waste accumulation.

Enema kits are available from the pharmacy, and you can do them by yourself at home, whereas colonics must be administered by a trained colon hydrotherapist as they require the use of specialized equipment.

Enemas and colonics are not very comfortable experiences. Often, they can be extremely uncomfortable and cause cramping, no matter how gentle the practitioner or how experienced they are. Feel free to incorporate either, but understand that they're unnecessary to detoxify your body.

Detox Herbs & Supplements

The supplement industry is full of detox pills, powders, meals, and liquids. Detox herbs work by overstimulating the colon, causing it to expel its contents at an accelerated rate. Some are highly stimulating and cause abdominal pain, loose stools, and a variety of other discomforts. Others are milder in their action.

Except for specific herbs being used to treat a deficiency or to remove (chelate) heavy metals from the body, detox herbs aren't necessary. Not only are supplement-based detox programs often expensive, many of these supplements aren't extracted from whole foods and aren't organic, and contain synthetic ingredients.

Many Chinese and Ayurvedic herbs, especially those purchased online, have been found to contain alarming amounts of heavy metals and other contaminants, the very things we must avoid when we're detoxifying. If you purchase these herbs, be especially careful and look for a third-party verification seal showing the herbs have been tested for heavy-metal contaminants.

Getting nutrients directly from a wide variety of fresh, whole foods is the best way to get your "supplements."

Our body knows how to detoxify itself, and it doesn't need to be hurried along. It'll purge at the fastest and best pace possible for our body at that moment in time. With chronic conditions, forcing the body to detoxify too quickly can overstrain the elimination organs, which then become flooded with more waste than they can handle. The rapid, forced detoxification symptoms can quickly overwhelm our body to the point of causing us to feel miserable, if not quite sick.

What Happens When We Detoxify

Now that we've talked about what detoxification is, let's explore what happens to our body once we start to clean it up and the cleansing process has begun.

DETOX SYMPTOMS

When we detoxify, our bodies begin to purge waste in large quantities. In the beginning, it's common to experience some uncomfortable symptoms. If you don't have a chronic health condition and you're simply changing your diet to a healthy one, you may experience symptoms that are short-lived and sporadic as the liver and kidneys get busy cleaning house.

Every toxin or substance released by the body will generate a purging reaction of some sort. Depending on how sick we are, detoxification symptoms can be intense, uncomfortable, mild, or sometimes barely noticeable. Detoxifying from a chronic illness can feel very uncomfortable and sometimes even overwhelming for a short time. These symptoms can last anywhere from a week to several weeks, depending on the amount and nature of the toxins, slowly diminishing as time goes by.

Common detoxification symptoms include:

Fatigue... One of the most common withdrawal symptoms you may experience is feeling tired. The body is very busy dealing with a mass release of waste and processing this waste for release through different bodily organs.

You might be concerned that your fatigue and weakness are due to a protein deficiency or the lack of foods you've given up, but this isn't the case. It's the result of the significant amount of energy being diverted toward neutralizing and releasing toxins. Your energy is doing some major housecleaning!

It's normal to feel tired, to want to nap, or to want to sleep longer than you usually do. If you're also experiencing withdrawal symptoms from giving up addictive habits such as caffeine, smoking, or processed sugar, it's common to feel even more tired. It's very important to honor the body during this process and give it all the rest and sleep it needs as your body chemistry normalizes.

Body odor... You also might experience unpleasant body odor, bad breath, foul-smelling stool and urine, and gas that can be so stinky it clears the room! These result from stagnant food that has been lodged in the intestines and colon for long periods of time finally being released. The good news is that this is short-lived, but in the meantime, it may send family members running for cover!

Very stinky stools are a sign of poor digestive health and are caused by either eating unhealthy foods or eating healthy foods in a combination that causes our digestion to become sluggish. When this happens, food stays in our system longer than it should and begins to ferment and putrefy.

Water loss... One of the first things that happens when we detoxify is that we begin to flush out all the excess water we've been holding onto from having too much salt in our diet. This water weight is significant and can range anywhere from 1 to 10 pounds or more. The sudden, dramatic weight loss we often see on the scales when starting a diet is due to our shedding this water weight.

Many dieters are disappointed by losing "only water" when they begin a healthy diet, but 1 pound of weight equals 1 entire pint of water. Losing this excess water is a dramatic, important change in our body! Turn that frown upside down and celebrate with a smile!

As a rule, sudden, rapid weight loss at the beginning of a diet or detox is almost always water loss. Losing 1 pound of fat requires burning 3,500 calories from either exercise, lowered food intake, or a combination of both (a higher metabolism from building muscle also stimulates the body to burn fat at a faster rate). Diets that advertise losing 10 pounds or more in a week are not referring to fat loss.

Withdrawal symptoms... Caffeine and nicotine withdrawal can cause emotional outbreaks, nervousness, irritability, headaches, and general anxiousness. These symptoms gradually lessen and disappear within 3-10 days—well worth the wait!

We can also experience withdrawal symptoms from eliminating refined sugar. Our moods fluctuate as our blood-sugar level finally begins to stabilize from the rapid rises and falls of the sugar roller coaster. This isn't the case with natural sugars from whole-food sources, such as fruits and vegetables.

Other common symptoms...

These include:

- Cold symptoms (mucus, sneezing, sore throat, postnasal drip, fever, chills)
- Skin conditions (acne, rashes)
- Headaches
- Digestive problems (diarrhea, constipation, gas, stomach aches)
- Mental fog
- Insomnia
- Joint stiffness
- Changes in blood pressure (as excess salt and water are removed from our body and salinity level begins to normalize)

Our body has its own individual cycles, just as nature has hers, and as it works to restore itself, it'll have up days and down days. On some days, as damaged tissue is being rebuilt, we might feel tired. On other days, depending on the toxins being released and from which part of the body, we'll experience different symptoms. We may feel awful for a short time, or suffer from a bout of acne, then rebound. Then the body will begin recycling older toxins that have been in the body for a longer time, and we may feel worse again. The cycle will continue until the work's done.

Healing from chronic health issues may take months, or it may happen much quicker. Regardless of how long it takes, your detox symptoms will progress until they're so mild you'll barely notice them while the work continues in the background. Making sure you provide your body with high vibrational foods is essential, as well as getting plenty of sleep and relief from stress.

Don't Suppress the Symptoms

All of these symptoms will gradually disappear on their own. Just as you shouldn't rush the detoxification with supplements that force the liver or other organs to expel waste quicker than they normally would, avoid taking supplements or medicines to reduce your discomfort unless you absolutely have to. Doing so interferes with the body's natural ability to regain its equilibrium.

A little discomfort is a very small price to pay for a healthy body. It took a while to build up the toxicity, and it will take some time to release it all.

Resetting Sensitivity to the Bad Stuff

When we eat enough of something unhealthy, the body "adapts" to it and becomes desensitized. In other words, it may no longer give us any obvious symptoms that tell us the food is bad for us, or we may become so used to the symptoms that we ignore them (such as that constant postnasal drip, acne, indigestion, or joint pain). We may also be unaware of which symptoms are tied to which unhealthy foods until they suddenly disappear when we change our diet.

After we clean house and our body detoxifies itself of the waste buildup, it no longer has a built-in tolerance for the unhealthy foods we used to eat. This is great news! It means that if we now suddenly reintroduce the unhealthy foods (especially a large amount), our body will immediately react with uncomfortable symptoms, which can range from mucus (in the back of the throat or nose, common with pasteurized dairy products), diarrhea, constipation, feeling bloated or uncomfortable, foul-smelling stools, etc.). The cleaner our body becomes, the quicker we experience these symptoms. In other words, the cleaner we are, the quicker we get sick, and the easier it is to figure out which food is the offender. How helpful!

The symptoms will disappear once our body eliminates the offending food. On the flip side, if we continue eating the offending food for a period of time, our body will again adapt to it and no longer give clear, immediate signs the food is unhealthy for us.

THE "TRIPLE A" NUTRIENTS

In the world of treating health conditions naturally, three types of nutrients are very important on our journey back to health:

Anti-inflammatories | Antioxidants | Anticancer

We'll talk about which foods contain these amazing nutrients, and how to also choose them in supplement form. The anticancer nutrients will be explored further down in the cancer section.

– ANTI-INFLAMMATORIES –

A big step we can take to reduce chronic inflammation common to most health conditions is to simply change our diet. A healthy diet full of antioxidant-rich and anti-inflammatory foods not only nourishes the body and reduces inflammation, but it also removes cellular waste and heals diseased tissue.

When we refer to an "anti-inflammatory diet," it's not really a diet. It simply means eating a variety of natural, whole foods that reduce inflammation. These include:

1. Omega-3 fatty acids
2. Antioxidants (fresh, raw, brightly colored fruits and veggies)
3. Whole-food anti-inflammatory supplements

Not coincidentally, foods that are naturally anti-inflammatory are also alkaline in nature (meaning that when we digest them, they have an alkalizing effect). In its natural state, the body is slightly alkaline. When we eat a diet of predominantly acidic foods (processed and refined foods, animal products), our body becomes more acidic and inflamed. By alkalizing our body with a variety of fruits, vegetables, nuts/seeds, fresh fruit and/or veggie juices, and smoothies, we help the body drastically reduce inflammation.

As a general rule, if you're in pain, alkalize your body. Disease finds it much more difficult to exist in an alkaline body.

Omega-3 Fatty Acids

Omega-3 fatty acids are potent anti-inflammatories found in both plant and animal foods. Contrary to popular belief, fish oil is only one of many sources of omega-3 fatty acids. In fact, there are some plant foods that contain more omega-3 fatty acids than fish oil.

Essential fatty acids (EFAs), also known as polyunsaturated fats, are considered "essential" because our body can't make them; we must eat foods that contain them. Eating omega-3 EFAs is one of the best ways we can naturally relieve inflammation.

EFAs play a very important role in growth and development (especially in infants and children) and make up the structure of every cell membrane in our body. They are also the backbone of many hormones needed for important things, such as the clotting and flowing of blood.

OMEGA-3 & OMEGA-6

The EFA families we are familiar with are:

- **Omega-3**: The two main types of omega-3 fatty acids are long-chain fatty acids (eicosapentaenoic acid, or EPA, and docosahexaenoic acid, or DHA) and short-chain fatty acids (alpha-linolenic acid, or ALA). The body partially converts ALA into EPA and DHA.
- **Omega-6:** Also known as linoleic acid (LA)

The Ratio of Omega-3 to Omega-6

Even though there's no established minimum recommendation for EFAs in our diet, we do know that the ratio of omega-3 to omega-6 is very important, and that the ideal ratio is 1:1 in our foods (an equal amount of each). Coincidentally, a balanced ratio of omega-3 and omega-6 is necessary for a healthy brain.[1]

Healthy foods = healthy omega-3 to omega-6 ratio

When we look at natural foods in a healthy diet, the ratio is very close to 1:1 for most of these foods. Modern, highly processed foods and refined oils and grains have a ratio seriously skewed toward omega-6. The average American now eats a diet ranging from 10:1 to 25:1 in favor of omega-6, a shift that contributes to chronic and inflammatory diseases. 10 population studies of 5 different continents revealed that American adults have by far the highest levels of omega-6 and the lowest levels of omega-3.[2]

Exhaustive studies have shown that the diets of traditional cultures contained close to equal amounts of omega-3 and omega-6 and none of our modern diseases existed. But these foods were natural foods and not processed, refined, genetically modified, irradiated, or covered with pesticides—the types of foods that now form the backbone of today's toxic food chain (and which are all part of the "dirty dozen" we talked about earlier in this section.

A deficiency of EFAs in the diet, along with an imbalanced ratio of omega-3 to omega-6, is linked to serious health conditions, including chronic diseases such as autoimmunity and cancer, dementia, memory and learning disorders, and premature aging. It's also been linked to an increase in bad cholesterol, premature birth, and an increased tendency to form blood clots.

The need for EFAs is lowest in healthy adults and highest for infants, children, women during pregnancy (and when lactating), people recovering from injury, and people suffering from a chronic disease. Foods high in EFAs (or short-term supplementation) can be used to help provide the body with what it needs during these times.

When it comes to purchasing liquid oils high in EFAs, always remember the following:

1. Liquid oils are fractionated products that are 100 percent pure fat. Aim to get your oils directly from whole foods (e.g., avocados vs. avocado oil, olives vs. olive oil, flax seeds vs. flax-seed oil, etc.).

2. If you do buy liquid oils, always choose organic raw or cold-pressed/expeller-pressed oils.
3. Aim for nut, fruit, and seed oils.
4. Look for the non-GMO stamp.

Get Rid of the Bad Fats

Bad fats reduce our ability to convert the ALA to DHA in our bodies, cause a DHA deficiency,[3] and can have a lasting effect on infants' cognitive and visual abilities during their adult years. Not only that, but animal experiments even suggest that these effects are multigenerational, with the DHA concentration in nervous tissue declining with each successive generation.[4]

Refined vegetable oils are terrible fats that contribute to heart disease. Even though experts have said for decades that consuming vegetable oils "prevents heart disease," randomized, controlled human trials have conclusively shown us the exact opposite is true. These studies suggest that refined vegetable oils are a probable cause of cancer and may also increase the risk of heart disease.

How EFAs Can Help Chronic Conditions

One reason EFAs (especially those high in EPA) are successful in treating various health conditions over the short-term is that they are anti-inflammatory. EFAs help the immune system reduce the continual low-level inflammation common in most degenerative diseases and unhealthy diets. Eating a diet high in both omega-3 fatty acids and antioxidants is a powerful way to help quickly reduce any internal inflammation in your body.

Studies have supported the following findings:

Heart Disease

Dozens of randomized, controlled trials have tested the effect of fish oil supplements on cardiovascular disease. These studies offer good news, along with a serious warning. 1 gram of omega-3 fatty acids per day may prevent arrhythmia in patients prone to heart failure or in patients recovering from a recent heart attack, but the long-term use of fish oil supplements for more than 4 years may actually increase mortality from heart disease.

This underlines the important point that the subject of supplements should never be taken lightly and should be replaced by nutrients from fresh, whole foods when possible. Use them judiciously, and only to help you correct an imbalance while you focus on improving your diet with nutrient-rich foods and removing all the offending items.

- Omega-3 fatty acids have been shown to reduce the risk of sudden cardiac death and heart attack, to slow plaque growth in the arteries by decreasing inflammation, to improve lipid levels, to help regulate blood pressure, and to reduce pulse pressure.[5] [6] [7]

Parkinson's Disease

- EFAs improve memory and reduce the risk of cognitive decline in the elderly.[8]
- A number of animal studies have shown that DHA has preventive and/or therapeutic effects against Parkinson's disease.[9] [10]

Autism

- Autistic children were found to have lower levels of DHA than those suffering from mental retardation, and a high ratio of omega-6 to omega-3 fatty acids.[11]

- Autistic children more often display symptoms of a fatty-acid deficiency. Supplementation with EPA-rich fish oil showed improvement in general health, sleep patterns, concentration, and sociability, as well as a reduction in irritability, aggression, and hyperactivity among autistic children.[12]
- Fish oil reduces certain autism symptoms such as stereotypy and hyperactivity.[13]

Rheumatoid Arthritis

- In rheumatoid arthritis, EPA/DHA supplementation reduces joint stiffness and soreness as well as improves joint flexibility.[14]

Alzheimer's Disease

- Low levels of DHA may be an important factor in the widespread increase in cognitive decline and dementia.
- EFAs reduce the risk of Alzheimer's disease in the elderly.[15]
- Studies show that those who have higher levels of silent inflammation are 3 times more likely to develop Alzheimer's than those who don't. Studies also show that high levels of fish oil can actually begin to reverse Alzheimer's. These studies have gained the attention of Harvard Medical School.

Here are the sobering statistics on Alzheimer's disease:

- By age 65, 10 percent of the US population will have Alzheimer's.
- By age 85, 50 percent of the US population will have Alzheimer's.

Sources of Omega-3 EFAs

There are two different ways to get our essential fatty acids: from either food sources (much more preferable) or supplements.

Under normal conditions and on a healthy diet, we should never have a reason to take omega-3 supplements. Evidence has shown that our need for EFAs is very small (below 0.1 percent of calories).

Whether you're a meat-eater, vegetarian, or vegan, it's easy to get all the EFAs you need from the following 3 sources:

PLANT SOURCES OF OMEGA-3 EFAS

- Sacha inchi seeds*
- Flax seeds, flax-seed oil (always keep the oil refrigerated)
- Walnuts
- Pumpkin seeds
- Chia seeds
- Hemp seeds, hemp-seed oil
- Brazil nuts
- Sesame seeds
- Avocados
- Dark-green leafy vegetables (spinach, kale, mustard greens, collard greens)

* Available in health-food stores, these seeds contain 9 g of protein and a whopping 6,000 mg of omega-3 per serving).

ANIMAL SOURCES OF OMEGA-3 EFAS

- Oily fish (wild-caught salmon, herring, mackerel, anchovies, sardines, albacore tuna)
- Shellfish
- Krill
- Eggs (from free-range / pasture-raised chickens)**
- Unpasteurized butter (from free-range / pasture-raised animals)**

** Free-range eggs and dairy have the proper balance of omega-3 to omega-6. Confinement animals, which are fed a genetically modified corn/soy diet, are much higher in omega-6.

Environmental Pollutants in Fish

Contrary to popular belief, even though fish has high levels of EFAs, this doesn't mean it's the best source. Many fish now contain harmful pollutants due to unsafe agricultural practices and factory-farming waste. Not only that, but our oceans are in a state of crisis, with many species of fish experiencing a rapid decline. If you eat fish, aim to buy it from a grocery store or fishmonger that can certify the fish is free of mercury (your local health-food store may offer this). Pregnant women are recommended to either limit their fish intake or avoid fish altogether to avoid the potential harm mercury can do to a growing baby's brain. There are many other wonderfully nutritious food sources that offer the EFAs you need during this time.

SUPPLEMENT SOURCES OF OMEGA-3 EFAS

The solution to getting enough EFAs in our diet is to eat the right foods that give us the right ratio. However, if you're experiencing acute (from an injury) or chronic inflammation, supplements can help because of the high dosage needed. Here are some helpful purchasing tips for EFA supplements.

Dosage. A standard recommended daily dose is 1–2 g (1,000–2,000 mg). For treating inflammatory conditions such as arthritis, a high dose of 2-3,000 mg of EPA daily is required. On the ingredient label, look at the EPA line item and make sure you take enough to equal 2,000 mg.

Take with Food. All fish oils should be taken with food to increase their absorption and prevent tummy upsets.

Capsule vs. Liquid. There's no difference, but for larger doses, you may have to take a large number of capsules. For example, 3 teaspoons of liquid oil equals 8 capsules!

Third-Party Verification. It's very important that the label confirms independent testing by a third-party company to certify it's free of mercury, PCBs, dioxins, and other dangerous contaminants found in fish oils. During purification, all these toxins are removed.

Some brands offer fish oils that are ultra-refined to not only remove toxins, but also to remove the fishy taste. Keep in mind that this refining also removes other constituents, leaving a product even farther removed from the original oil.

Tips to Increase Your Omega-3 EFAs

1. ELIMINATE all refined commercial vegetables oils from your diet.
2. CHOOSE FLAX SEEDS (or 1 tsp flax-seed or sacha inchi oil in salad dressing).
3. CHOOSE WILD-CAUGHT OILY FISH as the best fish source of Omega-3 EFAs.
4. CHOOSE RAW NUTS AND SEEDS in moderation, and soak them before you eat them to improve their digestibility.
5. CHOOSE EGGS from free-range chickens.
6. AVOID HEATING OILS as EFAs are destroyed by high heat and form free radicals at high temperatures.
7. STORE APPROPRIATELY as EFAs in oils are destroyed by light and oxygen. They should be kept in airtight, dark bottles.
8. AVOID supplemental fish oils entirely if you're pregnant unless they've been independently verified to be free of mercury and other contaminants.
9. ALWAYS BREASTFEED if possible as breastfeeding gives your baby many important health advantages over formula feeding, and DHA is one of them. Even though the concentration of DHA in breast milk is very small, the brains of breastfed infants accumulate 50 percent more DHA than infants fed formulas without these fatty acids. Studies show that when a mom improves her DHA levels by supplementing with EFAs during pregnancy and the first 3 months of lactation, her child's IQ improved.[16] [17]

– ANTIOXIDANTS –

Antioxidants are nutrients that protect the body's cells and tissues from the damaging effects of tiny little molecules called "free radicals." Found in many different fruits and vegetables, especially brightly colored ones, antioxidants are not only highly nutritious, but they're also natural anti-inflammatories, helping to purify our blood and lymph, as well as strengthen our entire lymphatic system.

What Exactly Is a Free Radical?

Free radicals are unstable oxygen molecules that cause aging, tissue damage, and other health issues, ranging from cancer to heart disease.

Some free radicals are naturally created by our metabolism and when our body burns oxygen. While the body metabolizes oxygen very efficiently, a small number of cells become damaged in the process. These damaged cells create free radicals in a process called oxidation. A healthy body easily eliminates these free radicals.

Other free radicals are created by environmental factors, such as stress, cigarette smoke, pollution, toxins, pesticides, chemicals in processed and refined foods, radiation, and other dangerous chemicals. These things react with our bodies, creating an overload of free radicals the body is unable to handle.

Antioxidants – How They Help

An antioxidant protects our cells by neutralizing the damaging effects of free radicals. There are thousands of different antioxidants, most of which fall into the following 4 well-known categories. Many fruits and veggies contain very large quantities of these antioxidants.

1. **Phytochemicals**
Phytochemicals are a class of compounds found in the plant world. Over 25,000 different phytochemicals (also called phytonutrients) are found in the plant foods we eat. Common ones include:
    - Flavonoids (found in brilliant blue, purple, emerald-green, and some yellow, red, and orange fruits and veggies)
    - Carotenoids (found in bright yellow, orange, and green fruits and veggies)
    - Polyphenols (founds in tea, grapes, berries, plums, and dark chocolate)
    - Allyl sulfides (found in onions, garlic, and leeks)

2. **Vitamins**
Several vitamins are very powerful antioxidants:
    - Vitamin A (beta-carotene)
    - Vitamin C (which we'll talk about in more detail)
    - Vitamin E
    - Folate (B9)
    - Coenzyme Q10 (a vitamin-like substance essential for energy production)

3. **Enzymes**
There are several different types of antioxidant enzymes. They all need the presence of various minerals such as selenium, manganese, and zinc to properly function:
    - Glutathione reductase
    - Superoxidase dismutase
    - Glutathione peroxidase
    - Catalases

4. **Amino Acids**
Amino acids, such as glutathione and cysteine, also have antioxidant properties.

A Rainbow of Goodness

I like to refer to antioxidant foods as rainbow foods because they come from foods with very bright, beautiful colors! Bright-red strawberries and tomatoes; bright-orange carrots and apricots; brilliant-yellow peppers, corn, and bananas; deep-purple eggplant, blueberries, and blackberries; and (don't forget) the many green veggies, ranging from kale and spinach to broccoli and artichokes. Antioxidants are almost exclusively found in the plant kingdom.

Raw nuts and seeds—including sunflower seeds, chia seeds, hemp seeds, flax seeds, pomegranate seeds, and pumpkin seeds—also contain antioxidants. Walnuts contain almost twice the antioxidants of other nuts. Fresh, commonly used seasonings such as basil, rosemary, oregano, mint, cinnamon, cloves, and peppermint also contain antioxidants.

Because our bodies are constantly exposed to toxins in our environment and our food chain, we're much more at risk of free-radical damage than in earlier years. Back then, the food chemicals and the high levels of toxic pesticides used today didn't exist, nor did the dangerous chemicals in household cleaning and personal-care products. Like an overworked factory, our bodies need antioxidants now more than ever as our immunity becomes seriously compromised.

Antioxidants & Microwaves Don't Mix

We talked about this earlier, but let's do a quick recap. When we microwave foods, we destroy many food nutrients, including antioxidants.

- A Japanese study revealed that 30 to 40 percent of vitamin B_{12} was destroyed in foods cooked by a microwave. This is a contributing factor to the increase in people showing a B_{12} deficiency.
- Microwaving causes a 97 percent decrease in vitamin C in broccoli alone.(1)
- Cancer-causing free radicals are formed in microwaved plants, especially root vegetables.
- An increase in structural degradation decreased the food value in 70 to 90 percent of all microwaved food tested.

"Antioxidants are both safer & healthier when from whole foods as compared to when isolated in supplement form."

Oxidative Medicine & Cellular Longevity

Whole Foods vs. Supplement Antioxidants

One of the best ways we can protect our bodies is to make sure we have plenty of antioxidant-rich fruits and vegetables every day, which is why these foods form the basis of the Body Healer Protocol.

While we're naturally raising our antioxidant level with the right foods, we can also temporarily use supplements high in antioxidants and sourced directly from whole foods (preferably raw-food supplements).

Studies show that not only is it safer to consume antioxidants in whole foods vs. supplements, but the health benefits of antioxidants are much greater when they are consumed from their natural food source compared to isolated supplements.(2) High-dose antioxidant supplements can also interfere with prescription medications.

Vitamin C

Vitamin C, also known as ascorbic acid, is the most famous of all the antioxidants, and because it's an important nutrient, it's often abused in supplement form. Vitamin C as an isolated nutrient is very different from the vitamin C we absorb directly from food. Studies have shown that when we isolate vitamin C, it doesn't have the same protective effect on the body. Let's check out why, and also discover which foods are our go-to foods for a healthy dose of vitamin C.

Why We Need Vitamin C

Vitamin C provides 3 very important health benefits:

- It helps prevent essential fatty acids from oxidizing.
- It can assist in treating iron deficiency and anemia.(3)
- It plays an important role in skin aging and is essential for building collagen. Without vitamin C, collagen formation is disrupted, creating a variety of problems in the body as collagen is the structural material for our skin, bones, blood vessels, and other tissues.(4)

Vitamin C can come from either food or supplements. Getting enough vitamin C from your diet by eating lots of fruits and vegetables is the best way to make sure you get the high vibrational vitamin C you need.

Vitamin C Food Sources

There are many fruits and vegetables that offer excellent sources of vitamin C (and not just citrus ones!), including:

Fruits	Vegetables
Oranges, lemons, limes, grapefruits, strawberries, mangoes, watermelon, papaya, cantaloupe, raspberries, blueberries, cranberries, pineapple	Tomatoes, spinach, leafy greens, red/green/yellow peppers, broccoli, potatoes, cauliflower, cabbage, Brussels sprouts, winter squash

AVOID COOKING WHEN POSSIBLE: **Vitamin C is easily destroyed by heat. Always avoid cooking fruits. If you need to cook any veggies containing vitamin C, very lightly cook them to preserve as many nutrients as possible. Also, submerging produce in water destroys vitamin C.**

PEEL FRUITS ONLY WHEN READY TO EAT: **Vitamin C is destroyed by light and air, so don't peel your fruits until you're ready to eat them.**

Vitamin C Supplementation

Many of the clinical studies conducted on vitamin C show that even though low levels of vitamin C are associated with various diseases, trying to fix these conditions with vitamin C supplements alone has been proven to marginally help except in certain acute conditions or the onset of colds and flus.

Studies have shown that the protective properties of vitamin C are found mainly in its original, whole-food form vs. from supplements.

Vitamin C supplements are either natural or synthetic. Tablets, capsules, and chewables are the most popular forms, but vitamin C also comes in powdered crystalline, effervescent, and liquid forms.

1. Always choose a raw-food supplement that contains vitamin C from whole foods (e.g. Vitamin Code's RAW Vitamin C, made by Garden of Life). The recommended dietary allowance (RDA) of vitamin C is 60 to 90 mg per day. As smoking reduces vitamin C levels in the body, smokers should consume more vitamin C.
2. Check the labeling and make sure your vitamin C comes from and is prepared in places such as the US, Canada, or Europe—not China.

Most vitamin C is derived from corn. If you find that it upsets your stomach, "buffered" vitamin C is extracted from beets and is gentler. An esterified form of vitamin C is also available and may be easier on the stomach for those who are prone to heartburn as it's less acidic. A small published study found no difference between esterified and non-esterified vitamin C in terms of absorption.

Treating Health Conditions with Vitamin C

The average American gets about 72 mg of vitamin C each day. To actively treat a health condition (especially colds and flus), aim for a therapeutic dose of between 4,000 and 6,000 mg/day (4-6 g) for several days.

For chronic health conditions, several doctors recommend very high doses of vitamin C for a short time. Nobel Laureate Linus Pauling, PhD, recommends the average adult take about 10,000–12,000 mg (10–12 g) daily. A well-known veterinarian in West Denver, Colorado, uses high doses of vitamin C to successfully cure parvovirus in dogs.

Vitamin C is generally considered safe because our body excretes what it doesn't use. But at high doses (more than 5,000 mg daily) it can cause diarrhea, gas, or stomach upset. If you experience these side effects, lower the dosage and slowly work up to a higher amount.

Studies have shown that providing your body with plenty of vitamin C can help a variety of health conditions:

Vitamin C & Colds / Flus

Even though vitamin C hasn't been shown in studies to prevent a cold, at high doses at the beginning of a cold, it can quickly reduce the symptoms and help our bodies heal quicker. Studies have also shown that those who exercise in cold climates (e.g., skiers) reduce their risk of getting a cold with higher levels of vitamin C in their diet.

Vitamin C & Cancer

Considered the most comprehensive study on nutrition ever conducted, the China Study looked at the relationship between vitamin C and cancer and found that when levels of vitamin C in the blood were low, families were more likely to have a higher incidence of cancer. Low vitamin C levels were heavily associated with a higher risk for esophageal cancer, leukemia, and cancers of the nasopharynx, breast, stomach, liver, rectum, colon, and lungs.

- Other population-based studies suggest that eating foods rich in vitamin C is associated with lower rates of cancer, including skin cancer, cervical dysplasia,(5) and possibly breast cancer.(6) It's unclear which exact elements in these foods are responsible as whole foods contain thousands of beneficial nutrients and antioxidants, not only vitamin C. ***However, taking vitamin C supplements has not been shown to have any helpful effect on these conditions as compared to vitamin C from whole-food sources.***
- Research conducted on cancer patients at the Mayo Clinic in a double-blind trial (meaning that neither the doctors nor the patients knew who was given the high doses of vitamin C) revealed that those who received synthetic vitamin C in high doses did worse than those who received a placebo. This is assumed to be due to the vitamin C (or any large dose of an antioxidant) interfering with chemotherapy medications as vitamin C helps stimulate the immune system, while chemotherapy drugs suppress it.(7) This is the big concern when we use chemotherapy drugs to treat cancer. They affect our ability to take in nutrients that are critical for a strong, healthy immune system.

Vitamin C & Heart Disease

Studies have shown that the presence of vitamin C protects arteries against damage by slowing down the progression of atherosclerosis. Other studies suggest that vitamin C may help keep arteries flexible. These studies found that people with low levels of vitamin C may be more likely to have a heart attack or stroke—potential results of having atherosclerosis.

But as with cancer (above), no studies show that taking supplemental vitamin C is protective, only that when it's low in the body, there's a higher likelihood of atherosclerosis. This may be due to the broad spectrum of other nutrients found in whole foods that contain vitamin C, and it's further proof that vitamin C is far more effective when taken in whole-food form.(8) (9) (10) (11)

Population-based studies suggest that people who eat foods rich in antioxidants, including vitamin C, have a lower risk of high blood pressure than people who don't.

Vitamin C & Asthma

Some studies show that low levels of vitamin C are more common in people with asthma, but it's not known whether this contributes directly to asthma. Other studies have shown that vitamin C may help reduce symptoms of exercise-induced asthma.[12]

Give Special Focus to These Foods

The following is a list of foods that are both antioxidant-rich and high in omega-3 fatty acids. They are our most powerful allies when it comes to reducing inflammation.

- VEGETABLES -

We need to include a wide variety of vegetables in our diet, focusing on dark-green leafy vegetables, brightly colored vegetables, bok choy, garlic, and onion.

Some people have an adverse reaction to corn and the alkaloids in nightshade vegetables (tomatoes, eggplants, potatoes, bell peppers, chili peppers, tomatillos, goji berries, gooseberries, and huckleberries). If necessary, omit these foods for 2 weeks, then reintroduce the ones you like one at a time and watch for any negative reaction from your body.

- FRUITS -

We need to make all fruits—especially citrus fruits, berries, papayas, tart cherries, pineapples (including the pineapple core which contains bromelain, a natural anti-inflammatory!), chili peppers (which contain capsaicin, another anti-inflammatory), and avocados—part of our diet. If you enjoy dehydrated fruits, eat them in small quantities. We should always avoid cooking fruits as the phytochemicals and other antioxidants are extremely heat-sensitive. Always enjoy them ripe, fresh, and raw.

- NUTS & SEEDS -

We need to focus especially on walnuts, sacha inchi seeds (the highest food source of omega-3 fatty acids), flax seeds, pumpkin seeds, chia seeds, hemp seeds, and sesame seeds.

Where possible, it's best to buy nuts in their raw form, available in most health-food stores. Remember to soak them for at least 6 hours before eating to neutralize enzyme inhibitors and improve digestibility. They should then be stored in the refrigerator as they will be perishable.

- SPICES, HERBS, & ROOTS -

We should especially include turmeric (see below), fresh ginger, oregano, rosemary, and green tea in our diet. The flavonoids in green tea have strong anti-inflammatory properties; however, green tea also has a stimulating effect on the body due to the caffeine content (25 mg per 8 oz. cup).

- MUSHROOMS -

All mushrooms—especially shiitake, maitake, enoki, and oyster—should be part of our diet. Several species of mushrooms also contain powerful anticancer compounds, as you will discover in the anticancer nutrients section.

Ergothioneine is an antioxidant and anti-inflammatory amino acid found in high concentration in mushrooms. Cooking the mushrooms releases ergothioneine from the mushroom cells so that we can absorb it. In addition, mushrooms contain high levels of polyphenols.

– ANIMAL-BASED FOODS –

Omega-3s are found in oily fish (salmon, herring, mackerel, anchovies, sardines), free-range eggs, and unpasteurized butter. Don't forget the many plant-based sources if you are a vegetarian or vegan. As we have just learned, the amazing antioxidants are almost exclusively found in the plant kingdom.

Anti-Inflammatory "Medications"

Aside from the help we get from the right food, some important supplements can help us relieve both acute and chronic inflammation. The most common ones—backed by health studies and proven to be effective—are curcumin, bromelain, boswellia, astaxanthin, and high-EPA omega-3 fatty acids.

Curcumin and bromelain are considered very strong natural anti-inflammatory nutrients, and both are available in most supplement stores. Randomized controlled studies have shown both to be as effective (and sometimes more effective) as drugs in reducing inflammation in the proper therapeutic dose.[13] [14] [15] They have been consistently shown to improve inflammatory diseases such as rheumatoid arthritis, IBS, psoriasis, and inflammatory eye disease.

Curcumin

Curcumin is the chemical found in turmeric, a popular curry spice; it gives turmeric its ant-inflammatory and antioxidant properties. The dosage shown to reduce inflammation is 1,000 mg+ of curcumin daily. We talk about curcumin and the many health studies confirming its ability to kill cancer cells in much more detail in the anticancer nutrient section.

Bromelain

Bromelain is an enzyme found in the center core of a fresh pineapple that acts as a powerful nonsteroidal anti-inflammatory. While it's always better to eat fresh pineapple for its bromelain, if we're actively fighting inflammation, we need the higher quantity available only in supplement form. The dosage shown to reduce inflammation is 500-1,000 mg daily. It's often found in combination with curcumin and other anti-inflammatory nutrients.

Boswellia

Boswellia is an Ayurvedic plant that has been found to significantly reduce inflammation. The boswellic acid and its derivatives not only reduce inflammation, they're also anticarcinogenic and antitumor. Boswellia is recommended for arthritic and joint-related issues as well as cancer (reducing cerebral edema caused by brain tumors) in both humans and pets.

Boswellia is best taken with food that contains fat. The therapeutic dosage is 400 mg per 20 pounds of body weight.

Astaxanthin

More than 700 naturally occurring carotenoids are responsible for the rainbow of colors in fruits and veggies (as well as in the beautiful, bright flowers in our gardens). Astaxanthin is a carotenoid that's both an antioxidant and an anti-inflammatory. It's found in the following two food sources:

- Microalgae (preferred)
- Sea creatures that eat the microalgae (salmon, shellfish, krill)

This pigment is the most commonly occurring red carotenoid in marine and aquatic animals and is what gives salmon their characteristic pink color.

We need to steer clear of synthetic astaxanthin, however, which is made from petrochemicals. Some aquaculture companies factory-farm their seafood using synthetic astaxanthin, which is why we need to make sure the seafood we choose is always wild-caught. Krill-oil supplements are a good source of astaxanthin and are also high in omega-3 fatty acids. In supplement form, the short-term therapeutic dosage for health conditions is 8-10 mg per day.

High-EPA Omega 3

In most clinical studies related to inflammation, especially arthritic conditions, the anti-inflammatory benefits of the omegas don't kick in until the daily dosage surpasses the 3,000 mg mark. Look for supplements that contain higher doses of the EPA component per capsule and aim for a daily dosage of at least 2,000 mg. For example, if the supplement you purchased contains 1,500 mg, of which 500mg is listed as EPA on the label, then 4 servings would equal the 2,000 mg of EPA.

PUTTING IT ALL TOGETHER

When it comes to healing the body and living a high vibrational life, we've talked about which foods to eat and which foods to avoid. We've also talked about the power of anti-inflammatories and antioxidants to help us on our healing journey. Let's do a quick recap:

FIRST: Kick-start with the Body Healer detox

As we have learned, the Body Healer detox is the single-most powerful way to detoxify and to begin immediately reducing and eliminating chronic inflammation in our body. When we eat highly nutritious foods that are anti-inflammatory and high in water content, while eliminating unhealthy foods, we begin returning the body to this natural state.

THEN: Change your diet

HIGH VIBRATIONAL: The majority of your diet (over 75%) should be

Fresh fruits and veggies
High water content / lighter / easy to digest

MED-LOW VIBRATIONAL: The minority of your diet (under 25%) should be

Legumes / nuts / seeds / sprouted grains / animal products*
Low water content / denser / more difficult to digest

*REMEMBER: If you eat animal products, always make sure they *do not* come from factory farms (confinement farms). These animals are not only live in deplorable conditions and routinely suffer acts of animal cruelty, but they are also fed medicated additives and an unnatural diet of genetically modified corn or soy. This significantly lowers the quality of the meat and makes it an unhealthy product to eat, contributing to inflammation. ALWAYS choose organic meat that has been pasture-raised (grass-fed), or completely eliminate animal products from your diet.

Pasteurized dairy is highly inflammatory and should always be avoided.

AND: Eat Plenty of Fresh, Raw Foods

Many antioxidants and some fatty acids are heat-sensitive, meaning they are either damaged or completely destroyed by heat and high-temperature cooking. Cooking foods at high temperatures (e.g., frying or charbroiling) has been conclusively proven to create cancer-causing chemicals, which result from the by-products of proteins and carbohydrates that become damaged at high temperatures. These chemicals are highly inflammatory.

Make sure your diet is filled with plenty of raw fruits and vegetables.

Always choose to get your nutrients from whole foods. For example, it's very easy to get all the vitamin C (antioxidant) and omega-3 essential fatty acids (anti-inflammatory) we need simply by eating the right selection of healthy food choices. In a double-whammy, foods such as walnuts are high in both omega-3 and antioxidants!

Cancer, Candidiasis, & Diabetes

Even though the principles we just covered for eating a diet filled with high vibrational foods hold true for most health conditions, we need to make a few minor tweaks specific to treating candidiasis, cancer, and diabetes. Let's take a look.

CANDIDIASIS, DIABETES, & CANCER
...FOR CANDIDIASIS

Candidiasis is a relatively common health condition caused by an overgrowth of a type of yeast called candida albicans. It's caused by a variety of different factors, ranging from eating processed foods or certain types of food, to taking medications such as antibiotics, birth-control pills, or other hormones. This condition is especially common in women.

Many women are completely unaware that they have candidiasis because the symptoms are similar to other health conditions:

- Chronic skin and nail fungal infections
- Chronic constipation and/or diarrhea
- Intense sugar cravings
- Excessive gas and bloating
- Skin issues (rashes, eczema, psoriasis)
- Headaches
- Brain fog, difficulty concentrating, memory problems
- Emotional outbursts or anxiety attacks, irritability
- Food allergies
- Extreme difficulties with weight loss
- Feeling tired or worn down
- Vaginal infections, vaginal or rectal itching

What Is Candida?

Candida is a type of yeast naturally occurring in our body that consumes sugar for food. The size of the candida colony in the blood is determined by its food supply, and when blood-sugar levels are normal, so too is the candida colony. The sugar we eat circulates through the body and is metabolized for energy, and any excess yeast quickly dies off.

If the blood-sugar level rises, the candida colony grows rapidly as it consumes the excess sugar. By doing this, the candida helps the blood-sugar levels return to normal and the candida colony itself then returns to normal. But if the sugar remains elevated in the bloodstream, it continues to feed the candida instead of being distributed throughout the body for energy. This causes us to feel tired and run down.

The candida acts as a backup mechanism for insulin, helping to bring the blood sugar down to normal levels, which is especially important if the pancreas is experiencing health issues. As we can see, candida plays an important role in our health, so we don't want to completely destroy it.

What Causes Candidiasis

Candidiasis is an infection caused by a species of candida. There are a few factors that can cause our candida population to grow out of control:

- Eating a diet high in processed foods (refined carbohydrates, refined fats)
- Eating inflammatory foods
- Drinking excessive amounts of alcohol
- Taking oral contraceptives
- Experiencing chronic stress
- Taking antibiotics (that kill the beneficial bacteria)

The High-Fat Connection

A healthy body digests sugars, and they pass through the intestines and into the bloodstream. They are then moved out of the bloodstream and into the cells of organs and tissues to provide fuel for the body (and the brain, which uses glucose as its primary fuel).

But when we eat a high-fat diet, the sugar remains in the bloodstream longer than it should because it's processed slowly. Let's see how:

1. The pancreas is responsible for producing insulin, which transports the sugar molecule from the blood vessels into the cells of the body.
2. When there's too much fat present in the blood, the fat forms a coating around the sugar molecules, the insulin, and the blood-vessel walls. This "insulation" prevents the insulin from effectively binding to the sugar molecule, reducing the movement of the sugar out of the bloodstream. Many type 2 diabetics produce enough insulin, but their high-fat diet affects how the body processes the sugar.
3. Blood-sugar levels then begin to rise as the sugar molecules aren't released to provide us with fuel when we need it.
4. When fat levels drop, the sugar is then distributed throughout the body again as fuel. The yeast levels drop as there is no excess sugar to feed on.

Those who follow a high-fat diet will always carry a high quantity of fat in their bloodstream, and blood-sugar levels may stay chronically high for long periods of time. This can lay the foundation for conditions such as candida, diabetes, chronic fatigue, and brain fog. This is also why many people on a low-carb diet can still have high blood sugar. Their high-fat diet causes a blood sugar imbalance.

It's not the fruit consumption or the sugars found in natural foods that cause the initial candida overgrowth. Fruit isn't the root cause of the problem, and avoiding fruit won't address this root cause. However, once you have candidiasis, natural sugars do make the situation worse. This is why treating candidiasis involves eliminating foods high in sugars and fats from the diet for a short time to normalize the candida and blood-sugar levels in the body.

Testing for Candida Overgrowth

The most common methods for testing for candida overgrowth are using a blood, urine, or stool test. As blood-test results can sometimes come back negative, a comprehensive stool test is considered more accurate.

Clearing up Candida

As the yeast thrives on sugar, until you have cleared your body of candidiasis, you will need to be especially careful about what you eat. This means starving the excess yeast.

Begin with the kick-start detox in the diet section of the protocol, following these guidelines:

FOCUS ON

- Choose high vibrational veggies (reduce or eliminate denser veggies)
- Making healthy fats 10 percent of your diet (giving special focus to coconut oil, as the combination of lauric acid and caprylic acid found in coconut oil can help eliminate candida)
- Eat plenty of fresh garlic, as the sulphur compounds can reduce candida[(1)]

ELIMINATE

- All processed and refined foods
- All legumes and grains
- Any food containing gluten
- All foods high in sugar, especially fruits (except for lemons, limes, and avocados)
- All alcohol

You'll also need to increase the good bacteria in your intestines with high-quality probiotics (which we'll talk about later in the supplement section). Avoid fermented drinks, such as kombucha, in favor of fermented vegetables.

Luckily, candida is a short-lived organism. By following this regimen, the yeast population can return to normal within as little as a week and the body will rebalance itself. This may not resolve any underlying health issues related to the pancreas or adrenals that contributed to the candidiasis, but by following the principles of high vibrational eating, you significantly improve (and often resolve) these issues too.

...FOR DIABETES

What Is Diabetes?

Diabetes is a disease where blood-sugar levels stay consistently above normal. There are two types of diabetes; the majority of people suffer from type 2 diabetes.

Type 1 Diabetes

The body is unable to produce insulin. People with type 1 diabetes must use insulin injections to control their blood sugar.

Type 2 Diabetes

Either the pancreas doesn't produce enough insulin, or the body doesn't respond to the effects of the insulin. As insulin is transported into our cells by insulin receptors, one theory is that those receptors are blocked in diabetics.

In the US alone, over 79 million people are considered pre-diabetics (with blood-sugar levels higher than normal, yet not considered diabetic). An estimated 40 percent of adults suffer from diabetes, yet are unaware of it. Left untreated, diabetes can take a serious toll on our health, damaging blood vessels throughout the body and laying the foundation for heart disease, stroke, and blindness.

There are several different blood tests to diagnose both type 1 and type 2 diabetes, with testing kits also available over-the-counter.

Treating Diabetes

Even though many conventional doctors still consider diabetes "incurable," this is absolutely not the case as evidenced by thousands of diabetics who have completely healed themselves on a diet of fresh, predominantly plant-based foods. In these individuals, diabetes was reversed and eliminated in as few as 30 days, with many diabetics no longer requiring any diabetes-related medications (including some patients who were insulin-dependent).

Let's take a look at just how effective a high vibrational diet is in curing diabetes.

A High Vibrational Diet Reverses Diabetes

Dr. Gabriel Cousen's is a world-renowned doctor, homeopath, Ayurvedic practitioner, and Chinese herbalist. He's also the author of the documentary *Simply Raw: Reversing Diabetes in 30 Days*.

Following this protocol, a study was done on 110 participants over 30 days. At the end of the study, the results were irrefutable:

- 100 percent of type 2 diabetics were off all diabetic medications after 3 weeks while maintaining a fasting blood sugar (FBS) of less than 100. Cure rate was 61 percent.
- 84 percent medication reduction among IDDM type 2 diabetics after 3 weeks, while sustaining a FBS of less than 100. Cure rate of 24 percent.
- 100 percent of pre-diabetics were healed.

There is no conventional approach or medication for diabetes traditional doctors can recommend that comes close to this type of success.

The Body Healer Protocol for Diabetes

The fastest way to eliminate diabetes is to follow a 100 percent high vibrational diet—meaning eating only foods that are high vibrational and eliminating medium and low vibrational foods.

All the foods in a diabetic's diet should be
100 percent fresh, 100 percent raw, 100 percent organic.

However, we do need to make a few tweaks to tailor our high vibrational foods for diabete which are outlined in the 3 phases below. If you're diabetic and are beginning this protocol, work with your physician to monitor your blood-sugar levels, progressing through each phase as your levels begin to improve and normalize.

PHASE 1: 30 DAYS

Fresh Vegetables

FOCUS ON

- Fresh salad veggies and the leafy greens, such as kale, lettuces, spinach, Swiss chard, cilantro, parsley, tomatoes, cucumbers, jicama, zucchini, and collard greens; include freshly chopped garlic.
- Sea vegetables, kelp noodles (which have no seaweed taste and are a delicious pasta alternative!)
- Sprouts, especially sunflower sprouts, watercress, broccoli sprouts, clover sprouts, and mung-bean sprouts
- Wheatgrass juice and other green superfoods, such as blue-green algae, spirulina, and chlorella

ELIMINATE

- Heavier starchy veggies, such as potatoes, yams, winter squash, butternut squash, and beets; also eliminate carrots and corn.

Fresh, Whole Fruits

FOCUS ON

- Lemons and limes

ELIMINATE

- All other fruits, including coconut meat

Fats

FOCUS ON

- Reducing your fat to less than 10 percent of your diet; choose only fats in whole foods, such as nuts and avocados.

ELIMINATE

- All liquid oils and refined oils

Fermented Foods

FOCUS ON

- Fermented veggies (e.g., sauerkraut)
- Apple cider vinegar

ELIMINATE

- Any other type of fermented food

Drinks

FOCUS ON

- Fresh vegetable juices
- Fresh water with lemon or lime
- Organic herbal teas

ELIMINATE

- All processed and fruit drinks
- Coconut water
- Coffee
- Kombucha

Spices, Seasonings, & Condiments

FOCUS ON

- Your favorite spices and herbs, especially cayenne, turmeric, and fresh ginger

ELIMINATE

- Any condiment that doesn't contain only whole-food ingredients
- Soy sauce products (except Nama Shoyu)

Avoid Completely

- Animal products (meat, eggs, dairy)
- All grains, gluten, and yeast (including nutritional yeast and brewer's yeast)
- Sweeteners (both natural and artificial)

PHASE 2: 30 DAYS

ADD

Fresh Vegetables

- Carrots and beets, whole not juiced

Fresh, Whole Fruits

- Blueberries, raspberries, strawberries, cranberries (fresh), cherries, grapefruits, pomegranates, coconut meat, and small quantities of grapefruit juice

Sprouted Grains

- Sprouted and ancient grains in small quantities (quinoa, chia, millet, oats, amaranth, teff, buckwheat, sorghum); if you experience any negative reactions such as digestive discomfort, fatigue, or skin issues, nix these from your diet.

Animal Products

- Wild-caught fish
- Free-range / pasture-raised eggs

PHASE 3: UNTIL DIABETES-FREE

ADD

Fresh Vegetables

- Small quantities of lightly cooked, dense vegetables, e.g., sweet potatoes, yams, winter squash, and root vegetables

Fresh, Whole Fruits

- Oranges, apples, blackberries, pears, plums, peaches

IN SMALL QUANTITIES

- All other fruits
- Dried fruits
- Fruit juices

Diabetes-Free

After testing confirms that your blood sugar has normalized, feel free to then expand your choices to the full Body Healer Protocol. If you experience any negative reactions when adding foods back into your diet, nix them completely.

...FOR CANCER

Cancer cells develop in all of us. In fact, they're present in every human being. When we're healthy and our immune system is strong, these cells are easily identified and destroyed before they progress to become a tumor. As long as our immune system is healthy, it will continue to protect us from the development of any cancerous condition.

If our immune system becomes compromised or overwhelmed, these cancer cells aren't destroyed—or aren't destroyed in a timely manner. As these cells multiply, they set the stage for cancer.

What Is Cancer

The body is made up of many different types of cells. When we're healthy, these cells grow and produce more cells when needed to replace other cells that have died or become damaged. On any given day, the body produces an estimated 500 million new cells; maintaining the health of these cells is very important.

They key to understanding why cancer cells overwhelm the body is understanding the DNA instruction for replicating our cells. If the DNA (the blueprint of the body) in the original cell becomes damaged in some way, then the copy will be damaged too. The damaged cells begin to reproduce a mirror image of themselves and begin to grow and divide abnormally. They also don't die when they should, creating new (abnormal) cells at an accelerated rate, even when the body doesn't need them.

These damaged cells can then collect to become a mass called a tumor. There are two types of tumors:

Benign: These tumors aren't cancerous and don't need to be removed unless they cause discomfort or pressure on other organs. If they're removed, they usually don't come back. Benign tumors don't spread to other areas of the body.

Malignant: These tumors are cancerous, invading nearby tissues and spreading to other parts of the body. When cancerous cells migrate to other areas of the body, this is called metastasis.

There are over 100 different types of cancers, and some, such as leukemia or bone marrow, don't form tumors.

What Causes Cancer

Far from being a disease of genetics, cancer has been confirmed to be a disease of our diet and of our environmental and lifestyle habits. It is *not* primarily a disease of genetics. If a family member has cancer, this doesn't mean you're likely to get cancer too. In fact, inheriting a cancer-causing gene is very uncommon and is responsible for a mere 5 percent of cancers.

The cell mutation responsible for cancer is primarily due to a combination of factors that cause chronic inflammation within the body and wear down the immune system. These factors should begin to sound very familiar.

1. **Chemicalized & Industrialized Foods**
   There's no doubt that the arrival of cancer correlates with the chemicalization of our food chain. Cancer and autoimmune conditions in general tend to thrive in industrialized countries where the diet is filled with:

   - Refined and processed foods
   - Food additives and chemicals
   - Pesticides
   - Genetically modified foods
   - Factory-farmed meat and dairy

   When we feed our body these "foods," not only do we harm our body, we also deprive it of the very nutrients that strengthen and protect it; we become malnourished.

2. **Cooking Methods**
   Also harmful to our body is eating a diet that primarily consists of:

   - Irradiated and microwaved food
   - Foods cooked at high temperatures

3. **Chronic Stress**
   As we've discussed, chronic stress is a primary cause of chronic inflammation, free radicals, and premature aging. It's a contributing factor to many serious health conditions, including cancer and autoimmune disorders, and can have a very serious, debilitating effect on the body.

4. **Environmental & Industrial Toxins**
   Many toxins in our environment are carcinogenic (cancer-causing) and are considered mutagens (they damage our DNA and trigger cell mutation). These toxins are found in:

   - The air we breathe
   - The water we drink

- Our household cleaning products
- Our garden pesticides
- In our personal-care products (soaps, shampoos, conditioners, cosmetics, etc.)
- Industrial pollutants in the area where we live
- Ingredients in some of the vaccines we're given

5. **Infections**
   The presence of some underlying infections can trigger cancer. These include the link between HPV and cervical cancer, candida and breast cancer, and chlamydia and lymphoma. When the infection itself is treated, studies have shown that the cancer progression resulting from the infection also stops.

6. **Drugs & Medications**
   Whether we're taking recreational drugs, prescription medications, or over-the-counter medications, when taken for extended periods, they suppress the immune system and damage bodily organs and tissues. Cancer is also a listed side effect on several commonly used medications, including chemotherapy medications.

7. **Stimulants**
   The continual forced stimulation of the body from stimulants in energy drinks, caffeine, supplements, and amphetamines has an overall depleting effect on the body. These stimulants manipulate the adrenal glands into pumping out cortisol and adrenaline, wearing down the body over time and contributing to thyroid conditions, adrenal fatigue, and chronic fatigue. These conditions can set the stage for cancer.

Why Can't We Pinpoint an Exact Cause?

The reason we're unable to pinpoint the exact cause of many cancers is that cancer is a breakdown of the immune system, and this breakdown is caused by a combination of the factors above. These factors set the foundation for many different types of diseases, including cancer, by creating hormonal imbalances and nutritional deficiencies, and by compromising the functioning of all our organs, especially the liver, kidneys, pancreas, and heart.

This is why preventing and treating cancer effectively requires a whole-body approach. For example, you can eat the healthiest diet on the planet, but if you remain chronically stressed or depressed, your chances of developing cancer or another chronic disease are high.

We know for certain that the factors listed above lower the resiliency of the immune system and set the stage for cancer. When we take a look at traditional cultures, we see a complete absence of not only cancer, but also other chronic, degenerative diseases. We also see a complete absence of these factors. Today, there are areas on the globe—areas that haven't been tainted by modern Western living—where there's never been one single incidence of cancer.

Why Cancer Treatments Work for Some, Not Others

There are many reasons why cancer therapies (whether traditional or natural) succeed in one person, yet appear to yield no positive results for others, as well as why some cancers remain in remission for many years (or permanently) for some people, yet return much sooner and more aggressively in others.

The main reason that a specific therapy can heal one person and fail to heal another is that each individual is different. The diet, lifestyle, and environmental factors that contributed to the development of their cancer are unique and specific to them. The short-term or long-term success of the treatment is dependent on:

- How far the disease has progressed
- How dedicated the person is to fixing the root cause of the problem

- The type of treatment chosen
- The mind-set with which the treatment is approached
- The successful management of stress
- The resiliency of their immune system

It's critical to address the root cause of cancer, while also treating the disease itself. Failing to address the root cause and the destruction of the immune system (caused by traditional cancer treatments) are the main contributors to cancer recurrence.

Cancer Treatments Approaches

When it comes to treating cancer, broadly speaking, therapies and protocols fall into the following three categories:

1. Conventional approach
2. Natural approach
3. Integrative approach

Conventional Cancer Treatments

Conventional medicine focuses primarily on chemotherapy drugs and radiation to treat cancer. It's a "trauma-based" response to the disease, meaning that once the body has succumbed to cancer, the medicine is used as a method of attacking or destroying the disease. This is done by using one or a combination of the following therapies:

Laser surgery. A beam of high-intensity light of a specific wavelength used to shrink or destroy tumors or precancerous growths; very precise, causing less damage to surrounding healthy tissue.

Chemotherapy. Uses drugs to destroy cancer cells; also damages healthy cells and causes unwanted side effects; several chemotherapy drugs (e.g., tamoxifen used for breast cancer) are cancer-causing agents.[1]

Radiation therapy. Uses high-energy radiation to shrink and kill cancer cells by damaging their DNA; also damages healthy cells and causes unwanted side effects.

Immunotherapy. Treats cancer by stimulating the body's immune system.

Cancer vaccines. A form of immunotherapy, usually made from the patient's own tumor cells.

Stem-cell transplants. Used to treat cancers affecting bone marrow; very high doses of chemo (often along with radiation) are used to destroy both cancer cells and stem cells in the bone marrow. New stem cells are then given to replace those destroyed.

Photodynamic therapy. One of the safest and least toxic of the conventional treatments, photodynamic therapy uses a photosensitizer drug injected into the bloodstream and a specific wavelength of light that "activates" the photosensitizer; when exposed to the light, the photosensitizers produce a form of oxygen that kills nearby cells. It's used for tumors on or near the skin as the light can penetrate only 1 cm of tissue.

Although most conventional treatments can help destroy cancer cells and remove tumors, they're focused solely on cancer destruction, not the root cause. They also don't place a primary focus on strengthening the immune system to prevent recurrence, which is why treating cancer without removing contributing diet and lifestyle factors falls far short of being called a "successful approach" to cancer treatment. Chemo and radiation can also seriously damage the immune system, which is why the recurrence rate of cancer is high, and why when it returns, it's much more aggressive the second time around.

Conventional medicine success rates are much higher when used in conjunction with natural methods of healing cancer.

Broadly speaking, traditional treatments are unquestionably toxic and are considered both highly invasive and destructive to the body. The agents used to destroy cancer seriously damage an immune system that's already compromised.

Often, chemotherapy drugs promise only a limited chance of success, while the drugs themselves cause side effects that seriously impact quality of life for the remaining time left. Sometimes, the treatment can be worse than the disease, and toxemia from chemotherapy drugs is a common cause of death in cancer patients. Sometimes, the disease is too advanced; therefore, the body is too weak to withstand the treatment, and the treatment destroys the quality of life remaining.

Patients are warned that failure to begin these treatments immediately can significantly reduce their chance of survival, yet not only do many cancer treatments fail, they can make the situation worse, with more doctors now on the fence about recommending treatment.

> **"Cancers destroyed by chemotherapy & radiation often return more aggressively after their initial treatment because when destroyed, they release substances that react with cancer stem cells."**
>
> Dr. Max Wicha, The Comprehensive Cancer

Dr. Max Wicha, the founder of the Comprehensive Cancer Center at the University of Michigan, is a pioneering researcher into why cancers recur and metastasize to other parts of the body. Cancers destroyed by chemotherapy and radiation often return more aggressively after their initial treatment because when they are destroyed, they release inflammatory substances that react with and can activate cancer stem cells. Dr. Wicha states that these stem cells can remain alive even after the tumor is eradicated by chemotherapy and radiation. The likelihood of hibernating cancer cells being signaled back into action in the future is high if no action is taken to support and strengthen the immune system, and to remove the diet and lifestyle factors that contributed to the original cancer.

Chemotherapy Drugs Are Highly Toxic

- The International Agency for Research on Cancer (a division of the World Health Organization) lists 9 chemotherapy drugs and 2 "combinational therapies" as known cancer-causing agents. Another 9 drugs are listed as "probable" and 10 as "possible" carcinogens. Most chemotherapy patients are completely unaware of this.
- A long-term study by the Netherlands Cancer Institute showed that modern radiation increases the risk of heart disease in women following breast-cancer surgery.(2)
- The federal government issued a detailed alert to the 5.5 million healthcare workers stating: The powerful drugs used in chemotherapy can themselves cause cancer and pose a risk to nurses, pharmacists, and others who handle them. A housekeeper who dumps the contents of a bedpan into a toilet might not realize that the waste is toxic. "Sometimes, 80% of the active ingredient in the drug goes right through the patient's system [and is excreted]," said Bill Borwegen, who served on the National Institute for Occupational Safety and Health work group.(3)

The highly destructive nature of cancer treatments is well established in the medical community. Although many oncologists treat their patients with these treatments, many say they wouldn't use the same treatments on themselves.(4)

Natural Cancer Treatments

More and more people are turning toward natural therapies to cancer as a first line of defense in recognition of not only the serious drawbacks of conventional treatments, but also the lack of education on addressing the underlying causes of cancer. The very challenging, sometimes fatal side effects of cancer drugs are also a significant motivating factor for a more natural approach to treatment.

Some choose natural methods in conjunction with chemotherapy or other conventional treatments. Others choose a natural approach as their primary—and only—cancer treatment.

A common reason for choosing a natural approach is when conventional methods either promise limited success, or have failed to successfully treat the cancer.

Whereas traditional medicine looks at symptoms with the goal of suppressing or eliminating them, natural medicine looks at both cause and effect with the goal of restoring the body back to a state of balance.

Natural Medicine Uses Natural, Noninvasive Treatments

This involves providing the body with the most nutrient-dense, nourishing foods on the planet, while incorporating specific lifestyle habits and natural whole-food supplements that contain powerful anticancer nutrients (we'll discuss these in a moment).

Natural Medicine Addresses Root Causes

Illness doesn't occur without a cause. Underlying causes of disease must be discovered and removed to not only treat an illness, but to also ensure the illness doesn't return. Cancer is a symptom of a problem, not the problem itself. Eliminating the symptom isn't the same as eliminating the cause. Failing to correct the cause of the cancer isn't a very effective approach to healing.

Traditional Chinese medicine and Ayurveda are two examples of natural healing systems that many people use to treat diseases such as cancer. There are also natural cancer treatment protocols offered by various clinics outside of the US with very high success rates.

Natural "Cure" Gimmicks

When it comes to treating cancer naturally, specific "foods" or "supplements" or "herbs" are marketed as cancer cures, but some aren't cures at all. Others may or may not help, but they aren't cancer cures.

By the time you've read through this protocol, you'll have a solid understanding as to why taking an herb or supplement as a cure isn't a path to health. You'll be able to easily sift through these "get-well" schemes because you'll know exactly what steps you need to take to restore your body to a state of balance.

Integrative Cancer Treatments

Integrative medicine blends conventional treatments that are much less invasive with natural treatments to create a far more holistic approach to curing cancer. An integrative approach focuses on strengthening the immune system and counterbalancing the damaging effects of conventional medicines.

For example, insulin potentiation therapy (IPT), using an integrative approach, uses insulin to deliver chemotherapy drugs to cancer cells in a targeted approach at microdoses (1/10 the standard chemo dose). Because the cancer cells are specifically targeted, and because the dosage is much smaller, little of the drug is left over to cause a toxic reaction in other healthy cells in the body. Nutritional support in the form of diet and supplements to strengthen the immune system is also provided throughout the treatment, resulting in far fewer side effects suffered by the patient.

The Body Healer Protocol Approach

The Body Healer Protocol is an example of a completely natural, whole-body approach to treating cancer that focuses on rebuilding your immune system and detoxifying your body of harmful elements. It's unique in that it teaches you that health isn't just the absence of disease, nor is it about healing via suppression. It's about achieving a mind/body balance, and understanding the difference between what a healthy body needs and what detracts from that health. It's about understanding the link between illness and the vibrational state of your body, and about how the mind is a key player in maintaining a healthy, high vibrational state.

Whether you're considering the Body Healer Protocol as your primary therapy, or whether you'd like to understand how to remove the causes of cancer while supporting your immune system during conventional treatment, you've come to the right place.

Used as the Main Treatment

Many people choose a natural approach to healing their body from cancer, and many of these people succeed. The Body Healer Protocol is a very powerful, complete healing protocol for healing your body from any chronic condition. The focus is on destroying the cancer while supporting your immune system so that when you've come through the crisis, not only will you have healed your body, but you'll also have a much stronger, more resilient immune system.

Used with Conventional Medical Treatments

Because cancer drugs are a leading cause of cancer recurrence, it's critical to combine any cancer therapy, especially chemotherapy, with a treatment approach of strengthening the immune system and providing the body with the high-quality nutrients it needs. In general, conventional medicine success rates are higher when used in conjunction with natural methods of healing cancer because conventional methods don't focus on root cause, prevention, or strengthening the body to prevent recurrence.

If you have stage 4 cancer, where the disease has spread to other areas of the body (metastasis), it's especially important to realize that treatment with chemotherapy alone will rarely cure the cancer permanently.

Regardless of which factors were the primary cause of your cancer, research now clearly indicates that how the disease progresses doesn't depend only on the type of cancer itself. It's the body's internal environment that plays the most significant role in influencing how the disease progresses.

Studies have shown that patients have dramatically better outcomes and that cancer recurrence is significantly reduced in patients who take specific steps to strengthen their immune system and address inflammation with anti-inflammatory foods—foods you'll be eating in this protocol—compared to those on conventional therapy who did not.

This protocol is aimed at helping you rebuild a compromised immune system damaged from the toxicity of chemotherapy and radiation, while you also consume a diet very high in specific nutrients that have powerful cancer-fighting properties – nutrients we discuss in the next section.

Used after Conventional Medical Treatments

The two primary reasons that cancers come out of remission are:

1. The cause of the cancer hasn't been addressed
2. The immune system has been severely compromised

The Body Healer Protocol addresses both. It's here to help you dig out the roots of *all* disease, cleanse the soil, and plant seeds of high vibrational radiance in their place.

Fighting cancer takes its toll not only your body, but on your state of mind and your entire life. You've been to hell and back surviving the ordeal. You've been through the worst of it and have come out a survivor. Now it's time to get your life back, rebuild your health, reclaim your peace of mind, and bulletproof your immune system.

The Protocol Is Both Treatment & Prevention

Cancer may be challenging to treat, but it's much simpler to prevent by following the Body Healer Protocol. You'll experience a level of health that far exceeds how you ever felt before you received your cancer diagnosis; in fact, your health quotient will far exceed that of the average American.

Walk Away from Cancer "Survival Rates"

Don't focus on what percentage of people survive what type of cancer. Countless people have not only significantly increased the survival time quoted by doctors, but they've also completely healed from stage 4 cancer.

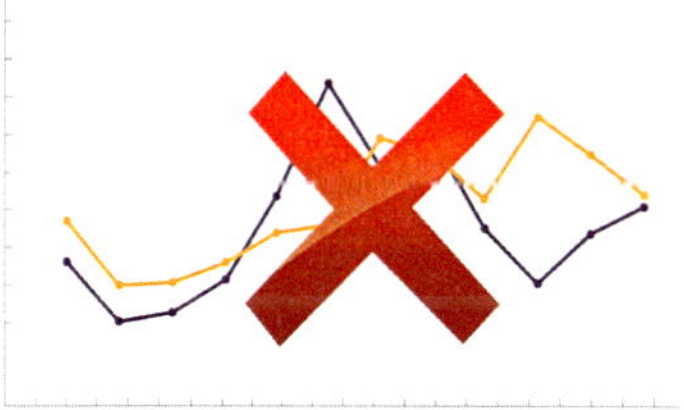

Time frames and survival statistics can have a very detrimental impact on our state of mind, and our state of mind is a critical component of our recovery. Few things in this world are more devastating, more catastrophic to our state of mind, than being given a "time frame for survival." It can mean the difference between surviving and thriving, or succumbing to the statistic.

ANTICANCER NUTRIENTS

Most of us have heard the claim "sugar feeds cancer," and this is true. Cancerous cells consume 16 times more sugar—the fuel source that helps the cancer cells to grow—than the other cells in our body. If you feed refined white sugar directly to cancer cells in a laboratory environment, they begin to grow quickly.

But with this knowledge comes an enlightened, powerful method of naturally treating cancer.

Insulin Potentiated Therapy

When we take cancer drugs, we take them with the goal of killing the cancer cells as quickly as possible because we know that cancer drugs are highly toxic to both the cancer cells and the cells in our body. Part of the challenge is making sure that drugs kill the cancer cells before they damage the body irreparably.

Insulin potentiated therapy (IPT) is an integrative therapy that involves a tiny dose of chemotherapy (about 1/10th) given with sugar. The cancer cells open up to grab and consume the sugar molecule along with the microdose of chemotherapy. Because the cancer cells consume 16 times more sugar than the body's cells, there is far less damage to the healthy cells as the cancer cells hoard the sugar, which is why IPT is far more effective than traditional chemotherapy. Not only that, but the side effects are much less—less nausea, less hair loss, and less muscle wasting.

We can take this knowledge and apply it to foods that are consider natural forms of chemotherapy.

Nature's Chemotherapy

A healthy diet and an active lifestyle free of chronic stress and unhealthy habits are by nature anticancer. Whole foods contain thousands of nutrients that provide our body with what it needs to stay healthy, but when it comes to cancer, specific nutrients in certain foods have been found in clinical studies to damage or destroy cancer cells. Others halt tumor growths and prevent metastasis (the spreading of cancer cells).

Just two of many examples include:

> **Resveratrol.** Found in abundance in the skin of red grapes, this powerful compound has been confirmed in studies to kill cancer cells on contact (known as cancer-cell apoptosis). Grapes also contain many other protective compounds, such as lycopene, beta carotene, quercetin, selenium, and catechin.
>
> **Ellagic acid.** Found in pomegranates, strawberries, and raspberries, ellagic acid is similar to resveratrol in that it causes cancer-cell death if it's extracted and applied directly to cancer cells. Ellagic acid can't be taken as a supplement because it's not absorbable in its isolated form. But when taken as part of the whole fruit, it's effectively absorbed by the cancer cells.

The sugar found in fruits rich in anticancer compounds is the delivery mechanism of these natural chemotherapy "drugs." These fruits raise the blood sugar, and the cancer seizes the sugar molecule and the anticancer compounds (such as ellagic acid or resveratrol, as well as others), which then attack the cancer cells. The diseased tissue is broken down and excreted from the body. When we eat a healthy diet filled with the right anticancer nutrients, we make this process of elimination much quicker and more efficient.

Many foods in nature contain anticancer agents. In fact, some fruits and vegetables are anticancer powerhouses.

When treating cancer, it's *very important* that we eat only natural foods high in sugar that *also* contain powerful anticancer compounds. Avoid all other natural foods high in sugar that don't (or take them with specific supplements high in these compounds) until you are cancer-free.

All concentrated sweeteners must be completely eliminated, such as honey, coconut sugar, or agave, unless you take them *only* in small quantities with specific and high doses of anticancer compounds.

Important Points to Remember

To maximize the vibrational frequency of the foods listed below, remember the following 4 golden rules:

— CHOOSE FOODS THAT ARE —
RAW | FULLY RIPE | ORGANIC | NON-GMO

1. The foods below should always be eaten in their raw, ripe form as this is when they contain their greatest amount of nutrients and are at their highest frequency. These foods are very high in biophotons, tiny units of light from the sun's energy that are absorbed within the plant's cells. The more sunlight food is exposed to (think ripe fruits and leafy greens and grasses), the higher their concentration of light energy and the higher their vibrational state. This is very important when treating and healing diseases such as cancer. Freeze-dried and frozen are alternatives when fresh is not available.
2. Always choose organic, where possible, as many pesticides are either carcinogenic or probably carcinogens. Organic also means non-GMO. If organic is not possible for some of these foods, choose non-organic and spray with white vinegar to remove the pesticides from the outer skin.
3. Freshly squeezed fruit and vegetable juices provide us with valuable enzymes and antioxidant nutrients that are very easily digestible. They provide the highest energy quotient of any foods on the planet while taking very little energy to digest. If possible, always make your juices at home. If buying from the store, make sure they are not pasteurized or commercially processed. Look for the words raw, "fresh pressed," or "cold pressed" on the bottle label and make sure they are not "from concentrate." There are now many brands of raw, cold-pressed juices that are available in health food stores.

All anticancer foods are classed as alkaline foods. The highly processed western diet is very high in acid-forming foods and low in alkaline foods, contributing to cancer and other chronic conditions. Eating a diet of predominantly alkaline foods keeps the blood at its ideal pH value of 7.4 and creates an inhospitable environment for cancer.

Many of the following foods are also naturally high in fiber which is very important in our daily diet. The typical western diet has far less fiber than it needs, and a low fiber diet is associated with several different types of cancers.

— GREEN FOODS —
LEAFY GREENS | GRASSES | ALGAE

Green foods are packed with chlorophyll and other important phytonutrients that detoxify our organs and systems and have been proven to be very beneficial in both cancer prevention and treatment. Chlorophyll is a blood-purifying phytochemical found in almost all plants and algae that gives them their green pigment.

Not only are green foods very beneficial for both cancer prevention and treatment, they also have a positive effect on our blood pressure and cholesterol levels. Studies have found that lutein and zeaxanthin, the carotenoids found in dark leafy green vegetables, reduce free radicals in the body and are protective against cancers such as lung, ovarian, colorectal, and endometrial.

The Foods

The green foods with the highest concentration of anticancer nutrients fall into 3 categories:

1. **Leafy Greens**
   These include greens such as spinach, kale, Swiss chard, arugula, collard greens, turnip greens, mustard greens, cabbage, and dandelion greens. The American Institute for Cancer Research confirmed that some studies identified chemicals in these foods that may limit the growth of some types of cancer cells. Leafy greens contain thousands of different antioxidants and other disease-fighting compounds that reduce inflammation and destroy cancer-causing compounds.

   Studies have consistently shown that people who have a high intake of leafy greens have a much lower risk of heart disease, digestive disorders, bone loss, dementia, and cancer.

2. **Grasses**
   Brilliant emerald-green in color, these include young wheatgrass and barley grass. As the grasses continue to grow, the chlorophyll and nutrient content declines rapidly to become far less beneficial to the body.

   Grasses are some of the most nutrient-dense foods on the planet. It is difficult to find so many vitamins, minerals, antioxidants, enzymes, and phytonutrients in a single food type. They repair DNA, reduce inflammation, increase healthy red blood cell count, and reduce the formation of lipids (fats). The gluten in wheat grass is only present in the seed, not the grass itself. Barley grass does, however, contain gluten.

   Wheat grass is so nutrient-dense that eating just 0.5 pound is the equivalent of eating 12 pounds of fresh vegetables.[5] Both grasses contain superoxide dismutase (SOD), a highly reactive form of oxygen that significantly reduces free radicals in the body, and also decreases LDL "bad" cholesterol levels. Other foods that contain SOD include cruciferous veggies, such as broccoli, cabbage, and Brussels sprouts.

   You can buy the grasses fresh from health-food stores in small trays, which can then be juiced or blended with other fruits and/or veggies. They can also be bought in powder, supplement, or capsule form. Fresh-juiced grass is higher in nutritional value and possesses the enzymes not found in dried supplements unless the supplements are raw. Always choose fresh as your first choice, followed by raw supplements as your second, and non-raw as your last choice.

3. **Marine Algae**
   These include chlorella and blue-green algae (AFA and spirulina). Chlorella is green algae, whereas AFA

(aphanizomenon flos aquae) and spirulina are blue-green algae. Spirulina is cultivated in fresh-water sources. AFA is naturally grown and harvested in specific places, such as Lake Klamath in Oregon.

Marine algae are a very rich source of antioxidants. Blue-green algae is an anti-inflammatory that has well-documented protective effects against viral and bacterial infections, cancer, allergies, and diabetes.

Important Points to Remember

When consuming green juices, aim to juice them at home. When purchasing, *always* choose freshly squeezed or those listed as "raw" or "cold-pressed" when buying from health-food stores.

The Studies

- Wheatgrass juice reduced the toxicity of chemotherapy in breast cancer, producing healthier blood levels during the chemotherapy, decreasing the need for blood-building medications. It didn't reduce the effectiveness of chemotherapy.(6)
- Studies concluded that wheatgrass can be an effective natural alternative to blood transfusions and can offer significant benefits to terminally ill cancer patients.(7)
- Multiple studies showed that wheatgrass and chlorophyll decreased the cancer-causing ability of compounds that cause cells to become cancerous by up to 99 percent.(8) (9)
- Wheatgrass has been found to significantly reduce the symptoms of ulcerative colitis (inflammatory bowel disease).(10)
- Laboratory tests have established that chlorophyll slows down or prevents the activity of carcinogens at a molecular level.(11)
- Studies have demonstrated the ability of chlorophyll-rich foods to reduce tumor growth.(12) (13) (14)
- Studies show that chlorophyll derivatives may play a significant role in cancer prevention.(15) (16)
- Superoxidase dismutase is effective at selectively killing cancer cells.(17)
- Some species of marine algae have anti-inflammatory and anticancer properties.(18)
- Blue-green algae spirulina decreased pancreatic cancer growth, showing promise as a chemotherapeutic (preventing cancerous cells from developing).(19)

— RED FOODS —
BERRIES | GRAPES | TOMATOES | CHERRIES | POMEGRANATES

Red foods are very high in immunosupportive antioxidants, the special guys that prevent the creation of free radicals in our body. Their high antioxidant content makes them an important part of any anticancer diet as they not only help prevent cancer from developing, they also stop it from growing and spreading. Some of these antioxidants specific to red foods (especially berries) have been confirmed to have a significant, detrimental impact on cancer cells.

Ellagic acid is a naturally occurring polyphenol found in over 40 different whole foods, but found in far higher concentrations in raspberries, strawberries, and pomegranates. This one single antioxidant has been found to not only kill cancer cells, but it also stops the growth of cancerous tumors. Not only that, but ellagic acid kills cancer cells rapidly—within 72 hours. It's important to note that ellagic acid must be taken as part of the whole food it comes with (and the spectrum of other nutrients present in that food) to be effective. In pure, supplement form, it's biologically unavailable.

The Foods

1. Berries

What nutrients in berries are cancer-preventative? There are many of them, including vitamins A, C, E, folate, calcium, selenium, beta-carotene, alpha-carotene, and lutein; polyphenols, such as ellagic acid, ferulic acid, p-coumaric acid, quercetin, and several anthocyanins; and phytosterols, such as beta-sitosterol, stigmasterol, and kaempferol. Anthocyanins in berries are bacteriostatic agents that help treat infections and are especially high in cranberries. All berries have been found to reduce inflammation.

There are many different types of berries on the market, including raspberries, strawberries, cranberries, goji berries, blackberries, blueberries, noni berries, and acai berries.

2. Grapes

Red, black, and purple grapes contain over a dozen cancer-destroying nutrients, such as resveratrol, anthocyanins, quercetin, and catechins. Resveratrol, a very special antioxidant found in dark-red and black grape skins, has been found in studies to be very effective in destroying different types of cancer cells and also preventing the cancer cells from spreading. It's been used with cancer drugs to reduce drug resistance.

Eating grapes (red, purple, and black) in high quantities is highly recommended to treat cancerous conditions; however, it's very important that the grapes be organic as the buildup of pesticides from eating large quantities of grapes is harmful.

When tested, microbes were unable to survive in fresh-squeezed grape juice.

3. Other Red Foods

Other red foods that are high in important anticancer nutrients include pomegranates, tart cherries, goji berries, and tomatoes. In tomatoes, the antioxidants beta-carotene and lycopene are confirmed to be directly related to both the prevention and treatment of cancer and heart disease. In a study of 13,000 California women who ate a 1/2 cup of tomatoes 5 or more times each week, the risk of ovarian cancer was reduced by up to 60 percent. Another Canadian study connected eating tomatoes to a reduced risk of pancreatic cancer.

Important Points to Remember

When consuming any of these red foods in juice form (such as cherry juice or pomegranate juice), always avoid commercial concentrated juices. They must be raw. **The anticancer nutrients are significantly lower (possibly nonexistent) in commercialized fruits and juices, plus, they provide the body with high quantities of sugar that can be very harmful without the important benefits of the anticancer nutrients in the original, unrefined foods.**

The Studies

- The Hollings Cancer Institute conducted studies over 9 years and discovered that consuming at least 1 cup of red raspberries or pomegranate daily prevents cancer cells from developing. In lower quantities, it slows the growth. In larger quantities, it causes cancer-cell death. Cancer-cell division was stopped within 48 hours, and cancer-cell death occurred within 72 hours.
- Resveratrol has been found to have cancer-preventative properties against several types of cancer and in studies was found to destroy human melanoma cells.[20]
- When used to treat breast cancer, resveratrol has been found to help prevent drug resistance experienced with rapamycin.[21]
- The antioxidant and antimutagenic effect of resveratrol shows anti-inflammatory and cancer-preventative properties.[22]
- When used with curcumin (another anticancer compound found in turmeric), resveratrol produces an anti-inflammatory effect that's beneficial for many health conditions, including cancer, heart disease, and type 2 diabetes.[23]
- The antioxidant activities of tomatoes, especially the round-tomato and potato-tomato varieties, have been found to be very beneficial in the treatment and prevention of both cancer and heart disease.[24]
- Gary Stoner, PhD, professor at the Medical College of Wisconsin, has studied the potential of berries for cancer prevention for more than two decades and discovered that both black raspberries and strawberries can inhibit esophageal cancer in rats 31–64 percent, and colon cancer up to 80 percent. The tests were completed with the fresh berries freeze-dried and taken in powdered form.[25]
- In a 6-month study, a diet of black raspberries was found to reduce breast-tumor volume in rats by 70 percent, with blueberries reducing tumor size by 60 percent.

—ORANGE & YELLOW FOODS—
VEGETABLES | FRUITS

As with the red and green foods, orange and yellow fruits and vegetables are packed with carotenoids and other disease-fighting antioxidants that detoxify the body from harmful substances. They also contain vitamins and phytonutrients that studies suggest are especially protective against cancers of the mouth, esophagus, stomach, and ovaries. Most orange and yellow foods are also high in vitamin C content, one of the most powerful antioxidants that protects against cancer in general when taken in natural, whole-food form.

Orange foods are especially high in a specific type of carotenoid called beta-carotene, the compound responsible for the orange pigment in fruits and vegetables. Beta-carotene is a precursor to vitamin A that protects cell membranes from damage and has an anticancer effect, slowing the rate of cancer-cell growth.

Falcarinol is a compound in carrots that acts as a natural pesticide to protect the carrot from disease and fungus. As a natural protectant, falcarinol has shown anticancer properties in rats. When given raw carrots, the rats were less likely to develop colon cancer, and rats with colon cancer that were given the carrots were one-third less likely to have those tumors develop completely. Falcarinol is sensitive to heat, so always aim to eat your carrots either raw or juiced.

Caffeic acid is yet another compound found in sweet potatoes and carrots that studies show slows down breast-cancer growth and promotes cancer-cell death.

The Foods

1. **Orange & Yellow Fruits**
   These include cantaloupes, apricots, mangos, papayas, peaches, persimmons, and nectarines. Tangerines, oranges, pineapples, bananas, lemons, and grapefruits contain lesser quantities of carotenoids.

2. **Orange & Yellow Vegetables**
   These include carrots, pumpkin, squash, sweet potatoes, yams, and orange and yellow bell peppers.

Important Points to Remember

Always aim to have your orange fruits and veggies raw, except for the winter and root veggies, such as butternut squash and sweet potatoes. However, do consider that these vegetables make a wonderful addition to fruit and veggie juices, so juicing them is a great option.

Avoid supplemental forms of beta-carotene and the carotenoids completely! As you will learn in the supplement section, most of the carotenoid supplements on the market are artificial chemicals and have been conclusively shown in studies to harm the body and may *increase* the risk of certain cancers. If you take supplements, always use supplements extracted from raw, organic foods (e.g., the Garden of Life RAW supplement line).

The Studies

- The carotenoids found in brightly colored fruits and vegetables have been found to have an anticarcinogenic effect on cancer tissue. They are also associated with a decreased risk of cancer (the higher the amount in your diet, the smaller the risk of cancer developing).[26]
- The falcarinol compound in carrots was found to delay or decrease the development of tumors.[27]
- Caffeic acid found naturally occurring in fruits, vegetables, olive oil, and coffee exhibited a potent anticancer effect and may be used as an anticancer agent.[28]

— GARLIC & ALLIUM VEGETABLES —
GARLIC | ONIONS | SHALLOTS | CHIVES | SCALLIONS

Alliinase is an enzyme found in allium vegetables such as onions, garlic, leeks, scallions/spring onions, and chives. Alliinase contains alliin, which is converted to allicin. The benefits of allicin are considerable. In studies, it's been found to have antioxidant, antimicrobial, antithrombotic, antiarthritic, anticancer, and lipid-lowering capabilities.

Allicin prevents cancer cells from developing by detoxifying the cancer-causing compounds, restricting blood supply to the cancer cells, and halting cancer-cell growth. The allium family, especially red and yellow onions and shallots, contains important antioxidants such as flavonoids and phenols. Red onions also contain anthocyanins and quercetin. Studies have shown these flavonoids can help prevent damaged cells from advancing to cancer and that they are also anti-inflammatory in nature.

Consuming allium vegetables is connected to lower levels of several different types of cancers. The polyphenols found in onions have anticancer effects on colon-cancer cells. Onions also contain anticancer nutrients such as apigenin, anthocyanin, myricetin, and quercetin.

Garlic in particular has been the subject of various promising studies concluding that compounds in garlic are protective against cancer, as well as against the side effects of radiotherapy and damage to DNA.

Important Points to Remember

Allium vegetables must be eaten raw and must be either chopped, chewed, or crushed to cause the chemical reaction that releases the allicin—the compound that also causes our eyes to tear when we chop up fresh onions. Add fresh, chopped/crushed garlic to your meals, and onions, garlic, and chives to your salads. Cooking and processing substantially reduce the protective compounds, which is why garlic supplements give us little anticancer benefit in terms of allicin content.

The Studies

- A large study conducted in Europe found that the higher the consumption of allium vegetables, the lower the risk of several common cancers.(29)
- In studies of breast-cancer cells, the phytochemicals in garlic and onion caused cell death or prevented cell division that prevented the cancer from multiplying.(30)
- Garlic has been found to reduce the development of mammary cancer in animals and to suppress the growth of human breast-cancer cells in culture.(31)
- The Iowa Women's Health Study of 127 foods tested with 41,387 women found that one or more servings of fresh garlic each week was linked with 35 percent less colon cancer and 50 percent less distal colon cancer.(32)
- Case-controlled studies in both China and Italy suggest that consuming garlic may lower the risk of gastric cancer, producing an inhibiting effect on cancer cells.(33)
- Compounds in garlic have been found to have inhibitory effects on chemical cancer formation and mutation. They have also been shown to reduce some animal cancers by 50–75 percent. In testing other animal cells, the compounds completely protected cells against a deliberate attempt to induce esophageal cancer.(34)

— CRUCIFEROUS VEGETABLES —
BROCCOLI | CAULIFLOWER | CABBAGE | KALE | BRUSSELS SPROUTS

Vegetables in the cruciferous family include kale, cabbage, broccoli, cauliflower, arugula, watercress, turnips, mustard plant, Brussels sprouts, and bok choy.

These vegetables are rich in 3 compounds that protect against the development and growth of cancer:

1. Phytochemicals called glucosinolates that produce protective enzymes when these vegetables are chewed, rupturing their cell walls.
2. An enzyme called sulforaphane, found in high quantities in broccoli and broccoli sprouts; not only are studies showing that sulforaphane has an anticancer effect, but it also helps detoxify harmful environmental substances and pollutants in the body (such as cigarette smoke) by operating as an antimicrobial agent against bacteria such as helicobacter pylori.
3. Glutathione (see later in this section).

Many clinical studies conducted by the World Cancer Research Fund and the American Institute for Cancer Research have found cruciferous vegetables to be very high in their anticancer effect. Indole-3-carbinole (I3C), a substance found in the broccoli family, has particular anticancer properties and, at a dose of 400 mg per day, was found to improve the chances of cervical dysplasia returning to normal.

Important Points to Remember

Aim to eat most of your cruciferous veggies in raw form. If you do cook them, opt to only lightly steam them. The sulforaphane in broccoli is easily destroyed by overcooking.

Many people are unaware that Brussels sprouts are not bitter when raw; in fact, they're quite bland, developing a bitter taste only after they're cooked. Simply cut off the stems, chop, roughly separate the leaves, and mix in with your favorite salads and healthy dressings.

The Studies

- Cruciferous vegetables contain detoxifying compounds called indoles and isothiocyanates that have been proven to help prevent human breast-cancer cells.[35] [36]
- Consuming Brussels sprouts has been linked to a decrease in cancer risk.[37]
- Consuming cruciferous vegetables is directly associated with a decreased risk of cancer by the following percentages: cabbage (70%), broccoli (56%), cauliflower (67%), and Brussels sprouts (29%). The study found the protection was associated with the presence of glucosinolates in these foods.[38]
- The anti-inflammatory compound sulforaphane found in broccoli was found to have a powerful cancer-fighting effect when eaten at least 3-5 times per week.[39]

— GREEN TEA—
JAPANESE GREEN TEA | CHINESE GREEN TEA

Green tea leaves are harvested from the Camellia sinensis plant. During preparation, they are quickly heated and dried to prevent oxidation. The tea is a pale-green color and has a slightly bitter, earthy flavor.

Because of how it's processed, green tea doesn't have a long shelf life (much shorter than other teas). From the date of packaging, the shelf life averages 6 months, and once opened, this drops to 2-3 months.

Green tea, of which there are several different varieties, is mainly produced in Japan and China.

Chinese green teas include:
Dragonwell | Anji Bai Cha | Mao Jian | Gunpowder | Pi Lo Chun

Japanese green teas include:
Sencha | Hōjicha | Genmaicha | Gyokoro | Matcha | Bancha

Green tea is very high in antioxidants called polyphenolic catechins, which studies have found can shrink tumors and reduce tumor-cell growth. A major component of green tea is the chemical epigallocatechin 3-gallate (EGCG), which accounts for 40 percent of the polyphenol content in green tea. EGCG has undergone many studies and has been confirmed to reduce free radicals from forming in the body (especially oxidation in the brain and liver); it also has potent anticancer effects.

Another key ingredient in green tea is caffeine, which is a stimulant but in a much smaller quantity than what's found in coffee. Green tea also contains the amino acid L-theanine, which increases the activity of GABA (an inhibitory neurotransmitter) to create an anti-anxiety effect. The combination of caffeine and L-theanine produces a different, far milder type of stimulation when compared to coffee. The average green tea has 24–40 mg of caffeine compared to the average brewed coffee, which has 95–200 mg of caffeine.

Important Points to Remember

Depending on the variety of green tea you buy, follow brewing/steeping directions carefully and remove the tea leaves when recommended. Brewing green tea for too long can cause it to taste very bitter.

Choose fresh: Not all green tea is created equal, and freshness is important to gain the benefits of the antioxidants present. Many mass-produced commercial brands contain very low levels of EGCG. Bottled green tea varieties such as Snapple contain almost no EGCG, while Honest Green Tea was found to contain only 60 percent of the catechins claimed on its label.[40] Additionally, some teabags contain undesirable elements, such as thermoplastics or PVC.

Choose Japanese over Chinese: When choosing a green-tea brand, aim for a Japanese green tea over Chinese green tea. China is an area with excessive industrial pollution and lax quality-control standards. Japanese green tea is also steamed, whereas Chinese green tea is pan-fried or roasted, which results in more nutrient loss from the leaves. A 2006 study found high concentrations of lead in Chinese tea leaves, with 32 percent exceeding the 2 mcg limit of lead per serving. The Japanese tea leaves contained no tea leaves that exceeded the limit.

The Studies

- EGCG in green tea reduces the number of leukemia cells and halts the spread of chronic lymphocytic leukemia in patients with CLL (a blood cancer), resulting in a 50 percent or greater reduction in lymph-node size. Only very mild side effects were experienced.[41]

- Green and black teas have been found to produce cancer-preventative activity in animal cancers, including skin, lung, mouth, esophagus, stomach, colon, pancreas, bladder, and prostate cancers.[42]
- The polyphenols in green tea produced apoptosis (cell death) in many types of tumor cells, including oral-cancer cells.[43]
- Green-tea extract inhibited breast-cancer-cell production. It also suppressed breast-cancer-xenograft size and decreased tumor-vessel density. The study also concluded that the EGCG in green tea may decrease the risk of cancer.[44]
- In relation to gastric and esophageal cancers, a study concluded that the polyphenols in green tea have "significant" anticancer properties. The study provided direct evidence that tea polyphenols may act as cancer-preventative agents against gastric and esophageal cancer development.[45]

—MUSHROOMS—
SHIITAKE | REISHI | MAITAKE | CORDYCEPS | BUTTON

Mushrooms are interesting in that they're classed as a fungus instead of a plant—a highly nutritious fungus that's been used for centuries in natural medicine.

Mushrooms contain vitamins B and C, calcium, fiber, and minerals and are an excellent source of antioxidants that are unique only to mushrooms. The bioactive compounds and fungal protein in mushrooms are responsible for their beneficial effect on our immune system.

The higher the number of mushrooms eaten, the lower the risk of various types of cancers (including breast cancer). Many studies have been conducted on the compounds of different varieties of mushrooms that have confirmed mushrooms kill cancer cells and have strong antitumor properties. There are over 100 different mushroom species; however, only the following have been found in studies to have these important compounds:

Shiitake | Reishi | Maitake | Cordyceps | Button

The shiitake extract "active hexose correlated compound" (AHCC) is one of the most popular alternative medicines used by cancer patients in Japan. Studies have found that AHCC enhances the immune system to help fight cancer, and Texas researchers also found that AHCC may also be effective in protecting against viruses and infections (including the flu).[46] [47] [48] AHCC can be purchased online from various retailers.

Important Points to Remember

I highly recommend adding a variety of mushrooms to your diet, but especially shiitake, reishi, and maitake. You can eat them either:

As fresh, whole foods (preferred): Eat them raw, cooked, or in dehydrated or powdered form and make sure they are certified organic. Powdered mushrooms can be bought as a powder or in capsules from reputable manufacturers. They can be taken straight or added to smoothies and salads. Dehydrated mushrooms need not be refrigerated and have a long shelf life.

As a concentrate or extract: Extracts are a concentrated source of the long-chain polysaccharides in the mushrooms. Methods of extraction (using hot water to boil for an extended time) do destroy or denature some of the temperature-sensitive bioactive compounds such as enzymes, amino acids, and proteins.

Always avoid picking mushrooms from the wild unless you are 100 percent confident you can identify them! Several species appear safe but are poisonous. Some of the deadliest mushrooms in the world are the unassuming ones that look very similar to the common button mushroom.

Please keep in mind that a fungus is a complex mixture of chemicals, and eating mushrooms in very large quantities should be approached with caution.

The Studies

- Shiitake mushrooms exhibited antitumor activity in both animals and humans. They were found to significantly suppress the spreading of breast-cancer cells as well as to stimulate the immune system.[49]
- Maitake mushrooms exhibited an antitumor effect on prostate-cancer cells, causing cancer-cell death. The study concluded that maitake has great potential as a therapeutic agent for prostate cancer.[50]
- Reishi mushrooms exhibited a suppression effect on highly invasive breast- and prostate-cancer cells, suggesting a potency at reducing tumor invasiveness. The study concluded that reishi mushrooms clearly demonstrated anticancer activity and show potential as an alternative therapy for breast and prostate cancer.[51]
- Evidence shows that not only do cordyceps militaris have an antitumor/anticancer/ antileukemic/ antimetastatic effect, but they're also beneficial as an anti-inflammatory, antifibrotic, antiviral, antifungal, antimicrobial, and antibacterial agent.[52]
- White button mushrooms show potential as a breast-cancer preventative, decreasing both tumor-cell reproduction and tumor weight.[53]
- Shiitake-mushroom extract was found to significantly reduce melanoma-tumor growth and to restore the immune response of melanoma-reactive T cells.[54]
- Maitake mushrooms have different bioactive compounds with anticancer and other therapeutic properties. They were shown to inhibit the growth of cancer cells.[55]
- The National Academy of Sciences published a paper that linked reishi mushrooms directly to cancer-cell death. The mushrooms were found to induce antibodies to recognize and kill antigens associated with cancer cells.[56]
- In a human trial, maitake mushrooms stimulated the immune system of breast-cancer patients. When combined with vitamin C, maitake mushrooms not only reduced the growth of bladder-cancer cells by 90 percent in 72 hours, but they were also highly effective in killing them.[57][58]
- Shiitake mushrooms contain a compound called lentinan. Clinical studies have found lentinan to be beneficial in terms of increasing survival rate and tumor death, and reducing the rate of cancer recurrence.[59]

— ROOTS & SPICES—
TURMERIC | OREGANO | GINGER

In the world of roots and spices, we can find many protective compounds, but there are 3 of great interest when it comes to the prevention and treatment of cancer:

1. Curcumin (from turmeric)

Turmeric is a popular Indian curry spice that the cancer world is taking very seriously. It contains several active components, all of which are anti-inflammatory and cancer-preventative. One in particular, called curcumin (not to be confused with cumin), is the yellow polyphenol in turmeric that has a potent effect on cancer cells. In fact, the MD Anderson Cancer Center in Texas states that no cancer has been found that's not adversely affected by curcumin. It's a powerful antioxidant, antiviral, and antibacterial compound.

Among all the natural nutrients studied, curcumin arguably has the most evidence-based studies to support its anticancer activity—over 300 published studies. Over the past decade, curcumin has been confirmed to be anti-inflammatory, cardio-protective, cancer-preventative, and chemotherapeutic.

The anticancer effect of curcumin has been shown in many cell and animal studies, and multiple studies have shown that curcumin can target cancer stem cells and prevent their regrowth. Several studies have also reported that curcumin suppresses all 3 stages of cancer: Initiation, promotion, and progression. It does this by targeting factors involved in cancer development, such as:

- Preventing tumor cells from spreading
- Preventing normal cells from transforming into cancer
- Preventing the synthesis of a protein for tumor formation
- Destroying cancer cells
- Decreasing inflammation

EuroPharma, Inc. has classed curcumin as an "anticancer herb" due to its ability to prevent cancer formation and replication, and many cancer treatment facilities (both traditional and natural) recognize curcumin as a very promising partner in cancer treatments.[60]

As an anti-inflammatory, curcumin is widely available and sold in supplement stores either alone or with other anti-inflammatory compounds such as bromelain. Unfortunately, the amount of curcumin in turmeric is very small. To meet the therapeutic doses necessary to affect cancer cells, a curcumin supplement must be taken (Curcumin C3 complex is a great example, and the one which I recommend).

2. Oregano

Even though you may be familiar with oregano as a cooking herb, it is a well-known medicinal herb that has powerful antibiotic, antiviral, antifungal, and other potent healing properties. In fact, when taken in therapeutic doses (e.g. as an extract), it is considered a broad-spectrum antibiotic with the benefit of not causing antibiotic resistance. It has been found to be effective against staphylococcus and E. coli as comparable to antibiotic drugs in its germ-killing properties.

Oregano extract a must on our anticancer nutrient list. The commonest varieties of oregano are Mediterranean oregano (also known as Greek oregano, Turkish oregano, and European oregano) and Mexican oregano.

Oregano contains vitamins A, C, E, and K, as well as fiber, folate, iron, magnesium, vitamin B6, calcium, and potassium. Additionally, fresh oregano has one of the highest antioxidant activity of any plant in the form of phytochemicals. It contains quercetin, a phytochemical shown in clinical studies to both slow cancer growth and kill cancer cells.

Carnosol and carvacrol, two powerful phytochemicals found in oregano, are confirmed to have anticancer and anti-inflammatory properties. Both are being tested for anticancer properties in various types of cancers with very positive results.

3. **Ginger**

   In traditional Chinese medicine, ginger has long been used for nausea and gastrointestinal problems. Its healing properties are largely due to active phenolic compounds such as shogaols, zingerone, gingerol, and paradol.

   Ginger is a well-known antiemetic (reduces nausea and vomiting) and reduces drug withdrawal symptoms. In vitro and animal studies have also connected ginger as protective against Alzheimer's disease and cancer. High concentrations of fresh ginger also show antiviral, anti-inflammatory, and antioxidant effects.

   Ginger has been confirmed to prevent chemotherapy-induced nausea and vomiting. Ginger supplementation also has cancer-preventative activities in the experimental initiation of cancer. In particular, it has been found to significantly decrease the number of tumors, as well as the incidence of prostate cancer in mice and colon cancer in rats.

Important Points to Remember

Clinical studies have shown that the amount of curcumin and oregano required to have an anticancer effect is far higher than the typical amount eaten in a daily diet. Because of this, they should be purchased as a supplement when treating cancer to benefit from a much higher and more concentrated amount. Both should also be taken with fats (e.g. olive oil or coconut oil) to increase their bioavailability in the body.

The dosage listed on the bottle is a general dosage, and clinical studies often show triple, quadruple, or greater quantities for a medicinal dose when treating cancer. The dosage for oil of oregano extract is 500mg, 4 times daily for bacterial and viral infections, and higher amounts for cancer under the supervision of a doctor (preferably naturopathic). Oil of oregano can be purchased in capsule or tincture form; remember to take it with an fats.

The dosage for curcumin should begin small and be slowly increased over time. Dr. Bharat B. Aggarwal is a pioneer in exploring curcumin as an alternate treatment for various cancers. He's published more than 600 scientific papers, and he recommends the following 8 week dosage schedule:

- Week 1: 1 g (1,000 mg)
- Week 2: 2 g (2,000 mg)
- Week 3: 4 g (4,000 mg)
- Weeks 4-8: 8 g (8,000 mg)

Split the dosage and take it twice a day. If you experience any negative side effects, don't increase the dose until the side effects have subsided. If test results show no improvement after 8 weeks, it is unlikely the curcumin is effective. If improvement is experienced, continue for an additional 4 weeks.

As very little curcumin is present in turmeric, it's important to buy curcumin (not turmeric) when treating cancer or other inflammatory conditions, such as arthritis. As a cancer preventative, the turmeric herb is a better choice so that you can benefit from other constituents present in the spice.

In large doses, curcumin may interfere with the effectiveness of stroke medications and blood thinners. It's also important to discontinue curcumin 2 weeks before any surgery. Work with your doctor when including curcumin in your cancer regimen.

The Studies

- Curcumin was found to inhibit the release of pro-inflammatory chemical messengers that cause cancers to spread throughout the body, helping to prevent metastasis. These findings relate to both prostate and breast cancers.(61)
- Curcumin inhibits breast cancer cell migration.(62)
- Curcumin can contribute to anticancer activity by targeting cancer stem cells by disrupting stem cell signaling pathways.(63)
- Curcumin has demonstrated cancer-preventative properties in cell cultures, animal models, and human investigations. It is safe and poses minimal adverse effects.(64)
- Curcumin causes death of cancer cells in the lining of the uterus and reduces the growth rate of uterine fibroids.(65) (66) (67)
- Oregano was found to selectively kill cancer cells.(68)
- Carvacrol, a component of oregano, was found to prevent the spreading of various human cancer cells lines, including breast cancer, hepatoma, leukemia, non-small cell lung cancer, and cervical cancer. It may also be a potential therapeutic agent for prostate cancer.(69)
- Carnosol, a component of oregano, was evaluated for its anticancer properties in prostate, breast, skin, leukemia, and colon cancer with promising results.(70)
- Ginger was found to reduce the spread and to increase the cell death of normal-appearing colonic mucosa in those with an increased risk of colon cancer.(71)
- Ginger significantly reduced the severity of chemotherapy-induced nausea in adults, as well as in children and young adults.(72) (73) (74) (75)
- Constituents in ginger were confirmed to have potent antioxidant and anti-inflammatory activities, with some exhibiting cancer-preventative activity in experimentally induced cancer.(76)
- Ginger supplementation was found to significantly decrease the number of tumors, as well as the incidence of colon cancer in the presence of pro-carcinogen DMH in male rats.(77)
- Ginger was confirmed to shrink prostate-tumor growth by 65 percent in mice while reducing the spread of the cancerous cells. No toxicity was seen in normal, healthy tissue.(78)
- Oil of oregano exhibited the greatest antibacterial action against common pathogenic germs, such as Staph, E. coli, and Listeria.(79)
- Carvacrol clearly demonstrated anti-tumor effects on metastatic breast cancer and has significant potential in treating cancer.(80)
- British researchers reported oregano oil had antibacterial activity against 25 different bacteria.(81)
- Carvacrol, one of oregano's chemical components, appears to reduce infection as effectively as traditional antibiotics, such as streptomycin, penicillin, and vancomycin.(82)

— GLUTATHIONE—

Glutathione is a very powerful antioxidant produced naturally by the body. It helps us detoxify and boosts our immune system, and it's very protective against growths such as cancer. It's a regenerator of immune cells and a very valuable detoxifying agent.

Glutathione is a combination of 3 amino acids: cysteine, glycine, and glutamine. It's important that we have enough glutathione, as without it, the functioning of other nutrients such as vitamin C and vitamin E is affected and our immunity can become compromised. Our production of glutathione can be significantly reduced by poor diet, stress, medications, environmental toxins, and other things that lower our immunity.

Low levels of glutathione are found in many diseases, including AIDS, Alzheimer's, arthritis, atherosclerosis, autism spectrum disorder, cancer, cataracts, diabetes, hepatitis, multiple sclerosis (MS), and Parkinson's disease.[83]

Luckily, glutathione comes from the very foods we talked about earlier. Eating foods rich in sulfur increases the body's supply of glutathione, including foods such as broccoli, cabbage, cauliflower, collards, garlic, kale, and onions. Most experts agree that glutathione in food is more effective than in supplement form.

USING SUPPLEMENTS

Our bodies are designed to get their nutrients directly from food. When we follow a healthy diet and lifestyle and are careful not to damage our body with unhealthy fats, chemicals in highly processed and refined food, and factory-farmed meats, as well as high levels of stress, then we rarely need supplements.

If your diet and lifestyle habits are unhealthy, first work on fixing them. Only take a supplement if you have a verified deficiency or a health condition that would benefit from it; when you have healed from that condition, stop taking the supplement.

Are you taking a daily multivitamin simply because you "think" you need it? If you fix your diet to include a variety of healthy foods and nix the pills, not only will this make multivitamins unnecessary and save you money, but you'll be doing your body a favor. Why? Because most multivitamins are synthetic supplements that can never cut it when it comes to providing your body with the nutrition it needs. They can also do the body more harm than good.

Today's Supplements

Over 90 percent of supplements in the marketplace are fractionated, synthetic products where a nutrient has been isolated and then a synthetic version of it's been made. Synthetic supplements are *not* the same thing as nutrients found in whole foods.

In whole foods, the vitamins, minerals, proteins, fats, carbohydrates, and important micronutrients (such as calcium and magnesium) are all packaged beautifully in a symphony with thousands of other micronutrients, synergistically working together. They're in their perfect proportions in whole foods for our body to best absorb and utilize them.

Nature doesn't isolate these nutrients because after they've been isolated, many no longer work as well and aren't absorbed as efficiently in the body. We can't simply extract a specific nutrient from its whole, make a synthetic version, and expect it to have the same impact on the body. It doesn't. This is the reason many multivitamin and mineral supplements have extremely poor absorption rates and do the body little good.

Why Supplements Are Not the Holy Grail

According to the multibillion-dollar supplement manufacturers, it's a wonder we can survive without chugging down daily supplements. The supplement craze has many people rushing to buy the supplement of the month. Buzzwords such as "St. John's wort," "Hoodia," "CoQ10," "EFAs," "vitamin C," "multivitamins," and scores of other substances are casually tossed around, with dosages varying greatly depending on what bottle you read and which expert you talk to. We enthusiastically believe the outrageous and sometimes bizarre claims of supplement manufacturers (in the absence of any independent studies to back them up).

Selling supplements is a billion-dollar, for-profit industry, with manufacturers routinely making false health claims.

We pop supplements every day even though we have no idea whether they do us any good; we just "assume" they must. Millions of people fall prey to supplement manufacturers' false advertising and misleading statements that have no truth to them. Sports enthusiasts and people trying to lose weight are the biggest targets.

"In a study, 4 of 7 common calcium supplements contained measurable lead content, an easily avoidable public health concern."

Journal of the American Medical Association

Taking supplements is a little like groping blind. We experience a health condition and look for a supplement based on Internet research, recommendations from a friend, or (more often) due to flashy, convincing supplement labels. Worse still, many of us take supplements when there's nothing wrong with us out of fear we're deficient or may become deficient if we don't.

Supplements are a tricky subject, and the wrong supplements can do more harm than good. Depending on whether they're synthetic or organic, where and how they were manufactured, whether they're from China (most are, including over 90 percent of the US supply of vitamin C), and how much we take over what time period, we can damage our organs and health with supplements.

It's also common for traces of lead, arsenic, and other heavy metals to be found in supplements, which build up in the body over time.

Heavy-Metal Contamination

Many supplements on the market have been found to contain alarming amounts of heavy metals. Because only a small quantity of supplements that arrive in the US are inspected, many formulations containing heavy-metal contaminants end up in the general marketplace.

Calcium Supplements Containing Lead

Many calcium supplements contain lead. Large amounts have been reported in popular over-the-counter calcium supplement ingredients including bone meal and dolomite.

Multiple studies have confirmed the presence of lead in calcium supplements. One study of 7 calcium supplements revealed that 4 of these contained measurable lead content, concluding that despite stringent limits on lead exposure, many calcium supplements still contain lead and pose an easily avoidable public health concern.[1][2]

Lead, Mercury, and Arsenic in Ayurvedic Medicinal Herbs

Lead, mercury, and arsenic have been detected in large quantities in traditional Ayurvedic medicines.[3]

- In a study, 193 of 230 herbs requested via the Internet were received and analyzed. The amount of metals in products manufactured in the US was 21.7 percent, compared with 19.5 percent in

Indian products.

Among the metal-containing products, 95 percent were sold by US websites, and 75 percent claimed "Good Manufacturing Practices."

All products containing metals exceeded 1 or more standards for acceptable daily intake of toxic metals.

- One-fifth of all Ayurvedic medicines purchased via the Internet contained detectable levels of lead, mercury, or arsenic.

The Problem with Self-Medicating

There are several problems with taking supplements to self-medicate:

1. When we take supplements, we may experience relief from one symptom but have no idea what other imbalance we may have created. This often happens when we take large quantities of some common supplements (or take them over an extended period time).
2. Most supplements are synthetic chemicals. They affect the body differently than their natural counterparts do, and because they're synthetic, they have very low absorption rates.
3. Many commonly used synthetic supplements, such as folic acid and vitamin A, are toxic to the body, and multiple clinical studies have concluded they can cause serious damage. More disturbingly, doctors and pediatricians recommend folic acid during pregnancy, instead of recommending the natural, non-synthetic version of this nutrient (folate) from whole foods. We talk more about folic acid in the next section.
4. Many people unknowingly use supplements (just like drugs) to suppress symptoms (such as inflammation), not realizing this masks the cause of the problem and fights the body's natural immune response to heal. Anti-inflammatories should be taken only for acute conditions, such as a muscle strain, and for chronic conditions while we focus on healing. Rarely are they required long term.
5. More is not better. In large quantities, some supplements deplete or affect our ability to absorb other nutrients, causing nutritional deficiencies where none existed. For example, excess iron can decrease zinc absorption (very important in human growth and for enzymatic processes).

A Poor Food Substitute

Unfortunately, because our food chain is largely a highly processed junk diet deficient in so many important nutrients, many people are becoming supplement addicts (instead of changing their eating habits) in fear of this deficiency.

With a nation that's getting sicker and fatter, and a healthcare system that's failing miserably in both preventing and curing the steadily rising rates of chronic disease, people instinctively know that something's wrong. Unfortunately, they're left to search for their own answers and cures.

Lack of confidence in traditional doctors has become serious, with patients instructing their own doctors on what medications they want based on TV and Internet ads. Medications and supplements are considered quick, easy fixes. Unfortunately, this isn't the case.

As traditional doctors are unfamiliar with many supplements on the marketplace today, patients are left to their own devices to choose which supplements they hope can help them. Often a doctor will recommend taking a daily multivitamin, having no idea that synthetic vitamins are far inferior nutrients, and that some very common ones have been shown in studies to be unhealthy. Doctors aren't dieticians, nor are they supplement specialists.

Synthetic supplements have now become part of the health problem, not the solution.

Supplements as Medicine

In the next section, we'll talk about how to use supplements as medicine and how to choose the best, high-quality supplements. We'll also explore why taking a high-quality probiotic is a good idea, and why this is especially important after taking a course of antibiotics to help repopulate the microflora in our gut.

When it comes to taking supplements, I recommend using them for:

Health Problems

While you work to restore balance in your body, supplements can be a wonderful friend in your journey. For long-standing health conditions, they can also be an important part of your recovery and are much preferred over toxic pharmaceutical drugs. However, once balance has been restored, if your diet is healthy, you should have little need to continue taking the supplements for most conditions.

Chronic Stress

Never underestimate the impact chronic and severe stress can have on your body. It weakens the immune system like nothing else can. If you're under severe stress, a high-quality multivitamin and minerals derived from natural food sources (*not* synthetic multivitamins!) is a great idea for the short-term to help give your compromised immune system a boost.

Common Deficiencies

No matter how healthy and varied your diet is, there are some common deficiencies to be aware of, such as vitamin D, vitamin B_{12}, where I strongly recommend taking supplements.

Let's spend a few minutes understanding exactly what synthetic supplements are and why it's very important we avoid them.

THE DANGERS OF SYNTHETIC SUPPLEMENTS

When we walk around the supplement section of a store, most of what we see are synthetic, lab-made chemicals that are health-depleting substances. Synthetic supplements are no joke, and we should never take them indiscriminately.

Most of us simply walk into a supplement store (or supplement section of the supermarket), choose a popular brand, and pop a pill or two every day, having no idea what the ingredients in the supplements are doing to our body. We have no understanding of the true biological impact of these ingredients.

Many commonly used synthetic supplements have been conclusively proven in multiple studies to harm the body.

Most of us have fallen prey to supplement fads and false advertising. Athletes, trainers, and people looking to lose weight are the most vulnerable. Athletes especially stock up on vitamins, minerals, amino acids, mass amounts of protein, and other specific substances that have few to no independent third-party studies backing up the manufacturers' claims.

Studies have linked large quantities of protein taken over time to serious health conditions, including osteoporosis and cancer. Regardless, many people take processed protein powders in en masse, mistakenly thinking these powders benefit their bodies.

If you take supplements based on marketing hype, you're volunteering to be a chemistry experiment.

Synthetic vs. Natural Supplements

Common nutrients, such as vitamin A, vitamin C, vitamin E, and folate, all play a role in the functioning of a healthy immune system, but not when taken as an isolated, synthetic nutrient and in high doses over extended periods of time. The body recognizes the difference between natural and synthetic supplements and treats them differently: synthetic supplements aren't digested the same way as natural supplements, and synthetic chemicals are considered toxins in the body. They have no place in high vibrational living.

Let's take a look at some of the most common synthetic vitamins millions of people take every day that aren't in the best interest of our health.

Folic Acid: Toxic in Supplementation

Folic Acid vs. Folate: Folate is an essential nutrient our body needs that's naturally found in many different fresh, whole foods. But folate is very different from the synthetic "folic acid" version found in supplements that's been clinically proven to increase the risk of various cancers. When taken during pregnancy, folic acid can also affect fetal health.

- In a 10-year research study, women who took folic acid (common during pregnancy) increased their risk of breast cancer by 20–30 percent.[1]
- Men increase their risk of prostate cancer by 163 percent when taking supplemental folic acid (alone or in multivitamin supplements).[2]
- Pregnant women taking folic acid supplementation increase the risk of their child developing childhood asthma by 26 percent.[3]
- Pregnant women taking folic acid supplementation increase the chance of respiratory-tract infections in infants.[4]

Avoid taking any multivitamin or prenatal formula that contains folic acid.

Unlike synthetic folic acid, folate (found in many veggies) is very healthy for us and contains compounds that naturally help protect us against various forms of cancer. The US daily recommended allowance for folate is 400 ug. The following is a list of just a few vegetables that contain over 200 ug of naturally occurring folate per average serving:

Folate (400-900 ug)	Folate (200-400 ug)
Spinach	Arugula
Green Lettuce	Brussels Sprouts
Endive	Celery
Asparagus	Soy Beans (fresh, non-GMO)
Collard Greens	Tomatoes
Mustard Greens	Cauliflower
Broccoli	Red Peppers
Bok Choy	Chickpeas
Okra	Red-Leaf Lettuce

Vitamin A: Toxic in Supplementation

Anybody on a reasonably healthy diet should never need to take vitamin A supplements. Also listed as retinyl palmitate and retinyl acetate on labels, studies on synthetic vitamin A have revealed very serious health concerns:

- Vitamin A is considered one of the deadliest supplements in large doses. The 2008 Cochran Report stated that in a review of 67 randomized clinical trials involving 232,550 participants over 3 years, the following three supplements significantly increased mortality:
  - Vitamin A: 16 percent increase
  - Beta-carotene: 7 percent increase
  - Vitamin E: 15 percent increase
- Vitamin A causes the body to lose calcium and can significantly contribute to osteoporosis. In a study, subjects taking 1,500 mg of vitamin A had double the hip-fracture rate of those taking 0.5 mg. For every 1 mg increase, hip fractures increased by 68 percent.[5]
- The most common effect of large doses of vitamin A in animals is spontaneous bone fracture.
- Large doses of vitamin A are toxic to the liver.

Beta-Carotene: Toxic in Supplementation

Synthetic beta-carotene is found in many supplements. It's a precursor to vitamin A, meaning it's needed to make vitamin A. It's been shown to increase the risk of several types of cancers when isolated and used in supplements.

The New England Journal of Medicine, The Lancet, and the National Cancer Institute all advise people not to take beta-carotene supplements.

- Beta-carotene supplements can interfere with our ability to absorb other very important carotenoids (e.g., lycopene and lutein), potentially increasing cancer risk.[6]
- A Finnish study concluded that beta-carotene supplements increased lung cancer by 28 percent in those taking it. Death rate from heart disease was also 17 percent higher.[7] [8]
- Beta-carotene supplementation increases the incidence of prostate cancer.[9]

Vitamin E: Toxic in Supplementation

Different forms of vitamin E (either tocopherols or tocotrienols) are available in supplement form. Large doses of vitamin E have been linked to an increased risk of prostate cancer.

- Multiple large clinical trials were conducted to test the effects of an antioxidant supplement with vitamin E, with doses ranging from 50 to 600 mg per day. The findings revealed that men who took vitamin E were 17 percent more likely to develop prostate cancer.[10]

What about Children?

Children on a healthy diet should never need supplements. Many parents develop and follow this terrible habit because of the misguided advice of others (including pediatricians) or because they "assume" their children need it. Most children's supplements are synthetically made and have no place in a child's body.

Unless your child has a DIAGNOSED DEFICIENCY, walk away from supplements and don't look back. If a deficiency is diagnosed, then buy a supplement sourced from whole-food ingredients and give it to your child only until a retest shows a healthy level of the nutrient is confirmed. At that point, your child no longer needs to take the supplement.

Many traditional pediatricians recommend supplements for no other reason than they think it's a good idea, instead of recommending a diet rich in the real nutrients children need. Pediatricians are not nutritionists, and unless they're naturopathic pediatricians, most traditional practitioners:

- Don't recognize the difference between healthy supplements and synthetic ones.
- Don't understand that most diseases are nutritionally preventable and controllable.
- Are unaware of both the serious damage that children can suffer from eating foods containing pesticides and the link confirmed in various studies between pasteurized milk products and an increase in childhood illnesses.[11] [12]

Supplements from China

Many synthetic supplements are now manufactured in China. Buying foods and supplements from China is a cause for great concern.

"More than 50% of food processing & packaging firms in China fail safety inspections. Rodent & fecal contamination was responsible for 10% of this figure."

Asia Inspection

From E. coli and salmonella outbreaks, to contaminated pet food that's caused illness in and the deaths of thousands of household pets and livestock, to infant-formula crises, China has some very serious issues when it comes to quality control. In China, food safety is in its infancy, and many foods are made in small backyard operations that are dirty and infested with rodents and insects.

Many wonderful supplements do come from China though, such as medicinal mushrooms and Chinese herbs used to treat many different health conditions. If you use these supplements, look for a verification seal on the bottle that it's been tested by an independent, third-party organization for purity and safety.

The Lure of Protein Sports Supplements

Sports supplements are a multibillion-dollar industry, and athletes are always looking for a way to achieve an edge with the perfect supplement. Athletes who consume extremely large amounts of protein on a long-term basis set themselves up for tissue and organ damage, as well as chronic degenerative conditions in the future due to metabolic acidosis (high acidity).

The Protein Myth

Protein may be an important part of exercise performance and recovery, but supplement manufacturers have capitalized on this by trying to convince us that much more is much better. Unfortunately, the exact opposite is true. Too much protein and amino-acid supplementation can result in calcium loss, dehydration, digestive problems, and in more extreme cases, kidney and liver damage.[13]

Many athletes consume far greater quantities of protein, in the form of protein powders, than their bodies need, believing it will increase muscle size and strength. There is now a significant amount of evidence showing that protein in excess of 10–15 percent of the diet is not only unnecessary, but very unhealthy. The amount of food and the number of calories an athlete needs may increase depending on activity level, but the ratio of protein should increase only slightly.

Not all protein sources are equal, and high-quality plant protein (organic and unrefined) and animal protein (small quantities from pasture-raised animals, never factory-farmed) provide us with the necessary spectrum of amino acids to build protein. There should rarely be any need for supplementation.

Many plant foods are very high in amino-acid content (amino acids being the building blocks of the protein our body needs), with some containing most if not all the essential amino acids we need. This isn't the case with meat.

Most people are completely unaware that once meat is cooked to 140°, the protein and nutrient content are denatured and/or destroyed.[14][15]

I am definitely not advocating raw meat! Rather, I'm illustrating that cooked meat is far from the high protein food most people think it is. The cooking process not only destroys nutrient content, but denatures the protein in a manner that is unhealthy for the human body.

When it comes to plant protein, raw hemp protein, pea protein, and cranberry protein are examples of plant foods that are very high in protein content and that are far less acid-forming and much healthier choices than meat, soy, and whey. Hemp protein is also naturally high in chlorophyll content (hence the green color). These and other raw, organic protein supplements are produced by brands such as Garden of Life and Sunwarrior.

Avoid Soy & Whey

Whey is a common protein supplement powder. As whey is the liquid remaining after pasteurized milk has been curdled and strained, it should be very clear by now why you should avoid it completely! Also, just as we talked about avoiding processed soy in the food section, nix all processed soy supplements and protein powders. Not only are they highly processed, most are from genetically modified soybeans. Talk about vibrationally dead food!

CHOOSING QUALITY SUPPLEMENTS

Choosing a supplement from the seemingly endless number available can seem daunting. We not only have to figure out which supplement to take, but also how to choose which one's the safest and most effective.

Are You Taking a Multivitamin?

If you're taking any daily supplement for no other reason than because you think you may be deficient, please stop. First, clean up your diet, and then get baseline nutritional testing to see if any deficiency exists. In most cases, if your diet is very healthy and is high in organic produce (which contains a higher amount of nutrients, especially trace minerals), you won't need the supplement.

Before you buy your next vitamin, herb, or other supplement, let's take a look at some important tips to help you choose the right one(s).

Tips on Choosing Supplements

When choosing a supplement, it's important to buy one that's high-quality, that's in its most natural state, and that comes from whole-food sources to avoid synthetic chemicals. Below are 10 tips to help you make the best purchasing decision possible:

#1: Look for a Reputable Manufacturer

A reputable manufacturer bases their claims on independent scientific research and uses high-quality ingredients tested by third-party labs to make sure these ingredients meet their claims. Many specialty health-food stores often have knowledgeable staff who can help guide you toward manufacturers with the best feedback and reputation.

Feel free to contact a manufacturer directly and ask them about third-party testing to verify the quality of their ingredients. Any good manufacturer will be very happy to speak with you on the quality of their products.

#2: Pay Close Attention to "Other Ingredients"

Pay close attention to "other ingredients" listed on the bottle that may include popular allergens, such as lactose, or unnecessary ingredients, including sugar, shellac, flavors, chlorine, or magnesium stearate (which offers no health benefit).

Always avoid any supplement that has artificial coloring or flavoring. High-quality manufacturers don't use these ingredients. Unfortunately, these are present in many sports supplements.

#3: Look for Supplements Sourced from Whole Foods

Whenever possible, choose organic supplements derived from whole foods, not synthetic elements. To identify supplements from whole-food sources, look at the ingredient list, which should contain food items you recognize, such as a fruits, vegetables, seeds, and nuts. If not, it's likely synthetic.

Choose "raw" whole-food supplements when possible as they're of much higher nutritional value. Several high-quality supplement brands, such as **Garden of Life**, produce supplements with raw, organic whole foods. This means the nutrients aren't destroyed by heat or processing.

The Body Healer isn't affiliated with Garden of Life; we just love their products! Many are organic, non-GMO, and dairy-, gluten-, and soy-free. Other reputable manufacturers also offer supplements with raw, organic, high-quality ingredients.

#4: Check Where the Ingredients Are Both Sourced & Prepared

Any reputable manufacturer will clearly display on their label where their ingredients come from and where they're prepared. If it comes from China, avoid it unless it's been independently tested by a third-party company.

#5: Is the Dosage High Enough?

Many manufacturers recommend much lower dosages than the amount shown to be effective in health studies. These smaller dosages do little to nothing for us. Sometimes the supplement amount is tiny compared to other unnecessary ingredients in the product.

For example, many people have heard that glucosamine sulfate has shown promise in treating arthritis and other bone-related conditions. Unfortunately, the dosage used in trials was approx. 4,500 mg, but many pills offer a dosage of 500 or 1,000 mg, far below what studies show provide health benefits.

Independent studies are easily found on the Internet that show what dose was used in successful health studies. Simply search for the nutrient followed by the term "health study" or "clinical study."

#6: Has the Supplement Been Tested for Heavy-Metal Contaminants?

This is especially important for the omegas, Ayurvedic herbs, and Chinese medicinal herbs. Look for the seal verifying it's been tested to be free of mercury and other contaminants. As we learned earlier, heavy-metal contamination in supplements is common.

#7: What about a "Seal of Approval"

Some products have a seal of approval on their label. This may or may not indicate a better product, depending on the seal they use (which may even be their own!). The following 3 seals are considered a gold standard and do carry weight:

- ConsumerLab.com
- USP
- Natural Products Association

Keep in mind that seals of approval can be very expensive, and some manufacturers choose not to pay for it. This doesn't necessarily mean there's something wrong with their product, or that it's worse than those that do carry a seal.

#8: Is the Supplement Sealed?

Make sure the supplement is sealed. There should be no evidence of seal tampering.

#9: Check the Expiration Date

Never buy a supplement without an expiration date. Unfortunately, the FDA doesn't require manufacturers to include this date on their products, but any reputable manufacturer will always include it on their product label. It may be printed on the bottom.

#10: Storage

Some supplements must be refrigerated, some don't. Most need to be stored out of sunlight and kept in a sealed container, especially herbs, tinctures, and extracts. Make sure you follow instructions on how to best store your supplement.

Nutrient Combos

Some vitamins are sold in combination with other nutrients or minerals. This isn't because manufacturers are trying to sell more products, but because some nutrients need the presence of others for the body to absorb and use them more effectively.

For example, calcium supplements often contain vitamin D. Your body requires vitamin D to absorb calcium or phosphorus, and if you're vitamin D deficient, this can affect how well you can absorb both of these nutrients.

SUPPLEMENTS FOR COMMON DEFICIENCIES

Even if your diet is healthy and you eat only organic foods, you still need to be aware of some common vitamin deficiencies. Let's take a close look at several that have reached epidemic proportions. Even on the healthiest of diets, we can still experience a deficiency of these nutrients in our diet.

— MINERALS —

Because nonorganic foods contain fewer nutrients than their organic counterparts, we can become deficient in various trace minerals. Organic foods can also be affected by questionable agricultural practices (though to a much smaller degree). I do recommend a high-quality mineral supplement to support the fact that even organic foods can be low in some trace and essential minerals.

— VITAMIN D —

Vitamin D is one of the most important nutrients in the body. Known as the "sunshine vitamin," it's the only vitamin our bodies can make simply by standing in the sunlight. In much smaller quantities, we also receive it from the food we eat.

The sun produces different wavelengths of light. Ultra violet-B (UVB) are short-wave rays, are the only wavelength associated with vitamin D production, and are available between approximately 11:00 a.m. and 1:00 p.m. during the summer months (except for those who live in the tropics). Rays produced at other times of day are UVA, which can harm the skin.

When your skin is exposed to sunlight, it produces vitamin D and sends it to your liver. It's then converted to a pre-hormone called 25(OH)D, which is what the doctor measures when they take a blood test to measure your vitamin D level. This pre-hormone travels to different tissues throughout the body, targeting over 2,000 genes.

Research now shows that this vitamin may also be important in preventing and treating a number of diseases. Internationally recognized research scientist Dr. William Grant, PhD, found that about 30 percent of cancer deaths could be prevented each year with higher levels of vitamin D. Taking vitamin D during the winter is one of the most effective ways to prevent cold or flu symptoms, far more effective than the flu shot (we'll talk about this in a minute).

Vitamin D is a very common deficiency, especially in northern countries.

Why We Need Vitamin D

Vitamin D is very important for healthy bones and the proper functioning of our muscles, heart, lungs, and brain. It also helps our body fight infection and is necessary for calcium absorption in our intestines. Without vitamin D, the body can't absorb calcium or phosphorus. In fact, no matter how much calcium supplementation you take or phosphorus you receive from food, it can't be absorbed without vitamin D. As calcium and phosphorus are essential for developing healthy, strong bones, a lack of vitamin D can severely impact the strength of our bones.

How We Become Vitamin D Deficient

There are several reasons we become deficient in vitamin D:

Not enough sunlight: Especially for those living in northern countries, a vitamin D deficiency is very common and is considered an epidemic in the US. An optimum level of vitamin D is considered a cancer preventative.(1)

> "There's no evidence to support that sun exposure is the direct cause of skin cancer. Studies show melanomas have been found to DECREASE with greater sun exposure & INCREASE with the use of chemical sunscreens."
>
> The Lancet

Overuse of sunscreen: Sunscreens (and SPF moisturizers) completely block the body's ability to produce vitamin D and play a large role in causing a vitamin D deficiency. An irrational fear of the sun causes many people to cover their skin with highly chemicalized creams containing a toxic cocktail of ingredients. Studies are finding that it's the chemicals in many of these sunscreens that contribute to the very skin cancer they claim to protect against (especially when these chemicals are baked into the skin by the sun).

Even weak sunscreens (SPF 8) block our body's ability to generate vitamin D by up to 95 percent. Sunscreens should be used judiciously. Our skin *needs* to breathe sometimes and absorb the UVB rays in natural sunlight!

Age: The older we get, the thinner our skin becomes, which in turns affects our ability to create vitamin D.

Obesity: People who are obese have lower levels of vitamin D.

Skin color: People with darker skin are more likely to be deficient than fair-skinned people.

Kidney and liver conditions: Both conditions can contribute to a vitamin D deficiency. As vitamin D is activated by the kidneys and liver before the body can use it, kidney or liver disease can greatly impair the body's ability to activate vitamin D.

Melanomas Are NOT Caused by Natural Sunlight

Rates of melanoma, the deadliest form of skin cancer, have been rising for at least 30 years, and this increase has been largely blamed on sun exposure, even though no long-term studies support sun exposure causing skin cancer. In fact, the opposite has proven true.

Melanomas have been found to decrease with greater sun exposure and increase with the use of chemical sunscreens. The UVB rays from natural sunlight are protective against melanomas (due to the vitamin D your body produces in response to the UVB rays).

- A study published in the British Journal of Dermatology indicated that natural sunlight is an innocent bystander in the development of melanoma and that cancerous melanomas are often misdiagnosed. A study of 4,000 cases of melanoma reported that many people are diagnosed with melanoma skin cancer, even though their lesions were noncancerous.(2)
- The Lancet published that outdoor workers have a decreased risk of melanoma compared with indoor workers, suggesting that increased sunlight exposure can have a protective effect.(3)

Flu Shot vs. Vitamin D

Thinking of getting the flu shot? Think again. Many people are told they should get a flu shot before each winter. Did you know that taking vitamin D is more effective for preventing the flu than getting a flu shot, making this vaccine completely unnecessary? Not only that, but some flu-shot manufacturers still use mercury in their vaccine.

Studies have shown that vitamin D is just as effective, if not more so, than the controversial flu vaccine. Let's look at the actual studies, not the hype, that show just how ineffective the flu vaccine is for both adults and children:

- During the 2012–2013 flu season, the flu vaccine's effectiveness was found to be just 56 percent across all age groups reviewed by the CDC—the statistical equivalent of a coin toss.
- In a review of 50 reports, including 70,000 adults, vaccination of healthy adults only reduced risk of influenza by 6%, and reduced the number of missed work days by less than one day (0.16 days). It did not change the number of people needing to go to the hospital or take time off work.(5)
- Vaccinating against one strain of influenza may increase your risk of exposure to related but different strains.
- In a review of over 51 studies involving 294,000 children, there was no evidence that

> "In seniors over 65, the flu vaccine was found to be only 9% effective. In a review of 64 studies of the elderly over 98 flu seasons, flu shots were non-significant for preventing influenza, ILI, or pneumonia."
>
> Cochran Database of Systematic Reviews

injecting children 6-24 months with a flu vaccine was more effective than the placebo, and it was found to be effective only 33 percent of the time in children over 2 yrs.[6]

- Children with asthma who receive the flu vaccine are more at risk for hospitalization than children who do not receive the vaccine.[7]
- A study involving African American postmenopausal women in New York found a 60 percent reduced risk of colds and influenza for those taking 800 IU vitamin D_3, and a 90 percent reduced risk for those taking 2,000 IU.
- A 2010 study demonstrated the effectiveness of vitamin D as a preventive strategy against influenza. Children taking just 1,200 IU of vitamin D_3 per day (considered a low dose) were shown to be 42 percent less likely to come down with the flu.[8]

The best protection you can give yourself against colds and the flu is to eat a healthy diet and to make sure you get enough vitamin D.

Sources of Vitamin D

Vitamin D comes from either the sunlight (our body makes it when exposed to natural sunlight), from supplementation (in the form of vitamin D_2 or D_3), or in very small quantities from food sources.

1. **Vitamin D from Sunlight – The Sun's Rays**

   When we avoid the sun, we lose out on this natural source of protection.

   The amount of vitamin D we can absorb depends on our skin color and our age, as well as the time of day and our location. The farther you live from the equator (e.g., Canada and the northern US, where vitamin D deficiency is an epidemic), the longer exposure to the sun you'll need to get enough vitamin D. People with dark skin need more sun exposure compared to fair-skinned people to generate the same amount of vitamin D.

   It's a common myth that to get enough vitamin D, you simply need to expose your face and hands to sunlight for 10 minutes every day. Remember that UVB is available only between 11:00 a.m. and 1:00 p.m. (approximately) during the summer months, except for those who live in the tropics. Aim to expose enough of your unclothed skin during your lunchtime to get a slight pink color from the sun, which is 15-20 minutes for most fair-skinned people. The healing UVB rays of natural sunlight that generate vitamin D in your skin can't penetrate glass, whether in your home or in your car.

   For the rest of the day, if you would like to spend time out in the sun, then follow these tips:

   - Use a mineral sunscreen with an SPF of at least 15 on uncovered skin to protect against UVA rays.
   - Choose shaded areas or cover the skin with clothing (white reflects the sunlight, which also helps keep you cooler).
   - Don't rely on glass to protect you from UVA rays, as they can penetrate glass.
   - Always avoid sunburn. If you do experience a burn, apply aloe-vera gel, available from most health-food stores and supermarkets. You can also buy an aloe-vera plant. Simply cut off a slice of the leaf and rub the raw gel in the leaf directly on the burn. Some generic brands of aloe-vera gel contain a variety of unwanted chemicals, so look for a bottle that has just the gel and any other natural ingredients (no chemicals).

Choosing Sunscreens

Choose Mineral Sunscreens: Zinc Oxide or Titanium Dioxide. When choosing a sunscreen, always choose a mineral sunscreen because minerals aren't absorbed by the skin; instead, they work by reflecting the sunlight. In a good mineral sunscreen, the active ingredient will be either zinc oxide, titanium dioxide, or a combination of both, and the rest of the ingredient list should be plant-based extracts.

Using the popular chemical sunscreens on the market not only increases your risk of skin cancer, but it also increases the amount of toxins that your body must then work to eliminate. They serve only to lower your vibrational frequency.

Toxic Ingredients in Sunscreen/SPF Lotions. When was the last time you looked at the ingredient list for your sunscreen? Most are filled with synthetic chemicals that haven't undergone any long-term testing, and others are hormone disruptors and carcinogenic or potentially carcinogenic. These ingredients include oxybenzone, 4-BMC, octinoxate, and many others. Over the past decade, dozens of studies have examined the potential health hazards of sunscreen chemicals, and experts caution that the unintentional exposure to and the toxic nature of their active ingredients erode any benefits of sunscreens.[9]

Sunscreens & Children. Never use these chemical sunscreens on infants and children! Toxic ingredients have no place on a child's skin. Always use mineral sunscreens, and check the ingredient list to make sure it contains no other synthetic chemicals.

2. **Vitamin D from Supplements**

   Vitamin D supplementation can easily be found at any supermarket, supplement store, health-food store, or online. Let's take a look at the two types of vitamin D available, as well as which one you should choose and what dosage you should take.

   - **Vitamin D_2:** Made by invertebrates (animals without a spine/vertebral column), fungus, and plants in response to sunlight; humans and other vertebrates do not produce vitamin D_2.
   - **Vitamin D_3:** Made in the skin when exposed to UVB rays from the sun; it's only when the UV index is greater than 3 that these wavelengths are present (typically around midday).

Always choose vitamin D_3. Vitamin D_2 is much less effective than Vitamin D_3 in humans.[10] Vitamin D_2 has also been associated with the softening of bones and hardening of organs and arteries. It's less absorbable and has a shorter life in the body. Because of this, it must be taken in a much higher dose than D_3.

Some doctors prescribe vitamin D_2 capsules if blood tests show a deficiency. This prescription is no different from the vitamin D found in stores; it's simply a higher dosage. If the prescription is for vitamin D_2, ask instead for vitamin D_3 or look for it in supplement stores.

Know What Dosage to Take

Even though it's never a good idea to assume you're deficient in any vitamin or to randomly guess at the dosage you should take, vitamin D is an exception because it's a very popular deficiency. The recommended daily dose is 2,000 IU per day, but experts agree that a higher dosage of 5,000 IU is safe (and often needed in northern countries in the winter). Full sun exposure for 30 minutes at midday alone generates about 20,000 IU.

A simple blood test at your doctor's office or at a lab will tell you if you're vitamin D deficient. Unlike many other nutrients, a vitamin D deficiency can't be reversed overnight. It can take several months of supplementation and/or sunlight exposure to rebuild a healthy level in your body.

If you're vitamin D deficient, your doctor will recommend a high dose for 2-3 months (often 5,000 IU/day), followed by a reduced amount, and then a vitamin D retest to make sure your level is where it should be. Many doctors will then recommend a maintenance dosage of 1,000 or 2,000 IU per day.

3. **Vitamin D from Food Sources**
Even though vitamin D is found in various food sources, it's nearly impossible to get enough from your diet. Sunlight exposure is the only reliable way to generate vitamin D in your own body, and high-quality supplementation is the only way to rebuild low levels if sunlight exposure isn't possible. Vitamin D is found in:

- Fatty fish / fish-liver oils / caviar / shellfish
- Shiitake mushrooms
- Insects / frogs
- Unpasteurized butter*
- Egg yolks*
- Organ meats*
- Animal fat* (bird and pig fat)

* from free-range / pasture-raised animals

"Pasteurized dairy contributes to allergies, type 1 diabetes, ear infections, chronic sinus infections, & is a leading cause of iron deficiency anemia & constipation in children."

The Lancet

Avoid "Fortified" & "Enriched" Vitamin D

Always choose natural sources of vitamin D and not fortified nutrients found in processed foods, such as pasteurized milk, processed soy products, and nondairy milks.

Fortified: The food never contained this vitamin to begin with and the manufacturer is including a synthetic version of the vitamin as an "add-on."

Enriched: The food used to contain the nutrient before it was processed and stripped away during refining, and it was then added back in synthetic form.

Milk: The Worst Way to Get Vitamin D

One of the biggest myths about vitamin D is that it's naturally found in milk. It's not, nor has it ever been. Synthetic vitamin D was added to milk to prevent rickets during the early 20th century.

The milk available today in stores is pasteurized and homogenized and comes from confined animals pumped with antibiotics and often hormones. It's then fortified with vitamin D_2. The final product in no way resembles a healthy food. As we now know, pasteurized milk and dairy increase acidity in the body, forcing the body to release alkaline minerals, such as calcium from bones and teeth, to balance this excess acidity.

Countries with the highest pasteurized milk and dairy intake also have the highest numbers of osteoporosis and bone-related disease. For every study showing processed foods fortified with vitamin D (or calcium) are good for you, more show that they're bad. The synthetic calcium added to "enrich" dairy and processed foods may increase heart-attack risk by 30 percent.[11] In addition, pasteurized dairy products are a direct contributor to common childhood illnesses.[12]

As we talked about earlier, nutritional differences between breast milk and pasteurized milk are significant, with the important bioactive components inactivated by pasteurization.

It's also important to realize that a person would have to drink 10 tall glasses of vitamin D–fortified milk each day just to get minimum levels in their diet.

— VITAMIN B_{12} —

Vitamin B_{12} is an important nutrient found in soil bacteria where plants grow. It's found in whole foods such as fruits and vegetables as well as in animal products (from animals that consume these foods). It's involved in synthesizing DNA, forming red blood cells, and maintaining proper brain and neurological functioning by assisting in the conduction of signals throughout our nervous system and brain cells.

While most vitamins can be made by a variety of plants and animal products, no plant or animal actually produces vitamin B_{12}. It comes from tiny microorganisms that include bacteria, yeasts, molds, and algae.

When our food chain became highly chemicalized and industrialized, the quality of our food and its nutritional content drastically changed. The widespread use of toxic pesticides and herbicides, common food-processing methods, and the antibiotics found in foods (especially factory-farmed meats) have caused a serious decline in many different nutrients. One nutrient especially affected is vitamin B_{12}.

Farmers have unknowingly sterilized the bacteria out of the soil—bacteria that's necessary for the production of B_{12}. Nutritional researchers are now unable to find vitamin B_{12} in plant foods grown in depleted, pesticide-ridden soils. However, organically grown plants specifically cultivated in highly composted soils rich with organic matter contain vitamin B_{12}.[1]

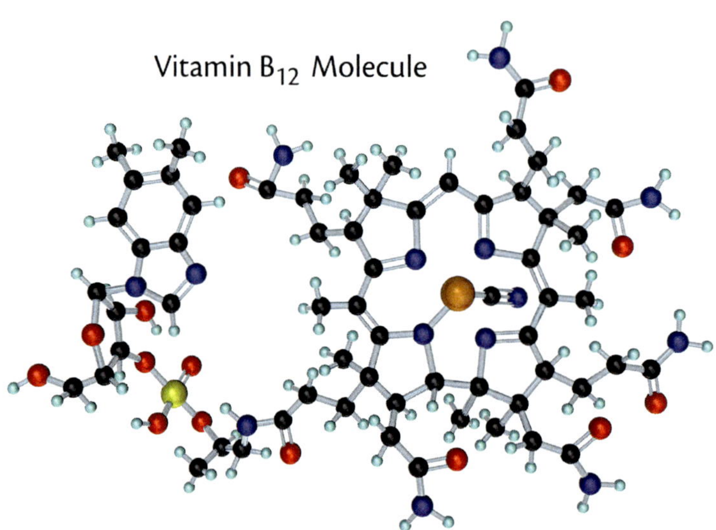

Sources of Vitamin B_{12}

If we need in increase our dietary intake of vitamin B_{12}, we can either include food sources in our diet, or we can choose a high-quality supplement. Our body also contains bacteria that produce approximately 5 mcg of B_{12} each day, but very little is absorbed by the colon.

1. **Vitamin B_{12} from Food**
   Plants grown in organic soils where pesticides haven't destroyed the bacteria necessary for vitamin B_{12} contain small quantities. Pasture-raised animals also contain the microorganisms that create vitamin B_{12} because they eat the plants on which B_{12}-producing microorganisms live. In addition, sea creatures also siphon large quantities of B_{12}-producing microorganisms from the ocean.

   - Plant Sources: Spirulina, chlorella, sea vegetables, tempeh, shiitake mushrooms, barley, nutritional yeast
   - Dairy & Egg Sources: Unpasteurized dairy products, eggs (organic pasture-raised) (note: egg whites don't contain any B_{12})
   - Meat Sources: Liver, beef, lamb, venison
   - Fish Sources: Mackerel, sardines, snapper, Chinook salmon, clams, scallops, oysters, shrimp, halibut, trout, crab, octopus

2. **Vitamin B_{12} from Supplements**
   There are 2 commonly found types of B_{12} in supplementation:

   - Active B_{12} (methylcobalamin): Methylcobalamin is the active form of vitamin B_{12} that exists in nature and is readily absorbed by the body.
   - Inactive B_{12} (cyanocobalamin): Most researchers agree that the use of inactive B_{12} (cyanocobalamin) can reduce, destroy, and interfere with active B_{12} by competing for the same cell-receptor sites. Some B_{12} and most multivitamin supplements contain cyanocobalamin. It's a cheap, synthetic chemical used by many vitamin manufacturers because it's far cheaper than the higher-quality methylcobalamin. Unfortunately, it leaves behind trace amounts of cyanide, which your liver must then remove. In short, it's slightly toxic!

     Always choose the active B_{12} in your supplements, most commonly listed on the ingredient label as methylcobalamin. Avoid multivitamins that contain cyanocobalamin.

Supplementation Absorption & Dosage

Vitamin B_{12} can be taken in several different ways, but the best methods are:

- Sublingual supplement (a small pill that dissolves under your tongue)
- Skin absorption (patch)
- B_{12} injections (requires a medical professional for each shot)

When choosing a supplement, avoid unnecessary and artificial ingredients and flavors that are very common with the chewable B_{12}. If you're a vegan, watch out for lactose.

Normal levels of B_{12} in the body are 200-900 pg/ml. Lower levels can be associated with symptoms (see below). If testing shows you're levels are less than 200, the typical dose is a 2 week loading of 2,000 mcg sublingually every day followed by 500-1,000 mcg daily for maintenance. Recheck after 2 months. Once you've reached a healthy level, reduce your intake and retest to find the lowest amount required. Many experts agree that 500 mcg each day is sufficient for maintaining health – similarly, 2,000 or 5,000 mcg weekly also works well (both commonly found supplement doses).

Vitamin B_{12} Deficiency

B_{12} supplementation is recommended by many natural healthcare practitioners, such as Dr. Joel Fuhrman, a best-selling author and American board-certified family physician who specializes in nutrition-based treatments for obesity and chronic disease. Dr. Fuhrman emphasizes that even if we follow a whole-food, predominantly plant-based diet, we need to be aware of our vitamin B_{12} intake because of how depleted our soils have become.

People who rely on plant-based foods alone may experience low levels of vitamin B_{12} if their diet isn't fresh and organic. This is because fruits and vegetables take up B_{12} only if they grow in healthy, organic soil because of the microorganisms present.

Yet Another Reason to Ditch Your Microwave!

We've talked about it before, but let's really hammer it home. If you use a microwave—ditch it! A Japanese study revealed that 30-40 percent of vitamin B_{12} is destroyed in foods cooked by a microwave.

Meat Eaters vs. Vegetarians vs. Vegans

Although vitamin B_{12} deficiencies are found in vegetarians, vegans, and meat eaters, a diet where all animal products are removed typically leads to a serum B_{12} drop if that diet isn't organic.

In a study of new vegans, results showed vegans had consistently lower serum B_{12} levels than meat eaters and vegetarians.(2)

- 4 students with a serum B_{12} in the 600-900 pg/ml range fell below 500 pg/ml in just 2 months.
- 10 students followed the vegan diet for 5 months, and their average B_{12} levels went from 417 to 276 pg/ml.
- After 5 months, 2 students went from normal B_{12} levels to below normal B_{12}.

These studies didn't review the quality of foods eaten by the vegans who participated in the study. A diet rich in organic fruits and vegetables (grown in soils with healthy bacteria) won't yield the same study results as a diet high in refined grains, vegan processed foods, and nonorganic produce. Many vegan processed foods on the market are filled with the same unhealthy ingredients that standard processed foods on a meat-based diet contain, and many vegans unknowingly adopt unhealthy vegan food choices.

Another important point to consider is how well we absorb vitamin B_{12}. According to Dr. Gabriel Cousens' research, although vegans show a lower level of B_{12}, their absorption ratio is 70 percent higher than that of meat eaters (26 percent); therefore, they don't need as much vitamin B_{12}.(3)

Our Ability to Absorb Vitamin B_{12} Is Important

Normally, active B_{12} is created and absorbed in the intestines. Intrinsic factor is a type of protein that helps us absorb B_{12} from food. However, when we have digestive problems (which millions of people do), are on medications, have an unhealthy diet, or take drugs or alcohol, we can significantly affect our ability to absorb any B_{12} from food by reducing or destroying bacteria in our intestinal tract. This is another reason why a B_{12} deficiency is now so common.

A deficiency in vitamin B_{12} is not only due to a lack in the foods we eat; it's also due to our inability to absorb it properly.[4][5]

Other factors include:

- Nutrients such as cobalt, folate, and B_6 must be present in the body for us to create and absorb B_{12}. A deficiency in these nutrients can cause a B_{12} deficiency.[6]
- Conversion of B_{12} from its nonactive form into its active form requires vitamin E. Individuals who are deficient in vitamin E may also show signs of a B_{12} deficiency.
- If the body has a problem absorbing nutrients such as B_{12} from food (such as with Crohn's disease and celiac disease), this can contribute to a B_{12} deficiency. In these cases, B_{12} supplementation won't help.

How Do I Know if I'm Deficient?

Unfortunately, requesting a vitamin B_{12} deficiency test from a traditional doctor will most likely result in a blood serum test that measures only your cyanocobalamin (inactive B_{12}) instead of methycobalamin (active B_{12}) levels, which doesn't help very much. Correct testing involves:

A UMMA test, which will be elevated if your B_{12} is low, and

A homocysteine (Hcy) test, which will be elevated if your B_{12} is low

The UMMA test (urinary methylmalonic acid) is considered the most reliable, accurate, and natural testing method for a B_{12} deficiency. It was developed by Dr. Eric J. Norman at the Norman Clinical Laboratory, Inc., in Cincinnati, Ohio.

Homocysteine is an amino acid normally found in our blood. When levels are elevated, this can indicate a B_{12} deficiency and an increased risk of heart disease and stroke. A B_{12} deficiency can cause homocysteine levels to rise if it isn't properly metabolized, which is why a high homocysteine level can help confirm a B_{12} deficiency. A homocysteine test is a standard test that your doctor can order.

Symptoms of Deficiency

Unfortunately, sometimes a B_{12} deficiency can cause no visible symptoms until serious problems occur, but certain types of neurological damage are quickly reversible with supplementation. Common signs of a B_{12} deficiency include:

- Tiredness or unexplained weakness, anemia
- Dizziness, trouble with balance, unsteady walk
- Confusion, memory loss, or dementia
- Chest pain or shortness of breath
- Coldness, numbness or tingling in the hands and feet
- Slow reflexes and reaction

- Pale skin or yellowing of the skin
- Sore mouth and tongue
- Diarrhea, constipation, or loss of appetite

A B_{12} deficiency often mimics many other conditions, including a variety of neurological or motor disorders, gastrointestinal disorders, blood disorders, psychosis/hallucinations, depression, personality changes, hypothyroidism, chronic fatigue, and autoimmune disorders.

Brain Shrinkage, Memory Loss, & Dementia

Brain shrinkage is a hallmark of declining memory and dementia, such as Alzheimer's disease. Dr. Susanne Sorensen from the Alzheimer's Society stated, "Shrinkage is usually associated with the development of dementia."

- A study revealed that a B_{12} deficiency was found in 2 out of 5 people and that a serious deficiency can cause brain shrinkage. People who had higher B_{12} levels were 6 times less likely to experience brain shrinkage compared to those who had lower levels of B_{12} in their blood.[(7)]

— PROBIOTICS & GUT HEALTH —

What Exactly Are Probiotics & Prebiotics?

"Probiotics" refers to the good bacteria that live in our intestines such as lactobacillus bacteria, which includes bifidophilus and acidophilus. These specific bacterial strains have been used as medicine for decades and are traditionally found in fermented food and drinks, such as yogurt and miso.

"Prebiotics" are plant fibers that the body can't digest, but which make an excellent food source for the probiotics (good bacteria) already in our digestive system. They're found in legumes, fruits, and raw honey.

Whereas probiotics are living microorganisms, prebiotics are nonliving and aren't affected by heat, cold, acid, or time. Prebiotics come mainly from carbohydrate fibers called oligosaccharides that our bodies don't digest, and they stay in our digestive system to help boost the growth of beneficial bacteria.

Who Should Take Probiotics?

If you're healthy, eat a nutritious diet with plenty of raw fruits and veggies, and suffer from no health issues, and if your bowel movements are firm and regular, then you don't need probiotics.

It is, however, very important to take probiotics during and after any treatment that can damage your intestinal flora, such as a course of antibiotics, laxatives, chemotherapy, radiotherapy, retroviral therapy, or after severe food poisoning, diarrhea, or a colonoscopy. During these times, probiotic foods and/or supplements provide our body with the friendly bacteria it needs to repopulate the lost bacteria in our gut. It can take anywhere from a few days to a few weeks for intestinal flora to take hold and fully repopulate after being reduced or wiped out.

It's impossible to be healthy if our intestinal flora is out of whack. A diet low in healthy, whole foods and high in processed foods will always compromise gut bacteria. In this case, the answer is to clean up our diet while taking a high-quality probiotic.

Those suffering from gastrointestinal disorders can also benefit from taking probiotic supplements that may not heal the health condition, but which can be a tremendous help in providing some relief and helping our body absorb nutrients in the food.

Sources of Probiotics & Prebiotics

We can quickly populate our gut with healthy bacteria by either eating fermented foods or taking a high-quality probiotic supplement.

Aim to get your probiotics from food, not supplements, where possible. Supplement probiotics are prepared in the lab and are proprietary strains, unless the supplements are raw probiotics (see below).

1. **Probiotics from Fermented Food & Drinks**

Natural sources of prebiotics include legumes, fruits, and raw honey. For probiotics, fermented foods are the food of choice. Some of these are prepared without heat.

Naturally fermented foods are a wonderful choice for probiotics that traditional cultures have been consuming for hundreds of years. Some fermented foods are high in sodium (because of the salt used during the fermentation process), whereas others are not. Many cultures today, including Japan and Korea, make a large variety of fermented foods.

Kombucha is a popular drink sold in many health-food stores and supermarkets that contains probiotics, as well as other beneficial nutrients. GTs Kombucha is a fantastic brand. Not only is it raw and organic, it also comes in many flavors that taste incredible! My flavor is Botanical #7; the ingredients are simply kombucha, hibiscus, orange peel, and lemon. As an added bonus, it comes in a glass bottle, not plastic. Unfortunately, many commercial kombucha drinks now contain all sorts of undesirables, so make sure you check the ingredient list carefully. Always look for raw and organic.

Other fermented foods include miso, natto, kimchee, tempeh, olives, sauerkraut, pickles, kefir, and yogurt. There are now several brands of raw sauerkraut that come in exciting flavors. Wildbrine makes a raw, organic dill and garlic version that our family loves!

What about Yogurts?

Traditional kefir and yogurt used to be fantastic sources of beneficial bacteria because of their raw, unpasteurized state. Unfortunately, most of today's yogurt is pasteurized unless specially purchased raw (only legal in some US states).

Most foods claiming to contain "live" or "active" probiotics have been highly processed and pasteurized. As we now know, pasteurization (including flash pasteurization) kills or sterilizes most of the beneficial elements of a food, including the good bacteria. This is true regardless of whether it's organic or not. Some yogurt manufacturers add cultures after pasteurization, but there are conflicting studies on how much bacteria in these products actually reaches the gut as many strains are unable to survive stomach acids.

Some types of yogurt (especially frozen yogurt) don't contain any live bacteria at all, but many do contain refined sugar, artificial flavoring and coloring, and other chemical additives. Even if they do contain any probiotics, any type of pasteurized yogurt isn't a healthy food.

Some products claiming to have live bacteria contain inulin instead, a soluble fiber additive that can act as a laxative. Inulin is harvested from plants and is used as a filler and stabilizer in processed foods. It may also be a potential allergen.[1]

2. Probiotics from High-Quality Supplements

Supplemental pre- and probiotics are widely available, easy to take, and most are inexpensive. They come in the form of liquids, capsules, and pills. Some need to be refrigerated, and some don't. The shelf life of refrigerated probiotics is 3-6 weeks, and about 12 months for freeze-dried probiotics.

False Claims by Probiotic Manufacturers

The probiotic supplement business is a big one, with many name brands cashing in on the profit. More and more products are falsely marketed as having probiotics, but it's a challenge to confirm whether these products contain any live organisms at all. Also, the number of organisms decreases over time. Some manufacturers claim their products contain far more CFUs (see more on CFUs below) than what are actually in their product.

Dead or Alive

Do Heat & Stomach Acid Kill Probiotic Supplements?

Some probiotics are very delicate and can be easily destroyed by heat, oxygen, stomach acid, and bile. Our stomach acid is specifically designed to kill the bacteria in the food we eat, so it will automatically kill many probiotic strains in supplements we take. For probiotics to survive until they reach the intestines, they must be resistant to both bile and stomach acid and survive any heat used during processing.

Probiotic supplements can also be shipped and stored poorly, with many of the cultures dead by the time they reach the consumer. Anything that's been heat-heated, such as pasteurized yogurt and dairy, may contain no live cultures at all.

Even though many experts believe that heat completely destroys the live bacteria in probiotics, research suggests otherwise.

- A study comparing the health impact using live bacteria vs. those treated with heat or UV radiation showed that one was just as effective as the other at stimulating an immune response in the body.[2]
- Studies have shown that probiotics in fermented foods survive stomach acid and intestinal bile.

Choosing Live Probiotics

Before we look at some very helpful tips on choosing the right probiotic supplement, it's important to understand "CFUs," a common probiotic term.

What Are Colony Forming Units (CFUs)

"CFUs" is a measurement of living vs. dead bacteria, which is found on probiotic bottle labels. It's the number of bacterial colonies in the preparation formed when cultured in the laboratory.

CFUs are best thought of as live bacterial cells that can multiply and form larger colonies of good bacteria. The number "5.5 billion CFUs" is the number of bacteria found in the product.

One of the problems with figuring out if a probiotic brand has what it claims is that it's impossible to prove it for yourself. Cracking open a pill and counting billions of CFUs, and then testing them to see if they're alive is ... well ... not likely on your to-do list!

- A Canadian study measured the viable organisms in 10 popular brands of probiotic preparations. *Not one matched the amount on their labels: 8 brands contained only 10 percent of the stated number, and 2 contained no viable probiotics at all.* Even foods such as pizzas are now being advertised as containing probiotics in an attempt to make the consumer overlook the list of unhealthy ingredients on their food labels. Fortified, processed foods claiming to contain probiotics are not only bad for your health, but will often cost more too.
- In 2012, ConsumerLab.com tested 29 popular probiotic products. 2 delivered far fewer than promised, containing only 57 percent and 65 percent respectively of the organisms listed on the label.[3]
- Consumer Guides analyzed several leading probiotic products, checking them for:
  1) CFU count
  2) Third-party verification
  3) Value
  4) Effectiveness

  Many "top" products, including both low-cost and expensive, failed to deliver on their claims.

  Very few manufacturers I researched could provide testing information on the survivability of the specific strains in their formulas, yet they were happy to make claims on their product labels based on this lack of information.

  Third-party verification is the only way to guarantee how much of the CFUs will make it into our intestines alive.

Choosing a Good Probiotic Supplement

Much of the beneficial bacteria in pricey probiotics will likely have been destroyed before it gets anywhere near our intestines. With all the confusion surrounding which probiotic to choose, how do we go about finding a high-quality product, and how do we make sure that what we buy contains any beneficial bacteria at all? Let's take a look at some handy guidelines to help us do just that.

Always Look for Independent Verification

First and foremost, look for products that show a third-party verification seal. Reputable manufacturers are proud of this verification and send their products to independent testing labs so that we can be sure we're getting what we pay for. This third-party verification is important because it's the only way to know for sure what's in each pill. Otherwise, we could find ourselves paying for dead cultures, tiny (no pun intended) amounts of bacteria, or unnecessary fillers and binders. The verification seal is printed on the product label.

Check the Number of CFUs

Look for a probiotic preparation with at least 5 million CFUs and 3 or more different strains of bacteria. Most of the randomized clinical trials have found better results from using multi-strain preparations. Multi-strain probiotics more closely match the natural ecology of our digestive system, rather than probiotics with only one or two strains. Check specifically for "lactobacillus acidophilus DDS-1," a highly effective strain of beneficial bacteria. Research at a major Midwestern university revealed that DDS-1 is especially beneficial because it colonizes well in the human gut.

Check for Allergens

Some probiotics contain common allergens such as dairy, corn, soy, wheat, or gluten.

Check the Expiration Date

Make sure the probiotic is well within the product expiration date.

Consider Raw Probiotics

Garden of Life is a great example of a reputable manufacturer who offers a raw line of supplements, including raw probiotic formulas for women, men, and children. Their formulas have not been heat-treated and contain no binders or fillers. They also contain over 30 different strains and over 85 billion CFUs.

NOTE! Raw probiotics should always be taken with food as they can cause discomfort if taken on an empty stomach.

What about Enteric Coating?

Some probiotic manufacturers claim that enteric coating protects bacterial strains from oxygen and stomach acid. Others claim the opposite, stating that strains of bacteria resistant to acid and bile can be made using high-quality manufacturing processes that don't need enteric coating.

It's more expensive to prepare enteric-coated probiotics, which typically means a more expensive product. Many enteric coatings also use synthetic ingredients. Studies have shown that the beneficial probiotic bacteria within fermented foods haven't had difficulties surviving stomach acid and intestinal bile, so why would a high-quality probiotic supplement need an enteric coating to increase the survivability of the contents?

Refrigeration

In general, microbes survive better at lower temperatures, and I recommend keeping yours in the refrigerator. However, technologies for keeping probiotics alive at room temperature have been developed by product manufacturers. It's not necessarily true that refrigerated products will be superior to unrefrigerated ones. If bacteria are dried and stabilized properly, they remain alive (and dormant) and start to grow again after they reach the moist environment inside our body.

Dosage & Time Frame

Probiotic dosage is based on general recommendations. Even though are no established guidelines, studies have shown that it can take 2-3 weeks to fully repopulate the gut with beneficial bacteria after it's been reduced or destroyed. Take the recommended dosage on the bottle for 3 full weeks after a course of antibiotics, food poisoning, chemotherapy treatment, or medical treatments such as a colonoscopy that damage gut bacteria. For chronic gastrointestinal disorders, continue taking probiotics until your condition has cleared up.

Each person has unique colonizing microbes, genetics, and diet; therefore, each person has the potential to respond to probiotics differently. It can involve trial and error to see what works best. Some probiotics can cause discomfort, such as bloating and gas, whereas others won't. With some, a noticeable relief of gastrointestinal issues may appear within just a day or two, but in general, it takes between 2-7 days to experience physical relief from digestive disorders that benefit from probiotics.

Can You Overdose on Probiotic Supplements?

The answer you'll typically hear is "no." In fact, several tablespoons of raw, fermented sauerkraut can contain more probiotics than an entire supplement bottle. But large doses of probiotics in supplementation form (especially if you don't have a health condition or any good reason for taking them) may cause more harm than good, especially since most are synthetic formulations.

- A study revealed that probiotic supplements can help stimulate an inflammatory response from the immune system to help fight infections, bacteria, and viruses. But in a healthy body, probiotic supplements also produce a similar inflammatory response, as though the body assumes the gut needs to prepare to fight infection.

ESSENTIAL OILS

It's time to explore a different type of supplement—the wonderful world of essential oils! We'll explore the benefits of their high vibrational frequency, and how they can be used medicinally to heal and rebalance our body.

The plant kingdom is the subject of an enormous amount of research and discovery. Many prescription drugs are based on the naturally occurring compounds in plants, with millions of dollars spent annually discovering new compounds for use as healing therapies and medications. Many essential oils have also been tested to be effective insect repellents.

Plant extracts have been used medicinally for thousands of years to provide a broad spectrum of therapeutic actions, and over 17,000 studies confirm the benefits of using essential oils. Research has shown that many viruses, fungi, and bacteria can't survive in the presence of many essential oils, especially those high in phenols, carvacrol, thymol, and terpenes. Some essential oils contain powerful antimicrobials and antivirals, and are more effective than broad-spectrum antibiotics.

> "From time immemorial, in every country, aromatic plants have been considered the most effective treatment for the diseases afflicting mankind."
>
> Dr. Rene-Maurice Gattefossé
> Father of Aromatherapy

Essential oils also provide many different fragrances (aromatics) that calm us, stimulate us, and energize us, and that create a relaxing, romantic atmosphere. Their use dates back to 4500 BC; the Bible itself has over 200 references to essential oils, including being burned as incense.

Even though essential oils are very potent, when used correctly, they rarely generate any negative side effects.

What Are Essential Oils?

Essential oils are very different from the traditional fruit, nut, and vegetable oils we're all familiar with in our kitchens. They contain highly concentrated compounds found within the plant that are far more potent than dried herbs. A very large amount of the plant is needed to distill only a very small amount of its essential oil. For example, it takes 1,000 lbs. of rose petals to produce only 6 oz. of rose extract, hence why pure, therapeutic-grade rose extract is very expensive.

A single essential oil can consist of a complex structure of hundreds of unique chemical compounds, and understanding these compounds and the effects they have on our body requires a sophisticated skill set. An essential oil can also have many variations of one compound, depending on the species of that plant. Some oils have much more volatile compounds than others, which dramatically alters the effect it will have on our body.

How Are Essential Oils Produced?

The extraction and distillation process has a significant effect on an essential oil's chemistry and medicinal qualities. Most are subjected to high heat and high pressure and are extracted with solvents, all of which damage the more delicate compounds. Therapeutic-grade (medicinal) essential oils, however, are normally extracted through steam distillation and are medicinally very different solvent-extracted oils.

Today in the US, many essential oils are completely ineffective as medicines because they're synthetic (or mixed with synthetic oils). These products are not healthy, nor are they high vibrational.

There are four different grades of essential oils:

1. Synthetic oils (created in the laboratory)
2. Fragrance oils (used for perfumes and to perfume products)
3. Natural oils (may or may not contain any therapeutic compounds)
4. Therapeutic- or medicinal-grade oils (pure, medicinal, and steam distilled)

The terms "therapeutic oils," "medicinal oils," and "aromatherapy oils" are often used interchangeably; however, there are big differences among them, and these differences lie in their quality and purity. Many aromatherapy oils are synthetic, produced simply for their fragrance, and usually contain other ingredients such as a carrier oil (an oil base). They may or may not be organically harvested, and many contain impurities or toxic contaminants such as methylene chloride, methyl isobutyl ketone, and methyl ethyl ketone.

There are over 300 essential oils, and thousands of their chemical constituents have been identified and registered. However, only 2 percent of these oils are produced for medicinal use; the other 98 percent are used in the perfume and cosmetic industries.

Synthetic Oils

Many chemical companies produce thousands of bottles of synthetic essential oils every year to mimic the scents of real essential oils. These synthetics are cheaply distilled with gum resins, alcohol, or solvents, such as dipropylene glycol (DPG) or diethyl phthalate (or DEP), to increase their volume. They may be heated to a high temperature to evaporate certain compounds, and then other synthetic ingredients may be added to them, such as linalyl acetate.

These synthetic essential oils have no medicinal qualities, and some cause allergic reactions, such as skin irritation and rashes. Back in the 1970s, a chemical known as AETT (acetyl ethyl tetramethyl tetralin) was used in a synthetic fragrance in many personal-care products. Even though animal studies revealed it caused brain and spinal-cord damage, the FDA refused to ban it; finally, the cosmetic industry voluntarily withdrew it.

Most of the essential oils you see in stores contain synthetic chemicals and fragrances—not any compounds from the original plant. Unfortunately, people often unknowingly buy these synthetic oils for health benefits and then conclude they're ineffective—and it's true! For example, several essential oils are used to help heal burns, yet the synthetic versions of these oils are not only missing the burn-healing compounds from the essential oil, but they also contain ingredients such as camphor that can *cause* skin burns and irritation.

Therapeutic-Grade Oils

Therapeutic-grade essential oils are prepared using a method that preserves as many of the healing compounds as possible. Most of these compounds are fragile and are destroyed by high temperatures, high pressure, or contact with chemically reactive metals (e.g., aluminum or copper), which is why they're prepared with low pressure and low temperature and in stainless-steel containers. No agricultural chemicals can be present during growth that contaminate the oil.

The purity and strength of the essential oil plays a very important part in its therapeutic benefits and its vibrational frequency. Purity depends on harvesting methods, distillation process, whether it's organic or whether chemical fertilizers are used, and the quality of the soil in which the plant grew. The altitude, climate, and time of the year also change how much of which compounds are in the oil. A plant grown in one region may differ in chemistry when grown in another region, which means it may or may not meet therapeutic standards. Plants that have been hybridized can have a very different fingerprint from the original species. After extraction, the chemical fingerprint of each oil is analyzed.

Growing

The original plant is wildcrafted (grown in the wild) or cultivated in virgin land that isn't contaminated by any chemical fertilizers, fungicides, pesticides, or herbicides. They shouldn't be grown near chemical pollutants, such as nuclear plants, highways, factories, and heavily populated cities. The plants are nourished with minerals, enzymes, and organic mulch to ensure their proper development, and they're watered via mountain spring water, reservoirs, or watershed as this water has a high mineral content. Municipal water (generic tap water) isn't used because it contains many contaminants.

Harvesting & Distillation

Plants are harvested in specific seasons and at specific times of day, both of which determine the strength of the various compounds in the plant. For example, a plant harvested in the morning may produce far more of one constituent than a plant harvested later in the afternoon. The percentage of plant bloom and its maturity are also important, as well as weather conditions during harvest. When harvested, plants are protected from environmental contaminants and distilled as soon as possible.

The quality of the equipment, the metals from which the equipment is made, and the distillation process can all impact the quality of the oil.

After harvesting, the plants are steam-distilled using the proper temperature and pressure for the right amount of time. Even small changes in the amount of pressure and the length of time the pressure is applied can greatly change the medicinally active compounds in an oil. Many commercial distillers cut costs by reducing preparation time (saving money on equipment use and equipment wear and tear), which can damage or destroy any therapeutic value in the oil.

No synthetic chemicals should be used or added to the water during steam distillation as they can affect the integrity of the oil, although some plant constituents must be extracted using a solvent such as alcohol.

Oil extracted from plants harvested at the wrong time of the day or from those that were incorrectly distilled might be pure but wouldn't be considered therapeutic-grade. To be considered therapeutic, the compounds specific to that oil must be present in the right percentage.

"Natural" or "Organic" Oils?

The terms "natural" and "organic" don't relate to whether an oil has therapeutic properties as organic standards have nothing to do with how the plant was harvested or prepared.

Therapeutic Oils Are Costly to Produce

As you can imagine, producing pure, therapeutic-grade essential oils is expensive. Hundreds or even thousands of pounds of raw plant materials may be needed to produce only a single pound of essential oil. This is why corporations that mass-produce synthetic oils use high pressures, high temperatures, and chemical solvents to distill the largest amount of oil in the shortest time possible. It's estimated that for every 1 pound of pure essential oil created, 110 pounds of synthetic oils are created.

Categories of Essential Oils

The chemical constituents used in essential oils are grouped into the following categories. The consituents in these compounds must be present in the right percentage to be considered therapeutic:

1. Phenols – antiseptic, antibacterial, very strong and can cause skin irritation
2. Terpenes - the most common, there are over 3,000
3. Alcohols - energizing, cleansing, antiseptic, antiviral
4. Carboxylic Acids - stimulating, cleansing
5. Ethers - balancing and calming, antidepressant effect
6. Aldehydes - antimicrobial, anti-inflammatory
7. Ketones - decongestants, analgesic benefits
8. Esters - soothing, balancing, antifungal, antistress
9. Oxides - respiratory decongesting, sinus clearing
10. Lactones - antiseptic, antiparasitic, anti-inflammatory
11. Coumarins - antiviral, antibacterial, antifungal
12. Furanoids - benefits of either lactones or courmarins

How Essential Oils Enter the Body

Essential oils penetrate cell membranes and diffuse throughout our blood and tissues. The fat-soluble structure of essential oils is very similar to the membranes of our cells, and because the molecules are very small, they can more easily penetrate the cells. When applied to our skin, they can travel throughout our body in minutes.

Whether essential oils are inhaled, taken orally, or used on our skin, the fragrance of a pure, therapeutic-grade essential oil can have a dramatic effect on our mind and body. When we inhale a scent, the odor molecules stimulate the lining of our nerve cells and trigger electrical impulses to different parts of our brain, including the limbic lobe—our emotional control center.

Essential Oil Certifications

The European community has very tight controls over the standards of botanical extracts and who can administer essential oils for medicinal purposes. **Only practitioners that have received the proper training and certification can practice as certified aromatherapists.**

In the US, however, it's a different story. Essential oils haven't been recognized medicinally, nor is any degree of training or education required to treat with or use essential oils. Anybody can call themselves an aromatherapist, even those who have little to no education on botanicals. This lack of recognized certification to therapeutically treat with essential oils has seriously damaged both the discipline and credibility of aromatherapy in the US.

Two standards have been established for the quality of essential oils:

The International Organization for Standardization (ISO)

The ISO is a worldwide federation based in Switzerland that sets the standards for a variety of products, not just essential oils.

Association Français de Normalization (AFNOR)

The AFNOR sets standards for a variety of products and services that represent the general standard set for a specific group of essential oils. They don't address the hundreds of minor trace components that are necessary for medicinal purposes. They only set the minimum standards for quality, safety, reliability, and performance.

The standards for both agencies with regard to essential oils are considered the same, and there are many essential oils for which neither agency has set standards. In recognition of this, several companies have developed their own standards using state-of-the-art equipment. Young Living is just one example of an essential-oil producer that has compiled a reference library of over 280,000 compounds and developed their own standards to guarantee the highest-possible medicinal value for their oils.

Highly sophisticated instruments are used in Europe to test the constituents present in essential oils, but within the US, few companies have the equipment to conduct a proper analysis of these oils. Most are used to analyze synthetic chemicals and are unable to analyze pure essential-oil constituents.

It's very important to buy oils from a reputable manufacturer that produces therapeutic-grade essential oils. My personal choice is **Young Living Essential Oils** as my research has shown me that they set very high standards for planting, harvesting, and distilling of their essential oils.

52 Essential Oils

There are many different essential oils to choose from; some are sold as single essential oils, and others are mixed into a blend. Thousands of clinical studies over several decades prove the powerful effects of essential oils and show their enormous potential to treat conditions ranging from acne to cancer. Following is a list of 52 oils commonly used to treat a wide variety of health conditions, each one backed by clinical studies. As the topic of essential oils can easily fill an entire book, detailed information on how to use these and many other oils for health conditions can be found in two guides I highly recommend: *Essential Oils Desk Reference, 6th Edition* by Life Publishing,[1] and the *Essential Oils Integrative Medical Guide* by D. Gary Young, ND.[2]

ESSENTIAL OIL	MEDICINAL PROPERTIES	USES
Angelica	Anticoagulant, relaxant	Respiratory infection, PMS, indigestion, anxiety
Anise	Anticoagulant, anesthetic, antioxidant, diuretic, antitumor	Arthritic conditions, cancer
Basil	Antispasmodic, antiviral, antibacterial, anti-inflammatory, muscle relaxant	Migraines, respiratory infections, insect bites
Bergamot	Antibacterial, antidepressant, hormonal support	Depression, anxiety, parasites, viral infections
Cardamom	Antispasmodic, antiparasitic, antiseptic, diuretic	Respiratory infections, skin conditions, water retention
Carrot Seed	Antiseptic, diuretic, antiparasitic	Water retention, skin conditions (psoriasis, eczema)
Cassia	Anti-inflammatory, antifungal, antibacterial, antiviral, anticoagulant	Fungal infections (candida, ringworm), arteriosclerosis, atherosclerosis, cataracts
Cedarwood	Antibacterial	Hair loss (alopecia), skin conditions (eczema, psoriasis, acne)
Celery Seed	Antibiotic, antirheumatic, diuretic	Arthritis, rheumatism, liver disorders (hepatitis)
Chamomile	Anti-inflammatory, antioxidant, antitumor	Arthritis, carpal tunnel syndrome, skin conditions (acne, psoriasis, eczema), arteriosclerosis
Cinnamon Bark	Anti-inflammatory, antioxidant, antibacterial, antiviral, antifungal, anticoagulant, antiparasitic, cardiovascular stimulant	Infectious diseases, viral infections, ulcers, heart disease
Citronella	Antibacterial, antifungal, antioxidant, anti-inflammatory, antiparasitic	Respiratory infections, skin conditions (acne, eczema, psoriasis), intestinal disorders, worms, anxiety
Clary Sage	Antioxidant, anticoagulant, antifungal, antitumor, relaxant, cholesterol-reducing, PMS	High cholesterol, leukemia, hormonal imbalance, circulatory disorders, insomnia
Clove	Antimicroblial, antifungal, antiviral, antioxidant, anti-inflammatory, anticoagulant, antiparasitic, antiemetic	Cardiovascular disease, parasites, respiratory infections, ulcers, acne
Coriander	Anti-inflammatory, sedative	Arthritis, intestinal disorders
Cumin	Anti-inflammatory, antitumor, antiviral, antioxidant, immune stimulant, cancer, infectious disease	Cancer, infectious diseases, digestive disorders
Dill	Antibacterial, blood sugar regulator, antispasmodic	Digestive disorders, diabetes
Fennel	Anti-inflammatory, antitumor, digestive aid, antiparasitic, antiseptic, antispasmodic	Cancer, parasites, arthritis, rheumatism, urinary tract infections, digestive disorders

Frankincense	Antitumor, antidepressant, immune stimulant	Cancer, inflammation, respiratory infections, depression
Geranium	Anti-inflammatory, antitumor, antibacterial, antifungal, antioxidant, antispasmodic, antiparasitic, circulatory stimulant	Skin conditions (acne, eczema, psoriasis, dermatitis), fungal infections, viral infections, hormonal imbalances
Ginger	Anti-inflammatory, anticoagulant, antiemetic, antitumor, digestive aid	Arthritis, rheumatism, cancer, nausea, respiratory infections, digestive disorders
Goldenrod	Anti-inflammatory, diuretic, antihypertensive	Urinary tract infections, high blood pressure, circulatory disorders
Grapefruit	Antitumor, antiseptic, diuretic, antidepressant, fat-dissolving	Depression, obesity, cellulite, Alzheimer's disease, fluid retention
Helichrysum	Antiviral, anticoagulant, antispasmodic, chelator, nerve generator	Arteriosclerosis, atherosclerosis, skin conditions (scar tissue, malassezia, pachydermatis), hypertension, blood clots, circulatory disorders, varicose veins, herpes simplex
Hyssop	Anti-inflammatory, antibacterial, antiviral, antiparasitic, decongestant	Respiratory infections, parasites, viral infections, circulatory disorders
Jasmine	Antibacterial, antidepressant	Anxiety, depression, skin conditions (eczema, psoriasis, acne)
Juniper	Antiseptic, circulatory stimulant, nerve regenerator, detoxifier	Skin conditions, urinary & bladder infections
Lavender	Antibacterial, anti-inflammatory, antifungal, antitumor, antiemetic, vasodilator, relaxant	Respiratory infections, skin conditions (acne, eczema, psoriasis), burns, arteriosclerosis, insomnia, anxiety
Lemon	Antitumor, antiseptic, relaxant, immune stimulant	Digestive aid, hypertension, arteriosclerosis, circulatory disorders, parasites
Lemongrass	Antifungal, antibacterial, anti-inflammatory, circulatory stimulant, antiparasitic	Respiratory infections, digestive disorders, parasites, salmonella, infections, halitosis
Manuka	Antibacterial, antifungal, anti-inflammatory	Skin conditions (infections, acne, dermatitis), fungal infections, respiratory infections (tonsillitis, sore throat)
Marjoram	Antibacterial, antifungal, antihypertensive, joint & muscle discomfort	Arthritis, rheumatism, circulatory disorders, respiratory infection, fungal infections
Mugwort	Antibacterial, antifungal, antiparasitic, digestive aid	Worms, digestive disorders, gout, headaches, malaria

Myrrh	Antioxidant, antitumor, anti-inflammatory, antiviral, antiparasitic	Cancer, fungal infections, skin conditions (cracked & chapped skin)
Myrtle	Antimutagenic, antibacterial, decongestant, prostate stimulant, thyroid stimulant	Respiratory & sinus infections, skin conditions (acne, psoriasis)
Neroli	Antiparasitic, antidepressant, antihypertensive	Depression, anxiety, insomnia, hypertension, menopause
Nugmeg	Anti-inflammatory, antiparasitic, antiseptic, circulatory & adrenal stimulant, growth hormone stimulator, antithrombotic	Arthritis, rheumatism, hypertension, neuropathy, thrombosis, Alzheimer's disease
Orange	Antitumor, circulatory stimulant, relaxant, anticoagulant	Cancer, arteriosclerosis, hypertension, insomnia
Oregano	Antiviral, antibacterial, anti-inflammatory, antiparasitic, immune stimulant	Infectious diseases, infections, arthritis, rheumatism
Palmarosa	Antibacterial, antifungal, antiviral, skin cell growth stimulator	Fungal infections, circulatory disorders, skin problems (acne, eczema, psoriasis)
Patchouli	Anti-inflammatory, antimicrobial, antitumor, antibacterial, relaxant	Skin conditions (acne, eczema), hypertension
Peppermint	Anti-inflammatory, antitumor, antibacterial, antiviral, antifungal	Viral & fungal infections, respiratory infections, skin conditions (eczema, psoriasis, dermatitis, acne)
Rose	Anti-inflammatory, relaxant, aphrodisiac	Anxiety, viral infections, skin conditions (scarring, wrinkles, stretch marks), uplifting
Rosemary	Antitumor, antifungal, antibacterial, antiparasitic, liver-protective	Infectious diseases, respiratory infections, impaired memory, liver conditions
Sandalwood	Antitumor, antiviral, immune stimulant	Cancer, viral infections, skin conditions (acne, scarring), herpes simplex
Spearmint	Anti-inflammatory, antiseptic, digestive aid, metabolic stimulant	Digestive disorders, hepatitis, obesity
Spikenard	Antibacterial, antifungal, anti-inflammatory, relaxant	Nervous tension, insomnia
Tea Tree Oil (Melaleuca Alternifolia)	Antibacterial, antimicrobial, antiviral, antifungal, antiparasitic	Fungal infections, skin conditions (acne), gum disease
Thyme	Antimicrobial, antifungal, antiviral, antiparasitic	Infectious diseases, heart disease, Alzheimer's disease
Valerian	Sedative, tranquilizer	Insomnia, anxiety, nervous tension
Wintergreen	Anticoagulant, anti-inflammatory, vasodilator, antispasmodic, antihypertensive	Musculoskeletal disorders, arthritis, rheumatism, arteriosclerosis, hypertension
Ylang Ylang	Vasodilator, antispasmodic, anti-inflammatory, antiparasitic, heartbeat regulator	Cardiac disorders, hypertension, depression, anxiety, intestinal disorders

Benefits of Essential Oils

Essential oils have the power to:

1. Raise the vibration of our body.
2. Destroy infectious diseases or slow the progression of diseases such as cancer; many are antibacterial, antiviral, antifungal, antimicrobial, anti-inflammatory, and antiseptic.
3. Act as broad-spectrum antibiotics (e.g., oregano oil); clinical studies have found some essential oils are more effective than traditional antibiotics and can kill viral and bacterial infections that have become antibiotic-resistant.
4. Help remove parasites, such as worms, from the body (antiparasitic); some are effective at repelling insects (insecticidal).
5. Be some of the most powerful antioxidants, as confirmed by ORAC testing developed at Tufts University.
6. Stimulate blood flow, which increases oxygen and nutrient delivery; some can reduce blood pressure and heart rate and decrease the thickness of the blood, increasing circulation.
7. Purify air space when diffused by increasing negative ions, eliminate bacteria, and eliminate cooking odors and odors from mold.
8. Stimulate the production of antibodies, endorphins, enzymes, and hormones.
9. Chelate toxins, such as heavy metals and petrochemicals, from our body.
10. Stimulate faster wound healing.
11. Break down potentially harmful chemicals and render them nontoxic due to their ionizing action (providing negative ions).
12. Reduce appetite by stimulating the hypothalamus, the area of the brain that governs how full we feel.

Eucalyptus oil is a great example of an oil that's been studied and found to have antimicrobial effects, while frankincense has produced antitumor effects. Clinical research shows us that these and other oils have a tremendous potential to help treat a wide range of health conditions.

Because the molecules of essential oils are so tiny, they quickly penetrate the tissues of the skin and circulate throughout the entire body, where they are then metabolized like other nutrients.

Essential Oils Raise Our Vibrational Frequency

As we discovered earlier, everything has a vibrational frequency—our food, our bodies, and every type of disease. Pure essential oils emit some of the highest vibrational frequencies of any natural substance on earth. Using these oils helps create an inhospitable environment for disease, bacteria, viruses, and fungi and helps raise the frequency of our body.

To emit their naturally high frequencies, these essential oils must be medicinal- (therapeutic-) grade, and they must not contain any impurities or contaminants. They should be organically harvested from their natural environment, such as forests, prairies, and deserts.

Highly sophisticated frequency-measuring devices show us that several essential oils resonate at some of the highest frequencies of plants on the planet:

Rose (Rosa damascena) – 320 MHz
Lavender (Lavendula angustifolia) – 118 MHz
Myrrh (Commiphora myrrha) – 105 MHz
Blue chamomile (Matricaria recutita) – 105 MHz

Juniper (Juniperus osteosperma) – 98 MHz
Sandalwood (Santalum album) – 96 MHz
Angelica (Angelica archangelica) – 85 MHz
Peppermint (Mentha piperita) – 78 MHz

These high frequencies make them an important part of our high vibrational journey. By using these oils, we can help raise the frequency of our body, which in turn improves both our health and our state of mind.

Essential Oils & Drug-Resistant Bacteria

Drug-resistant bacteria are germs on steroids. Due to the overuse of antibiotics in both the healthcare system and in our food (especially in the meat industry—over 80 percent of the US supply of antibiotics is pumped into confined farm animals daily), we now have an epidemic of drug-resistant bacteria. However, essential oils such as lemongrass, lemon myrtle, and cinnamon can inhibit drug-resistant bacteria such as staphylococcus aureus (MRSA). Spanish oregano and cinnamon essential oils were tested to be above 95 percent efficient against candida albicans, E. coli, and streptococcus.

As with using herbal medicine, there is no evidence of built-up resistance when using essential oils due to the intricacy of the hundreds of chemical constituencies within the oil.

- In testing 13 essential oils against different bacteria, all 13 oils completely inhibited the growth of helicobacter pylori. No resistance developed to either lemongrass or lemon verbena, even though resistance to the antibiotic clarithromycin developed under the same conditions.[3]

The complexity of essential oils makes them powerful in preventing the spread of bacteria because bacteria have a difficult time mutating in the presence of so many different antibacterial constituents.

Essential Oils Help Detoxify the Body

The chemicals in personal-care products, such as lotions and moisturizers, can stay trapped in fatty tissues under the skin for years until a topical substance such as an essential oil starts to remove them. Chemicals in the water we drink and the air we breathe also create a toxic buildup, as does exposure to household chemicals that, by their nature, contain highly toxic ingredients. When we use essential oils, they react with these chemicals to help detoxify them from our body. At the same time, drinking plenty of fresh water while eating highly nutritious foods helps the essential oils work quicker and more effectively on our body.

- In a 6 month clinical trial of 3,000 patiets, specific scents were used to trigger significant weight loss in those who achieved no success with other programs. Average weight loss exceeded 30 pounds.[4]
- In a double-blind, randomized sexual-arousal study, 31 male volunteers were given 30 different essential oils. Each one experienced a marked increase in arousal (based on penile blood pressure). The two scents that produced the most excitement were lavender and pumpkin. The study concluded that the fragrances increased sexual desire by stimulating the amygdala.[5]
- Essential oils have been found to increase levels of oxygen in the brain by as much as 28 percent, which can have a dramatic impact on our emotional state, our learning ability, our ability to concentrate, and our hormonal balance.

Essential Oils Are Safe & Noninvasive

When used correctly, essential oils are a safe, gentle, powerful healing method that can be used on us adults, our children, and our pets. Unlike the synthetic chemicals used in most essential oils, pure essential oils don't disturb our body's balance. Even if one constituent in the oil is too strong, another will often counteract it. Synthetic chemicals, however, often contain ingredients that are biological irritants.

When used correctly, it's rare to experience any side effects from using therapeutic-grade essential oils, except for general detoxification symptoms (temporary irritation, nausea, or headaches) as toxins are released from the body. Symptoms depend on how long the toxins have been in the body, how much have accumulated, and what type of toxins they are.

How to Use Essential Oils

Essential oils are most often:

1. Diluted in various "carrier" oils (commonly used for massage)
2. Used undiluted, either orally or topically
3. Inhaled [research shows this has a strong effect on the hypothalamus (the hormone command center of the body) and the limbic system (the seat of our emotions)]

Depending on what condition is being treated, one method may be more effective than another. For example, inhalation is the best method to use for increasing the production of growth hormones, but a topical application works better for joint and muscle disorders.

Now, let's go over the basics of how to use essential oils.

Diluted vs. Undiluted

Although some essential oils are used undiluted, most need to be diluted in a carrier oil when used either internally or on the skin, with some requiring more dilution than others. Dilution is shown as a ratio, for example:

1:1 ratio = an equal amount of carrier oil and essential oil
4:1 ratio = 4 parts carrier oil and 1 part essential oil

Essential oils are oil-soluble, not water-soluble, so they must be diluted in oil. When using essential oils, it's a good idea to always keep a bottle of organic, unrefined, cold-pressed oil available to dilute them if they cause skin irritation. Some essential oils (considered the "hot" oils) should always be diluted, including cinnamon, thyme, oregano, eucalyptus, lemon, and orange oils.

When mixing blends or diluting in a carrier oil, use glass or earthenware containers. Avoid plastic as plastic particles can leach into the oil and the skin.

Skin Testing the Oil

Always do a skin test before applying any essential oil to your skin.

1. Before testing essential oils, it's important to clean your skin first. The rashes and allergic reactions some people experience from using therapeutic-grade essential oils are sometimes the result of the oil interacting with synthetic, petroleum-based chemicals on the skin from lotions, moisturizers, soaps, shampoos, hair-care products, and deodorants. Lauryl sulfate and propylene glycol are two very common examples found in thousands of personal-care products.
2. Using a chemical-free and fragrance-free soap or cleanser, clean a small, sensitive area of your skin (e.g., on the inside of your wrist or the bottom of your foot) and apply several drops of the oil. If using more than one oil, apply one at a time. Allow 15 minutes between applying each oil to see how your body responds.
3. Some essential oils can cause skin irritation when applied undiluted. If you have any negative skin reaction, dilute 1-3 drops of the essential oil in a half teaspoon of carrier oil, then do a second skin-patch test. If redness or irritation occurs again, immediately apply the carrier oil to reduce irritation and then apply the essential oil only on the bottoms of your feet.

How to Apply Essential Oils

Oils can be used anywhere on the body except around the eyes or in the ears. The following are some of the most common methods we can use to apply them, along with important usage guidelines.

Note: If you accidentally swallow an essential oil, immediately eat or drink an oil-based food such as avocado or a teaspoon of liquid oil. Also, if you have high blood pressure, use extra caution with high ketone oils (such as basil, rosemary, sage, tansy, and mugwort).

Applied to Skin: Use 1-2 drops of oil on 2-3 different locations twice each day, increasing to four times if needed. Allow the oil to absorb for 2-3 minutes before getting dressed. For disorders that aren't location-specific, apply the oil(s) wherever it's convenient or on the bottoms of your feet.

Most oils are safe to apply directly to your skin. If any irritation occurs, dilute it with more carrier oil. The bottoms of the feet are considered safe locations to apply essential oils topically, but it's always recommended to test for skin sensitivity by applying 3-6 drops of a single or blended oil and spread over the bottom of your foot or on your wrist. Some essential oils are photosensitive and can cause skin rashes when exposed to sunlight or UV rays.

Inhaled/Diffused: When inhaling directly, place 2-3 drops in the palm of one hand and rub both hands together. Cup your hands over your nose and mouth and inhale deeply, being careful to avoid your eyes. Several drops can also be added to a bowl of hot (not boiling) water; you simply then inhale the steaming vapors. Draping a towel over your head and the bowl can increase the intensity of the vapors.

For therapeutic benefits, inhale 2-3 times daily, or diffuse 2-3 times daily (see below) for 30 minutes.

Internally: Some oils can be diluted and taken internally, whereas other cannot; therefore, use extreme caution when using internally. Even a single drop of some essential oils can be toxic, while in larger doses, others can be fatal.

Most essential oils taste unpleasant. Add them to standard-size gelatin capsules (size 0) available at most health-food stores or online. This way, you can simply swallow the oil-filled capsule. If you're taking more than a few drops of any essential oil each day, I strongly recommend working with a health professional.

Massage: For massage, apply 2 drops of a single oil or a blend of oils on the skin and massage. For a large area, mix 2 drops with 1 teaspoon of carrier oil. Some oils, such as almond, olive, coconut, or jojoba, can leave grease stains on fabrics.

Acupuncture/Acupressure: Many licensed acupuncturists use essential oils to increase the effectiveness of their acupuncture treatments. Essential oils can also be used in conjunction with acupressure by applying the oil and then pressing firmly and releasing.

Warm Compress/Cold Pack: For deeper penetrations, soak a cloth or towel in hot water. Wring it out, and place it on top of the area where 1-3 drops of the essential oil have been applied. Cover the hot, damp towel with a dry towel for 15-30 minutes. If you feel a burning sensation that causes any discomfort, add a little carrier oil to the area.

Similar to a warm compress, after applying the oil, use a cold pack or ice pack that forms to the body (such as a bag of peas) when treating swollen or inflamed tissue.

Bathing: This is more challenging as oils don't mix with water. If more than 2-3 drops are needed for therapeutic benefits, the oil should first be mixed with Epsom salts or an unscented bath-gel base before being added to the water. Adding more than 10 drops of undiluted essential oil directly to water can irritate the skin as the oil floats, undiluted, on top of the water.

Vaginally or Rectally: Oils can also be taken vaginally (for health problems such as vaginitis or candida) or rectally. To use it vaginally for infections, mix 10 drops of essential oil in 1 tablespoon of coconut oil and freeze until solid before inserting at bedtime. If used during the day, insert a tampon after applying to prevent leakage. For external lesions, mix 20 drops of essential oil to 2 tablespoons of carrier oil and add to sanitary pad. To use rectally for hemorrhoids, candida, or colon-related conditions, mix 10-15 drops of oil in a tablespoon of carrier oil, pour it into a small plastic syringe, and inject it into the rectum before sleep to retain the mixture for as long as possible. Clean and disinfect the syringe after each use.

Using Diffusers: Many essential oils and oil blends are extremely effective for eliminating and destroying airborne germs and bacteria. Cold-air diffusers spray a microfine mist of essential oils into the air where they can remain suspended for hours, no burning or heating required (heating can reduce the therapeutic benefits of the oil). If the oil is too thick though, it may plug the diffuser.

Diffuse either 30 minutes 2-3 times each day or once for 1-2 hours, and diffuse one blend at a time if you're using different blends. Wash the diffuser with water and natural, unscented soap only.

If you don't have a diffuser, add several drops of the oil to a spray bottle with one cup of fresh, pure water and shake well before spraying throughout the day.

Oils can also be added to humidifiers and vaporizers.

Storage & Shelf Life

If you take care of your essential oils, they'll hold their potency for years. Therapeutic-grade essential oils don't go rancid.

1. Essential oils should always be stored in a cool location in dark-colored glass bottles to protect the oil from any light that can chemically alter or degrade it. Unlike plastic, glass will not leach any chemicals into the oil. Store away from light. The darker the storage area, the longer your oil will maintain its original chemistry.
2. The lid should always be tightly sealed to prevent oxygen in the air from oxidizing the oil.

Even though many essential oils can be used on children and pets, treat these oils like medications and keep them well out of reach.

Whew! We've Learned a Lot about Food!

Congratulations! You've just finished exploring the incredible power of food and essential oils to detoxify and raise your vibrational frequency. Now it's time to take a breather—literally—and move on to the next part of the protocol to talk about the power of breath. Did you know that the way you breathe not only determines how well oxygenated your body is, it also directly impacts your vibrational state? Let's explore the link between breath and energy.

BREATH

BREATH & ENERGY

The first and last act of physical life is to breathe. From the moment we're born, we begin to breathe. We instinctively draw the breath into our lungs and infuse our body with life-giving oxygen. Our life is entirely dependent on our ability to breathe oxygen, and this is true not only for both the human and animal worlds, but also for all plant life.

Although we may go for many days without eating, we can measure in minutes how long we can survive without breath.

Breath Is an Energetic Food

It's not only the act of breathing itself that's important for our life, the quality of our breath directly relates to the quality of our health and our emotional and mental state of mind. Our posture, stooping shoulders, and shallow breathing significantly reduce the amount of oxygen we take in, which in turn affects the cellular integrity of our entire body.

Breath is an energetic food, a rhythmic flow of oxygen and subtle energy continually infusing our entire body. Systems of healing such as Ayurveda and traditional Chinese medicine understand and respect the power of breath and the impact that reduced oxygen flow has on our body.

Prana

In Sanskrit, the term "prana" means "life force" or "vital energy." This refers not only to the life-giving oxygen in the air, but also to the essence of energy that gives life. It refers to something much subtler—the primal essence of life force that distinguishes a living thing from a lifeless thing.

In Ayurveda, absorbing as much prana as possible from breathing, food, and our surroundings is vitally important. The practice of breath control and simple breathing techniques are used to absorb a much greater amount of prana than what we receive during mainstream, shallow breathing. Deep, mindful breathing more fully oxygenates and increases our body's ability to rid itself of waste products and toxins. These breathing techniques are known in Sanskrit as "pranayama," translated to mean "mastery of the breath/vital energy."

Qi/Chi & Acupuncture

A very important part of the vitality equation and a founding principle of health in Oriental medicine is breathing deeply and fully oxygenating the body. This principle is based on the understanding that disease stems from an imbalance of Qi flowing throughout the body. There are various points on the skin where the flow of Qi is closest to the surface, which are called acupoints, and they're stimulated using acupuncture and acupressure.

We commonly hear today that "acupuncture stimulates the flow of energy in energy meridians throughout the body." But it would be more accurate to say that "acupuncture stimulates the flow of oxygen throughout the blood vessels." Let's take a look at how a simple mistranslation led to a misunderstanding of what Qi is.

A French monk named Georges Soulie de Morant lived in China from 1901 to 1917. During his stay, Morant translated the original Chinese medical texts, despite having no medical training nor any training in the ancient Chinese language. His translation is the one the Western world is familiar with today and is the source for all the textbooks used in Western schools of Chinese medicine.

Translation of Qi = Oxygen. Although Morant translated "Qi" as energy, the concept of Qi in China doesn't resemble the Western concept of "energy." In the original texts, the term "da qi" refers to "great air," which translates to "oxygen." Qi is defined as "air" or "the essence of air." It doesn't mean energy. The Chinese knew that something in the air we breathe is essential to life and that something in the air circulates throughout our body in our blood. At the time of the original text, the term "oxygen" hadn't yet been defined. Today, the closest translation of Qi is "oxygen." Despite this translation, many practitioners feel that, similar to prana, "great air" also relates to a more vital essence within the air itself, in addition to oxygen.

Translation of Xue Mai = Blood Vessel. The original texts also described Qi as flowing through "Xue Mai," which translates as "blood vessel." But Morant translated "Xue Mai" to mean the French word "meridian."

The air we breathe contains more than simply oxygen, hydrogen, and nitrogen, and breathing does more than simply oxygenate our blood and our body's systems. Rhythmic breathing brings us into a harmonious, higher vibration with both ourselves and the natural world around us; it increases our levels of awareness and intuition, focus, and concentration; and it literally dissolves stress. It's a very important part of the health equation.

How We Breathe

Our respiratory system consists of:

- Two lungs and the air passages leading to them
- The trachea (windpipe)
- Two bronchi (air tubes that branch off from the trachea to each lung)
- Diaphragm (dome-shaped muscle that contracts when we breathe in and relaxes when we breathe out)

As we draw air into our nose or mouth, it's warmed and drawn into our lungs. Our diaphragm then contracts to increase the size of our chest cavity and our lungs as we inhale air. It then relaxes, exhaling air from our body.

The muscles we use for breathing control the movement of the ribs and the diaphragm. When we breathe in, these muscles expand our chest capacity, allowing our lungs to expand properly. Without them, our lungs can't expand. The health and strength of these muscles and their ability to expand our lungs are very important.

When we inhale, oxygen fills our lungs and enters our bloodstream through tiny vessels in our lungs. The oxygen then combines with hemoglobin (a red protein that transports oxygen) and travels to every single cell and tissue to oxygenate our body. This assists in cleansing, renewing, and replacing each cell as necessary. As we exhale, waste products are released.

The greater the amount of oxygen we bring into our body, the more oxygenated our body becomes, and the more waste is removed from our body.

When we breathe shallowly, our body becomes oxygen-deficient and less waste is removed.

It's very important that our blood is purified by breathing deeply and fully; otherwise, impurities build up in the system and contribute to disease because our cells and tissues (and, in turn, our organs) aren't sufficiently nourished. Not only that, but the oxygenation of our blood affects our digestive system.

The less oxygenated our blood is, the darker and more "bluish" and acidic it becomes. The more oxygenated our blood is, the richer and brighter the red color and the more alkaline it becomes.

The act of breathing also "massages" our organs and exercises the muscles in the trunk of our body. This is an important form of exercise necessary for our internal health.

Energy & Nerve Force

From the limited medical (Western) perspective, we breathe in oxygen, and it's then distributed throughout the circulatory system.

When we begin to breathe more mindfully and use the entire capacity of our lungs to oxygenate our cells, we naturally begin to not only cleanse and strengthen our entire body, but we also begin to raise its vibration.

The subtle energy that exists in the air we breathe infuses our body in higher and higher quantities. This isn't a "chemical" that traditional science can measure; it's an imperceptible ether. A noticeable difference in the quality of our health simply "happens" as a by-product of deeper breathing.

In earlier times, doctors commonly recommended that their patients travel "out to the country to breathe fresh country air" to help them heal from an illness. This is not only because the air is free of pollutants and industrial chemicals, but also because the energy of air around nature will always be more balanced and harmonious.

Nerve Force

The energy transmitted from our brain throughout our body by means of our nerves is known as "nerve force" and can be compared to an electric current. This nerve force causes our heart to beat, our lungs to breathe, our brain to function, and all involuntary systems of our body to work.

The oxygen in our blood not only cleanses the systems of our body, it also stimulates this nerve force. It increases the subtle energy that permeates us at a higher level and stimulates the functioning of our entire nervous system. The increase in this subtle energy is what helps raise our vibrational frequency, elevate us to a higher functioning, and causes us to experience higher states of consciousness.

Nose VS. Mouth Breathing

Our respiratory system gives us the ability to breathe through either our mouth or our nose, but there's a big difference between the two when it comes to the quality of our breath.

Apart from our ability to smell, there's another important reason we have our nostrils. Before air enters our lungs, it's first filtered by the nasal cavity. Without the benefit of this filtering, we're more likely to catch infections and contagious diseases through mouth breathing. Here's why:

- When we breathe through our nose, air is filtered and strained of dust, dirt, and other foreign substances before it reaches our lungs. When we breathe using our mouths instead, the air is carried straight to our lungs without the benefit of any filtering.
- Air is warmed to a greater degree when taken in through our nose by the warm mucous membranes. When we breathe in cold air through our mouth, it's more likely to dry out our throat during the night when we sleep, which is why we sometimes experience throat dryness when we wake up.

When animals in nature are at rest or sleeping, they always breathe through their nasal cavity. They instinctively know this is the natural and preferred way for the body to breathe.

The Three Types of Breathing

Let's take a look at the three different ways we breathe and which one we should focus on:

1. **High Breathing (shallow breathing)**
   Shallow breathing involves using only the upper part of our chest and lungs. It's considered the least desirable form of breathing as the upper lungs have a small air capacity. This results in our body absorbing smaller amounts of oxygen, which in turn leads to a host of problems, such as the buildup of toxins, reduced mental clarity, and lower nerve energy.

   Shallow breathing is the most common breathing style, primarily due to posture, stress, and a high-paced lifestyle. Tight-fitting clothes, intense concentration, anger, and other intense emotions also cause us to breathe shallowly. The more we breathe shallowly, the more likely we are to also breathe through our mouth.

   When we practice shallow breathing, we use only a small portion of our lungs, instead of their full capacity. Our body is then under-oxygenated because we're built to be nourished by the oxygenation of our entire lung capacity.

2. **Middle Breathing (thoracic breathing)**
   It's not as shallow as high breathing, but middle breathing is still far from ideal as our abdomen is engaged to only a small degree. When we're relaxed and not stressed or anxious, we often move from high breathing to middle breathing.

3. **Deep Breathing**
   Deep breathing (also called abdominal or diaphragmatic breathing) involves using not only our entire lung space, but also fully engaging our abdomen. Each time we inhale, not only are our lungs expanded, but our stomach and abdomen are gently pushed out to intake a larger amount of air. When we exhale, our lungs, stomach, and abdomen return to their normal positions. Deep breathing is far superior to high or middle breathing because we absorb far more oxygen due to the increased surface area and capacity of our lungs. The abdominal organs are also massaged by the diaphragm as it rises and falls, and our overall circulation improves.

In Ayurveda, the practice of deep breathing is also known as the "complete breath" and is considered fundamental to achieving a higher level of awareness. Let's take a closer look at deep breathing and learn how to practice the complete breath.

DEEP BREATHING

The more we actively practice deeper breathing, the more it becomes our natural and preferred way to breathe, and the more we experience a healthier, higher vibrational state. First, let's talk about two things that can significantly affect how we breathe: our clothing and our posture.

Clothing

The first thing to address is our clothing. We need to avoid wearing tight or constrictive clothing because it's not healthy for our circulation, nor for our breathing habits. If you must wear tight, constrictive clothes, wear them only when necessary and for as short a time as possible. For women, tight waistbands on pantyhose are especially constrictive. Look for brands that don't have tight, elasticized waists, or consider wearing stockings (not only are they better for you, but they're fun and sexy too!).

Posture

Posture is one of the biggest contributors to shallow breathing, so let's address how to improve our posture by becoming conscious of straightening our spine. Many of us have grown accustomed to sitting with slouched shoulders at our office or on the couch in the evenings, often because we're hunched over a computer, laptop, tablet, or smartphone. Let's start by actively relearning and practicing improving our posture.

1. Either stand up tall, or sit erect with your arms at your sides.
2. Raise your shoulders and collarbones up slightly while bringing your shoulder blades back and closer together. This helps open the chest.
3. Lengthen your spine by imagining the crown of your head energetically "reaching" up toward the sky. This tiny movement helps both lengthen and straighten the spine.
4. Slowly and deeply begin to inhale into your lungs to a count of 6, all the way down into your belly as you feel it expand, hold for a count of 3, and then slowly exhale throughout your nose to a count of 6 while gently drawing your belly in.
5. Now, let your shoulders slouch forward and inward again, and allow your lower back to curve as your stomach sinks back. Try the inhalation and exhalation exercise again, and you'll notice how much more difficult it is to breathe the air deeply and down into your abdomen.

Deep breathing begins with practicing it several times a day, and then more often, to the point that you naturally begin to breathe deeper throughout your day until it becomes a habit. Simply draw in longer and deeper breaths by expanding both your chest and your stomach each time you inhale.

Paying attention to posture and breathing deeper go hand in hand. The more you remember to adjust your posture each time you consciously deepen your breath, the sooner your body will naturally adapt to this correct posture.

The Complete Breath

Although there are many different types of breathing exercises, the one we're going to learn is a form of deep breathing based on an Ayurvedic technique called the "complete breath." It's very easy to learn and takes only 5 minutes to do each day.

The Complete Breath

The complete breath engages your entire respiratory system, expanding the lungs to their fullest capacity. The first time you practice this exercise, place both your hands lightly on your belly to feel it gently rise and fall. This helps you more fully connect with the action of your breathing and the impact it has on your body.

1. Sit or stand with an erect spine, pulling your shoulders slightly back to open the chest. If you prefer a seated position, sit cross-legged and rest your wrists on your knees with palms facing up (called the "lotus pose" in yoga).
2. Inhale through your nose and draw the air down into your belly, feeling it gently expand as air is drawn down. As the intake of breath continues, your mid-chest is then expanded, followed by the upper chest. Feel your chest expand in all directions.
3. At the height of the breath, pause for several seconds.
4. When you exhale, draw your belly in and up, slowly expelling the air from your body. Your upper chest is the last to deflate.
5. Begin by inhaling to a count of 6 seconds, pause for a count of 3, and exhale to a count of 6. Increase the number of seconds as your lung capacity increases. Work toward inhalation and exhalation seconds of 8-4-8 and 10-5-10.

In the beginning, you should do this type of breathing only during breathing exercises as it can cause dizziness or light-headedness.

Deep breathing is never a forced or uncomfortable breath. On the contrary, it's a very natural, rhythmic, fluid movement that you'll come to love as you feel a calmness and clarity infusing your body. You'll also develop a deeper connection with your body and how you feel.

If noises around you are distracting, instead of feeling annoyed, see these distractions as a great opportunity to practice tuning out the background noise. Turn your focus toward the sound and the experience of your breathing, and on counting the seconds. This will help you master your breath regardless of your surroundings.

Benefits of Deep Breathing

Breathing deeply throughout the day offers us several important benefits:

- When we use our lungs properly, we increase the health of our lung tissue. Healthy lung tissue resists germs and respiratory illnesses. By practicing deep breathing when we have a cold or the flu, we can significantly speed up our recovery time (especially when combined with essential oils).
- By more fully oxygenating our blood, we reduce the toxic load in our bloodstream, which reduces the toxins that circulate throughout our body.
- We transmit nerve currents more efficiently, which has a positive impact on our brain, spinal cord, and entire nervous system.
- We exercise the muscles of our respiratory system, which in turn massage and stimulate the liver, stomach, and other internal organs to help them function optimally.
- Most importantly, we increase the flow of energy, which helps elevate the energetic frequency of our entire being.

HOMEWORK

What better homework than to breathe ... deeply! Let's talk about a schedule for improving the quality of your breathing throughout the day.

Deep Breathing

Begin by practicing deep breathing each morning for 5 minutes when you wake up and each evening before you go to sleep. Simply lie on your back in bed and lengthen your body into a straight line. (Your eyes can be open or closed.) Begin to breathe deeper to a count of 6-3-6 (inhale for 6 seconds, hold for 3 seconds, exhale for 6 seconds). What a wonderful way to begin and end each day!

Throughout the day, look for occasions when you can take at least 1 minute to breathe deeply (while walking, working at a computer, going to the restroom, or watching TV, for example). Work up to once per hour, and then several times each hour. Soon, your breathing will naturally and permanently adapt to this deeper rhythm, and you won't need to count the seconds.

The more conscious you become of your breathing (the more you pay attention to it and remind yourself to practice it), the more it will become an automatic part of your daily life.

Introduce Distractions

After you've settled into a schedule of incorporating deeper breathing into your day, begin to practice deep breathing while surrounded by noises and other distractions (eyes open!), and during times of stress or frustration. Purposefully choose areas that are full of activity, such as a mall, a busy beach, or a subway, or when walking through a busy shopping street. You could also turn on an action movie or put on some loud music in the background.

One of the first things you may notice is how quickly your breathing becomes shallow when your environment changes and you become distracted.

The Complete Breath

Every day, at whatever time works best for you, practice the complete breath for 5 minutes. No matter how busy your day—even if it means doing it in the privacy of the bathroom—make sure you find time to practice.

Now that we've taken the time to relax, and we've learned that by breathing deeper we not only improve the flow of oxygen throughout our body but also the flow of energy throughout our entire being, it's time to move on to the next section and talk about taking action of the more energizing kind!

MOVEMENT

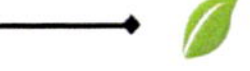

GETTING A MOVE ON

When we think of exercise, let's face it: the first thought that comes to mind is effort, and the first sound out of our mouth is a groan. When we think about spin classes, CrossFit, weight lifting, running, jogging, stair climbers, and ellipticals, we quickly turn on the TV and change the subject. What's worse—many of us don't enjoy the workout activities we do. For most people, fun and excitement fly out the window!

Even though we may feel invigorated after working out, we literally have to drag ourselves out the door to do it. This is why even though we all know that exercise is good for us, the average person ends up leading a very sedentary lifestyle. This isn't what exercising our body is about.

The key to exercise is to understand that our body primarily needs to move, and that the goal of exercise is to increase the flow of oxygen throughout our body to keep it both limber and flexible. The type of exercise our body needs should never spell misery. Exercise is about finding different ways to be active that we enjoy and to include these activities in our life.

Exercise is another area where the old paradigm no longer works. To add insult to injury, many slave away at the gym only to feel exhausted and run down. Continually overtaxing an already overstressed body isn't in the best interest of our health, nor is it in the best interest of high vibrational living.

Before we talk about both a healthy *and* enjoyable approach to exercise, let's first dispel some common myths.

MYTH #1: Aerobic exercise can get rid of my cellulite

Losing cellulite isn't about spending several hours a week on exercise machines or slaving away doing aerobics. Many people who exercise religiously suffer from cellulite, just as many who don't exercise have none. Losing cellulite is about healing connective tissue and releasing cellular congestion by normalizing the flow of nutrients into the cells and the flow of waste products out of the cells.

We do this by:

1. Eating the right foods that hydrate the body and release cellular congestion
2. Getting the body moving, and especially by incorporating stretching exercises
3. Skin brushing, which stimulates our skin (the largest organ of our body)

All 3 of these activities also mobilize and oxygenate our entire system. Exercise contributes to eliminating cellulite, but alone it rarely eliminates it because it doesn't address the root cause—cellular congestion.

The Sodium/Potassium Balance

Sodium and potassium work closely together to maintain a delicate balance within the cells of our body, making sure that nutrients are efficiently absorbed by the cells and tissues and that waste is removed. When our body retains excess fluids because there's too much sodium in our diet, this balance becomes damaged, and waste can't be effectively removed, creating cellular congestion.

The cells in our skin are held in a fibrous mesh, and when these cells become waterlogged from excess fluids, they expand and damage this fibrous mesh. The result is that our skin becomes less elastic and more prone to conditions such as cellulite. Potassium levels also fall due to unhealthy eating habits, leading to fatigue and irritability.

When the sodium/potassium ratio is changed, becoming heavily disproportionate toward sodium, a degeneration takes place. A severe potassium deficiency caused by excessive salt intake can also cause the muscles, valves, and arteries of the cardiovascular system to adapt by shrinking, calcifying, and scarring tissue. A long-term potential result is congestive heart failure.

When we take a look at the ratio of sodium to potassium in refined foods, the sodium content is far higher. In comparison, fresh fruits and vegetables are naturally either higher in potassium than sodium or found in a similar ratio.

Water Weight Loss

When we start a healthy diet, we often lose a dramatic amount of weight in the first 2 weeks because excess water stored by our body is now released as the sodium/potassium balance normalizes.

Even though early weight loss is mostly water and not fat, never downplay the loss and say, "Oh, it's just water" because ridding our body of all this excess water is just as important as fat loss. At the same time, the high-quality nutrition begins rebuilding the damaged fibrous mesh, helping to eliminate cellulite.

MYTH #2: Weight-bearing exercise prevents bone loss

Weight-bearing exercise is the type of exercise where our body works against gravity. It includes high-impact exercise (jogging, running, stair climbing, dancing, tennis, aerobics) and low-impact exercise (elliptical machines, brisk walking, some styles of yoga, Pilates, using weight machines, lifting our own body weight, using elastic exercise bands, isometrics).

Many women engage in weight-bearing exercise to build bone mass in fear of suffering from osteoporosis or other bone-related conditions, but lack of exercise isn't the primary cause of bone-related diseases such as osteoporosis. The primary cause of osteoporosis is eating a diet heavy in acidic foods, especially refined foods and pasteurized dairy products.

When it comes to bone loss, diet is just as important as weight-bearing exercise.

Can weight-bearing exercise help reduce bone loss? Is exercise important? Yes, absolutely. But if we're talking root cause here (and this program is *all* about getting down to the root cause of the problem and then digging up that root!), then diet is the big culprit.

Contrary to the milk industry's babbling, pasteurized milk products are big offenders when it comes to acidifying the body and contributing to osteoporosis; this includes milk, yogurt, butter, cheese, ice cream, and frozen desserts that have been pasteurized. As we learned earlier in the protocol, the process of pasteurization damages protein content, destroys the enzymes in the milk that help us digest the milk proteins, destroys calcium and other nutrients, and creates a highly acidic food.

- When we consistently eat a diet of overly acidic foods, our body must neutralize this excess acid by releasing alkaline minerals, such as calcium, from our bones and teeth. This calcium is then excreted in our urine, ultimately contributing to osteoporosis.[1][2][3]
- The more acidic our diet, the higher the risk of hip fractures. Incidentally, the countries with the lowest ratio of vegetable-to-animal protein have the highest incidents of hip fractures. This may be due not only to the animal protein, but also to the pasteurization of dairy protein.[4]

There are many different types of weight-bearing exercise; the key is to do what you enjoy. Using inexpensive resistance bands is one of the simplest ways to include strength training in your day. Not only are they easy to use, but they're wonderful when you travel as they're small enough to fit into luggage.

MYTH #3: Aerobic exercise is necessary to lose weight

Weight gain is caused by incorrect eating habits and general inactivity from a sedentary lifestyle (i.e., sitting in front of a computer or TV all day). Losing weight is about eating the right type of food and being more active throughout the day. When we give our body the fuel it needs and take away the toxins that damage it, our body weight will naturally begin to normalize.

Being active is an important part of being healthy and speeds up weight loss, but as we'll soon learn, this doesn't mean you have to engage in an hour of exhausting aerobics every day that you dread doing!

MYTH #4: I need more protein when I exercise

We touched on this earlier in the supplement section. Buying into the belief that we need to fill up on protein shakes (processed soy, whey, and other highly processed protein drinks), protein supplements, and amino-acid supplements when we exercise is not only totally unnecessary and a waste of money, it's also very damaging for our health.

As we now know, the quickest way to acidify our body and bog it down is to fill it up with refined or synthetic proteins. By now, some simple truths should be staring you in the face. All of these protein supplements are dead foods that clog our cells and tissues ... and what happens when we feed dead foods to our body? We cause it to degenerate and age quicker, and we lower its vibrational frequency. When it comes to health and nutrition, steer clear of synthetic and refined protein supplements.

If you have an intense workout schedule, yes, you'll need to increase your overall food intake. But the RATIO of your protein should change very little, as testified to by world-class athletes such as Brendan Brazier, who are the best in their class and who thrive on the healthy levels of protein recommended in the Body Healer Protocol.

Why We Need to Be Active

We gain many important benefits from exercising our body. Regular activity strengthens our muscles and improves the functioning of our entire body—especially our circulatory system. This automatically translates to a reduction in our risk of major diseases. Activity can add years to our life. All it takes is just 30 minutes of physical activity each day, and a general increase in daily activities to reap both the physical and psychological rewards.

Let's take a look at the 7 most important benefits of regular exercise:

1. **It Increases Our Oxygen Content**
   The most important thing that exercise does is increase the oxygen content of our body. It increases the number and size of blood vessels that carry blood and nutrients to our cells and tissues. As we increase the capacity of our lungs to take in more oxygen when we exercise, we not only strengthen our circulatory system, we also increase the oxygenation of every single cell in our entire body.

2. **It Increases the Flow of Lymph**
   The more we stimulate lymphatic flow, the more we increase our capacity to transport nutrients to tissues and waste from tissues, which reduces and eliminates the cellular congestion that contributes to cellulite. When we much more effectively remove toxic waste from our organs and tissues, we naturally prevent disease from settling in (more on lymph later).

3. **It Strengthens Our Immune System**
   Exercise reduces our likelihood of catching infections. The more active we are, the less sick we get. This translates not only to better health, but also to a cost saving for doctor appointments, medications, and over-the-counter products.

4. **It Helps Strengthen Our Heart and Reduce Arterial Inflammation**
   Exercises reduces our risk factor for heart attacks and strokes. It is a very important (and free!) health insurance policy we can give ourselves!

5. **It's is a Natural Antidepressant**
   Exercise lowers levels of stress hormones and can relieve depression as effectively as antidepressant medications. It triggers our body to release morphine-like chemicals called "endorphins" that create feelings of pleasure and euphoria, and which also act as a natural anesthetic to pain. Our levels of serotonin—a natural antidepressant that makes us feel positive, upbeat, and more optimistic about life in general—also increase. We feel better about ourselves and our self-esteem blossoms, especially as we begin to see our bodies transform.

6. **It Improves Our Sleep Quality**
   Exercise helps us sleep, contributing to feeling more rested and less stressed, which also allows our body the downtime it needs to repair and restore itself.

7. **It Increases Our Metabolism**
   The more active we are, the higher our metabolic rate because muscle tissue is metabolically more active than fat tissue (muscles burn up far more energy compared to fat, which is relatively inactive). As we increase muscle, we have our own internal "furnace" to consistently burn up more calories 24/7.

What Kind of Exercise Do We Need?

Not the kind you might think. We need exercise that keeps us moving, stretches our limbs, and keeps us flexible—the kind that increases our capacity for oxygenation. And it's *not* the miserable kind!

Let's talk about the 2 types of exercise that will give us the important health benefits we need:

1. The stretchy kind
2. The active kind

If you do more exercise than you need to for your health, or choose forms of activity that are not necessary to be healthy simply because you love them, then go at it! Enjoy yourself and embrace that optimism and enthusiasm! Just make sure that you do not overtax your body.

Before we go into the types of exercise we'll be doing, let's spend a few minutes talking about one of the most important benefits of exercise ... the stimulation of our lymphatic system.

LYMPH – LOVE IT & MOVE IT!

It's important that we have a basic understanding of our lymphatic system and the role it plays in keeping us healthy.

The word "lymphatic" comes from the Latin word "lymphaticus," meaning "connected to water." Also known as the sewage system of the body, the lymphatic system is a vast drainage and filtration system that removes waste and larger particles that can't be absorbed by the blood capillaries or removed by the circulatory system. Its two primary jobs are to:

1. Transport a clear, colorless fluid called "lymph" containing white blood cells to help eliminate toxins, waste, and other unwanted materials.
2. Produce immune cells, such as lymphocytes and monocytes; it also transports white blood cells to and from lymph nodes located in different areas of the body.

When the lymphatic system disposes of waste products and toxins through our bladder, bowels, lungs, and skin, it's performing a vital function for both detoxification and for our immune system. If it doesn't work properly, a wide range of illnesses can develop.

The lymphatic system is essential to our body; without it, we would die. *The Tibetan Book of the Dead* describes a method of bringing on death within 7 days by simply becoming completely inactive. American Indians assisted their transition into the next world by sitting very still and fixing their eye on an immovable object. This helps stop the movement of lymph. In the American culture, many people practice a similar ritual during "retirement" by becoming more and more inactive, which causes sluggish lymphatic flow, disease, and other disorders now commonly related to old age.

How Exercise Impacts Lymph

We can now see how important it is to keep our lymph moving. Without a strong circulation of this fluid, waste can build up in our body quicker than it can be eliminated, and the more waste builds up, the more toxic our bodies become. The more toxic our bodies become, the lower our vibrational state and the more we become susceptible to disease. One of the best ways to improve our circulation and the circulation of lymph is through exercise.

The lymphatic system has no "pump" like the heart to force lymph throughout our body. Not only that, lymph must be able to flow uphill to our lymph nodes. The reason it always moves in the right direction, even when it has to flow upwards, is because of the large number of valves in our lymphatic vessels that allow the lymph to flow in only one direction. We stimulate the flow of lymph through two types of muscular contraction:

- Muscular contraction when we exercise; during exercise, lymphatic flow can increase as much as 10-15 times compared to when we're resting. Every time our tissues compress during exercise, the lymphatic system pumps fluid with toxic waste and acidic proteins out of tissue spaces. The exercise doesn't have to be high impact; in fact, low-impact exercises, such as rebounding on a mini-trampoline and swimming, are fantastic ways to increase the flow of our lymph.
- Muscular contraction during deep breathing.

Rebounding

Rebounding is one of the best ways to stimulate the flow of lymph throughout our body. It's also a fun, easy, low-impact exercise!

Also known as a mini-trampoline, a rebounder averages $30–$80 and can be bought online or from most sports stores. You can use your rebounder outside, or inside while watching TV as it's small. Most come with detachable handles for stability.

To rebound, gently bounce up and down with small movements that are so gentle your feet barely lift off the rebounder. Even though the movements are small, the effect on the lymphatic system is significant. The gentle up-and-down movement propels the lymphatic fluid throughout the body in the same way it does during any other form of exercise.

The more you rebound, the more you help your body with waste removal. Rebounding can also help those with poor circulation and with legs that are prone to swelling because it helps break up the congestion and toxic waste that contribute to poor circulation.

The 3 Things That Stimulate Lymph

Exercise is very important when it comes to stimulating the movement of lymph, but there are other important factors too.

Hydration
Hydration is very important when it comes to lymphatic flow. This is one of the reasons we always make sure our diet is filled with healthy, high vibrational foods that are high in water content and naturally hydrate our body.

Nutrients
The enzymes and nutrients in fruits and vegetables play an important role in our lymphatic health. Chlorophyll and the thousands of antioxidants found in green, leafy vegetables and many fruits help to purify both our blood and lymph, strengthening our entire lymphatic system.

Dry-Skin Brushing & Massage
By massaging our skin and lymph nodes and spending a few minutes each day dry-brushing our skin, we can increase the circulation of lymph up to 70 percent or more.

Lymphatic drainage is a special type of massage that also works to specifically stimulate the flow of lymph.

Speaking of dry-skin brushing, how about we spend a few minutes talking about some simple dry-skin brushing techniques we can use at home before we continue to explore exercising?

DRY-SKIN BRUSHING

Our skin is the single-largest organ of our body, and one of the best ways to stimulate our skin is through skin brushing. Not only does it feel wonderful, it's easy to do and takes only a few minutes each day.

Our skin plays an important role in detoxification, so when we help to stimulate our skin to remove waste more efficiently, we increase its ability to detoxify.

Here are 4 important benefits we get from dry-skin brushing:

1. It stimulates our lymphatic system and our lymph nodes, which assists in the removal of waste from our body.
2. It exfoliates our skin by helping to remove dead skin cells, which in turn stimulates cellular renewal.
3. It reduces cellulite by increasing circulation and relieving cellular congestion. It does this by stimulating the flow of nutrients into the cells and the flow of waste products out of the cells.
4. It's refreshing and invigorating. A good skin brushing wakes up our skin and makes us tingle all over. It feels wonderful!

Types of Brushes

When it comes to dry-skin brushing, we can use several different types of brushes. The main tool of choice is a high-quality natural-bristle brush. The bristles should feel firm but not too hard, or they'll hurt. Dry-skin bristle brushes can be purchased online or at most health-food stores.

Some brushes are double-sided and have large "knobs" on the back that also help stimulate and massage our skin. They offer a different way to help break up cellular waste beneath our skin that contributes to cellulite. Feel free to use the knobby side first, but then finish with the brush side.

Massage sponges are also another milder way we can stimulate and exfoliate our skin.

How to Do It

Incorporate dry-skin brushing into your daily routine at any time when you're undressed. Before putting on your clothes or taking a shower is a great time because you're already naked. You can brush your entire body (avoiding the face and private parts as the firm bristles are too abrasive for these delicate areas—ouch!). Also, avoid irritated skin and varicose veins.

If you dry-skin brush when you take a shower, do it beforehand rather than after, as our skin is more sensitive to the bristles immediately afterwards.

In general, use firm pressure and long, sweeping strokes. For areas containing cellulite, give them more of your attention by first using circular motions to help break up the cellular congestion.

Brushing Direction

The direction in which we brush is determined by the location of our major lymph nodes:

Arms: Brush from wrist to elbow, and then from elbow to armpit.

Legs: Brush from feet to knee, and then from knee to groin. For cellulite-prone areas, use circular motions, followed by sweeping motions to the groin.

Tummy: Use small, circular strokes, followed by sweeping strokes toward the groin.

Back: Brush from your lower back up toward the lower shoulder and armpit.

Buns: Use large, circular strokes, followed by sweeping strokes toward the groin.

When you've finished, your skin should have a fresh, pink glow. If your skin is very red, then lighten up on the pressure next time.

Now that we've talked about the importance of lymph, let's get back to the two types of movement our bodies need to both increase the flow of oxygen throughout our body, and maximize our energy potential.

STRETCHING & FLEXIBILITY

Stretching always feels good. Not only is it both relaxing and therapeutic, it's also one of the key elements of movement.

Increasing Our Flexibility

As we get older, our muscles become tighter and shorter, which means the range of motion in our joints is lessened. One of the best ways to eliminate general joint and muscle aches first thing in the morning (as well as pulled muscles in general) is to work on limbering up our body.

The important benefits of stretching include:

- Increased flexibility
- Increased range of motion
- Stabilization of our joints
- Improved posture and sense of balance
- Increased circulation to different parts of the body
- Tension relief
- Reduced exercise-related injuries
- Relief from muscle and joint aches and pains
- Decreased muscle soreness when practiced after other forms of exercise

The key to limbering up is to stretch regularly and not to stretch our body to the point of pain. We can include stretching in our lives on a daily basis in two great ways: do a set of stretching exercises or practice yoga (especially hatha yoga or restorative yoga).

The only pieces of equipment you'll need are an exercise mat and foam blocks, which will help you ease into stretching/yoga poses that may be difficult in the beginning.

Stretching Exercises

Stretching is important before we begin any type of exercise, but stretching is also an activity by itself.

Stretching is low impact, requires little effort, and is performed doing slow movements. Including a few simple stretching exercises in our day is very easy to do. It's something we can do while watching our favorite TV show, listening to music, or working in the garden. If you live in an apartment and have a balcony, consider making it a stretching place, and add plants and other items to create a beautiful, tranquil space.

Let's take a look at some stretches you can begin to include in your day. Whether you're an absolute beginner or you practice yoga or other forms of stretching regularly, these stretches can effectively help you increase your flexibility and stabilize and strengthen your joints.

Guidelines for Stretching

While some poses may be easy for you, others may be more challenging. You may need to do a simpler variation or bend your knees to ease into the posture. The following examples are for you to work up to; it's important to allow your body to loosen up at its own pace. It took me many months to ease into the full expression of some poses, and some were still challenging even after a year. All in good time ...

1. Ease slowly into each stretch. Never bounce or force yourself into a stretch because this causes the muscle to involuntarily tighten and increases your risk of injury.

2. Stretch to the point of mild discomfort while breathing in a deep, rhythmic manner. You'll soon discover that the deeper and more rhythmically you breathe, the easier it is to ease into a stretch more deeply and the longer you'll be able to hold each stretch.
3. Begin holding each stretch for 20 seconds, and then repeat 2 more times. As your flexibility increases, progress deeper into the stretch and increase the hold time to 60 second, 1 time.
4. If any exercise feels uncomfortable or causes you pain, pass on it.
5. Never "lock" your knees or elbows into any position.
6. Use props if you need to.

As always, check with your healthcare practitioner before beginning this or any type of exercise or stretching program.

15 STANDING EXERCISES

Standing Pose

Forward Fold

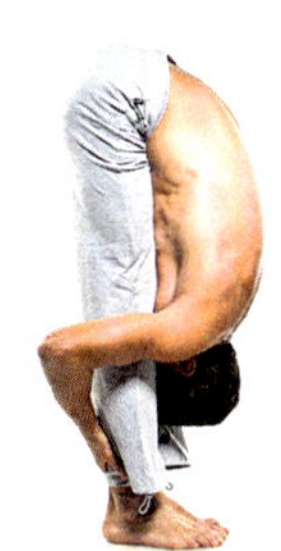

Side Stretch

Quad Stretch

Dancer's Pose

Triangle Pose

(modify: place hand on shin)

Half Moon Pose

(modify: use block)

Half Moon Quad Stretch

(modify: use block under hand)

1-Legged Side Stretch

Wide Legged Forward Fold

Runner's Lunge

Downward Dog

Crescent Lunge

Warrior II

Reverse Crescent Lunge

(modify: use block under hand)

15 SEATED EXERCISES

Cow Pose

Cat Pose

Forward Fold

Forward Fold II

(aim to straghten legs)

Forward Fold III

(progress after achieving I & II)

Side Forward Fold

Half Splits Pose

(aim to straighten legs)

Splits Pose

(modify: use block under groin)

Cobra Pose

(modify: turn toes under & drop knees to ground)

Bow Pose

Wide Leg Happy Baby Pose

(modify: bend knees)

Boat Pose

Hero Pose

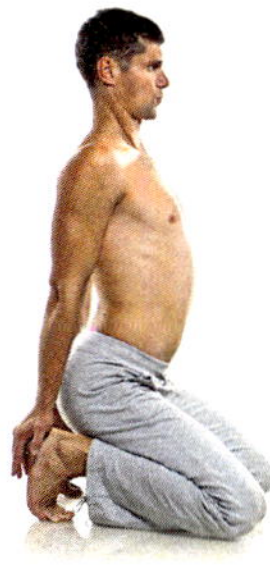

Reclining Hero Pose

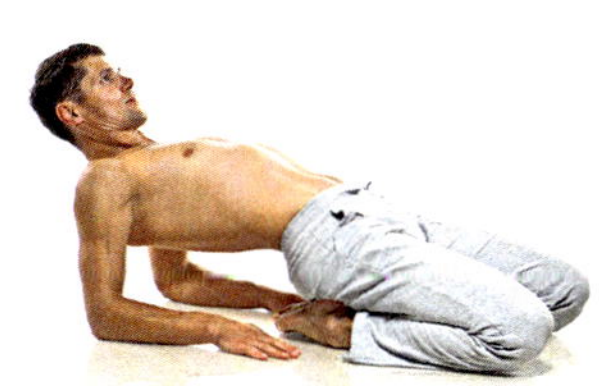

Reverse Table Pose

Practicing Yoga

The word "yoga" comes from the Sanskrit word "yuj," meaning "union" or "to merge." It's based on the Indian philosophy of achieving a balance of the mind, body, and spirit with the goal of enlightenment.

Although yoga is practiced with a much more spiritual focus in India, in the Western world it's become more sports-oriented with less focus on the spiritual side. People from all walks of life practice yoga.

Many styles of yoga have emerged:

- Some emphasize the strict alignment of the body, while others focus on coordinating breath (pranayama) with movement.
- Some hold poses for specific lengths of time, while others flow from one pose to the next in a fluid motion. Some lead you much deeper into stretches than others.
- Some styles of yoga are distinguished by the name of the Yogi who developed that particular style.

Whereas a hatha class is gentle and restorative and will leave you feeling peaceful and meditative, a vinyasa power yoga or ashtanga yoga class is more physically demanding and aerobic.

Hatha Yoga

Hatha yoga is the branch of yoga most commonly practiced worldwide today. It's best known as a set of physical poses that include gentle stretches (many of which are in the "stretches" section above), deeper breathing practices, and progressive relaxation. If you decide to take yoga classes, I recommend this style. The poses in hatha yoga form the basis of most other yoga styles.

Because many yoga styles vary greatly, you can bet that if one style doesn't float your boat, another will because there's a yoga style for everyone. Have fun exploring the differences and see what clicks!

Yoga Classes – What to Look for

Whichever style of yoga you choose, here are some important tips to follow when choosing a class:

Try One Class. Most instructors and yoga studios will invite you to try your first class either for free or at a significant discount. Before you buy a package or monthly membership, always try out the class to see if you like it. Introduce yourself to the instructor and let them know you're new to their class.

Find out the Costs. Some studios will be more expensive than others. Most offer different pricing packages ranging from a more expensive, single-class drop-in to a "package" of classes or monthly membership that's cheaper. Make sure the class is within your budget to practice it regularly.

Choose a Style of Yoga That Suits You. If you're looking for a calming, relaxing style of yoga to reap the benefits of stretching, then a hatha yoga class would be a great class for you (or a style of yoga based on hatha yoga). Similarly, if you're in good shape and looking for a challenging, more aerobic workout that also provides you with the stretching you want, then power vinyasa flow or ashtanga yoga may be a better choice. These styles of yoga help increase flexibility, but they don't focus on holding or deepening into poses.

If you want to experience the benefits of a heated environment to help you ease into and experience a deeper stretch, then Bikram yoga and heated vinyasa flow are great choices. My favorite yoga class is a heated power vinyasa flow.

Is the Instructor Knowledgeable & Hands-On? When it comes to yoga poses, correct alignment in postures is crucial in understanding how to stabilize joints and prevent injury. Chiropractors and physical therapists make a fortune from students who have hurt themselves either practicing yoga poses incorrectly or trying to push their body too far too fast. From pulled back muscles to wrist tendonitis, tweaked necks to shoulder strains, yoga injuries are a dime a dozen. When we practice yoga without guidance on how to properly move into and out of each pose, we set ourselves up for injury either now or in the future as we progressively weaken a joint through repetition.

A good instructor will always make continuous rounds throughout the class to help students correct their postural alignment. In a beginner's class, verbal cues should be given on each posture. For example, in a pose called Warrior II, you should hear tips such as, "front knee over ankle, back foot flat on the ground, fingertips reaching, shoulders centered over hips, gaze past your fingertips." These cues are important and very helpful, especially for a beginner.

If the class you're considering is hands-off and the instructor doesn't cue postures, I'd strongly recommend you look elsewhere. Before taking my teacher training course in power vinyasa flow, I practiced yoga for several years. It wasn't until I took my course that I became aware of my poor alignment in several poses, and how much I was increasing my risk of future injury. When I now attend yoga classes, I never fail to see students yanking back their necks, overextending their joints, and stretching to the point that they're falling out of the pose and aren't reaping its benefits. Some instructors pay no attention or are dealing with too many students to effectively help all those who need alignment help. Avoid these classes, especially as a beginner.

Ask about Your Instructor's Experience & Background. Ask how long your instructor has been practicing yoga. Also ask if they're a Registered Yoga Teacher (RYT). The RYT designation means they've followed a program that's been endorsed by the Yoga Alliance, an independent body that sets a minimum standard for yoga teacher training.

Is the Instructor Engaging? Do You Feel a Connection? No matter how knowledgeable an instructor is, if you don't feel a connection or particularly enjoy their style of teaching, then you won't have a great yoga experience. Similar to a math or art teacher, you may love the subject, but the instructor can either make or break the class for you. Some teachers are abrupt, whereas others are more fluid in their style. Some may simply have a voice that annoys you or play a music style that's too distracting. Attend classes with several different instructors so that you can experience different styles of teaching and see what you prefer.

In Parker, Colorado, I attended a weekly class with an instructor named Sara Ewing who made each class a truly unique, incredible experience. As the class began and we settled into Child's Pose, Sara set an intention with either a little story or a poem. Throughout each pose during class, we were brought back to the intention, and as we deepened each pose, we deepened our commitment to the intention. I was always excited for each class!

How Does the Studio Look? Most yoga studios are created to be warm and inviting, usually with wood floors and a relaxing ambiance. They should be kept clean and free of clutter. Some are quite beautiful, with plants, simple nature-oriented décor, and bamboo floors.

Look for Mirrors. Most studios have mirrors, and I highly recommend choosing a studio that uses them. They help students observe themselves and especially help beginners recognize if they aren't in alignment during a pose. In the beginning, it can "feel" like you're doing a pose correctly, when in fact you aren't. You may "think" that your shoulders are balanced above your hips in Warrior II, but when you look in the mirror, you discover you're actually leaning forward. Your knee may "feel" like it's directly over your ankle, but after a quick peek in the mirror, you realize it's extended beyond your ankle.

The longer you practice, the sooner you'll know when your body is in correct alignment, and you'll then use the mirror as a point of focus instead of as a guide. Where possible, I always choose to practice in studios with mirrors.

How Large Is the Class? Yoga classes should be small, with 20 or fewer students and room to comfortably move in your own space. Smaller classes give instructors the opportunity to effectively guide the class and address alignment corrections. This is especially important in a beginner's class. It's very difficult for an instructor to be hands-on and help students correct their alignment if there are too many students.

Some classes pack 30 or more students in spaces so tight that yoga mats are almost touching. Not only is it unsafe, but sweaty arms and legs waving in your face isn't a very fun or pleasant experience.

Common Yoga Terms

In yoga, there are several terms commonly used in yoga classes:

Asana

Each yoga pose is called an "asana," and different poses have different effects on the body depending on which areas and organs they stimulate.

Vinyasa

Some yoga styles perform poses in a flowing sequence called "vinyasa" flow where breath is synchronized to movement (inhale for one pose, exhale for the next pose).

Namaste

In yoga, a gesture called "Namaste" is said where the palms of both hands are brought together before the heart, as within prayer, with the head lightly bowed.

Namaste represents the belief that divinity is within each of us and recognizes everyone as equal. The essence of the word conveys, "The God within me sees the God within you." It's an acknowledgment of the soul in one person by the soul in another. After a yoga class, the teacher will often close with the word "Namaste," and the students will respond likewise, each acknowledging and giving thanks to the other for the experience together.

Namaste can also be performed by bringing your hands together in front of your third eye (between the eyes), bowing your head, and then bringing your hands down to your heart. This is considered an especially deep form of respect.

Energizing Movement

Stretching exercises are one of two types of movement our body needs. Let's take a look at the importance of exercise that's more active and upbeat.

ENERGIZING MOVEMENT

In contrast to the very low-impact, gentle activity of stretching, energizing movement is just that—movement that wakes us up and makes us feel energized and upbeat ... a splash of fresh oxygen to our body and our brain cells!

It could be taking a brisk walk or a slow jog, or getting on a cardio machine at the gym. It could be going for a swim, or vigorously dancing around the house to our favorite music. Whatever active exercise we choose, it's important to energize our body. The more immobile and sedentary we are, the slower our metabolism, the more sluggish our lymph, and the less oxygenated we become. This contributes to the lowering of the vibrational state of our body. We literally become "devitalized."

We're going to increase our activity in two ways. The first is to increase our general activity throughout the day, and the second is to choose specific types of exercise we enjoy that we can do every day. If you're new to any exercise program, remember to always check with your healthcare practitioner to make sure that you're working at a pace and level that are best for you.

Increasing Your General Activity

By making just a few simple changes in how you approach your daily schedule, it's much easier than you might think to increase your activity level throughout the day. Let's take a look at a few examples:

- Take the stairs instead of the elevator.
- Take the parking spot at the mall or office that's farthest from the door. No more scouting for parking spots—woo-hoo!
- Take the dog for a long, very brisk walk. Your pup will appreciate it as much as your body will.
- If you can walk or bike to the store or a friend's house, then forego the car.
- Make it a point to walk briskly on your lunch break and around your office building several times each day. Each time you need a bathroom break, take the longest possible route to get there and back.
- When you take a walk, who says you have to just walk? Incorporate skipping, twirling, little dance moves, light jogs—whatever strikes your fancy. Not only will you feel great, but you'll also bring a smile to the faces of people around you ... guaranteed!
- While watching a movie at home, every time a commercial comes on, make it your time to do a fun, wild, wacky mini-workout. It may be a few dance moves or as many push-ups or ab crunches as you can fit in. Maybe some squats or lunges. Make it something different for each commercial. You also don't have to wait for the commercial as there are many exercises you can do while watching the TV screen.
- Look for any opportunity you can to move, move, move!

Choose an Exercise Activity You Enjoy

When it comes to doing exercise, you have so many choices. If you're considering a gym, community center, yoga or Pilates studio membership, or something similar, look for a location near your home or on the way to and from work so that it's convenient for you. Make sure the atmosphere and facility are welcoming and pleasant because this is an important part of the experience. Take a look at what they offer in terms of machines, classes, swimming, and other activities. The more they offer, the more variety you'll have.

If getting on a machine at the gym isn't your thing, then consider taking up a new hobby that involves exercise, such as tennis, volleyball, or racquetball. Community centers often offer training, and some have teams you can join. This is a great way to not only get some exercise, but also make some new friends. Another great way to begin an active hobby is to join a local Meetup group.

There are many different activities to choose from that are aerobic in nature, including:

- Basketball
- Cardio machines (ellipticals, stair climbers, stepmills, treadmills, bikes, arc trainers, versaclimbers, etc.)
- Circuit training
- Classes (zumba, spin, yoga, kickboxing, cycling, etc.)
- CrossFit
- Cycling
- Jogging or running*
- Jump rope (skipping rope)
- Pilates
- Plyometrics
- Racquetball
- Rollerblading
- Swimming
- Tennis

* Running and jogging are considered high-impact activities. They place a greater strain on our joints and should be approached with care and with the right equipment.

If you try something and don't like it, then try something different. Keep experimenting until you find something you enjoy. Also make sure you give yourself some variety. A long, brisk walk one day, followed by a yoga or cycling class the next day, then a workout at home the day after that... Switch it up.

Exercise can also be an opportunity to reconnect with nature, perhaps by briskly walking in a park or on a trail, going for a run or jog, taking a bike ride, or going rollerblading (one of the best butt exercises you can do!). If you have access to more rural environments where you can breathe clean, fresh air on a regular basis, this can be incredibly healing. As we know, healthy air quality is one of the essential elements our bodies need to rebalance.

Invest in a good pair of jogging/running shoes and get properly fitted to make sure you minimize joint impact. Stores that specialize in running shoes offer professional fittings for free that involve filming you for up to a minute while you run on a treadmill. This helps the fitter analyze your gait and choose which running shoes will benefit and protect you the most.

Brisk Walking

For many people, joining a gym or doing team sports just isn't appealing (or funds may be too tight). With jogging and running, the high impact of the activity also turns some away. With every step, the impact generates a force several times our body weight, and the long-term wear and tear on joints can be a deterrent.

In contrast, brisk walking is one of the best types of exercise we can do: We can do it anywhere. It requires no special equipment, it's easy and low impact, and it does the job! Brisk walking doesn't jar the body with the impact of running or jogging. Because it's a lower-intensity workout, we should focus on a longer duration, aiming for 60 minutes (or 30 minutes twice each day). We can also increase the intensity by incorporating hills or stairs.

Brisk walking doesn't have to engage only your lower body. Make your arms as active as your legs by using wrist weights, and include some bicep curls on your walk. If you enjoy listening to music, bring along your headphones.

If you have a dog, then by all means, include them because they also need daily exercise, and walking together is a great bonding time!

Contraindications

The more intense the activity, the more we should approach it with caution if we have any contraindications, including these or other conditions:

- Heart disease
- Recent heart attack
- High blood pressure
- Heartbeat irregularities, or disease of the heart valves
- Certain respiratory disorders
- Conditions that produce pain during exercise

If you have a health condition, consider working with a naturopath or a doctor that strongly encourages natural lifestyle habits and exercise for rehabilitation as opposed to medications, and one who is willing to work with you to reduce and eliminate any medications. A good rule of thumb is to judge a doctor by their willingness to spend time educating you on how to prevent health conditions, and how to heal from health conditions as naturally as possible.

How Much?

When it comes to how often and how intensely you should exercise, avoid rushing out to buy a heart monitor or worrying about keeping track of your BMI. Here are 4 golden rules to help you decide if your workout is effective:

1. It should stimulate your muscles enough that you're a little sore the next day—soreness that feels good when you stretch the sore muscle, not the type of soreness that leaves you barely able to move and has you groaning with every step. This is a sign that you've pushed too far. The exception is that you may feel overly sore during the first few days of beginning an exercise program while your body adjusts to the activity.
2. Focus on a goal of 30-60 minutes, 5 times each week. Two separate, 30-minute intervals during the day (of two different activities, if you like) work just fine.
3. If you find your workout is too easy and doesn't challenge you, step it up a little until it does. Then give your body 1-2 weeks to fully adapt (until you experience no soreness) before increasing the challenge.
4. For weight training, when you can push yourself to do 3 extra repetitions beyond your current schedule still maintaining good form, then either increase the weight or the repetitions.

Any Time That Suits You

When it comes to exercise, any time of the day is just fine (except right after eating). Pay no attention to the mandates that it "should" be done first thing in the morning, or in the midafternoon, or in the early evening, or before a meal ... or whenever the particular expert-of-the-day deems appropriate. The right time for exercise is the time you do it—just make sure you do some every day.

There have been times in my life when I preferred to work out from midnight to 1:00 a.m. at 24 Hour Fitness because I'm a night owl and love an empty gym—that worked just great for me. At other times in my life, first thing in the morning felt best.

Rigid schedules are unnecessary unless they benefit you personally and help keep you on track. Take note of what times during the day are easier and more convenient for you to exercise (and when you feel more energized) and capitalize on them. The best time is when you feel the most motivated.

The Importance of Our Environment

Let's move on to the next section of the protocol and talk about how the 80,000 chemicals in our personal-care products, household cleaning products, the water we drink, and the air we breathe detrimentally impact our immune system and lower our vibrational frequency. Not only are many of these chemicals carcinogenic (cause cancer), they also cause hormonal disruption.

You'll discover how to create your own natural, nontoxic cleaning cabinet; the wonderful health benefits of houseplants; and how to make natural, safe choices when it comes to all your personal-care products.

CREATING A HEALTHY HOME

Today, there are over 80,000 chemicals in our food, personal-care products (shampoos, soaps, deodorants, sunscreens, toothpaste, etc.), household cleaning products, vaccinations, the air we breathe, and the water we drink.

Many of these chemicals are toxic. Exposure to industrial and environmental chemicals over time can cause us serious harm, and when they build up in our body, they've been conclusively linked to serious conditions, such as cancer, neurological disorders, and autoimmunity. These chemicals significantly impact our energy frequency, especially when we put them directly onto and into our bodies.

Creating a healthy home environment free of these chemicals is a very important part of a healthy, high vibrational body. This is especially the case if you're healing from a chronic disease such as cancer.

We'll be going over:

Cookware & Food-Prep Utensils. We'll talk about what to ditch and why, and what to use instead. We'll also hammer home why you should never use a microwave to prepare or warm food.

House & Garden Chemicals. You'll become enlightened (after recovering from the shock!) on the highly toxic nature of common household cleaners, chemicals, and pesticides. Learn why you should remove them all from your home in favor of nontoxic cleaning products.

Becoming a Masterful Mixologist. Natural cleaning products are not only effective, they're also far safer for yourself and your entire family. You'll learn how to build your own natural, nontoxic cleaning cabinet using just a few inexpensive products from the local grocery store.

Freshening Up the Air. The air we breathe plays an important role in our health. Artificial air fresheners are filled with hormone-disrupting chemicals, dozens of air pollutants, and harmful synthetic fragrances. Learn how to eliminate household odors by filling your home with lovely aromas using essential oils and other natural products.

Personal-Care Products. Not only do they contribute to skin cancer, acne, and allergies, they also contribute to toxic buildup in the cells and tissues of our body. Most of the chemicals in personal-care products have no place on our bodies.

Transforming your home into a healthy, high vibrational haven is a simple, rewarding experience! You'll discover just how easy it is to create a much better environment for yourself and your loved ones, both the human and furry kind.

Before we do that though, let's spend a moment talking about why leaving shoes and boots at the door is a great idea.

Leave Shoes & Boots at the Door

The bottoms of our shoes house a collection of all sorts of organisms, such as bacteria and molds. The same shoes that walk on dirty pavements, in public restrooms, and on grass that's the public bathrooms for pets and wildlife are the ones walking in our home.

Simply leave your shoes at the door, and create a cleaner environment for your children and your bare feet. It's a much better, healthier alternative than first covering the floors with all sorts of bacteria, which you then try to wipe out with a variety of toxic household floor-cleaning chemicals.

In many cultures (for example, European, Middle Eastern, and Asian), removing shoes in the home is standard for both the cleanliness of the floors and for health.

When it comes to guests, have several pairs of slippers in assorted sizes next to the door, and politely explain to them that your household doesn't typically wear shoes indoors; however, they're welcome to keep their shoes on if this makes them feel more comfortable. If you're gracious and polite when you make your request, most guests will happily oblige and appreciate that you care about your home and its cleanliness. I've found that guests are astute enough to recognize when hosts aren't wearing shoes and take their cue when they see shoes placed next to the door.

Be Accommodating

Some guests may not feel comfortable removing their shoes. Perhaps someone is wearing orthotics and finds it difficult to spend time on their feet without them. Others may be very self-conscious, especially women who wear stilettos to make them taller or to help complete an outfit. Some feel inexplicably "naked" without them. It's important that your guests feel comfortable, so just go with the flow. Etiquette is a two-way street, and after all, enjoying their company is more important than a pair of shoes.

COOKWARE & FOOD-PREP UTENSILS

When it comes to all the different materials available for cooking and preparing food, some are much healthier and safer than others.

The ones we want to remove are the ones that leach chemicals into our food. These chemicals have been shown to biologically impact our bodies, some causing hormone disruption, while others are known cancer-causing agents. Over time, these chemicals accumulate in our cells and tissues and degrade our health.

Ditch It

Plastic

Where possible, avoid plastic utensils and accessories when cooking as these leach chemicals and can melt or flake with extreme heat. They also wear down over time, potentially causing chemicals to migrate into food. If you need to use them, always make sure they contain the BPA-free logo (BPA is a developmental, neural, and reproductive toxin commonly used in plastics such as plastic food containers, utensils, and plastic bottles).

Scientists have linked very low doses of BPA exposure to cancers, impaired immune function, early onset of puberty, obesity, diabetes, and hyperactivity.

NEVER use plastics in the microwave, even if they are BPA-free ("microwave-safe" means only that the plastic won't actually melt, but the extreme heat will increase the transference of chemicals from the plastic into food). Unfortunately, all plastics contain chemicals that can leach into our food. We increase the risk of chemical migration when we heat this plastic or wash the containers in the dishwasher, both of which accelerate plastic breakdown.

Melamine (Plastic Tableware)

Melamine is a chemical approved for use in cooking utensils and is commonly used in plastic tableware (plates, knives, forks, and spoons). The melamine in the product can migrate slowly into the food—especially so if the melamine is heated to high temperatures, increasing the likelihood of contamination.[1]

> "Melamine is linked to kidney stones, kidney failure, and cancer in animal studies."
>
> World Health Organization (WHO)

Teflon

Avoid Teflon and any other chemical nonstick coatings. Teflon is manufactured using perfluorooctanoic acid (PFOA). It's considered a likely human carcinogen and is also linked to male infertility, high cholesterol, and ADHD.

When heated, cookware coated with Teflon and other synthetic nonstick surfaces emit fumes toxic enough to kill birds. In a 2013 study, Teflon was linked to Alzheimer's, ALS, and autism spectrum disorders. Overheating nonstick pans and any scratching or chipping of the materials can also cause these chemicals to be released.[2]

Aluminum

Aluminum is a soft, highly reactive metal that can migrate in measurable amounts into food during cooking. It's been linked to brain disorders as well as behavioral abnormalities, and it's considered a toxic substance.[3] Anodized aluminum is aluminum that's been dipped into a chemical bath to create a more durable layer so that the aluminum can't leach as easily into food; however, it can still break down over time. This toxic substance is also used in many child and adult vaccinations.

Deep-Frying Cookware

Get rid of it. There's nothing healthy about deep-fried foods!

Microwave

Ditch it! We talked about microwaves earlier. Landmark studies show how microwaved food can significantly affect not only our blood, but also the various systems throughout our body when we eat microwaved food on a daily basis. Many key nutrients are also destroyed when they're microwaved, and the availability of others is reduced.

Purchase

Glass

Ovenproof glass is inexpensive, reusable, and recyclable. Keep in mind that while it's great for baking, most glass cannot be used on the stovetop.

Ceramic

Make sure it's lead-free, and skip painted ceramic dishes in particular unless you're certain they don't contain lead.

Copper, and Enamel-Coated Cast Iron

These are durable, nontoxic materials.

Stainless Steel, Cast Iron

Aim for stainless steel if possible. It's the least likely to leach components into cooking foods. Cast iron does have the potential to leach iron into food. The amount varies greatly depending on the food, its acidity, how long it was cooked, and how old the cookware is.

Accessories

For cookware accessories, choose stable materials, such as wood, bamboo, silicone, or stainless steel.

DANGERS OF HOUSEHOLD CHEMICALS

The ingredients found in many common household cleaning products not only pollute the air in our homes, they are also directly linked to asthma attacks, allergies, neurological conditions, and serious diseases such as cancer. These products have become very dangerous items in our homes as they're loaded with toxic chemicals, artificial colors and fragrances, harsh cleansing agents (like bleach and ammonia), and other ingredients that legally don't have to be disclosed on the label.

Many "natural" cleaners are also not as green as you may think. They can contain chemicals that irritate our eyes and lungs, especially in children and pets. They also contain unnecessary antibacterial agents (pesticides, technically) that can create strains of bacteria resistant to antibacterial drugs.

These products are not only unnecessary, they can also be expensive! All our cleaning basics can be replaced with some simple, nontoxic ingredients that are not only just as effective at cleaning, but are also cheaper and much safer for our entire family, pets included.

The trade-off is that we'll not only protect our health, but by replacing antibacterial chemicals in our home with natural disinfectants, we'll also develop a stronger immunity against illness and disease (more on this later).

Dangerous Chemicals in Household Cleaners

The EWG (**Environmental Working Group**) is a nonprofit agency that tested 21 common cleaners and the level of air pollution created after the products were used according to directions[(1)]:

- **Febreze Air Effects (Hawaiian Aloha)**
  Contained 89 irritants, including:
  - Ethyl acetate (toxic to the brain and nervous system)
  - Acetaldehyde (a known respiratory irritant and possible human carcinogen)
  - Butylated hydroxytoluene (toxic to the immune system, interferes with hormones)

- **Pine-Sol Brand Cleaner (Original)**
  Contained 18 air contaminants, including high levels of formaldehyde, a known carcinogen and asthma trigger. Pine oil contains chemicals called terpenes that react with ground-level ozone to form formaldehyde.

- **Comet Disinfectant Powder Cleanser (Regular)**
  Contained 146 air contaminants, including:
  - Formaldehyde, toluene, and benzene (3 chemical components of gasoline)
  - 7 chemicals linked to cancer
  - 2 chemicals linked to reproductive damage
  - 2 chemicals that interfere with hormones
  - Chloroform (previously used as a surgery anesthetic, which can cause dizziness)
  - Quartz (poses a threat if inhaled in powdered form)

Comet is an abrasive powder that can easily and effectively be replaced with baking soda or borax. To disinfect, follow up with a spray of hydrogen peroxide or vinegar, both of which are powerful germ-killing ingredients.

EWG Cleaners Hall of Shame

The Environmental Working Group has gathered compelling evidence that hundreds of common cleaners, even some of those hyped as "green" or "natural," can inflict serious harm.

- Some are banned in other countries.
- Some can burn or blind.
- Some emit toxic fumes.
- Some are fatal if inhaled.

Did your cleaner make the list? Check it out at: www.ewg.org/guides/cleaners

Say No to Bleach

Just because bleach can kill germs, mold, and bacteria doesn't mean we should use it. Chlorine bleach is rated as a highly toxic, lethal cleaning agent at levels ranging from a few drops to a teaspoonful if swallowed. Bleach containers are legally required to be labeled with a skull and crossbones and the words "DANGER – POISON" because the bleach is both dangerous and poisonous.

Both the EPA and CDC state that spraying surfaces with simple white vinegar followed by hydrogen peroxide is just as effective (99.9 percent) as using bleach.

> **"Spraying surfaces with vinegar followed by hydrogen peroxide is just as effective at killing bacteria as bleach."**
>
> EPA & CDC

Soaking sponges for 5 minutes in white vinegar has been shown to destroy 99.6 percent of bacteria (almost identical to full-strength bleach, rated at 99.9 percent).[2]

If this is the case, then why do millions of people—unaware of the dangers—purchase them? We can write it off to very savvy advertising by product manufacturers, the failure of the FDA to ban these chemicals, and to a medical industry that encourages us to overly disinfect our homes and our children.

There's never a good reason to buy and use the hoard of dangerous household chemicals in cleaning products on the market today. As you'll soon discover, there are much safer and more natural ways to clean our homes and remove germs.

Disposing of Household Chemicals

When it comes to getting rid of all your old toxic household cleaners, **NEVER pour them down the drain!** When disposed of in this manner, these chemicals are carried through the wastewater, damaging the fragile ecosystems of our waterways. They can then make it to our drinking water. Contact your local trash or recycling company to find out where you can dispose of them at local hazardous waste sites.

Okay, let's spend a few minutes talking about why oversterilizing, oversanitizing, and overcleaning can lower our immune system and damage our health.

GERMS – AN UNHEALTHY PHOBIA

Due to the aggressive marketing campaigns of cleaning manufacturers, the American public has developed a neurosis when it comes to the subject of bacteria. This fear-mongering has millions of Americans needlessly spending large sums of money on antibacterial products, believing that we must all lead highly sanitized lives. This obsessive need to destroy all germs has degraded our immune system and does far more harm than good.

Bacteria are single-celled microorganisms that are crucial to our health and well-being. As we learned earlier in the protocol, bacteria are essential for a healthy gut, and billions of these organisms are necessary to break down food into elements we can absorb. Some strains of bacteria are beneficial, while others can be potentially harmful.

But in today's chemicalized world, we've been conditioned to fear germs to an unhealthy, irrational degree. Product manufacturers convince us to clean our homes with household products designed to eradicate *all* bacteria (with no mention of the highly toxic nature of these products that can cause far worse damage).

Our unhealthy obsession with germs and the constant sanitization by scouring, bleaching, disinfecting, scrubbing, and spraying dangerous chemicals around our household are not only dangerous for our health, these behaviors have been shown to increase the likelihood of allergies, asthma, and other health conditions.

Why the Fear?

In 1878, scientist Louis Pasteur published "The Germ Theory of Disease," which states that many diseases are caused by the presence and actions of specific bacteria within the body. Unfortunately, this knowledge went on to cause not just a fear, but an unintended, full-blown phobia of germs among the public.

People began cooking foods that were never previously cooked. Many food items are now irradiated, and milk and other dairy products are pasteurized. Earlier, we learned all about pasteurization and how it removes potential pathogens, but also destroys nutrients and the enzymes we need to digest milk proteins.

This phobia continues today and has contributed to the increasingly toxic products we use to clean our homes and bodies.

A Healthy Body Is Inhospitable to Disease

Our bodies are full of bacteria, viruses, and various microorganisms. They feed upon the toxic waste inside us and aren't a problem when our bodies are healthy. For example, each day cancerous cells are routinely created and destroyed by a healthy body, preventing these cells from developing a cancerous condition.

Disease gravitates to an unhealthy, low vibrational body in a way that's similar to bugs gravitating toward unhealthy soils and rotting produce. The healthier we keep our body, the less we'll succumb to health conditions because our immune system will be strong and our bodies not toxic.

How Germs Help Strengthen Our Immune System

To understand how germs help play an important role in our health, we need to understand what germs are and how the immune system responds to them. Germs are tiny microorganisms that include bacteria and viruses. When they enter our body, they look for the best environment to start reproducing. Our immune system stops them from invading our bodies by destroying them. Sometimes, this results in a fever or cold symptoms, such as coughing, sneezing, and mucus buildup, while the immune system clears these germs away. As we learned earlier in the protocol, using anti-inflammatory medications suppresses this natural immune mechanism, and our body takes longer to complete the immune response.

When the immune system removes the bacteria or virus, it creates something special called an "antibody," which quickly destroys the bacteria or virus if it later returns. Because an infant doesn't yet have a fully mature immune system, it relies on its mother's milk to pass on these antibodies (which are naturally present in breast milk). As we grow older, exposure to different germs helps our immune system learn and become stronger. Each infection results in new antibodies to help fight against future infections.

Overly disinfecting our children and our homes is unhealthy and can lower our children's immune system, making them more susceptible to allergies and illnesses.

Being exposed to common microbes such as the cold or flu helps teach our immune system to respond appropriately with antibodies so that when we're exposed to more serious strains of bacteria, viruses, and allergens, our body is better prepared. Exposure to basic germs and dirt, such as in the garden and around the home, is important. Of course, it's also important to maintain basic cleanliness, such as washing our hands after going to the bathroom and keeping our homes clean. But obsessively worrying about cleanliness and overusing hand sanitizers are very unhealthy behaviors that negatively impact our health.

It's impossible to eradicate germs and bacteria entirely from our homes, and we wouldn't want to anyway because a clinical, antiseptic environment isn't healthy.

Say NO to Antimicrobial Soaps

According to the AMA (American Medical Association), antibacterial and antimicrobial products can encourage bacterial resistance to antibiotics and lead to new superbugs that can no longer be treated with antibiotics. Some are also harmful if swallowed by small children.

Triclosan

As well as containing synthetic fragrances and dyes, many hand sanitizers contain antimicrobial chemicals, such as triclosan, which are banned in Europe. This chemical has been linked to endocrine disruption, altered hormones in animals, and it may also be damaging to the thyroid. It's irritating to the eyes and skin and has been known to accumulate in women's breast milk.

In 2006, there were over 12,000 cases of hand-sanitizer poisoning reported in the US.

A meta-analysis of 27 studies revealed that soaps with triclosan were no more effective than plain soap in preventing infections and reducing bacteria on the hands.[1] More concerning is that there are now virulent strains of bacteria that are resistant to triclosan (e.g., E. coli, salmonella, staphylococcus, and tuberculosis).

There is zero evidence that excessive use of antibacterial soap results in fewer illnesses for our families. Even the FDA states that regular use of simple hot, soapy water works just as well without the associated risks of triclosan.

Under pressure, the FDA finally banned triclosan in 2016, but only banned it from soaps. It's still used in many other personal care products such as body washes and toothpastes.

ALLERGIES & CHILDHOOD ILLNESSES – AN EPIDEMIC

It's no secret that American children are fatter and sicker and suffer more allergies and chronic childhood illnesses than children do in any other country. This isn't because of germs. It's because they're exposed to thousands of dangerous chemicals in their food, homes, schools, and on their skin.

Bacteria are an essential part of a healthy gut and for the development of a strong, robust immune system. Children need to be exposed to some germs to strengthen their immunity and develop the ability to fight back against common bugs. Many doctors now believe that children growing up in sterile environments are far more likely to develop allergies and childhood diseases than those who are not.

When I was a kid, many of my friends grew up on farms filled with cows, sheep, chickens, dogs, and many other creatures. There was no such thing as a sterilized environment, and the chronic childhood sicknesses rampant today were practically unheard of. Allergies were rare, and these kids were healthy and rarely sick.

Food Allergies & GMOs

Studies now link the increase in childhood allergies with the consumption of both GMOs and foods treated with pesticides. As GMOs themselves are heavily treated with pesticides, this double-whammy creates a recipe for disaster.

The DNA of an organism contains instructions for making proteins, but when food is genetically altered, the altered DNA can, in turn, create new proteins. GM foods are designed to produce their own insecticidal toxins (to deter bugs) and introduce foreign proteins in foods that never existed before. Because the DNA of GM foods have been altered, the new proteins created may create new allergies to that GM food that did not previously exist, or allergies to similar food proteins. Children are especially susceptible as 70% of a child's immune system is found within their digestive tract.

- A 2005 allergy and asthma study found that human subjects exhibited an immune response to GM soy, but not to non-GMO soy. This is because GM soy contains a different protein.[(1)]

In the absence of any long-term health studies, the only way to tell if GM foods contribute to health conditions is to completely remove them from the diet and see if a health condition improves or clears up. Labeling GMOs is critical to give people the choice to opt out of these foods and their potentially hazardous health implications, rather than be part of one huge chemistry experiment.

Childhood Vaccinations

Childhood vaccinations contain ingredients that are highly toxic and can cause severe neurological damage and autoimmune conditions. In 1986, Congress recognized that vaccines may have the ability to injure and kill children, and passed the National Vaccine Injury Act in response to a large number of lawsuits filed claiming vaccines were causing adverse reactions, including brain damage and death.

Since 1988, the government has awarded over $2 billion in payouts to more than 1,300 families whose children suffered brain damage from vaccines. In March, 2011, the US Supreme Court ruled that you cannot sue drug companies over vaccines because vaccines are considered "unavoidably unsafe."

There are both pros and cons to vaccinations. On one hand, they are an important part of our health and protect us from dangerous diseases. History has shown that vaccinations have both halted and prevented serious health epidemics. On the other hand, there is definitive proof that vaccinations and their schedules/dosages given to infants at an age where their immune system is not fully developed, can have devastating health consequences, including both brain damage & death.

- An ongoing study of 12,583 participants showed that unvaccinated children are far less affected by common diseases than vaccinated children, most likely due to an uncompromised immune system.[(2)]

- A New Zealand survey of children born during or after 1977 revealed that none of the unvaccinated children had asthma events, yet nearly 25% of vaccinated children were treated for asthma by age 10.[2]
- In some studies, a vaccine does not always prove more effective than non-vaccination. In 2001, 13 children in the Smithdown school district of Long Island in New York were infected with whooping cough. Health officials stated that all 13 had been vaccinated against the illness. They did, however, suffer milder cases of the illness due to the vaccination.[3]
- According to the CDC, up to 98 million doses of the polio vaccine were exposed as containing a cancer-causing virus now believed responsible for causing millions of cancers in the US.[4] Though the CDC denies a definitive causal link between SV40 and cancer, it implies that the virus was problematic in relation to cancer development. "More than 98 million Americans received 1 or more doses of polio vaccine from 1955 to 1963 when a proportion of vaccine was contaminated with SV40," admits the CDC. "It is estimated that 10-30 million Americans may have received the contaminated vaccine."
- In 1992, a New Zealand group called the Immunization Awareness Society (IAS) surveyed 245 families with a total of 495 children. The children were divided with 226 vaccinated and 269 unvaccinated. 81 of these families had both vaccinated and unvaccinated children. The differences were dramatic, with unvaccinated children showing far less incidences of common childhood ailments than vaccinated children.[4] Is the manipulation of the immune system with more and more vaccines in early life setting some children up for future chronic disease and disability? Evidence points in that direction. Fully vaccinated children are NOT healthier than non-vaccinated children. The opposite has been proven to be true. Vaccinated children suffer more chronic illnesses, rates of autism, asthma, allergies, and infections that are as much as 30% higher.[2]
- In January 2016, the CDC publicly admitted that flu vaccines **are only 50 percent effective** at preventing influenza requiring medical care – the statistical equivalent of a coin toss (we talked about this earlier in the Vitamin D section). In addition, a CDC analysis of flu vaccine effectiveness for the past decade demonstrated that over half the time, flu shots are **less than 50 percent effective**. Unfortunately, the public remains largely unaware of this fact, as do the doctors and clinics recommending the vaccine.[5]

Some of the ingredients in vaccines are highly toxic and can cause severe neurological damage and autoimmune conditions. Vaccine ingredients (e.g. aluminum) may also be the primary reason for some vaccine-related injuries.

Making an Educated Decision

Parents are now faced with conflicting studies and serious concerns about the dangers relating to vaccinations, which they do not fully understand. The key to making the right decision about whether to vaccinate is to weigh the consequences of (and likelihood of contracting) the disease in question against the potential adverse effects of the vaccine. Arm yourself with as much information as you can to make the best decision possible.

When I was young, any child who contracted chicken pox or the measles were brought to spend time with other children so that they, too, would contract it and develop a natural , long-term immunity (unlike the vaccines which fail to provide long-term immunity). A vaccination was were never part of the equation. Also, the CDC reports that no one in the US has died of measles in the last 12 years, yet 98 measles vaccine-related deaths were reported since 2003.

No vaccination is without risk, but some of the diseases they prevent are more serious than others. Knowing this, you can choose to vaccinate against one disease, but not another. You can also spread them out a little to avoid giving your children a batch of shots that can overtax the immune system. Consider following the schedule of other countries and not vaccinate any child under the age of 2, the point at which their immune system is stronger and more resilient.

Here are some important questions to consider before moving forward with any vaccination:

1. Is there a high likelihood of contracting the disease in your area? If so, the risk of the vaccine may be

worth the potential consequence of the disease. If the disease is rare or does not exist (which is often the case), then why consider the vaccine? This is common with pet and childhood vaccinations.

2. Ask whoever is administering the vaccine what other ingredients are included. Some vaccine additives, such as mercury and aluminum, are more toxic than the viral component itself.
3. What are the potential risks and side effects of the vaccine? If you suspect any adverse reaction, notify your doctor immediately and report the adverse reaction to the Vaccine Adverse Event Reporting System (**vaers.hhs.gov**).

If you or your child are sick, your immune system is compromised. Never vaccinate during this time. Wait until your health is clear. If you or your child suffered a bad reaction from a prior vaccine, the risk from further vaccination should be seriously reconsidered.

Whether you have to vaccinate child also depends largely on what state you live in. For up-to-date state laws on vaccination, visit the National Vaccine Information Center (**NVIC.org**).

THE NATURAL, NONTOXIC CLEANING CABINET

Are you ready to ditch the dangerous household chemicals and poisons? Of course you are! Let's trade products covered with warnings such as "corrosive" and "danger" and "extremely flammable" and "poison" for more natural solutions that are safe and just as effective at cleaning up.

Creating a nontoxic cleaning cabinet is very easy and involves buying just a few common products available from your local supermarket, health-food store, or pharmacy. The great news is that they're much less expensive than traditional cleaning products!

Becoming a Masterful Mixologist

Okay, let's take a look at our shopping list. These are the essentials, and to make it even more cost-effective, you can buy them in bulk.

1. **Sponges, Brushes, & Spray Bottles**
   You'll need an assortment of sponges, scrubbing brushes, a microfiber cloth, a toothbrush, and several empty spray bottles. Sponges carry more bacteria than anything else in the kitchen, but as we just learned, soaking them for 5 minutes in white vinegar destroys 99.6 percent of bacteria.[1]

   Toothbrushes are great for cleaning grout lines and around taps. Dishcloths or reusable wipes can be washed in the laundry, and microfiber cloths are formulated to penetrate and trap dirt.

2. **White Vinegar**
   Vinegar is a natural disinfectant that kills many types of germs. The white vinegar you buy in the store contains 5 percent acetic acid, which has antimicrobial properties.

   Studies have shown that vinegar (especially when used after hydrogen peroxide) is so powerful it can inhibit the growth of some strains of E. coli. It's nontoxic, and while it can smell strong, the smell fades very quickly. It's also effective in killing mold and can remove odors, mildew, and wax buildup. Vinegar is safe to use on all sorts of surfaces, such as countertops, floors, and windows.

   Concoction: Fill a spray bottle with a 50/50 ratio of water and spray onto surfaces. This spray is strong enough to clean even the grimy outsides of your windows.

3. **Hydrogen Peroxide**
   Hydrogen peroxide is a great disinfectant because it rapidly breaks down in the environment to plain

oxygen and water, and it's not dangerous to humans when used according to label directions. *Concoction:* Fill a spray bottle with a 50/50 ratio of water and spray onto surfaces. It can also be added to laundry as a bleach alternative. A cup of hydrogen peroxide will brighten your whites (as well as take stains out of mattresses when poured onto the stain and left for at least 1 hour).

4. **Baking Soda (instead of Comet)**
   Baking soda is a mild abrasive and acts very similar to Comet. It's used to clean, deodorize, soften water, and as a scouring agent. It can also be added to your rinse cycle as a fabric softener.

   For drain blockages, pour a half cup baking soda, a half cup vinegar, and add 2 cups of boiling water, and allow time for the fizzy chemical reaction to break up the blockage. Follow with a flush of boiling water.

5. **Lemon Juice**
   One of the strongest of the food acids, lemon juice is very effective against many types of household bacteria, for removing mineral deposits from faucets, and as a sink cleaner. The scent is very refreshing and fills your home with a citrus aroma. Depending on what you're cleaning, lemon juice can be combined with water, vinegar, salt, or baking soda.

   For furniture polish, combine 1/2 cup lemon juice, 1/4 cup of olive oil and 2 drops of lemon or orange essential oil. Citrawood is also a great natural wood polish brand.

6. **Castile Soap**
   Castile soap is made from 100 percent plant oils (no animal products, such as tallow, which are present in most commercial soaps). It's completely biodegradable and very earth-friendly. Because of its natural ingredients, castile soap is a common choice for those who want to be environmentally conscious. It's very gentle and can be used:

   - On the skin and as a body wash
   - By people who have sensitive skin
   - As a pet shampoo
   - On delicate surfaces and fabrics, such as silk

   Dr. Bronner's is a well-known, respected brand of castile soap (liquid or bar soap) that's available in many health-food stores. It comes in several different scents depending on the essential oils it contains, including lavender, almond, rose, and citrus orange.

   Although olive oil is the traditional base oil for castile soap, it can also be made with coconut, avocado, help, almond, walnut, or other oils. It can be unscented or scented with essential oils and florals. Mixed with oatmeal, it can also be used as an exfoliant. It's a fantastic replacement for commercial soaps!

7. **Essential Oils**
   These oils not only give natural cleaning products different scents, but they also offer another solution for disinfecting. Adding a few drops of lavender and tea tree oils in a spray bottle of water creates an antiseptic and antibacterial cleaner (and is a fantastic syoga mats, too!). It also leaves behind a pleasant scent when added to baking soda or hydrogen peroxide. Experiment with different scents in your mixture to see which ones you like best.

8. **Salt**
   Salt offers an incredible variety of benefits. From preserving and flavoring food, to soothing aches and pains, to cleaning our homes, salt is a household essential. Depending on what you're cleaning (see below), it can be used in different amounts with other products.

ALL-PURPOSE CLEANER RECIPE

For a great, all-natural, safe general-purpose cleaner, mix the following ingredients together in a spray bottle. Simply spray onto surfaces, let sit for several minutes, then wipe away with a sponge or cloth.

Ingredients:

- 1/2 cup white vinegar (vinegar alone has natural germ-killing properties)
- 2 cups hot water (hot water to dissolve the ingredients properly)
- 2 tablespoons baking soda

10–20 drops tea tree oil (a natural oil with powerful germ-killing abilities—oil of oregano is effective at killing germs) and another essential oil of your choice to balance out the tea tree scent which some people may find overpowering. Lemongrass is a great choice!

Store and keep the mixture in a spray bottle for future use.

Whole House Cleaning Tips

Now that we know about the healthy ingredients we need to buy for our cleaning cabinet, let's take a look at how we can use these ingredients to clean different areas of our home:

For countertops

Use a spray bottle with a 50/50 mix of hydrogen peroxide and water, followed by a good shining with a microfiber cloth. For tougher stains, mix baking soda or salt with water to make a mild abrasive. Keeping the baking soda in an empty sprinkle container (e.g. a Parmesan cheese container) is a great way to sprinkle it on surfaces.

To completely sanitize an area, spray first with 50/50 mix of water and hydrogen peroxide, followed by 50/50 water and white vinegar. This approach is just as effective as bleach and also works great for stainless steel sinks, cutting boards, refrigerators, oven tops, and more.

For sinks & faucets

Combine lemon juice and salt and mix to the consistency of toothpaste. Apply this to brass, copper, or stainless steel sinks and fixtures. Scrub gently, then rinse with water. This mixture is also great for removing rust stains. If you have mineral deposits on your faucets, spray on lemon juice and let it sit for several minutes before scrubbing off.

For dish & hand soap

Make a dishwashing soap using a 50/50 mix of water and castile soap, along with your favorite essential oil(s). For hand soaps, choose a naturally scented castile soap.

For mirrors & windows

Create a 50/50 mix of white vinegar and water in a spray bottle, using a cloth to wipe. Greasy windows?

Spray with a mix of 2 tablespoons lemon juice, 1/2 cup white vinegar, and 1 quart of warm water and watch them sparkle.

For stove tops, baths, showers, porcelain, & tile

For a soft scrub, dilute 1 part castile soap and 3 parts water. Sprinkling the area with baking soda, then spray the castile mix on top. Scour with a sponge to get rid of even the toughest stains and give a bright shine. If you have mineral deposits, spray on lemon juice and let it sit for several minutes before scrubbing off with a mildly abrasive sponge.

For tile and grout mold, spray with a 50/50 mix of hydrogen peroxide and water. Wait at least one hour before rinsing or using the shower.

For silverware

Keep your silver shiny with this ingenious method. Line a bucket or heat-safe bowl with aluminum foil and drop in tarnished silver. Pour in boiling water, a cup of baking soda, and a dash of salt. Let sit for a few minutes. The tarnish will transfer from the silver to the foil.

Now that we've ditched those toxic household chemicals for good, it's time to clear the air ... literally!

FRESHEN UP THE AIR

Fresh air is an important element of any healthy home, not only to clear out offensive odors, but also to remove stagnant air. Fresh air is vital to good health!

When it comes to the air in our home, never underestimate the importance of circulating fresh air, not only during the summer months, but also when the temperature drops. We may not realize it, but the air quality in our homes is often anything but fresh, especially when you consider dust, cleaning-product residue, germs from illnesses such as the cold and flu, cooking odors, and mold or mildew.

Open Your Windows

Come rain or shine, cold or heat, aim to throw open your house and car windows (unless in smoggy areas) for at least 15 minutes each day to circulate fresh air and replace the old, stagnant indoor air. If it's cold outside, put on a sweater. If you have the cold or flu, it's especially important to breathe in clean air because not only does it help get rid of accumulated impurities, but a well-oxygenated body emits a higher vibrational frequency and heals quicker.

Never Allow Cigarette Smoke in Your Home

If family members or friends smoke, encourage them to smoke outside. Secondhand smoke (SHS) contains hundreds of contaminants that negatively affect the health of both people and pets. SHS kills children and adults that don't smoke. Take a look at the following statistics, all of which relate to SHS:[1]

- SHS contains 7,000 chemical compounds. More than 250 of these chemicals are harmful, and at least 69 are known to cause cancer.
- There is a definitive link between SHS and lung cancer.
- Evidence suggests SHS is linked to lymphoma, leukemia, brain tumors in children, and cancers of the larynx (voice box), pharynx (throat), nasal sinuses, brain, bladder, rectum, stomach, and breast in adults.
- SHS contains about 20 chemicals that, in high concentrations, cause breast cancer in rodents. In humans, chemicals from SHS reach breast tissue and can be found in breast milk. A report from the

California EPA in 2005 concluded that the link between SHS and breast cancer is "consistent with a causal association in younger women." This means it acts as if it could be a cause of breast cancer.

In the US, the cost of extra medical care, illness, and death caused by SHS are over $10 billion per year:

- SHS causes between 150,000 and 300,000 lower respiratory tract infections (lung and bronchus) in children under 18 months of age, with 7,500 to 15,000 hospitalizations each year in the US.
- SHS causes an estimated 42,000 deaths from heart disease.
- SHS causes an estimated 3,400 deaths from lung cancer in adults.
- SHS causes worse asthma and asthma-related problems in up to 1 million asthmatic children.

There's never a good reason to allow anyone to smoke in your home or around your pets and children.

Air Fresheners Using Natural Scents

When it comes to using an air freshener, we have the choice of using natural air fresheners or commercial ones. Always aim for natural choices. Commercial air fresheners not only contain hormone-disrupting chemicals to create that artificial smell, but they also contain dozens of air pollutants, petroleum-derived propellants, and harmful synthetic fragrances. These fragrances are created to "copy" the scents of nature, scents that are naturally found in something called essential oils.

Let's talk about how you can use essential oils to naturally freshen the air in your home, and how to create your own air-freshening spray that beats the commercial stuff, hands down! But first, here are some tips on getting rid of tough house odors.

For kitchen odors

- Boil a pot of water with some orange and/or lemon peels, cloves, and cinnamon sticks, and let it simmer on the stove for a while. Simmering orange and lemon rinds creates a fresh, festive scent. Feel free to then pour the cooled water into a spray bottle for future use as a spray air freshener.

For garbage disposals

- Quarter a lemon, put all four pieces in the garbage disposal with running water, and leave the garbage disposal on for around 10 seconds.
- Pour a half cup of baking soda with 1 cup of distilled white vinegar into the disposal. Let it sit for 10 minutes before running the water and the garbage disposal.

For cooking odors

- Simmer 1 tablespoon of vinegar with 1 cup of water on the stove while cooking.
- Wiping cutting boards and utensils with vinegar is also a great way to get rid of pungent smells, such as fish.

For musty smells & gasoline spills

- Use a tray of cat litter! The main ingredient is diatomaceous earth, a naturally occurring mineral that absorbs odors. It also absorbs moisture in the air and kills pests that come in contact with it. If you prefer not to use cat litter, then buy a box of diatomaceous earth, fill a few bowls, and place them in the corners of musty rooms. You can find diatomaceous earth in garden supply stores.

Natural, all-purpose air fresheners

- Dissolve 2 tablespoons of baking soda in two cups of hot water and a half cup of lemon juice for an instant air freshener.
- For all you coffee lovers, keep a bowl of fresh or used coffee grounds on the counter. Some coffee shops give their used coffee grounds away for free, so stop by your favorite coffee joint and offer to relieve them of their stash.
- Mix 1 cup of water with 2 tablespoons of vodka and 20 to 30 drops of your favorite essential oil(s).
- Create a potpourri by collecting fragrant, dried flowers and herbs in a bowl. Common favorites include passion flower, hibiscus, orris root, orange peel, juniper berries, and sandalwood. Sprinkle with a few drops of your favorite scented essential oil.
- As we'll find out in the next section, houseplants are natural air purifiers that help remove subtle odors in the home. They're also known to remove formaldehyde (found in some paints, glues used on wood, and in furniture finishes).

Using Essential Oils

As we discussed in detail earlier, essential oils are a highly concentrated liquid extract of plants that not only provide fragrance, but also offer a range of therapeutic benefits. They're available in many natural-food stores, supplement stores, and online. The bottles may be small, but a little goes a long way as you'll be using only a few drops at a time. Just one little bottle may last you a year or more.

Essential oils are one of the best ways to add fresh scents to your home, while eliminating your exposure to harmful chemicals found in synthetic scents. You can add a few drops to just about anything, ranging from vinegar-based household cleaners to candles and bath water.

You can completely customize your scents based on what you like, and you can have fun mixing and matching your favorites. Various oil blends are also available. Here are some common essential oils used for natural home air fresheners:

- Orange/mandarin
- Lavender
- Lemon
- Bergamot
- Sandalwood
- Basil
- Rosemary
- Clary sage
- Rose
- Clove oil
- Neroli
- Peppermint
- Eucalyptus
- Cinnamon
- Ylang-ylang
- Juniper

When purchasing essential oils for air fresheners, always choose a reputable source that uses only natural, organic ingredients, or ingredients that are free from pesticides and chemical residue. Completely avoid products containing synthetic ingredients. The ingredient label should list only the plant(s)—nothing else.

If possible, buy from companies that use wild-harvested plants collected from their natural environment, such as forests, prairies, and deserts. The plants are often reseeded, or the roots are left to restock native populations. These companies include:

Young Living Essential Oils
VedAroma Essential Oils
Mountain Rose Herbs
The Herbalist Organic Essential Oils
Organic Infusions

HOMEMADE AIR FRESHENER

To make your own air-freshener spray, mix the following in a clean spray bottle:

- 1 cup water
- 2 tablespoons vodka (purchase a tiny bottle—unflavored and undiluted)
- Your favorite essential oil(s)

Some essential oils are much stronger than others, so begin conservatively when creating your special concoction. Screw on the top, shake well, and you're ready to go!

Homemade Oil Diffusers

Oil diffusers are another great way to infuse your home with natural, subtle scents you love. Many inexpensive infusers are on the market. Some can be used with tealight candles, with some of the prettiest made of soapstone. Simply place a few drops of essential oil in the upper bowl, and place a lighted tealight candle inside the burner base. As the candle burns, a gentle aroma of the oil infuses the air. For other types of diffusers, simply follow the manufacturer's instructions.

Moving on

Before we talk about personal-care products, let's explore the importance of houseplants and indoor trees. Not only are they a way for us to connect with nature and appreciate its beauty while indoors, but plants offer us other benefits too: they filter the air of pollutants, release oxygen, increase air humidity, and reduce dust. Some are even natural insect repellents!

HOUSEPLANTS

Who doesn't enjoy the feeling of being surrounded by plants and flowers? They instantly transform a room, bringing warmth and life, contributing to a Zen-like feeling of peace and tranquility. But there's a lot more to plants than meets the eye!

Let's take a look at why you shouldn't underestimate the importance of wonderful plant life in your home, as well as the benefits of creating your own herbal kitchen.

Plants Filter the Air around Them

According to NASA, plants help remove harmful contaminants in the air, including VOCs (volatile organic compounds) that can cause headaches and nausea. While some are better than others at absorbing various pollutants (chrysanthemums top the list), all show this behavior to some degree. Plants also help reduce airborne chemicals from cigarettes.

Plants Absorb Carbon Dioxide & Release Oxygen

By creating oxygen and lowering the carbon-dioxide content of the air, they can help improve our ability to sleep, reduce incidences of headaches, and reduce feelings of drowsiness (associated with excess carbon dioxide).

Plants Increase Air Humidity & Reduce Dust

These natural air humidifiers increase the moisture level in our homes, which can provide various health benefits, including a 30 percent reduction in cold-related illnesses, a reduction in dry skin, and a reduction in dust-related allergies. Some plants can help clear congestion—especially the eucalyptus plant, which is often used in cold and congestion remedies.

Plants Reduce Stress & Improve Mental Health

People that own houseplants suffer less from depression because caring for living, beautiful things naturally makes us feel happier and less lonely. Less stress translates to lower blood pressure. Plants and flowers contribute to our feelings of optimism and well-being.

Studies have shown that hospital patients who have rooms filled with plants and flowers, or who have a room with a garden view, recover more quickly than those without either.

Plants Have Healing Properties

Herbalism shows us that many plants have healing properties. Plant and plant combinations are used in thousands of remedies in traditional Chinese medicine, Ayurvedic medicine, Bach flower remedies, homeopathy, and Western herbalism. Aloe is just one example of a popular plant that can be applied directly to sunburn and other skin conditions to help our skin heal quicker. Echinacea is an herb commonly used for infections, and to relieve cold and flu symptoms.

Many Plants Are Natural Insect Repellents

Citronella, marigold, catnip, lavender, eucalyptus, and rosemary are just a few examples of plants that naturally repel mosquitoes.

If you've ever doubted the power and energy of plants, I strongly recommend reading *The Secret Life of Plants* by Peter Tompkins and Christopher Bird. Described as a fascinating account of the physical, emotional, and spiritual relationship between plants and man, the book takes us on a journey into a world where we realize that plants are so much more than they appear. Another wonderful book is *Plant Intelligence & the Imaginal Realm* by Stephen Harrold Buhner.

Tests conducted in laboratory conditions show that not only do plants have "humanlike" feelings for the people they interact with, but they also immediately react and respond to changes in their environment, including the moods and thoughts of people around them.

AN HERBAL KITCHEN

You may have a variety of herbs and spices in your spice cabinet, but how often do you make salads and cook meals with fresh herbs? Many common herbs can now be found in the plant or produce section of supermarkets or in home-improvement stores and nurseries for under $5.

Place a variety of your favorites on your window ledge or around your kitchen, and include them in your salads and other meals. For a nice display, create an herbal basket. All you need is a large basket, organic potting soil, and your favorite herbs! Make sure you purchase organic herbs free of harmful pesticides and neonicotinoids (pesticides that kill bees).

— THE HEALING POWER OF HERBS —

Herbs are a potent source of disease-fighting antioxi PDF/X-1a dants. Oregano alone has 42 times the antioxidant capacity of apples,[1] and we now know that oregano oil is a broad-spectrum antibiotic containing carvacrol, a compound with powerful antimicrobial properties effective in treating the drug-resistant staph infection and E. coli.[2]

Herbalists and natural healthcare practitioners often recommend plant extracts and herbs in place of antibiotics. In his book *Healing with Whole Foods*, Dr. Paul Pitchford lists herbs and extracts that contain antiviral and antibiotic properties, including:

- Aloe gel
- Black-walnut extract
- Chaparral leaf
- Cinnamon
- Clove
- Colloidal silver
- Colostrum (bovine or goat)
- Echinacea root
- Eucalyptus lemon/radiata
- Garlic bulb, raw
- Ginger root, raw
- Goldenseal root
- Lavender
- Lemon/lime
- Nutmeg
- Oil of oregano
- Olive-leaf extract
- Onion
- Tea-tree oil
- Thyme

Because these products are highly concentrated, it's important to make sure they're organically harvested and not treated with pesticides. If you're interested in using medicinal herbs, follow your natural healthcare practitioner's advice on dosage based on your specific condition.

Caring for Your Plants

You don't need a green thumb to have thriving plants in your home. Most plants need very little care, and the details of what they need should be on their information/care tag. If that's missing, ask the store attendant to find one for you. When buying your plants, remember 5 important things:

1. Look for plants that don't contain bee-killing pesticides (labeled as containing "neonicotinoids"). The neonic levels in plants sold at many hardware stores and nurseries are high enough to kill bees outright. Retailers are now beginning to take steps to no longer sell plants with bee-harming pesticides. Some retailers, such as Home Depot and BJ's Wholesale Club, require warning labels on plants treated with neonics. The European Union has banned the use of neonicotinoids on flowering plants and crops.
2. Check to see if your plant needs sun, shade, or partial shade. Then make sure that you place them in the best area of your home, depending on the light available. A plant that needs full sun won't survive in a shaded area. Conversely, a plant that needs shade will suffer in an area that has too much sun.
3. Check to see how much water they need, and put their watering schedule in your calendar. Their watering schedule may need a little tweaking depending on where they're placed. Simply check the soil by sticking your finger into it. If the soil's moist, no water is needed. If the soil's dry with little to no moisture, it needs watering.
4. Check to see that the plant(s) you've chosen aren't toxic to children or household pets (if you have children or pets in your home).
5. For finicky reasons known only to plants, sometimes they do well in one area of the house, but not in others. If your plant appears to be struggling and has the correct amount of light and water, try relocating it to a new area. Many times my plants have looked sapped of all life in one room, only to become much happier and perkier when moved somewhere else!

Personal-Care Products

Now that we've removed all the toxic chemicals from our home, discovered healthy air-freshening alternatives, and learned about the healing power of plants, let's move on to the last part of this section and make some important changes when it comes to the products we put on our body every day.

PERSONAL-CARE PRODUCTS

Even though it may seem obvious to us that the quality of the food we put into our body is important to our health, what may not be so obvious is that the quality of the personal-care products we put on our bodies every day also plays a very important role in our health and our vibrational state.

Personal-care products contain thousands of chemicals, many of which have been shown in animal studies, human studies, or both to damage our body. Many have never been tested for safety. Exposure to these ingredients is linked to rising rates of neurological disorders such as autism, as well as to cancer, asthma, autoimmunity, and reproductive problems.

Some of these chemicals are illegal in other countries because studies have confirmed they're hazardous to our health. Europe, Canada, Australia, and New Zealand have stricter standards in general when it comes to banning dangerous chemicals in personal-care products than the US, where the FDA has done very little to regulate dangerous ingredients in personal-care products. Even known offenders such as formaldehyde, triclosan, and phthalates are still legally permissible in US product formulations, while banned in other countries.

Because we use some of these products every day, the toxic elements inside them accumulate in our cells and tissues. Over time, this buildup degrades our body.

Every day, the average woman absorbs approximately 110 artificial chemicals from the use of personal-care products before leaving the house for work. The average man absorbs approximately 88 artificial chemicals.

Let's take a look at the 12 categories of products we use the most:

- Soaps
- Deodorants
- Moisturizers, lotions, lip products
- Beauty masks
- Shaving/after-shave products
- Cosmetics
- Sunscreens
- Shampoos and conditioners
- Hair-styling products
- Nail polish
- Toothpaste
- Mouthwash

It's very easy to take for granted that these products are "safe" and "nontoxic," but the opposite is true for over 80 percent of the products on the market. For example, studies show that some of the most commonly used sunscreens contain very toxic ingredients that are not only dangerous for our skin, but are direct contributors to the skin cancer they claim to protect against. When they're absorbed by our skin, they pose far more danger than the sun itself when it comes to skin cancer.

Clearing Out the Junk

Let's get started by cleaning house.

First...

Just as we did with our food, the first step is to collect all our personal-care products into one big pile so that we can take a good look at what's inside them.

Don't forget to check gym bags, purses, cars, and work drawers for any stray bottles.

Then...

We'll learn how to read product ingredient labels so that we can separate the good products from the bad. We'll also create a "not so good" pile that may not be the worst offenders, but are products we should plan not to repurchase (or that we should use only in very small quantities on rare occasions).

Cancer-causing chemicals are found in many different types and brands of personal-care products. In fact, some of the biggest brands out there (ranging from cheap to very expensive, high-end brands) are the worst offenders. There's nothing "beautiful" about using cosmetics that contain cancer-causing agents.

Categories of Chemicals

Generally speaking, industrial chemicals fall into one of the following 7 categories:

1. Hormone disruptors (disrupt or mimic hormone production in the body)
2. Carcinogens (cancer-causing agents)
3. Allergens (can cause an allergic reaction)
4. Neurotoxins (toxic to the nervous system)
5. General toxins (considered toxic to the body in general)
6. Reproductive toxins (adversely affects reproductive system and the developing fetus)
7. Pesticides (named so because they're designed to "harm life")

Nearly all personal-care products on the shelves of supermarket and pharmacy chains, cosmetic stores, and department store cosmetic counters contain *at least* one toxin from these categories, with most containing several. Let's take a look at some of the common offenders.

BHA & BHT: The National Toxicology Program classifies butylated hydroxyanisole (BHA) as reasonably anticipated to be a human carcinogen. It can cause skin depigmentation. In animal studies, BHA produces liver damage and causes stomach cancers such as papillomas and carcinomas, and it interferes with normal reproductive-system development and thyroid hormone levels. The European Union considers it unsafe in fragrance. It's found in food, food packaging, and personal-care products.

Boric acid / sodium borate: These chemicals disrupt hormones and harm the male reproductive system. Men working in boric acid–producing factories have a greater risk of decreased sperm count and libido. In animals, high doses cause testicular damage to mice, rats, and dogs. The cosmetic industry's own safety panel states that these chemicals are unsafe for infants and that they damage skin because they're easily absorbed by our skin. Despite this fact, boric acid is found in some diaper creams.

Cyclomethicone / cyclotetrasiloxane (D4 & D5): These are silicone-based compounds used to smooth, soften, and moisten. They help make products such as deodorants slide on more easily. These toxic ingredients are classed by the European Union as endocrine disruptors and possible reproductive toxicants that may impair fertility. High doses have been shown to cause uterine tumors and harm to reproductive and immune systems.

Dibutyl phthalate (DBP): This is used in some nail products and as a fragrance. It's been shown to cause reproductive and developmental defects and is classed as a suspected endocrine disruptor by the European Union. Health Canada states there's evidence to suggest phthalates may cause health effects such as liver and kidney failure in young children if these products are taken in by mouth. It's highly toxic to aquatic organisms and has been banned by the European Union in cosmetics and children's products.

Diethanolamine & DEA-related ingredients: These are used to make foamy, creamy products. They can react to form nitrosamines, which in turn may cause cancer.

Formaldehyde: This is a potent preservative considered a known human carcinogen by the International Agency on Research on Cancer. Formaldehyde, also an asthmagen, neurotoxicant, and developmental toxicant, was once mixed into many personal-care products as an antiseptic. Its use has declined, but some hair straighteners depend on formaldehyde's hair-stiffening action and release substantial amounts of the chemical.

Formaldehyde-releasing preservatives / formalin: These can be labeled as DMDM hydantoin, bronopol, diazolidinyl urea, imidazolidinyl urea, methenamine, and quarternium-15 and are cosmetic preservatives that form formaldehyde to kill bacteria growing in products. The preservatives—and the formaldehyde they generate—can trigger allergic skin reactions. Formaldehyde releasers are widely used in US products.

Fragrance / parfum (listed as an ingredient): Such an innocent word, yet this single ingredient can contain dozens of hormone-disrupting elements. Federal law doesn't require companies to list any of the chemicals in their fragrance mixture on product labels. Recent research from EWG and the Campaign for Safe Cosmetics found an average of 14 chemicals in 17 name-brand fragrance products, none of which were listed on the label. Fragrances are among the top 5 allergens in the world. Always buy fragrance-free wherever possible, unless the scent is from plant-based extracts.

Oxybenzone / benzophenone: According to the CDC, sunscreen agents are now found in the bodies of nearly all Americans. In human epidemiological studies, oxybenzone has been linked to irritation, sensitization, and allergies. During pregnancy, it's also linked to decreased birth weight in newborn girls and greater birth weight in newborn boys. Studies on laboratory animals show that oxybenzone and its metabolites may disrupt the hormone system, and it's been linked to renal adenomas in rats (a precursor to cancer).

Parabens: Parabens are a group of compounds very commonly used in personal-care products that have been found in measurable concentrations in breast tumors. UK researchers found measurable concentrations of 6 different parabens in 20 human breast tumors. Parabens are estrogen-mimicking preservatives used widely in cosmetics. The CDC has detected parabens in virtually all Americans bodies. According to the European Commission's Scientific Committee on Consumer Products, longer-chain parabens, such as propyl and butyl paraben and their branched counterparts isopropyl and isobutylparabens, may disrupt the endocrine system and cause reproductive and developmental disorders. Examples include:

- methylparaben | propylparaben |isopropylparaben | isobutylparabens | ethylparaben | butylparaben | propyl-p-hydroxybenzoate (E216)

PEG compounds (polyethylene glycol): This is a family of conditioning and cleaning agents that go by many names. These synthetic chemicals are often contaminated with 1,4-dioxane, which the US government considers a probable human carcinogen and which easily penetrates the skin. Cosmetic makers could easily remove 1,4-dioxane from ingredients, but tests document it's still a common presence in many products.

Petrolatum (a.k.a. petroleum jelly): This is used to create shine in hair products and as a moisture barrier in skin-care products. It may be contaminated with PAH (polycyclic aromatic hydrocarbons), which have been directly linked to cancer when used over extended periods of time. The European Union classes petrolatum as a carcinogen and restricts its use in cosmetics.

Petroleum distillates: These are petroleum-extracted cosmetic ingredients commonly found in mascara. They may cause contact dermatitis and are often contaminated with cancer-causing impurities. They're produced in oil refineries for automobile fuel, heating oil, and chemical feedstocks.

P-phenylenediamine: These are coal-tar-derived hair colorants linked to cancer, immune-system toxicity, and other health effects. They're listed as:

- C.I., followed by 5 digits (e.g., C.I. 77000)
- D&C, followed by a number or color (e.g., D&C Orange 4)
- FD&C, followed by a number or color (e.g., FD&C Blue 1)

Coal tar is a recognized human carcinogen that may also be contaminated with low levels of heavy metals. The US National Cancer Institute has linked p-phenylenediamine to tumors, and epidemiologic literature has confirmed statistically significant associations between hair dye and several types of cancer.

Phthalates: These are plasticizing chemicals that are considered probable reproductive or developmental toxins and endocrine disruptors. They've caused reproductive birth defects in animals (especially males), are sometimes hidden under the ingredient "fragrance," and are found in some nail products. Two common phthalates used in the US (yet banned in Europe) are dibutyl phthalate (DBP) and diethylhexyl phthalate.

Polyacrylamide: This is used to help hair hold its style and keep makeup in a compressed tablet or cake form, as well as in sunscreens to cause the skin to retain water. Acrylamide is considered so toxic it's given the highest hazard rating by the Environmental Working Group. It's carcinogenic and linked to developmental and reproductive toxicity, allergic reactions, neurotoxicity, endocrine disruption, and is a skin and eye irritant. Despite its high toxicity, it hasn't been banned in the US.

Polytetrafluoroethylene (PTFE): Previously found in kitchen pans—and the main component of Gore-Tex—this chemical is now found in many personal-care products, including skin creams, mineral makeup, injectable wrinkle fillers, and nail polish. It's used as a bulking and binding agent and as a skin conditioner. The concern is the potential contamination with perfluorooctonoic acid (PFOA), which has been directly associated with cancer, reproductive toxicity, and endocrine disruption.

Resorcinol: A common ingredient in hair color and bleaching products, it's a skin irritant and is toxic to the immune system. In animal studies, resorcinol can disrupt normal thyroid function. The federal government regulates exposure to resorcinol in the workplace, but its use isn't restricted at all in any personal-care products.

Sodium laureth sulfate (SLS) / sodium dodecyl: A detergent found in over 90 percent of shampoos, it's been shown to damage protein formation in eye tissue in young animals and to penetrate systemic tissues (e.g., the heart, brain, and liver), which raises serious concerns for infants and children. A single drop can cause retention in tissues for up to 5 days, and it can react with other ingredients to form cancer-causing compounds. SLS is also a skin irritant implicated in scalp irritation, dandruff, itching, and premature hair loss.

Styrene / acrylates copolymer: Associated with organ-system toxicity, styrene is listed as "reasonably anticipated to be a carcinogen" by the National Toxicology Program as it's been linked to leukemia, lymphoma, stem, blood, and bone-marrow cancers. It's considered "safe based on low absorption" due to claims that the molecules don't penetrate the skin. Evidence shows this isn't the case.

Thimerosal (mercury): Examples include the word "mercury" within any ingredient, and more obscure terms such as 2-mercaptobenzoato-s, ethylmercury, sodium o-mercapobenzoato, and ingredients beginning with ethylmercurithio-. Mercury-based preservatives are used in some cosmetics for eye products, as well as in vaccines. They're considered very toxic, and any products containing them should be completely avoided. The FDA states that mercury compounds are readily absorbed through the skin and tend to accumulate in the body. They are neurotoxic, can cause allergic reactions and skin irritation, and are especially toxic to the developing fetal brain during pregnancy and infancy. Many flu shots still contain thimerosal.

Toluene: This is a volatile petrochemical solvent, paint thinner, and potent neurotoxicant that acts as an irritant, impairs breathing, and causes nausea. A pregnant woman's exposure to toluene vapors may impair fetal development. In human epidemiological and animal studies, toluene has been associated with toxicity to the immune system. Some evidence suggests a link to malignant lymphoma.

Triclosan / Triclocarban: An antimicrobial pesticide in liquid soap (triclosan) or soap bars (triclocarban), as well as in antibacterial cosmetics, toothpaste, and deodorants, it's very toxic to the aquatic environment and is often found in the cells and tissues of the body due to widespread use of antimicrobial cleaning products. Triclosan disrupts thyroid function and reproductive hormones. The American Medical Association and the American Academy of Microbiology say that soap and water are just as effective in preventing the spread of infections and reduction in bacteria. Overuse of triclosan/triclocarban may promote the development of antibiotic-resistant bacteria.

Triethanolamine & TEA-related ingredients: Used to allow oil- and water-soluble ingredients to blend, they're associated with organ-system toxicity and are immune, respiratory, and skin toxicants or allergens; they also cause dryness of hair and skin. Animal studies show sensory organs are affected at very low doses, especially when used around the mouth, eyes, and lips. When used on mammalian cells, they showed positive mutation results. They've been shown to cause bladder and liver cancer, as well as changes in testicles. The Cosmetic Ingredient Review (CIR) determined triethanolamine is "safe" for use in skin-care ingredients if used briefly and followed by a thorough rinsing unless the concentration is under 5 percent.

Lack of Studies

Because safety studies don't exist on most of the chemicals used in personal-care ingredients, there's no trail of cause and effect to show to what degree these chemicals damage our health. We're unable to say, for example, that the parabens in a skin-care cream used for years caused breast cancer in a 35-year-old woman with no family history of the disease. But what we *are* able to say is that:

1. Parabens are found in high concentrations in breast-cancer tissue, and studies have linked them to breast cancer, and
2. This being the case, they may contribute to or cause breast cancer, and applying them regularly may increase our risk of developing breast cancer.

Walking Away from Chemicals

Now that we have a very good understanding of what bad ingredients are (and we know to avoid any products containing ingredients we doubt), let's talk about ingredients that are much healthier and safer choices to put on our skin. We'll also talk about why we should never trust beautiful pictures and flashy label advertising, why we should choose organic ingredients where possible, and other important things to keep in mind when making our purchases.

MAKING NATURAL & SAFE CHOICES

When it comes to making the right choices for our personal-care products, now that we know what to avoid, let's take a look at the type of ingredients to look for instead.

Generally speaking, healthy ingredients are those that come from:

Botanicals
These are plants that provide us with the extracts, oils, butters, thickeners, and emulsifiers.

Minerals
These are naturally occurring elements formed by geologic processes that occur in nature.

Let's see what these ingredients look like on product labels and make sure they're the *only* types of ingredients we see on any product that we use on our face and body.

Plant Ingredients & Extracts

Many plant extracts are used in skin-care products. Some are especially high in antioxidants and nutrients that are very beneficial for our skin. Examples include:

Aloe Vera | Arnica | Berries | Calendula | Chamomile | Chlorophyll | Courmarin | Geraniol | Kelp | Lavender | Oats | Passion Flower | Pomegranate | Rose | Vanilla

Keep in mind that just because an ingredient is natural doesn't mean it's necessarily best for your skin. Some plant extracts such as tea tree oil can be irritating and/or drying for some people, yet may work well for others.

— PLANT OILS —

Plant oils are found in almost every natural skin cream or lotion. Examples include:

Acai | Almond | Apricot Kernel | Argan | Avocado | Coconut | Evening Primrose | Hemp | Jojoba | Lemongrass | Lemon | Macadamia Nut | Olive | Pomegranate | Rose | Rose Hip | Sesame Seed | Spearmint | Sunflower | Sweet Almond | Sweet Orange | Tamanu | Tangerine | Tea Tree

— PLANT BUTTERS —

Plant butters are soft, creamy substances that contain antioxidants and other phytonutrients in varying degrees and are wonderfully nourishing to our skin. The most common ones include:

- Shea butter (fat extracted from the nut of the shea tree)
- Cocoa butter (fat extracted from cocoa beans)
- Mango butter (fat extracted from the mango fruit kernel)
- Avocado butter (fat extracted from the flesh of avocado fruit)
- Coconut butter (fat extracted from coconut flesh)
- Cupuacu butter (fat extracted from the cupuacu fruit)

For people with acne-prone skin, some plant butters may trigger acne flare-ups when used on the face.

— PLANT-BASED EMULSIFIERS & THICKENERS —

Emulsifiers are the basis of creams and lotions. They allow water and oil to mix and form a cream, creating an effective method of providing moisture to skin as the water attaches to the oil for deeper absorption. Examples include:

Beeswax | Caranuba Wax | Guar Gum | Sclerotium | Rolfsii Gum | Soy Lecithin (nonorganic will likely be genetically modified) | Xanthan Gum

When we choose nonorganic skin-care creams, we're likely using a product that has synthetic emulsifiers, many of which are unhealthy for our skin.

— MINERALS —

Minerals are now used in lotions, sunscreens, and cosmetics. Unfortunately, many of these products also contain other undesirable ingredients, so check the ingredient label very carefully. The two commonly used minerals are:

Titanium Dioxide | Zinc Oxide

When it comes to sunscreens, ONLY choose mineral sunscreens that contain one or both of these minerals and nothing else except natural ingredients. This is especially important when applying sunscreens to infants or children (more on this below).

— ANTIOXIDANTS / ANTIAGING —

Many chemicals found in skin-care products are considered antiaging. In reality, the best contain antioxidants found in plant oils and extracts. These antioxidants are also found in concentrated amounts. Examples include:

Alpha Lipoic Acid (ALA) | Vitamin C (preferably fat-soluble vitamin C ester) | Vitamin E (tocopherol) | Yucca Extract | Vitamin A (Retin-A products) | Green Tea Extract | Sea Buckthorn | Dimethylaminoethanol (DMAE) (an anti-inflammatory nutrient) | Hyaluronic Acid

A Word about Acne Products

Specific ingredients used in acne treatments, such as salicylic acid, benzoyl peroxide, and Retin-A products, can be very harsh and cause irritation, but in small quantities can help keep acne under control. Although the ingredients were originally naturally derived from plants (e.g., salicylic acid is naturally derived from the willow bark tree), most are now synthesized in a lab.

By far, acne breakouts are most attributable to our diet and hydration, skin care products, and hormonal fluctuations. On the Body Healer Protocol, many skin conditions automatically clear up, and there will no longer be any need for acne products—especially when pasteurized dairy products, fried foods, and synthetic chemicals in processed and refined foods are removed.

Natural vs. Unnatural Ingredient Lists

Now that we know the difference between unnatural and toxic ingredients and the healthy ones we should be looking for, let's take a look at some practical examples of good ingredient lists vs. bad ones.

GOOD VS. BAD MOISTURIZER

NOURISH ORGANICS LIGHTWEIGHT MOISTURIZING FACE LOTION

Organic Aloe Barbadensis Leaf Juice | Organic Shea Butter | Autolyzed Yeast | Organic Argan Oil | Organic Cupuacu Butter | Organic Rose Flower Distillate | Xanthan Gum | Organic Rice Bran Extract | Organic Sweet Orange Essential Oil | Organic Vegetable Glycerin | Organic Sweet Almond Oil | Organic Acai Fruit Oil | Organic Soy Lecithin | Tocopherol (vitamin E) | Ascorbic Acid (vitamin C)

-VS-

VERY COMMONLY USED FACE LOTION

Water | Cyclopentasiloxane | Glycerin | Polyethylene | Niacinamide (vitamin B_3) | Dimethicone Crosspolymer | Dimethicone | Stearyl Dimethicone | Propylene Glycol | Butylene Glycol | Panthenol (pro-vitamin B_5) | Palmitoyl Pentapeptide 3 (amino-peptide) | Tocopheryl Acetate (vitamin E) | Lavender Extract | Arnica Montana Flower Extract | Green Tea Extract | Alanine | Arginine | Betaine | Glycine | Lysine | Proline | Serine | Threonine | Glutamic Acid | Sodium PCA | Sorbitol | PEG 10 | Dimethicone Crosspolymer | Sucrose Polycottonseedate | Allantoin | Petrolatum | Bis PEG|PPG 14|14 Dimethicone | Cetyl Ricinoleate | Disodium EDTA | PEG 100 Stearate | Phenoxyethanol | PEG 10 Dimethicone | Benzyl Alcohol | Butylparaben | Ethylparaben | Isobutylparaben, Methylparaben Propylparaben | Fragrance | Red 40 | Blue 1

GOOD VS. BAD SOAP

A WILD SOAP BAR - PASSIONFLOWER

Organic Extra Virgin Olive Oil | Organic Coconut Oil | Sustainable Organic Palm Oil | Organic Sunflower Oil | Organic Castor Oil | Organic Passion Fruit Oil | Distilled Water | Organic Oat Flour | Essential Oils (orange, ylang-ylang, patchouli, rose geranium, clove) | Sea Salt | Passion Flower | Cosmetic Grade Earth Pigments

- VS -

VERY WELL-KNOWN SOAP BRAND

Triclocarban | Sodium Cocoate | Sodium Palm Kernelate | Sodium Palmate | Sodium Tallowate | Water | Talc | Coconut Acid | Palm Acid | Tallow Acid | Palm Kernel Acid | Peg-6 Methyl Ether | Fragrance | Glycerin | Sorbitol | Sodium Chloride | Pentasodium Pentetate | Tetrasodium Etidronate | Yellow 5, 8, 4

What an enlightening experience! Did you count the number of toxic chemicals we already talked about that are listed in the unhealthy products? What about other items you don't recognize that sound questionable?

Putting It All Together

Let's put all we've learned together so that we're fully prepared when we get to the store to purchase new products. Here are 5 important tips when choosing *any* personal-care product, especially skin or beauty products we put on our body every day.

#1 – Read the Ingredient List

When you pick up any personal-care product, look first at the ingredient list. Generally speaking, if you see an ingredient you don't recognize as natural, question it. If it contains one of the toxic ingredients we talked about earlier, or if the ingredient list is very long and filled with unpronounceable and unrecognizable chemicals, definitely ditch it.

If you're not sure of any ingredients (i.e., they may "sound" natural but you don't recognize them), you can look up its level of toxicity by searching for it in the Environmental Working Group's Skin Deep Cosmetic Database (**www.ewg.org/skindeep**). This database is continually updated and contains nearly 69,000 personal-care products and growing, searchable by product type, brand, or ingredient. It's the most comprehensive database in existence to help us find the rating on the ingredients in our personal-care products.

#2 – Natural? Safe? Probably Not

Similar to food packaging, when it comes to the labels on personal skin-care products, take each claim with a grain of salt. Thanks to the lax labeling laws on these products, "natural" and "safe" mean very little, and product manufacturers use these terms indiscriminately based on their own definitions.

It's very common for manufacturers to claim their products are "all natural" even though they contain dangerous and cancer-causing ingredients in proprietary formulations. These ingredients are hidden behind generic terms such as "fragrance" or "parfum" on the label.

Many skin-care products are considered safer in places such as Europe and other countries where regulatory standards are much stricter. To add insult to injury, many companies offer safer versions of the exact same skin-care products in these countries than they do in the US.

#3 – Where Possible, Choose Certified Organic

The one claim you can trust on product packaging is the USDA certified-organic seal. On any personal-care product label, this seal indicates that 95 percent or more of the ingredients in the product must be organic.

Not only are organic products far better for your health because of the absence of dangerous chemicals, they're also environmentally responsible choices. They contain no synthetic chemicals and fertilizers that have a destructive effect on our soil, water, and our health, and ingredients are often harvested with sustainable farming practices. Our bodies also assimilate organic and truly natural ingredients better.

Organic ingredients are far less likely to cause irritation and allergic reactions on our skin as compared to synthetic ingredients. If organic products do cause irritation (e.g., an essential oil), it's due to the natural compounds in the plant, not to toxic compounds that cause much more serious harm.

#4 – Look for Products That Are "Cruelty-Free"

"Cruelty-free" indicates that the product wasn't tested on animals. In 2004, the European Union banned animal testing for cosmetic products and now bans the sale of cosmetic products with ingredients tested on animals. Israel and India followed suit in 2007 and 2013 respectively. This sadly isn't the case in the US.

Europe, Israel, and India have banned animal testing for cosmetic products. The US hasn't implemented this ban, nor does it give these animals any protection under the Animal Welfare Act.

Investigators have found product-testing animals kept in deplorable, cruel, inhumane conditions. These animals are deprived of medical care and are given no protection under the Animal Welfare Act (a fact most people don't know). Animal testing should *never* play any part in personal-care or "beauty" products.

The FDA does not require any cosmetic to undergo animal testing. It's entirely up to the product manufacturer, whether they ***choose*** *to test their products on animals. Many do.*

Animal testing involves:[1]

- Skin and eye irritation tests where chemicals are rubbed onto shaved skin or dropped into the eyes of restrained animals who are offered no pain relief
- Repeated force-feeding to look for signs of illness, cancer, or birth defects
- "Lethal-dose" tests where animals are forced to swallow large amounts of a test chemical to find the dose that causes death

At the end of the testing, the animals are killed, normally by asphyxiation, neck-breaking, or decapitation. No pain relief is given.

Many personal-care product companies don't test their products on animals and produce a large variety of high-quality, very effective skin-care and cosmetic products. There are also thousands of ingredients tested to be both safe and natural for use in personal-care products that have a long history of use, and for those that haven't yet been tested, a number of nonanimal tests can be used to assess their safety.

There is zero justification for animal testing.

How to Choose Cruelty-Free

Always choose products that are cruelty-free. Look for the "Leaping Bunny" logo certification to make sure the product hasn't been tested on any animals.

The words "not tested on animals" or an image of another bunny may only refer to the finished product, yet animal testing occurs at the ingredient level. Companies also often contract with other companies that do test on animals. The only way you can be 100 percent certain that the product is completely cruelty-free is to make sure the product's been certified by the Leaping Bunny Program, which requires no animal testing be used in *any* phase of the product's development.

Many cruelty-free products can be easily found at health stores and online.

#5 – Be VERY Wary of Sunscreens

Sunscreens are some of the worst offenders when it comes to toxic chemicals, and many of us apply these creams in large quantities. Even though we learned about sunscreens and SPFs earlier in the protocol when we explored the benefits of vitamin D, let's recap what to look for when we make our next purchase.

When it comes to sunscreens, a great deal of misinformation is circulating. An unhealthy fear of the sun has caused many women to significantly overuse sunscreens, contributing to the vitamin D epidemic. Many of these sunscreens contain very toxic chemicals that not only damage the skin, but studies now show that when they're absorbed into the skin, the sun then bakes these chemicals into our skin, contributing to skin cancer.

Clinical studies have shown that melanomas have been found to *decrease* with greater sun exposure and to increase with the use of chemical sunscreens. You have far more to fear from today's chemicalized sunscreens and their dangerous ingredients than from the sun itself. Disturbingly, most dermatologists are unaware of these studies.

When choosing a sunscreen:

1. Always choose mineral sunscreens. The active ingredient will be either titanium dioxide or zinc oxide, both of which work by reflecting UVA and UVB rays, rather than synthetic ingredients that are absorbed by the skin.
2. It should contain very few and only plant-sourced inactive ingredients.
3. If possible, choose organic.

Badger Organic SPF 15 Sunscreen is a great example of a mineral sunscreen that contains only natural ingredients. Let's take a look at both the active and inactive ingredient list:

Active: Non-Nano | Uncoated Zinc Oxide 18.75%

Inactive: Organic Sunflower Oil | Organic Beeswax | Tocopherol (Sunflower vitamin E) | Seabuckthorn Fruit Extract

When applying any product to a child's skin, it's especially important to choose only products that contain natural ingredients. Most sunscreens on the market should never be allowed anywhere near a child's skin.

HEALING WITH ENERGY

Before we begin learning how to directly use the flow of high vibrational energy to heal our body and balance our emotional and psychological state, let's talk about what energy medicine is and how it works, as well as the common pitfalls that prevent many people from experiencing any success when visiting energy medicine practitioners.

The Human Energy Field

As we know, at a fundamental level our entire body is composed of energy that emits an energy field. This field of energy expands out from our body several feet and can be photographed using a special type of photography called Kirlian photography. This energy is an electromagnetic field sometimes called an "aura" that can be seen by the naked eye with a little training and practice.

All the systems of our body are interconnected and reflect our state of health via the human energy field. Disease is the result of a disturbance in this energy field.

Stress – The Missing Link

A significant, powerful connection exists between stress and disease, and many health-related problems are either a result of or are aggravated by stress.

Our emotional state dramatically impacts how our immune system functions, effectively suppressing it during times of high stress. Our thoughts are pure energy that use the brain as their interface with the rest of our body. Changes in our thought processes create changes in our physical body by affecting and sometimes impeding the flow of energy.

Stress-triggered neurological and hormonal activities are the primary causes of organ wear and tear, and they create a foundation for nervous-system and immune-system disorders.

Disease isn't a cause; it's an effect. The energy disturbance is the cause, creating a cascading effect on the body. The energy behind our thoughts and our perceptions, as well as in the quality of the food we eat, the lifestyle choices we make, and the chemicals we expose ourselves to all cause biological changes in our body for good (health) or for bad (disease).

"The body is the battlefield for the war games of the mind."

Brian Luke Seaward
Author, Speaker

Thoughts are things, invisible and powerful. They are particles of energy that interact with their surroundings.

WHAT IS ENERGY MEDICINE

The definition may surprise you! When it comes to energy medicine, there is a great deal of confusion. It's a branch of medicine that uses energy and its spectrum of vibrational frequencies to diagnose and heal different diseases. Common diagnostic methods such as X-rays, radiation therapy, and electromagnetic field stimulators used to heal fractured bones are all forms of energy medicine. When doctors use full-spectrum light therapy to treat those suffering from seasonal affective disorder, they're using a form of energy medicine.

Energy medicine, also known as vibrational medicine, is based on the principle that when the energy frequency of our body (or individual organs) drops below a healthy range, it becomes susceptible to diseases that resonate at lower frequencies. Energy medicine works by rebalancing the energy field that caused the body to generate abnormal cells and tissues. When the organs and systems of our body are restored to their correct frequency range, our body's energy equilibrium is restored. Cell and tissue growth normalizes, cellular congestion clears up, and tumors and any other diseased tissue are shed from our body.

Understanding how our health directly relates to our energy state isn't a new concept. In fact, it traces back thousands of years to various ancient civilizations, and it's a founding principle in both traditional Chinese medicine and Ayurvedic medicine (the chakra system). Ancient Egyptians made use of color therapy by using solarium-type rooms filled with windows of colored glass. Sun shining through the glass would flood the patient with specific colors. Energy healing techniques have also evolved from Native American and other traditions.

Different Approaches to Energy Medicine

Today, the term "energy medicine" refers to several different types of treatment. Even though these treatment models may differ from each other in their approach to treating our body, they're all based on the principle that disturbances in the human energy field have resulted in illness or imbalance, and that this energy disturbance must be addressed.

The following energy-based treatment methods can be used as a complement to traditional medical care, or, depending on the condition, alone as a complete system of healing. It's important, however, to use these methods as part of a whole-body approach to health, as we do in the Body Healer Protocol.

Energy Healers

The term "energy healers" refers to practitioners that use their hands and their intention to detect any imbalance in our body and to focus streams of energy on the imbalance to correct it. As well as using their hands, practitioners may also use crystals, sound, light, and color to channel the energy. This channeled energy is known as "life-force energy" (US/Europe), "chi" (China), "qi" (Japan), or "prana" (India). The energy is channeled through the body of the practitioner and into the body of the patient to normalize the frequency of the patient's energy field.

Energy healers typically follow a system of healing that may or may not involve formal training or certification programs. Popular systems include:

Reiki | Hands-On Healing | Therapeutic Touch | Quantum Touch

Homeopathy

Homeopathy is a gentle, natural system of healing that involves using a highly diluted version of a plant-based substance (or substances) that, in higher doses, would cause the illness or symptom being experienced. It acts as a natural "vaccine" to stimulate our body's healing mechanism to heal from the disease. Arnica montana is a very common homeopathic medicine used to treat bruising and swelling.

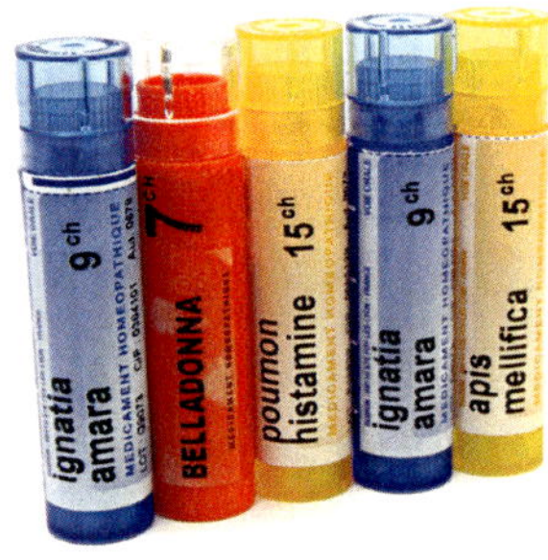

Homeopathy is fully recognized by the traditional medical community in many other countries. Homeopathic remedies are routinely prescribed by MDs and DOs worldwide, especially in Europe, including 30-40 percent of French and 20 percent of German medical doctors. In France, 35 percent of the cost of homeopathic remedies prescribed by an MD are reimbursed by health insurance. Homeopathy is not endorsed by the US healthcare system as traditional doctors have no formal training in homeopathy.

Bach Flower Remedies / Essential Oils

Similar to homeopathy, Bach flower remedies are another gentle, nontoxic, subtle method of healing using either one or a combination of 38 different flower essences.

The remedies work on the premise that all disease results from a state of emotional or psychological imbalance. The flower essences stimulate the internal healing mechanism of the body to restore balance, which in turn, heals the body of disease.

Earlier, we talked about the power of therapeutic-grade essential oils to heal and raise our vibrational frequency.

Frequency Generator Devices

These devices are machines that scan our body to locate sickness based on the different frequency ranges that radiate from different areas of our body. The machine is then used to restore the correct energy frequency to the organs and tissues in that area by breaking down diseased tissue.

Today, sophisticated devices are used successfully in medical settings. Unfortunately, many aren't widely advertised within the US due to a severe backlash from the FDA toward any method that conflicts with traditional medicine—in spite of the many failures of traditional medicine and its highly toxic side effects suffered by millions. In other countries, medical doctors with a more holistic approach to medicine are now beginning to use frequency generator devices in their practices.

Controversy & Skepticism

Traditional medicine is failing miserably in the treatment of many diseases now rampant in the Western world. On one hand, it's quick to deny that the human energy field plays an intimate part in the health or sickness of our body, yet on the other hand, it can offer no rational explanation for the power of the placebo effect. Traditional medicine may acknowledge that the mind has a powerful effect when it comes to placebos, but it denounces that same power when it comes to how the mind affects the state of our body and the role it plays in disease.

Regardless of the failures of traditional medicine in treating chronic diseases, traditional practitioners are very quick to write off energy medicine as "quackery" with no scientific evidence to back its claims. Because energy medicine cannot be quantified, spliced, and diced, and because it belongs to a newer branch of science they don't understand (quantum physics), it's simply discounted.

A Paradigm Shift: The Realm of Quantum Physics

We can't look toward science to explain something that, at the current time, is not easily understood by traditional science. When we talk about energy healing, we're entering the world of quantum physics, which is exploding the current limitations of evidence-based science.

Quantum physics has shown us that the energy and intention behind our thoughts are powerful enough to impact not only our physical body, but also the world that surrounds us. This isn't something that can be easily or effectively "measured." On the flip side, we can very effectively measure the significant failure rate of traditional healthcare treatments and medications.

But the reality is that energy medicine also has a significant failure rate. While some achieve success and have used energy-based treatment methods to completely cure themselves of serious and terminal diseases such as cancer, others have experienced no success at all after visiting energy healers. Not only does their health fail to improve, but medical tests both before and after treatments conclusively show that the treatment has failed to induce any healing. This lack of success fuels the fire against energy-based medicine.

Let's talk about these apparent failures.

Root Cause

When it comes to healing our body, focusing energy of different frequencies into our body is only one part of the equation. If the energy practitioner doesn't work with their patient to understand what caused their patient's energy field to become imbalanced to begin with, so that these causes can be addressed, then the chances that the energy medicine will be successful are small at best. This is also the main reason that many cancers treated with chemotherapy come out of remission, and the chemotherapy fails the second time around. Not only is the immune system seriously damaged from the first round, but the cause(s) of the cancer were also never addressed.

The energy frequency of a person's body will always reflect the frequencies they expose their body to. An energy medicine practitioner may spend an hour focusing a higher frequency of energy into their patient's body, but as soon as their patient leaves the room and returns to their daily environment, their body again resonates to these surrounding frequencies. Do you see the problem?

Let's use a simple analogy. Assume you live in a small apartment filled with cigarette smoke from two smoking roommates. You spend all day and all night in this house. You leave the house for 1 hour each day and experience a welcome relief from the cigarette smoke. You breathe in fresh, clean air, and you feel better. But then you return to your smoke-filled home and again breathe in the same smoke-filled air. How effective do you think that 1 hour break was for you?

Many energy medicine practitioners may understand how to channel energy, but they are completely unaware of the interconnected nature of diet and lifestyle habits as they relate to the energy state of the human body. Their training has taught them to simply channel energy into their patient's body to restore the energy balance (usually over a series of appointments) and stop there. The patient then returns to their daily life and their energy frequency will always reflect this life. Of course nothing changes! The patient then views the treatment(s) as a failure.

When it comes to using energy to heal your body, you not only need to learn how to effectively focus a high frequency of energy into your body (which is not difficult, as you will soon learn), but you *must* also address the causes in your life that contributed to your condition in the first place, and remove those causes! An energy medicine practitioner who does not approach healing from the perspective of removing root cause energy factors is doing their patient a great disservice.

The Knowledge & Experience of the Practitioner

Unfortunately, the exploration of energy medicine is in its infancy when it comes to fully understanding the relationship between the human energy field and disease. Through trial and error, and through working with many clients, some practitioners are far more effective than others and have a much stronger track record when it comes to being able to help their patients heal from disease.

As energy medicine is not formally recognized, there is also no standard of accreditation for any energy healing modality. This means that the only way to gauge the competency of a practitioner is to read patient reviews and talk to patients who have experienced success in curing their health condition. Some practitioners keep case studies they share with prospective patients (omitting sensitive and personal information, of course).

You Are All You Need

I often get asked the question, "don't I need to go to a professional energy healer to learn how to use energy to heal my body?" Not if you follow this Protocol, you don't! Working with energy is both easy to learn and requires no special equipment or lengthy courses.

Detailed and easy-to-follow instructions and exercises are included in this section of the protocol. The only thing required from you is a commitment to dedicate some time and attention to daily energy exercises in order to perfect and fine-tune your ability. As you become proficient, you will find you only need to spend a few minutes each day doing a couple of different exercises to maintain the higher frequency of vibrant health, and just a little longer to address acute or chronic health issues.

Despite what you may have heard about energy medicine, learning how to use energy to heal your body from disease:

- IS NOT complicated, nor is it difficult to learn.
- DOES NOT require taking long courses and getting expensive certifications.
- DOES NOT require a Master Healer or Certified Healer to train you.

Unless you are using a physical device (such as a frequency generator), the energy we use for energy medicine comes from an inexhaustible source that supplies energy to all life on this earth. It cannot be limited by anything or anyone because, by its very nature, it is limitless. It does not belong to anyone, and it is not exclusive to anyone.

Energy medicine is simply the result of a high frequency of this energy directed and focused into the body. Whether this is done by someone else or you learn how to do it yourself makes no difference. What *does* make a difference is that you learn how to properly develop the skill to work with energy.

Are you ready? Then let's get started.

Lights... Camera... BREATHE!

We all know how important the simple act of breathing is and how important it is for our health and well-being. With each breath, our body is flooded with life-giving oxygen and energy. But our breath is also a very powerful tool we can use when it comes to developing our ability to work with energy to raise our vibrational state.

In this section, you'll learn how to:

1. Use your breath to build and direct energy into specific areas of your body.
2. Use your breath and hands to intensify this energy.
3. Learn how to work with energy of different colors.
4. Successfully use 4 powerful energy exercises to heal your body.
5. Explore and fine-tune techniques that work best for you.

Earlier in the protocol, we talked about the power of breath. Let's dive right in and learn the basics of how to use breath to build energy within the body.

DIRECTING THE FLOW OF BREATH

In preparation for your energy work, you'll learn how to breathe "into" different areas of your body. Not only will this help you develop a much more direct, intimate connection with your body, but by paying attention to how you breathe and where in your body your breath is going, your focus is automatically brought into and kept in the present moment.

IMPORTANT! After you learn how to direct the flow of breath, it's important that you practice each exercise in the order given as they build upon themselves.

Where the Mind Goes, Energy Flows

At any given moment in time, whatever you focus your intention on is where you automatically send your energy. Whether you're working on a task, having a daydream, thinking thoughts of stress or worry, or watching a TV show, whatever you focus on is where your energy flows. This is why it's very important to learn how to control where your mind spends its time, and especially important for your energy work and high vibrational living.

The present moment is always your point of power.

We must always focus our energy and attention in the present moment. Many people find it challenging to learn how to control what their mind focuses on because the mind has a tendency to wander in many directions. This is very common for those of us who have an overactive mind, an attention deficit disorder, or who are used to multitasking. Also, the more stressed we are, the more our mind has a tendency to be distracted by the source of our stress.

Luckily, I'm going to teach you a sneaky trick that will help you easily keep 100 percent of your focus on the following exercises. You're going to begin by deepening your breath to a rhythmic count, use your breath to draw energy into your body on every inhale, and then channel that breath into a specific area of your body on every exhale. You'll quickly find that if you want to accomplish this task, you must focus all your attention on your breath and where it flows.

THE BODY BREATH

This exercise will take approximately 15 minutes.

Please make sure you're in a quiet area where you won't be disturbed.

You can be either standing or in a seated position. As we learned earlier, posture is important, so make sure your spine is straight, with your shoulders pulled back slightly to expand your chest. This exercise can be done with your eyes open or closed. Some people find it easier to focus with their eyes closed, whereas for others, eyes open is best. Experiment both ways to see what works best for you.

We always begin our breathing and energy exercises by mindfully deepening the breath, which helps us enter a state of internal calmness and stillness. But this stillness isn't the absence of energy, or life, or movement. It's a very dynamic, powerful stillness where we begin to experience the harmony of being fully present in the moment and, as you'll soon feel, the interconnected nature of all life.

Okay, let's get stated!

1. **Begin to Deepen Your Breath**
   Settle into a rhythm of inhaling to a count of 6, holding to a count of 3, and exhaling to a count of 6. Continue with this steady, rhythmic breath, keeping your focus in the present by silently keeping the count for approximately 5 minutes.

2. **From Without to Within**
   With each inhale, begin to visualize "drawing" your breath, and the energy that surrounds you, into the center of your chest area. From all directions, visualize and "feel" this breath and energy filling your chest every time you inhale. On each exhale, visualize and "feel" the energy then infusing your chest.

   INHALE draws the air and energy into your chest.

   EXHALE expands and infuses it throughout your chest.

   With several more inhales and exhales, continue to breathe the air and energy into your chest, and expand and intensify it on every exhale. Use the rhythm of your breath to continue building and intensifying this energy.

3. **Expand Your Breath**
   Continue breathing the air and energy into your chest, but now, with each exhale, feel this energy begin to expand and radiate out from your chest into the other regions of your body. Expand the energy slowly, taking 3-4 exhales to send the flow into your shoulders and down to your abdomen. Continue expanding the flow into your arms and legs, and up into your head on each exhale. When the energy has filled your entire body, spend several minutes continuing to pull energy in on the inhale, and intensifying it throughout your body on the exhale.

4. **The 5-Pointed Star**
   Stand with your feet at hip's width distance apart and raise your arms out to each side, reaching as far as you can with your fingertips. Continue breathing energy into your chest, but now, with each exhale, allow the energy to not only fill your body, but also gently flow out through the bottoms of your feet, out through your fingertips, and out through the top of your head. You're the center of a 5-pointed star, radiating energy out through your 5 points. The energy naturally dissipates as it exits your body. Continue radiating this energy for several more minutes.

USE YOUR HANDS

You're now going to repeat numbers 1 thru 3, but this time, you're going to use the movement of your hands, along with your breath, to "guide the energy" where you'd like it to go.

As you draw the energy into your chest area, use the movement of both hands to pull your breath toward your chest. Use your hands to gather the air and draw it toward and into your chest on the inhale (as if you're beckoning someone to come to you). On each exhale, expand your fingertips across your chest while visualizing the infusion of air and energy expanding and filling your chest area.

As you continue to draw energy in, experiment with hand and finger movements that work best for you to help you visualize and draw the energy to you, breathe it into your chest, and then expand it throughout your chest. Now, use your hands and fingers to expand and "pull" your energy and breath into other areas of your body. Play with the movements that work best, and have fun experimenting.

THE GOLDEN SPHERE

In the next exercise, you're going to "brighten up" by streaming golden light into your body and then radiating this light out from the center of your chest. This exercise should also take approximately 15 minutes.

This is an incredibly powerful exercise. The sheer intensity and power of this light will not only naturally serve to raise the vibrational frequency of your body, it will also fill you with a sense of inner calm, help clear your mind, and dissolve stress.

1. **Begin to Deepen Your Breath**
   Settle into a rhythm of inhaling to a count of 6, holding to a count of 3, and exhaling to a count of 6. Continue with this steady, rhythmic breath, keeping your focus in the present moment by silently keeping the count.

2. **Breathe in the Light**
   Bring your awareness to the area above your head and begin to visualize a beautiful golden light above you. Using the skills you learned in the first exercise, with each inhale, begin to breathe in this golden light through the crown of your head and into your chest area. With each exhale, expand this golden light in the shape of a sphere to fill your entire chest area.

   Don't rush this exercise. Spend all the time you need to visualize and feel the golden light entering your body and flow into your chest. It may take a few minutes, or it may take longer. It may take several days of practice. Use your hands to help you direct the light down through your head and into your body.

   INHALE draws the golden light into your chest.
   EXHALE expands and intensifies the golden light.

   When the golden light is a brilliant, intense, glowing sphere in the center of your chest, progress to the next step.

3. **Incorporate Sound**
   Each time you exhale, begin to use the sound of your breath to help you intensify the light. An audible exhale, similar to the whooshing sound of the wind, is a very simple yet powerful tool that will help you expand and intensify the golden energy—especially when used along with your hands.

4. **Expand the Light**
   Continue breathing the golden light energy into your chest, but now, with each exhale, begin to expand the sphere of golden light out from the center of your chest. Continue breathing rhythmically, visualizing this sphere growing larger and larger until it's encompassed your entire body and you're at the center of the glowing sphere. Every inhale pulls more golden energy in, and every exhale expands it out to encompass your body.

   Use your hands to help direct this energy into and out of your body. Enjoy bathing your body in the glow of this intense, powerful golden light.

5. **Infinity**
   Continue inhaling the golden light and expanding the sphere with each exhale. Begin by slowly expanding it to encompass the room you're in, followed by your entire home. Again, don't rush this exercise. Give yourself the time and patience you need to feel and visualize the light radiating farther and farther outward. Continue expanding it to encompass the street and then the town where you live, with yourself remaining at the center of the sphere. Use the forceful sound of your audible breath when you exhale to help shoot the light out farther and farther beyond.

   Continue slowly expanding the light out until it expands beyond any geographic limits to encompass the earth, and out into infinity.

The Breath of Power

As you continue to practice the Golden Sphere exercise, you'll soon be able to breathe the light into your chest and radiate it out into infinity in just a few breaths. Soon, you'll have mastered this exercise to the point where, with only one single inhale and one powerful and audible exhale, you'll be able to shoot the light out into infinity. This is what we call the Breath of Power, as it quickly and powerfully vitalizes your entire being.

HOMEWORK

The Golden Sphere exercise is your daily homework.

10-15 Minutes Daily

Make sure you're alone and undisturbed. A great time is early in the morning when you first wake up, or before you go to bed, or even in the bathroom. When I first learned to work with energy, I often did this exercise in the shower. I used the flow of water hitting my skin to help me visualize and intensify the energy entering my chest. That little trick helped provide an instant "boost" to my visualization skills (as well as to my confidence!).

No matter how busy you are and what distractions are in your life, you must find the time to practice this exercise every day. By doing so, you set an important cycle in motion: The more you practice, the more skilled you'll become at moving breath and light through your body until it becomes second nature. The more you practice, the higher your body's frequency will also become, which also boosts your ability to direct and control the energy. It's a win-win!

Getting "Lighter" & "Brighter"

So far in the protocol, we've covered some very important prerequisites that are fundamental to high vibrational living and to your success when working with energy. You also understand the importance of breath and are working on mastering your ability to direct breath and energy into your body. Are you ready to learn how to use energy to heal yourself from physical, emotional, and psychological imbalance?

THE ENERGY EXERCISES

By now, we have a basic understanding of the human energy field. We know that this energy field animates our entire physical body, and that any disturbance in this energy field will eventually cause a corresponding negative effect in our cells and tissues. This energy disturbance is what sets the stage for health conditions.

Let's talk about this energy field in a little more detail and discover how it connects to and affects our physical body.

The Energy Centers

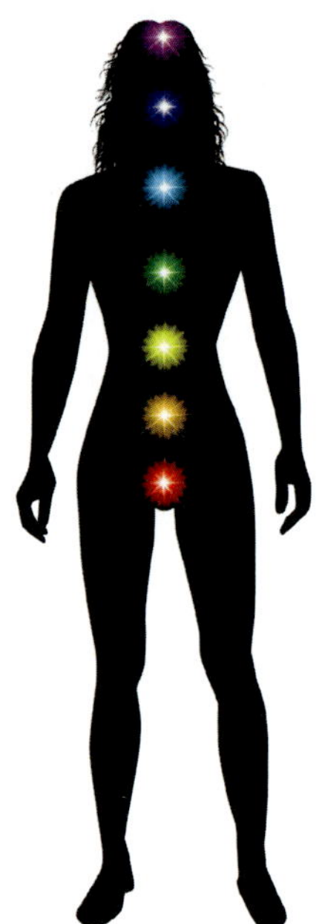

Similar to the way that blood flows throughout the circulatory system of the body and is regulated by the heart, the flow of energy in the body is regulated via 7 energy centers (also known as chakras in Ayurvedic medicine). These energy centers are located on a "powerline" that runs down the center of the body from the top of the head to the base of the spine. Each energy center receives, stores, and transmits energy throughout our entire organism.

The word "chakra" translates from the Sanskrit word "wheel" or "vortex" because each energy center is a whirling mass of energy.

The unobstructed flow of this energy determines our emotional, psychological, and physical health. When we engage in habits that affect our vibrational frequency, our energy system is affected in the form of chaotic, congested, or weak energy patterns. This impacted energy flow also reduces the flow of oxygen throughout our entire system, causing congestion in the blood. Depending on which energy center(s) are affected, we'll experience physical symptoms in different organs or parts of the body.

Acupuncture is a branch of traditional Chinese medicine that focuses on stimulating the flow of oxygen throughout the blood, which in turn, increases the flow of energy and resolves energy constriction. Acupuncture recognizes over 2,000 "acupoints" throughout the body beneath the surface of the skin where the flow of blood rises closest to the body's surface.

By stimulating an acupoint, blood flow is increased, energy congestion is cleared, and the oxygen content of the blood increases dramatically. This, in turn, assists in the removal of unhealthy cells and the generation of new, well-oxygenated, healthy cells.

Acupoints can be stimulated using several different methods, including acupuncture (tiny needles), acupressure, shiatsu massage, and various massage techniques involving pressure. Of the 2,000 acupoints, more than 400 are classified by the World Health Organization (WHO). Each point is listed by name, number, and the blood vessel to which it corresponds.

Energy Center	Location	Color	Related Gland
Base	Root of tailbone	Red	Adrenal (personal security)
Sacral	Below the navel	Orange	Ovaries/Testes (self-esteem)
Solar Plexus	Above the navel	Yellow	Pancreas (anxiety)
Heart	Heart	Green	Thymus (anger)
Throat	Throat	Blue	Thyroid (self-expression)
Third Eye	Forehead center	Indigo	Pituitary (cognitive issues)
Crown	Top of head	Violet	Pineal (spiritual issues)

Many books have been dedicated to explaining the relationship between the energy centers of the body and the different organs and systems they relate to. They explore which energy centers are linked to the development of common diseases and how to address these diseases by working on the corresponding energy center.

While studying this information may be interesting—and to some, enlightening—it's not at all necessary when it comes to energy healing. In fact, we can quickly get bogged down in the details and get distracted with unnecessarily complex exercises involving trying to fix the individual energy centers, instead of spending our time and attention addressing our energy structure as a whole.

I find that the more my clients learn about these energy centers, the more they trip themselves up. They can't see the forest for the trees and mistakenly assume that specific conditions are associated with only one energy center; then they spend time working on only that energy center. This may have been the old premise, but we know this is no longer the case. Our knowledge of energy has progressed beyond this basic understanding.

To work effectively on the human energy field, we must address the entire organism.

To successfully direct and control energy to heal your body, all you need is a very basic understanding of energy as it relates to your body, and only to the extent we've discussed above. Now, that wasn't too complicated, was it?

Preparation

We'll be learning 4 energy exercises, each of which offers different benefits and is used for different reasons. For each of these exercises, let's talk about 6 preparation steps, which help put us in a receptive state and send a clear signal to our mind and body that important work is afoot.

Remove All Distractions

It's very important that you're uninterrupted during your energy exercises. Let everyone in your family know you don't want to be disturbed, and use a private room or section of the house. Pets, children, the TV, and any other distractions should be taken care of.

Settle into a Calm, Positive Mindset

As you prepare your space, spend a few minutes removing any thoughts of stress, worry, negativity, or distractions so that you can much more effectively focus on your energy exercises. Whatever may be going on in your day, put it aside. This is a very small piece of your day dedicated *to* yourself and *for* yourself. Make it count!

Get Barefoot

Whenever possible, remove socks and shoes and work barefoot. The more direct your connection to the ground, the easier you may find it to send energy either down or up through your feet. Some people find it especially beneficial to stand on an area of grass or earth, or with a connection to the earth that's as direct as possible—for ease of visualization and because it simply feels wonderful to be directly connected to nature. The more adept you become at working with energy, the less important clothing or location becomes as these things will have no bearing on your effectiveness.

Do It on an Empty Stomach

Trying to do energy work with a full stomach is more difficult than when it's empty, just like trying to work out on a full stomach. A significant portion of your energy is diverted towards the process of digestion, lowering your overall energy level. The bodily process of digesting a large meal also distracts us on a subtler level. Constant snacking and "grazing" throughout your day is also a big offender in energy depletion and should be avoided when doing energy work.

Begin with Deepening Your Breath

We always spend several minutes deepening our breath before beginning any type of energy exercise because our brainwaves automatically move into a different frequency; we become deeply relaxed, and can take advantage of being in a much more receptive state.

Keep a Pen & Notebook Handy

Always keep a pen and paper (or smartphone or tablet) handy when doing your energy exercises. After you finish each exercise, make a note of any sensations and feedback you receive from your body both during and after the exercise. Write down anything you experience, no matter how small or unimportant you think it may be, such as a shiver down your spine or a sensation of warmth or coolness. If you feel nothing, that's perfectly fine!

With just a little practice, you'll begin to tune in to the subtle differences each color has on your mind and body. Keeping a journal of your experiences with energy not only tracks your progress, it also helps you build confidence as your knowledge and abilities flourish.

Let's Get Colorful!

Let's begin our energy exercises with "the color meet 'n' greet." This exercise will introduce you to the 7 energy center colors and help lay the foundation for working with each one. You'll also begin fine-tuning your ability to sense how each color feels and to take note of any physical or psychological effects you feel when working with these colors.

EXERCISE 1
THE COLOR MEET 'N' GREET

This exercise will take approximately 15-30 minutes. Keep your pen and notebook nearby. Take off your socks and shoes and stand with your feet hip's width apart.

Straighten your spine and pull your shoulders back slightly to expand your chest. Your eyes can be either open or closed.

1. **Begin to Deepen Your Breath**
   Begin breathing to a 4-2-4 rhythm, and deepen to a count of 6-3-6. Keep your focus in the present by silently keeping the count. Continue with this steady, rhythmic breathing for several minutes.

2. **Meet Red**
   Begin to turn your attention to the color red. Visualize a glowing red sphere of light several feet in front of you. This is a visualization, therefore let your mind play with building this sphere of light in your mind's eye. Play with the shade and the intensity of the red until it's a deep, vibrant, velvety shade, similar to a red velvet rose. Visualize this sphere expanding to the size of a beach ball. Play with the size and color of the ball and have some fun getting to know it. Use your hands and your breath to help create and intensify it. Then, release it and let it dissipate.

3. **Invite Red Inside**
   As you continue to breathe deeply and rhythmically, begin to feel the air alive and electric around you. You're surrounded by billions of molecules of energy, each alive and responsive. Begin to focus on the color from your red sphere and visualize a ray of red light above you, shining into the crown of your head. Spend a moment to build the visualization of this shining ray of light. With each inhale, begin to draw this energy down into your body, and with each exhale, feel it radiate and intensify throughout your body.

   As you first begin to breathe red into your body, it may be very weak and barely visible in your visualization. This is why we use our breath and hands to intensify it.

   INHALE draws the red light in.
   EXHALE radiates and intensifies the color.

   It's very important not to rush this process! It may take you several minutes before you're able to visualize the ray of light shining into your head. It may take 10 minutes or more. It may take completing the exercise several times. The more relaxed you are and the deeper and more rhythmic your breath, the easier this visualization will become. You may find you can "feel" the red enter your body, but you may find it difficult to visualize it as a ray of light above you; that's perfectly okay. This is a new skill, and you're just beginning to test the waters. Be patient, and don't expect or demand "instant" success; be kind and supportive of yourself in your learning experience.

4. **How Does It Feel?**
   How does the color red make you feel as it fills your body? Do you feel calm or agitated? Do you feel distracted? Energized? Emotional? Tired? If you feel no different, that's okay! Often, it's a subtle feeling that becomes more perceptible with practice, especially after breathing in different colors and then being able to compare them.

   Allow the red energy to slowly dissipate and write down anything you may have experienced.

5. **Meet the Rest of the Gang**
   Repeat the entire exercise, but each time you do it, visualize a different color in the following order:

   Red > Orange > Yellow > Green >
   Blue > Purple > Violet

   Remember to write down and detail any thoughts, feelings, and experiences you have with each of the colors.

6. **Finish with Gold**
   After breathing in each of the seven colors, repeat the exercise one last time with the beautiful golden light from your "golden sphere" exercise.

How did you do, and more importantly, how do you feel? Please make a note of your entire experience.

Tips & Tricks of the Trade

When you first begin working with breath and energy, it's normal to experience challenges. You may feel like you have no idea whether you're doing it right, and you may doubt your ability. This is perfectly natural; we all experience this in the beginning. It will take some practice before it finally begins to "click" and become much easier. Let's talk about some of the most common challenges and how to work through them.

How do I know if I'm doing it right?

If you're following the directions, you're doing it right. As you repeat the energy exercises and they become more and more familiar, you'll soon have no doubt you're doing them correctly.

Is this real, or is it all in my mind?

Yes, to both. Remember, your thoughts are real. Your mind is incredibly powerful; it's the tool you use to direct and control where energy flows and what energy does. Your body constantly reflects the predominant energy of your thoughts in the form of colors that radiate out from your body. If you visualize a ball of light, that light now exists. You've created it. You may not be able to physically "see" it, but using Kirlian photography, the energy field around all living things, and any energy that you consciously create, can be instantly captured and made visible.

Several years ago, while in Santa Monica, California, a friend and I walked down the 3rd Street Promenade to see the many street performers who set up temporary stalls each weekend. That particular day, a store was advertising Kirlian photography photos for $15 each. We both decided to have some fun!

We each had our photo taken, and my photograph revealed a red and orange glow surrounding my entire upper body. My friend had a more bluish/reddish glow. I sat down for 10-15 minutes on a bench and visualized a beautiful golden sphere hovering right above my head. I held this image clearly in my mind and built the gold up to be very intense and bright, and then I had a second picture taken. Sure enough, a big, hazy golden sphere was right above my head (although bigger than I'd visualized it, and it had infused the top half of my head).

Meanwhile, my friend had fun filming her green sphere. We spent a good 2 hours building all sorts of shapes in different colors, with our proof in the photography.

Always remember: Thoughts are things. Just because you can't see them doesn't mean they don't exist. Welcome to the world of quantum physics!

Help! I'm not good at visualizing!

The visualizations are in your mind's eye (such as when your mind wanders or when you daydream about something), and some of us are much better at visualizing than others.

The good news is that it really doesn't matter whether you're good at visualizing or not. You're using focusing your intent, and using your hands, your words, and your breath to guide the energy down into your body. It makes no difference whether you can clearly "visualize" it or not.

I'll let you in on a little secret: When it comes to visualizing things in my body, I'm a terrible visualizer! I use my hands and "pull" the energy down and focus on "feeling" the energy flow into my body. That's what works best for me, and it's all I need.

I also can't visualize with my eyes closed—only with them open. As soon as I close my eyes and try to imagine anything specific, I get nowhere fast. If I try to picture a quiet meadow, a tornado suddenly appears and starts pulling everything out of the ground. But the moment I open my eyes, the tornado instantly disappears and the meadow is beautiful and green and perfectly calm. If I close my eyes and try to visualize a line of sheep jumping over a fence, every single one of them trips, chews on the fence, walks around the fence, or turns into a deer or some other creature! But the second I open my eyes, those sheep line up like obedient little soldiers and hop right over the fence one by one.

Experiment. See what works for you and what doesn't. We each need to find what method "clicks" best with us. If what works for you seems weird or strange, run with it!

Use words of power

Along with using your hands, one of the best ways to feel the energy flow and intensify in your body is to use words that make you feel strong and powerful. This is a very important tool of the trade. I place great emphasis on statements such as "I INFUSE my ENTIRE BEING with the INTENSITY of the GOLDEN LIGHT." I repeat key words over and over again each time I draw the energy in and expand it. My voice becomes more intense, more urgent, more commanding ... and that's what triggers the energy to become so much more powerful for me.

While building energy, I often alternate the following statements and place greater emphasis on the words in all caps:

I AM POWERFUL and STRONG.

The energy I draw in GROWS in INTENSITY.

The energy INFUSES my ENTIRE BODY.

The energy EXPLODES with POWER and INTENSITY.

I AM a BRILLIANT GOLDEN LIGHT.

Experiment with different phrases and words to see what works best for you and what helps you generate a sense of power.

How do I know if the color "shade" is right?

As long as the color is clear and bright, you're doing just fine. The color shade will adjust to be the right shade for your body and for your body's needs at that moment. You may benefit from a shade of green that's the bright green of grass, or perhaps a deeper "hunter green" shade. Whatever shade the color becomes is the right shade for you.

When it comes to color, the important thing is for the color to be CLEAR (not murky or spotted) and BRIGHT (not dim or dull). If the color is murky or dim, simply keep drawing down that color and exhaling it until it becomes clear and/or bright.

I don't physically feel anything. Does that mean I'm doing it wrong?

Not at all—especially in the beginning while you're learning. With practice, you'll soon become sensitive enough to feel the sensation of the energy as you draw it into you. It often feels like a little "shiver," such as when you get goose bumps, or it may feel like a gentle wave.

The more intense and excited you become during your energy work, the more animated your hands and the more you use words of power, you cannot help but begin to feel the energy course through your body.

The Projection Technique

This is a different technique used to visualize energy flowing through your body. It involves visualizing yourself as a separate person standing before you and directing the energy to flow into that image. I prefer this technique and use it often. You may find that you also prefer it.

In your mind's eye, visualize a reflection of your body standing before you. The image can be either facing you or facing forward. It's not important to visualize any details or features or articles of clothing. You're simply projecting a generalized image of yourself. I often visualize myself as an outline of white light.

Following the instructions in Exercise 1, use your hands to draw the energy down into the crown of your image's head. Then expand the energy out through the heart center. Because this is an image of yourself, you'll find that with practice, as you draw energy down into the image, you'll feel the corresponding "energy rush" in your own body.

Have some fun with this technique and see if you like it! When you're ready, let's move on to the next energy exercise and do some spring cleaning of the colorful kind.

EXERCISE 2

THE COLOR CLEANING SPREE

This exercise will take approximately 15-30 minutes. Keep your notebook and pen handy. Take off your socks and shoes, and stand with your feet hip's width apart.

Straighten your spine, and pull your shoulders back slightly to expand your chest. Your eyes can be either open or closed.

1. **Begin to Deepen Your Breath**
   Begin breathing to a 4-2-4 rhythm, and deepen to a count of 6-3-6. Keep your focus in the present by silently keeping the count. Continue with this steady, rhythmic breathing for several minutes.

2. **Begin with Red**
   Focus your intention on a brilliant shade of red light shining down on your body from above. With each inhale, breathe this red light in through the crown of your head and into your lower pelvic region to the base of your tailbone. As you exhale, this red light expands into a glowing red sphere.

   Take your time as you visualize the red light flowing into the red sphere. At first, the sphere may be a pale red, and then grow deeper and deeper until it's a bright, deep red sphere of light. Let the sphere shine and grow out to be the size of a baseball or greater.

   With each inhale, pull the red light down, and with each exhale, strengthen the color and intensity of the red sphere. Pay attention to how the red looks. Is it bright and clear, or is it dull and murky? Is it streaked with other colors? Is it pale? Is it too dark? How does it make you feel? Continue breathing out the red sphere until the light sparkles with a beautiful, clear red glow.

   Enjoy several more breaths, then let the red sphere slowly dissipate as you replace it with the brilliant white light you originally breathed into your body. Write down anything you may have experienced.

3. **Repeat with the Following Colors**
   Repeat the exercise above, but this time visualize the following 6 colors glowing in the following 6 regions of your body:
   - Orange > Pelvis
   - Yellow > Stomach
   - Green > Heart
   - Blue > Throat
   - Purple > Between your eyes and 1 inch up
   - Violet > Crown of your head

   Remember to write down and detail any feelings you experience with each color.

4. **Finish with Gold**
   After breathing in each of the 7 colors, finish by infusing your body with a beautiful golden light.

How did you do? How did the colors make you feel? Please make a note of your entire experience.

Light of a High Vibrational Kind

Now that you've learned the basics of breathing in energy and are getting comfortable working with the colors of the 7 energy centers, it's time to master a very important exercise when it comes to raising the frequency of your body and balancing your mental, physical, and emotional states. Practiced daily, this exercise will not only prevent disease, it will also dissolve stress and tension.

EXERCISE 3

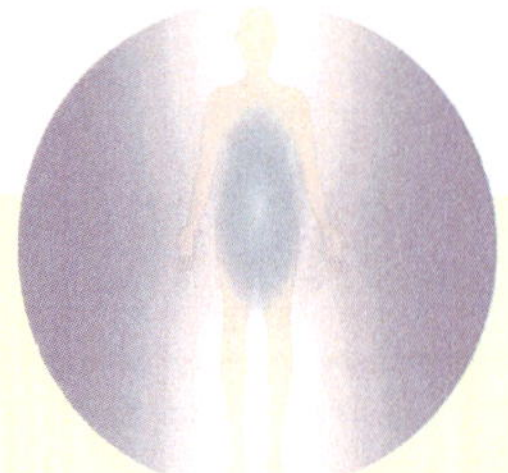

THE VIOLET FLAME

This exercise will take approximately 15 minutes. With practice, this time frame will grow much shorter, and you'll be able to draw in and infuse your body with violet light within moments. Keep your notebook and pen handy for after the exercise.

Take off your socks and shoes and stand with your feet hip's width apart. Straighten your spine, and pull your shoulders back slightly to expand your chest. Your eyes can be either open or closed.

1. **Begin to Deepen Your Breath**
   Begin to deepen your breath. Similar to the Complete Breath, draw the air into your abdomen, feeling your belly rise, followed by your chest. Slowly exhale, contracting your abdomen, then chest. Continue this deep-belly breathing for several minutes as you enter a state of deep relaxation. Allow any thoughts to come and go, and keep bringing your attention back to your body and your rhythmic breath.

2. **Build the Flame**
   Begin to visualize a flame, approximately 2-3 feet high, before your body. It's a beautiful flame of bright, violet light. It's not necessary that you "see" the flame, only that you focus on visualizing it in your mind's eye, your imagination. Spend several minutes visualizing the luminous, beautiful glow of this violet flame.

3. **Synchronize Your Breath**
   Begin to synchronize your breath while increasing the size and intensity of the flame before you. With each inhale, pull brilliant white energy into your body, and with each exhale, send this energy out into the flame and see it growing larger, stronger, and more intense.

   Every inhale draws more energy into your body, and every exhale makes the flame grow larger and larger, and more and more powerful as it becomes energized. After each inhale, begin to repeat the following words:

   "I now transform all fear to light."

   As the flame grows in size and intensity, it may begin to "roar" like a fire, or it may stay quiet as it grows in power. It may be explosive or sizzle or crackle, or it may be perfectly calm. It may begin to engulf you in the power of its light. All of these are wonderful signs. Let the light be what it will be.

   Don't try to exert any control over how the flame manifests. Simply continue exhaling energy into the flame while repeating the phrase above. Feel it grow more powerful with each repetition and each breath.

4. **Breathe in the Flame**
   When the flame before you has grown larger than your body, open your arms toward it. With each inhale, draw it to you and begin to feel it envelop your entire being. The following words can be very helpful:

   "With every breath, the violet flame infuses my body."

   As you continue to breathe rhythmically, feel the flame fill your entire body. You may experience some very intense sensations, ranging from a high-pitched tingling to a sensation of floating or weightlessness. You may feel a quivering throughout your body or a gentle warmth. It may be a soothing coolness. Some people feel the flames begin to rush through their body, emblazoning them in light. In the beginning, you may feel and sense very little or nothing at all, and that's just fine.

5. **Need Help? Just Ask**
   If you're having a specific problem, ask the violet energy to transform the problem to light. For example, if you're experiencing severe stress from an event, ask the violet light to transform the stress energy from that event into light. If you've had an upsetting disagreement with someone, ask the violet light to transform the disagreement to light. If you're feeling upset or angry or depressed, ask the violet light to infuse your entire body and transform that negative energy into the highest vibration of light.

   Continue breathing in the flame after you've made your request. Release any emotions you may feel into this light.

6. **Release Control to the Flame**
   When the cleansing process is complete, the violet flame will naturally begin to retreat and burn down to a gentle, quiet simmer. This may take a few minutes, or it may take much longer. Bask in the glow for as long as it takes, enjoying this beautiful, very powerful energy. Then, allow the energy to slowly dissipate.

The violet flame is much more than an energy exercise. It's one of the most powerful methods on this earth for transforming lower vibrational states of mind (stress, tension, worry, anger, frustration, envy, sadness, grief, guilt, etc.) into a much higher frequency, effectively dissolving them. As these emotional and psychological states lay the foundation for disease, we actively prevent disease from developing when we use the violet flame.

The color violet is the highest frequency in the visible spectrum of light; the next octave of light transitions to ultraviolet. Violet is also the color of the seventh energy center located at your crown. When you focus on and infuse this extremely high vibration into your body on a regular basis, you'll naturally begin to raise the vibration of your body to its highest frequency.

How did the violet flame make you feel? Do you feel more emotionally settled? Do you feel a sense of clarity and peace? Do the room and the air around you feel any different? If so, in what way? When I work with the violet flame, the room around me always seems to take on a calm "milky smoothness" (that's the best way I can describe it!).

Make a note of your experience.

When dealing with chronic health issues, or with emotional issues such as grief or guilt that have taken very deep hold of your psyche, repeat the violet flame exercise every day. The effects of using this energy are very powerful and quite dramatic in terms of a psychological transformation (how you begin to feel about the issue, and how it begins to resolve naturally and to your benefit).

It's necessary to reactivate this energy on a regular basis to help your body begin resonating to this higher frequency. You'll need to use the violet flame regularly to thoroughly penetrate and transmute long-standing issues.

Practice, Practice, Practice

Once you're very familiar with this exercise and have practiced it on a regular basis, you'll find you no longer have to spend time "building" the violet flame before you. By calling it into being either mentally or verbally, it will quickly infuse your body.

Simply begin to breathe rhythmically, inhale the white light, and exhale the violet flame throughout your entire body, intensifying it with each exhale. Mentally or verbally state,

"I now draw into my body the violet flame to transform (your issue) to light."

Verbalize your statements when possible as you'll find this much more empowering.

Release the Need to Control

Try not to exert too much control over what you see, feel, and experience during your energy exercises. Release any expectations you may have about what "should" or "should not" happen. Too much control can prevent the energy from expressing itself in ways that it needs to, depending on your body and your health.

Your job is to draw the energy into your body and let it go to work. This energy is highly intelligent and doesn't need you to tell it how to heal and what to fix. It flows intuitively where it needs to go, reestablishing harmony and equilibrium. All your body's systems begin to effortlessly respond to this higher frequency, triggering healing on every level. As viruses, toxins, and diseases vibrate at lower frequencies, the high-energy frequency of the violet light helps raise your body's frequency and prevent lower vibrational states from continuing to exist within your body.

Doing this exercise on a regular basis is wonderful for health maintenance.

Treating Disease

When it comes to treating a physical disease within your body, you're now going to take the knowledge you've gained from all the previous exercises and learn how to draw into your body the right type of energy for your condition.

It's much easier than you think.

In the previous exercise, we talked about how energy is inherently intelligent. When it comes to healing disease, your job is to bring the energy to you with the directive that the energy heal your body. You don't need to worry about how the energy chooses to do that and what colors it may or may not use (and that's great news!). Whether you suffer from cancer, heart disease, diabetes, obesity, or an autoimmune disorder, the basic principles of this exercise remain the same. Your job is to state your goal—the end result—and specify that the energy work toward that end.

Let's talk about how to do just that.

EXERCISE 4

THE COLOR OF HEALTH

This exercise will take approximately 15-30 minutes and should be done every day to address any physical disease. Have your notebook and pen handy to take notes when you've finished.

Take off your socks and shoes, and stand with your feet hip's width apart. Straighten your spine, and pull your shoulders back slightly to expand your chest. Your eyes can be either open or closed.

1. **Begin to Deepen Your Breath**
   Begin to slow and deepen your breath. Similar to the previous exercise, use the Complete Breath to draw the air into your abdomen, feeling your belly rise, followed by your chest. Slowly exhale, drawing your belly in and up, followed by your chest. Continue this deep belly breathing for several minutes as you enter a state of deep relaxation. Allow any flitting thoughts to come and go, and keep bringing your attention back to your body and your rhythmic breath.

2. **State Your Intent**
   Begin by clearly stating your health goal. Because you use your mind to draw energy into your body to heal, giving it a very clear directive is essential. Consider the following simple phrases:

"I now infuse my entire body with the energy of vibrant health."

"My body now fully restores itself to health."

"My body is now healthy, strong, and radiates health."

Always make your statement in the present tense using words that show what you want to achieve, not what you want to remove. For example, compare these phrases:

"I am free of disease." vs. "I am healthy and strong."

"I no longer suffer from diabetes." vs. "I fully restore my body to health."

The mind always communicates using words and pictures, and it automatically tunes in to each word you say, magnifying its energy—including words such as disease, suffer, and diabetes. Words are incredibly powerful little energy vessels, and we only want to focus on and give power to words of light.

3. **Draw down the Energy**
   As you continue to breathe deeply, begin to visualize a clear, bright light above you, shining into the crown of your head. Don't exert any control or expectation on what color this light should be. Simply feel the warmth of the glow enter your head and slowly move down throughout your entire body.

   Begin to use your breath to intensify this energy. With each inhale, draw the energy down through the crown of your head and into your core, and with each exhale feel it radiate and intensify throughout your body. Settle into a slow, steady rhythm. Inhale brings the energy in, exhale increases the power and intensity of the energy throughout every single cell of your body.

4. **Use a "Power Word"**
   You're now going to use a single word on every exhale throughout the exercise. This word guides the intent (the purpose) of the energy and keeps you 100 percent focused on that intent.

   On each exhale, repeat ... HEAL.

   Such a simple, yet powerful word, yet it begins to fill your consciousness. Take the entire length of each exhale to whisper this word as it begins to power the energy working its way throughout your body. If you prefer a different word, then choose what works best for you, but choose a short word that you can easily say on your exhales. Settle into the rhythm of exhaling the energy while using your power word.

5. **Become the Watcher**
   In this relaxed state, take on the role of a detached observer, and watch/feel the color and movement of the energy. This little trick helps prevent you from trying to unintentionally control what the energy does. As you begin to fill your body with energy, it may begin as a white light, or it may immediately appear as a color. It may be a combination of colors, or it may change from one color to another throughout the exercise. It may appear to intensify in one area or several areas of your body, or it may flow evenly throughout. It may become explosive or be calm and even. It may even begin as a white light and stay white throughout the entire exercise. Let the light do what it will and behave as it needs to.

   Regardless of the color, the energy you breathe in should always be bright and crystal-clear. It should "feel" and "look" vibrant. As you expand it throughout your body, it may become muddied or dull, or it may weaken as it enters and interacts with your energy system. It may enter your body as a bright light and then become barely visible as you expand it. All of these things are perfectly okay and are to be expected, especially when treating a health condition. Simply continue pulling in the bright, clear energy and breathing it throughout your body until all the energy you exhale becomes bright and clear.

   How does the energy feel in your body? Pay attention to any physical sensations you experience, as well as how the energy affects your emotional state. You may have an unexpected welling of emotion, or you may feel nothing but a sense of calm. Throughout the exercise, continue to pay attention to both the behavior and color of the energy and the effect it has on you.

6. **Use Your Tools**
   On each exhale, continue to verbalize your power word. I like to verbalize it as a quiet yet powerful whisper, with my breath sounding like the wind. Occasionally, when I feel a surge of power, I'll blast the word out loud as a powerful statement and feel the energy explode throughout my body. Experiment with what feels right for you and what works best when it comes to building and intensifying the energy. Use your hands, too!

7. **Bring It to a Close**
   When the energy reduces to a gentle rhythm of clear, bright light, the cleansing process is complete. This may take 5 minutes, or it may take 20 minutes. Don't rush the process. Simply wait until the cycle of healing is complete, and let the energy slowly dissipate.

Write down in your notebook what you experienced during the exercise.

Practice Daily

When dealing with any health issues, it's very important to repeat this exercise every day. If possible, repeat it twice or more each day. This is a very powerful exercise that has a profound effect on your body on a subtle level. The energetic disharmony that created your health condition didn't happen overnight, and raising the frequency of your energy requires repetition while it builds upon itself.

As with all the exercises you've learned, practice makes perfect. The more you practice, the quicker the energy will have a cumulative effect and raise the frequency of your body, restoring it to the original blueprint of health.

Mini Sessions

The more you repeat this exercise and tie it to your power word, the easier it will become and the faster you'll be able to generate the energy. When you reach this point, in addition to your daily exercise, also take 2-3 minutes several times throughout your day and give yourself "mini" sessions.

Over the space of several deep inhales and exhales:

1. State your intent.
2. Inhale the energy into your body.
3. Exhale it throughout your body.
4. Use your power word with each exhale.

Even though it's a mini session, it's a very powerful exercise you should never rush.

Expect the Unexpected

You may have different experiences each time you repeat the exercise. The color that appears today may be completely different from the color that appears tomorrow. The way the energy behaves may also change. This is perfectly normal.

Maybe you have a health condition localized in one area of your body, but the energy seems more focused somewhere else. This is very common as the organs and systems of your body are intimately connected. For example, we may have a growth in our spleen, yet the energy may be focused on detoxifying the blood throughout the circulatory system or strengthening a specific aspect of the immune system that, in turn, triggers healing of the spleen. Similar to acupuncture, even though pain may be localized in one area, the corresponding acupuncture needles are often inserted into other regions of the body.

YOUR DAILY ENERGY SCHEDULE

Let's Recap

Let's take what we've learned about using energy and create a daily schedule. Let's also talk about which exercises to do and how often you should do them, based on your needs.

#1 - Practice Mindful Breathing

We now know that the act of breathing has far more to do with our state of health than we may have thought. The way we breathe can either provide us with a much greater quantity of oxygen and energy, or it can severely deplete it over time because breath is an energetic food. The oxygen stimulates our nerve force, in turn generating a greater quantity of energy.

When breathing, make a conscious effort to inhale through your nose. As we talked about earlier, our nose acts as a filter to remove contaminants such as dust, dirt, and other foreign substances.

AVOID shallow breathing—breathing that uses only the upper part of your chest and lungs. It drastically reduces oxygen intake, which translates to an under-oxygenated body and a depletion of energy.

INSTEAD, practice belly-breathing throughout your day. On each inhale, draw the oxygen and energy all the way down to your core, expanding your abdomen, followed by your chest. Exhale in reverse, drawing in your abdomen, then your chest.

WATCH YOUR POSTURE. Throughout the day, pay attention to your posture, and make a conscious effort to straighten your spine and bring your shoulders back to open your chest.

DO THE COMPLETE BREATH once each day. The easiest times are either each morning when you rise or each evening before you go to sleep.

#2 - Do Your Energy Exercises

Let's talk about which exercises to do for general health maintenance and which ones to do for health conditions.

The Golden Sphere (daily)
This exercise is a fantastic "maintenance" exercise and should be done every day. The more you do it, the of your day. You'll find that you begin to feel calmer and both your perspective and attitude toward life become more relaxed and balanced. What used to aggravate you or cause you distress simply slides away. Any negative mind-set will fall by the wayside and be replaced with a more open, expansive, positive state of mind.

The Color Cleaning Spree (weekly)
This is an exercise to do on a weekly basis to help you identify which color(s) seem congested, dull, spotty, or weak. Each time you do the exercise, work with each color until it becomes bright, strong, and clear. You may notice that one energy center needs more work than the others. Always finish with the golden sphere.

The Violet Flame (daily, as needed)
It's the most powerful of all the energy exercises for emotional or psychological stress. It helps those who use it to properly assimilate the lessons provided by difficult times and then rise above the entire experience. The violet flame has a profound calming effect. It can cause us to feel a slight sense of

detachment from our surroundings as we begin to see things from a higher perspective. It's also the single-best energy exercise to increase our intuition, help achieve higher states of consciousness, and develop our extrasensory abilities.

The Color of Health (daily, as needed)

This is the daily exercise to do for specific physical health conditions and should be continued at least once each day until your health condition has been fully resolved. You may find that the color of your energy and how it behaves vary every time you do the exercise, and that's perfectly okay. At times, the energy may be the golden light from the golden sphere exercise, or a violet light from the violet flame exercise. It will become whatever it needs to be to raise your frequency and dissolve the disease.

Tips & Tricks to Remember

- Use phrases and words of power. Experiment to see what works best for you.
- Release the need to control how the energy flows and what the energy does.
- Expect the unexpected. Each person is different, and what you experience will be unique to you because your energy needs are unique to you.
- Use your breath and your hands to move and guide the energy. They're very powerful tools.
- The pure energy you inhale will always be bright and clear. If the energy turns dull, murky, or spotty when it enters your body, continue breathing it in and exhaling it throughout your body until it becomes bright and clear.
- Experiment with your body movements, eyes open and closed, and any other instinctive behavior that helps you move the energy.

The golden sphere is my go-to exercise and a permanent part of my daily ritual. I often do it while working out, using the beat of a steady rhythm to help me (such as the rhythm of walking, being on an elliptical machine, of a vinyasa yoga flow, etc.). If I'm going through a stressful period and feel unsettled, depressed, or anxious, then I head straight for the violet flame.

Change the Way You Think

Your thoughts directly affect both the quality of your body and the quality of the life you live. You can never escape the fundamental truth that the energy behind your thoughts is continually rearranging billions of molecules to create both your body and your life's experiences. Whether that energy creates vibrant health or a body receptive to disease more it will steadily raise the frequency of your body and help you rise above general worries and stresses is largely determined by the way you think.

If you remain unaware of the energy behind your thoughts or do not actively guide them in a positive direction, then the best you can hope to experience is a life of mediocrity and average to poor health.

True Power

It's now time to move on to the most important part of this entire protocol, the part where you'll begin exploring the inner workings of your mind. You'll learn how to tune in to the energy source that surrounds you, and direct it toward manifesting your goals, exploding your limitations, and breaking through any barriers to quickly and effectively achieve the life of your dreams. Get ready to take an unforgettable journey and fulfill your potential to become the limitless person you were born to be.

How does that sound? Interested? Of course you are! Then let's get going on a discovery trip.

MIND

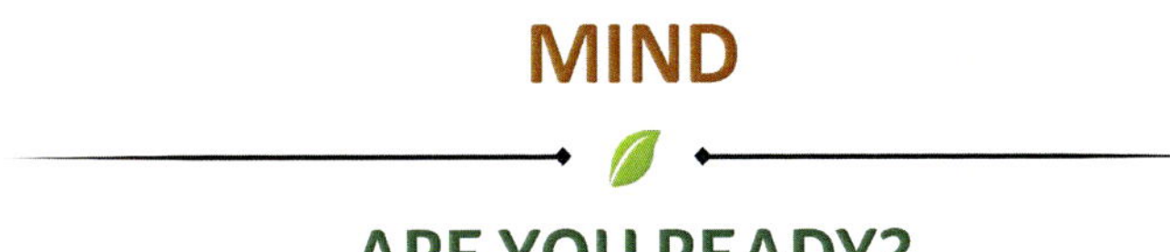

ARE YOU READY?

When it comes to personal change, health, and transformation, rest assured that at every moment in time, you always possess everything you need to achieve your infinite potential.

Until you take your last breath on this earth, you're on a journey. Whether you sit by the wayside and let life pass you by or whether you walk with purpose on the path, being an active participant in managing your health and creating your own destinations and life experiences is entirely up to you.

The only person responsible for creating the reality you experience ... is you.

Now that's a pretty serious statement. Many people are shocked by the thought that they could possibly be responsible for the difficulties they're experiencing or for the unwanted aspects of their lives. Whether we're consciously or unconsciously aware of it, the energy produced from our thoughts and from the people we attract to us and surround ourselves with affects the type and quality of the life we manifest. Any time we want to gauge our state of mind, all we need to do is look at our current environment and see what's reflected back to us.

But with that understanding, there comes another: If you have the power to create your life's experiences, then you also have the power to change them. If you have the power to create a mess, you certainly have the power to create order. If you have the power to create misery for yourself, you have the power to create happiness. The only person responsible for feelings of love or hate, a state of wealth or poverty, social involvement or loneliness, frustration or contentment ... **is you**.

Are you really so powerful that you can simply change your life by changing the way you think? Yes! You really are that powerful. All it takes is an understanding of the energy behind your thoughts and how to *consciously* begin working with it.

> "Mastering yourself is true power."
>
> Lao Tzu
> Chinese Philosopher

Your Starting Point

We begin with understanding that it doesn't matter where you are at this moment in time.

Your starting point is wherever you find yourself right now. Whether you're 150 or 400 pounds, whether you're healthy or chronically ill, feeling lost and lonely, sad or depressed, it's time to embrace the NOW, this moment, as your starting point for change because that's all you need to begin.

All you have to do is commit.

We begin by exploring how creation physically happens. We'll talk about our beliefs and perceptions and how they not only shape our body, but also shape the world around us that we experience. We'll then talk about the practical steps you'll take to immediately begin creating what you want and removing what you no longer want. These steps include becoming familiar with the "tools of the energy trade" and learning the "7 golden rules" of working directly with energy for the purpose of manifestation.

You'll soon discover that every person has the power to:

Create health OR create disease

Create happiness OR create misery
Create wealth OR create debt
Sustain the environment OR destroy it
Evolve OR stay stagnant

Will it be difficult? No, not at all. In fact, it'll be enlightening and fun! Will it require you to commit your time and effort to the process? Yes, absolutely, and you'll have homework assignments that you need to complete. But I'll let you in on a little secret ... the sooner you start and the more dedicated you are, the swifter the changes take place. As momentum builds, you'll begin to see solid proof in your ability to create major change, and you'll become so swept up in the excitement that you'll become unstoppable!

HOW CREATION HAPPENS

We've all heard the terms "thoughts become things" and "be careful what you wish for because you may just get it." But have you ever stopped to consider how this actually happens? If not, now is the time to think about it very seriously.

"With our thoughts we make the world."

Buddha

We are made up of pure, radiant light energy that we draw from an infinite source. Each of us is an individual expression of this energy, which is intelligent, alive, and responsive, and every one of the trillions of cells in our body possesses this same innate intelligence. Some choose to call this source of energy divine intelligence, some call it the Universe, and others call it God. Whatever we choose to call it, it's a part of who we are, and it expresses itself through us. It provides us with the raw material to be, do, and have whatever we want, and what we choose to do with that raw material is up to us. We can choose to survive and simply get by, or we can actively participate in creating whatever we'd like to experience and achieve.

Through this energetic connection, we're continually creating and recreating not only our bodies, but also our life's experiences based on our ability to interact with and shape this energy. We do this by using only one tool—our thoughts.

Just because thoughts aren't "physical" objects doesn't mean they don't exist within a framework of principles. They absolutely do. Thoughts are real. They may not look like a tree or a cup or a plate, but they're just as real. Every single thought we think carries with it a vibrational frequency that's creative by its very nature and comes into expression as determined by our thoughts.

Our outer world—the physical world we experience—is always an expression of the thoughts stored in our subconscious mind. What we physically "see" is the *result* of the way we think, not the *cause*. You can never get away from your own thoughts, nor the fact that every thought you think today determines your tomorrow and your future. It's your own thinking that sets you apart from every other being around you. We all use the same creative energy as the source for what we manifest, but how we choose to express this creative energy is what makes some people healthy and others unhealthy, some wealthy and some poor, some happy and some depressed.

The quality of the thoughts we think determines the nature of our experiences.

If you don't like your outer world, what you physically see in terms of your body, the state of your health, or the life you're experiencing, you always begin by looking within for the cause. You use the *same* power (energy) to bring out difficult situations and circumstances you don't want that you use to create the wonderful experiences you do want. This is the very nature of your existence. What you are—right now—is a result of the beliefs and perceptions you've embraced up until this point in your life.

We Are Evolving

Because we're intelligent beings, we have the ability to play an active part in directing energy and raising our vibrational frequency, which, as we now know, can heal us from disease. But with this same energy, we can also change the type and quality of our life's experiences. We can literally "play" with energy, just like a child who's surrounded by Lego pieces that they can use to build and create objects and scenes. We already do this unconsciously, often creating experiences we don't want. But now it's time to become active, conscious creators of our lives.

We're all continually evolving in a sea of vibrational frequencies. As we evolve, we have access to abilities and higher states of consciousness that we were previously unaware of, and through diet, lifestyle habits, and thinking habits that raise our energy frequency, we can begin accessing these abilities and states of consciousness. Evolving into these abilities is part of our DNA.

The higher our vibrational frequency, the more intuitive we naturally become. Other abilities surface that are extrasensory in nature, but that are perfectly natural and a part of who we are born to be. Just because we're unaware of them or don't know how to use them doesn't mean that they're unnatural or impossible. Like a child who hasn't yet been taught how to swim, we simply need to learn how to use these extrasensory gifts.

The source of energy from which we pull is limitless and inexhaustible. Our only limit to its use is the limit we impose. Accessing this energy is automatic; it lies at the source of who we are.

The rules of engagement for creation work the same for everybody. They don't favor one person above another. We're *all* equally natural creators and manifestors of our lives.

But How Does It Work?

When you think a thought, it sends out energy. Depending on what the thought is and on the strength of the energy (the emotion) behind it, it may emit a weak or strong energy. When thoughts are backed by a strong energy, or when we think them repeatedly, the energy builds upon itself to the point that it externalizes and physically manifests in our lives. Conversely, we weaken the energy behind our thoughts and intentions if we don't give them focus or direction.

We'll always bring into our lives the experiences that reflect our dominant thoughts and beliefs. Lower vibrational thoughts tend to attract to us the types of food, general lifestyle habits, situations, and people that are also low vibrational in nature, and which lower the quality of our life, compromise our immune system, and open us up to disease. The opposite is also true: higher vibrational thoughts attract that which is higher vibrational in nature, bring us happiness and peace of mind, and protect our body from disease.

Let's explore an example of using the same energy two different ways with two very different outcomes. We'll use the fun example of a car, but it can be an example of anything we want to have or achieve, from a physical manifestation in our life to healing our body from health condition:

I wish I had it ...

Your car has been struggling for some time, and you've decided you need a new one. The one you want isn't quite in your budget, but secretly you really wish you could have it. You're driving down the street and pull up to a red traffic light. You stop, your eyes roam around, and you spot the exact car you want and in a color you love—it literally makes your mouth water. Your thoughts focus on how great the car is and that you wish you had one of your own. You wistfully look at the driver and think how lucky they are. You smile and dreamily think of how you'd love to own one, and that maybe one day in the future you may be able to afford it. Then the light changes, and you progress on your merry way, with thoughts of the car occasionally crossing your mind.

Now, let's take a look at the same example and create an entirely different result:

I claim it as mine ...

You're at the same stoplight, looking at the same car, and you've made a decision: You want that car, and there's no doubt about it—you're going to make sure you get it. It doesn't matter that you have nowhere near the amount of money it costs to get the car. That's the least of your worries because you know that the sooner you focus on getting it, the sooner the circumstances in your life will rearrange themselves to allow that car to become part of your life's experience.

The car becomes a major focus in your thoughts, and you become excited and expectant. You write down a couple powerful affirmations, and throughout the day you repeat those affirmations. In fact, whatever you do, thoughts of that car are always foremost in your mind. You may not know how quickly you'll have that car, but you do know it won't be long.

You start "living as if" the car is yours. That very evening, you go to the dealership and talk to the salesperson. You test drive it—touch it, smell it, breathe it in. You look at the selection of colors to see which one you like best, and you bring the sales brochures home with you. The excitement you've generated within yourself is very strong, and it's very "expectant" and very "insistent." You cut out your favorite pictures from the brochures and carry them around with you, looking at them at least 20 times a day.

You're now ready and waiting. You instinctively know that circumstances are rearranging themselves to prepare you for having the car, and you're on the lookout. New people may appear in your life, or you may be drawn to drive a different route to work that leads to a chance experience or meeting with someone. You have an urge to browse through magazines or newspapers you normally never look at. You don't know how the events in your life will be orchestrated to bring the car to you, nor do you care. You don't have to worry about that (and that, unfortunately, is where many people falter—fretting and worrying about the "hows" and "wheres" and "whos"). Your job is to simply direct the energy, fuel the energy, and wait for it to manifest. The only thing you need to do is pay attention to urges to do something or go somewhere or say things that may not be typical for you, and follow those urges.

There's no part of you—absolutely no part of you—that believes the car won't be yours. You've claimed it—mind, body, and soul—as yours, and you know with every fiber of your being that it will be. On an energy level, the car's already been created and it already belongs to you. It simply needs enough energy and time to project itself into your life.

Do you see the big difference in these two ways of thinking? Depending on the energy behind the thoughts we think, they'll either be strong enough to create the car into physical manifestation ... or they won't.

- If more and more of the same thoughts are created, the energy builds upon itself and becomes stronger. It begins to intelligently transmute itself into physical form for us to experience as our physical reality.
- If random thoughts (such as daydreams or transient wishes) are generated that are weak, and aren't repeated over and over in our mind, then they can't gain the energy they need to become strong enough to appear in our physical reality.

Remember: The quality and type of thoughts we think determine the vibrational frequency of the energy we use to create and re-create our bodies. They also determine which objects, people, and situations enter our lives.

Every moment of the day, we automatically and unconsciously generate thought energy that determines our future. Until we learn how to consciously control our thoughts, we have little control over what shows up. Not only that, but we're also at the mercy of other energies around us that may be much stronger and more focused and directed than ours. We become swept along on a sea of surrounding energies, feeling helpless and at the mercy of people and circumstances in our environment. Our life appears out of our control, and so is born the "victim" mentality.

Let's take a look at some fundamental truths.

We alone are the makers of our destiny.
We have never been a slave to circumstance.
We alone are responsible for all that we create.
We have always been the master of our own fate.

The lower and more chaotic your vibrational frequency, the more likely you'll be to unconsciously create negative, undesirable experiences, circumstances, and health problems because you become energetically drawn to make decisions and take action that bring these types of things to you. You begin to eat foods that aren't in your best interest and make poor choices. You draw relationships into your life that cause you stress and unhappiness. You then think even lower vibrational thoughts and create more imbalance, and a vicious cycle is created.

Once we begin to take conscious control and use our natural ability to be the director of what we want to experience, then we're no longer at the mercy of our own negative, limiting thoughts (or the stronger, more focused thoughts of those around us). We alone decide what we choose to experience, not anyone else. We begin by thinking about what we want and then fueling thoughts of these things with energy. This sets in motion all the changes necessary to bring these situations, objects, or accomplishments to us.

Getting in the Way of Ourselves

We often feel we're committed to getting the things we want. We consciously focus on them and do our best to bring them into our lives. We work very hard to get that promotion, save up as much money as we can to get that house, and try diet after diet in a never-ending effort to lose weight ... yet we often either struggle to accomplish these things, or we fall far short of the goal. The two biggest culprits that stand in our way are:

1. **We Sabotage Ourselves & Put out the Fire Before It Begins to Burn**
   This is where most people slip up. You can't spend a few minutes each day thinking about that new career, that promotion, that weight loss, that new relationship, that new house, or anything else you want, and then spend the rest of your day stressed and focused on the opposite. If you want a new job and you spend your drive to work feeling depressed about the day ahead and most of your day wallowing in the misery of your current job duties, feeling stressed that it won't ever change, then where are you directing the majority of your energy? Right on the very thing you're trying to walk away from.

   Spending 5 minutes a day "visualizing and affirming" a new job ain't gonna cut it. If you continue to identify and focus your attention on where you are, instead of seeing your current condition as temporary and focusing your energy on *where you're headed*, then you'll simply create more of what you have.

2. **We're Lazy**
   Many people can't be bothered to put the time and energy into focusing on what they want. They're too busy feeling sorry for themselves, stuck in their current situation, to have the "energy" to put into anything else. They procrastinate and put it off until tomorrow, and when they finally focus for a few minutes on their goal, it's wishy-washy at best. I'll let you guess what wishy-washy energy creates.

For some people, even the arrival of a serious health condition isn't enough to make them take action. They continue doing the same things they always have (perhaps half-heartedly making some changes they never fully commit to) while expecting things to change.

Whether you're consciously aware of it or not, your life's experiences are simply a collective reflection of all the thoughts and beliefs you've "chosen" to cultivate up until this moment. They're also, to a lesser degree, the collection of stronger energies around you that you've allowed to shape your environment. Whether you like it or not, your life will *always* reflect the predominant energy that fills your thoughts each day.

You can gauge your state of mind at any moment by simply looking at your surroundings and at what is reflected back at you.

Nobody is going to do the work of creating your life's experiences for you. That's your job. It's your responsibility. Recognizing that you're an incredibly powerful being that can manifest things simply by thinking about them is an amazing, awe-inspiring discovery. The reason many people can't be bothered, or see this as a chore, is that they haven't really embraced the concept of their true power. They don't truly believe in it. Why should they put any effort into something that will probably just be a waste of their time? And they're right. If they doubt their ability to be a conscious creator of their experiences, then they'll accomplish very little, and it *would* be a waste of their time. This is called a self-fulfilling prophecy.

Luckily, you do not fall into that category. You are much, much smarter (and more powerful) than that.

Conscious vs. Unconscious

When we create, we do so either consciously or unconsciously, so let's talk about both in a little more detail.

The conscious part of us is the part that thinks, reasons, judges, and chooses. It determines how we decide to express the energy we have unlimited access to.

The deeper level of our mind, called the unconscious mind, is linked to the intelligent source of energy that's responsible for the involuntary processes of our body: it causes our heart to beat, our lungs to breathe, and each cell to intelligently function as it should. It's the home of our core beliefs and the perceptions we have of ourselves and the world around us. It also acts as a gatekeeper to determine whether what we've asked for is possible based on our current beliefs (what we believe is possible).

The unconscious part of us doesn't judge us; it's amoral, nonjudgmental, and completely impartial. It's simply there. It receives our conscious thoughts and either accepts or rejects them based on our beliefs and perceptions. Every single thought that enters our conscious mind is either accepted as true or rejected by our unconscious. If accepted, the request becomes a driving force, and, depending on how much energy we put into it, it's then brought into physical creation in our lives. The unconscious can create based only on what we provide it. If we don't really provide much, it will autogenerate our everyday experiences simply based on our beliefs and perceptions stored up until this point in time.

As we mentioned earlier, the higher our vibrational frequency, the more intuitive we become. The more intuitive we become, the less our unconscious mind remains "unconscious" to us. This means we can much more effectively and quickly dig out any obstacles, such as limiting beliefs or perceptions. They become immediately clear to us and very easy to change.

Inside Out, Back to Front

We've grown accustomed to doing things backwards. We get busy trying to change the physical circumstances around us instead of changing what creates those circumstances: the way we think. We assume we have to go through all the hard work of trying to muddle through changing the things we don't like in our lives. We do our best, but we flounder.

If we took a step back and realized that all we had to do was change our mind about what we want, life would become so much easier (and more pleasant!).

But I Would Never Choose This Misery!

We've all experienced things we know we would never in our right mind have asked for—things, in fact, we wouldn't have even wished on our worst enemy—such as a debilitating illness or an emotionally devastating experience that's caused serious consequences to both our state of mind and our health. Let's take a look at what causes these troubling times:

1. There are some things we do unconsciously create. Depending on the environment in which we were raised and how we feel about ourselves and what we deserve, our predominant thoughts may generate scenarios of debt, ill health, unhappy or destructive relationships, and a lack of accomplishments.
2. We're all affected by energies around us, and sometimes those energies can be very powerful. Like a boat tossed on a stormy sea, if you're unaware of your ability to create the experiences you want or how to transform current experiences into something different, you'll be at the whim of all the stronger energies around you. Those energies (especially from people who don't have your best interest at heart) may be destructive and harmful. They lower your vibrational state, and this lower state attracts negative experiences.
3. We've drawn the experience to us because we need it. It carries a very important learning experience for us so that we can learn, grow, and evolve beyond where we are.
4. We don't have control over how the people we love positively or negatively create their own life's experiences—experiences that can, in turn, significantly impact us. We only have control over how we respond and react to their actions.

It may not seem like it, but the Universe is always perfectly balanced. Whatever experience we're having, there are never any accidents. Every event that happens, happens for a reason, and it can exist only because of the energy that generated it.

BELIEFS & PERCEPTIONS

If we could create events in our life by simply thinking about them (and we can) then the truth is that these things are just a thought away. The stronger our belief in our ability to create what we want, and the more fully and completely we embrace that belief, the easier it becomes to bring it into our life. Not only that, but with each success, our confidence in our ability grows, and results appear quicker and quicker with more practice.

"All things are possible to him who believes."

Mark 9:23

Our beliefs and perceptions are a critical piece of the puzzle. They lay the foundation not only for how we perceive and judge the world, but also how we perceive and judge ourselves. They determine the quality of our thoughts and whether those thoughts are limiting or expansive.

There is nothing more powerFUL than the belief that we are powerLESS!

We'll always think thoughts that are in line with our beliefs. Most people's lives never change much because their thoughts ... their beliefs ... remain relatively constant and unchanging.

Where Do Our Beliefs Come From?

Beliefs come from many different places. We adopt the beliefs of our parents, our teachers, our friends, and our family members. Unfortunately, some of these beliefs may not be in our best interest. We also become jaded by life's experiences and by the mass media. We allow the perceptions of other people to define us and change how we feel about ourselves. We buy into these illusions, and then we give these illusions power. Most of us are heavily affected by the beliefs and perceptions of a select few people who we then allow to have a strong influence over us.

The only thing that defines you, is you.

Our beliefs can become so rigid that even in the face of proof that these beliefs are unhealthy or proven to be incorrect, we still staunchly defend them. They become deeply ingrained, and we refuse to release our need to believe in them.

When we're young, we really don't know any different. But as we get older, and as we become more self-aware and start taking stock of our lives, it's important to begin questioning the beliefs we hold and why we judge things the way we do.

All our actions (or inactions) are based on our beliefs. To master our thoughts, we must first change our beliefs, or we'll continue to be limited by them. But beliefs are tricky creatures. They distort the true nature of life and cause us to embrace illusions that limit our ability to see things as they really are. They can take a fundamental truth such as "we're powerful creators" and cause us to believe we are powerless.

Any lack we experience is man-made.

What someone thinks or believes about you is just that—their own opinion. It's their own perception of you and nothing more. If someone believes you'll amount to nothing, this is simply a belief they've chosen to hold. You then have a *choice*: will you accept their perception and believe it ... or not? If you do, you've allowed their perception to define who you are. When you choose to allow someone else's perceptions to define (limit) you, you must take full responsibility for that choice and how it impacts you. Feeling victimized as a result of how someone else feels about you is not self-serving. In fact, it's very disempowering.

One of the first things we'll toss in the garbage is any habit we have of feeling like a victim. The great news is that whatever labels you've chosen to place on yourself, you can also remove—and there's no time like the present!

Getting to Know Yourself

At some point, "to thine own self be true" (as Shakespeare so eloquently put it) must come into play, and that point is now.

Getting to know yourself is about getting to know what makes you tick and what ticks you off. It's about recognizing the things in life that cause feelings of stress and why they cause stress, which comes back to the beliefs and perceptions we have that caused the stress in the first place.

Even though it's unnecessary to spend all our time tracking down the root of why we believe the things we do, it *is* important to get to know ourselves.

Mirror, Mirror, on the Wall

You may have heard the phrase "life reflects back to you who you are." Even the book of Proverbs (27:19) tells us, "The heart of man reflects man." At first glance, that statement may not make any sense at all, but now we have a new understanding of energy and creation. We know that what surrounds us is a "reflection" of the types of thoughts and feelings and beliefs we've embraced, either consciously or unconsciously.

This is great news! The quickest way we can get to know ourselves is to simply take a look around us. **This is ALWAYS our starting point.** It makes getting to know ourselves much easier because we always begin by looking at our life, the people in it, and the things we've surrounded ourselves with.

We also begin "watching" ourselves think by paying close attention to the everyday thoughts that we think on a continual basis. This helps us gauge our state of mind and just how positive—or negative—we really are. It then becomes much easier to make corrections.

It's time for some homework that requires us to roll up our sleeves. The assignment will take two full days: one day when you're working, and one when you're off work (if you're not currently working, then any two days is just fine). The only supplies you'll need are some paper and a pen, or a tablet or smartphone. You'll need to always keep them handy.

HOMEWORK

The purpose of this 2-day assignment is to learn about your state of mind and how you think, and to recognize the areas that need some work.

You'll need to keep on your toes and pay very close attention to your thoughts, especially the ones that are repetitive, popping up continually. They're underlying currents that often cause us to feel unsettled and are the true cause of our stress.

Activities You Do on a Daily Basis

What are your daily activities, and how do you feel about them? Do you enjoy them, or are they a chore? Do you wish you didn't have to do them? Do you find yourself wishing you were doing different things instead, and if so, what things would you prefer to be doing?

Becoming an Observer

From the moment you wake up until the moment you fall asleep, consider yourself on watch patrol. The person you're "watching" is yourself. Pay close attention to how you feel about and react to things that happen throughout that day. Listen to the chatter of your inner voice, and pay very close attention to the quiet thoughts, the ones that sneak up on you and have a sobering effect. Listen to how you talk to yourself and other people, as well as how you perceive them. Are you critical? Judgmental? Self-deprecating? Negative? Short-tempered? Irritable? Always on the defensive? Over-emotional? Controlling? Easily controlled? Bored? Listless?

Don't judge yourself for your thoughts or the things you say or do. That isn't the purpose of your homework. You're simply the watcher, and your task is to watch and listen and take note.

How Did Your Day Make You Feel?

At the end of each day, ask yourself the following questions and write the answers down in a notebook:

Did you find yourself expressing negative opinions about yourself and/or others?
Did you gossip, and if so, what fuels that gossip—jealousy, boredom?
Did you spend time worrying and stressing? If so, about what?

How You Feel about Your Life

When you objectively look at your life and the way you spend your time, how do you feel? Do you feel a sense of accomplishment, or do you feel unfulfilled? Do you feel content and happy, or do you feel empty, wishing for more? If there are elements that make you unhappy, what are they?

Question Your Beliefs about the World

When you consider your beliefs, do you find that any of them stem from the beliefs of other people, beliefs that were handed down to you that you simply adopted as your own without questioning them? Consider how you feel about things such as religion, politics, your career and food choices, expectations you have of yourself or others have of you. You are the one who must live with the consequences of those beliefs, not your parents or your teachers. Therefore it's your responsibility to question which beliefs serve you and which don't.

Paying attention to the thoughts roaming your mind is one of the best ways to get to know who you truly are. After all, your thoughts created your current life.

Make it a habit to always:

- Question anything that limits.
- Question anything that's contracting, that's not expansive in its nature.
- Question anything that brings you down, rather than raises you up.
- Question why you believe the things you do.

Why does it seem so easy to attract misery and hardship, while the good stuff seems so elusive? It really isn't; this is simply how we've been conditioned to think. We're so used to thinking in limits because it's what many of us were raised to do. This is often a by-product of the limiting beliefs imposed on us by parents or teachers or by a religious faith. Raised in a very strict religious school during my childhood, I may have received an excellent education, but it took me many years of soul-searching and questioning to release some of the rigid, self-deprecating beliefs and feelings of guilt I had adopted as a result of my religious education.

For many people, getting to know themselves is a sobering experience. I often hear comments such as, "Gee, I didn't realize I was so down on myself!" or "Wow, I really obsess about what people think of me," and "I didn't realize how overly sensitive I am and how easily I fly off the handle." How about, "I don't like to admit it, but I can be very controlling and bossy." Coming face-to-face with—and accepting—what makes you the person you are is the best way to begin raising yourself out of your current energetic space.

The quicker you get to know yourself and the things that throw you off-balance, the quicker you can get to work and change them. If you're thinking about judging yourself; if you feel ashamed or guilty about the way you think or the things you've done, or for past failures and you want to beat yourself up, don't bother. Recognize that self-punishment and self-judgment don't help you; becoming a better person and learning from your experiences as a result, do. Every single person on this earth has an obligation to be the very best person they can, and by doing that, they automatically move themselves into a higher vibrational space. In doing so, they also become a shining example to those around them.

Wallowing in misery does both yourself and those around you a great disservice. The sooner we move into that higher vibrational space, the sooner we benefit ourselves and positively impact the lives of those around us, helping them on their journey too. We'll talk more on that subject later, but meanwhile, if you feel a need to engage in a self-pity party, then do it quickly, get it over with, and join me right back here!

Changing Our Beliefs

We overcome limiting beliefs by gaining a higher understanding of how they came to exist and how they can be changed. The more we focus our time and energy toward new beliefs, the more the old beliefs will lose their energy and simply dissolve. You *do not* have to devote time and energy to discovering what those old, outdated beliefs are. This will only hamper your progress.

You Don't Have to be a Hunter

Because beliefs are invisible, we don't really know what our beliefs are, but by paying attention to the thoughts we think on a daily basis, we can find out what some of them are.

Is it necessary, though, to figure out what all our ingrained beliefs are in order to change the ones that are limiting? No, not at all. Trying to uncover a life's worth of beliefs buried in our psyche can seem like a daunting task and is completely unnecessary. Contrary to the popular and outdated approach of many psychologists and psychiatrists, it's not necessary to discover each belief, deconstruct it, and change it. We have much better things to do with our time and energy than to dig into and get hung up on our past.

Where the mind goes, energy always flows, and we certainly don't want our energy focused on the past.

There's a simple yet very powerful trick when it comes to changing beliefs. When we begin focusing our attention (our energy) on what we want, we automatically lessen the energy going toward generating what we don't want. Limiting beliefs quickly weaken and lose their power because we no longer give them any of our precious energy. Without energy to sustain them, they begin to dissolve.

When we begin to change the way we think, we automatically begin to change beliefs. In the beginning, these new beliefs aren't habitual because they're new. We've just introduced them into our life and need to cultivate them with our energy. It may take a little time before we fully embrace them and accept them as true. There's an adjustment period as we begin the process of replacing the old with the new, even though we'll quickly begin to experience flashes of insight and understanding that enforce our new beliefs.

Cultivating a new mind-set is progressive. I may tell you that you can think away an illness, but such words won't hold too much weight with you because they don't yet resonate with who you are. You don't yet truly believe them. You have to think on the concept, chew on it, let it marinate in your mind, and give it time to fully sink in before you decide its level of truth. Then, when you begin to dip your toes into the water and begin thinking differently, you find that your health condition begins to improve. Either that belief will strengthen, or you'll write it off to coincidence and it'll take longer for you to embrace the truth.

How best do we cultivate a new mind-set? Luckily, I have some wonderful "tricks of the trade" coming up that will help you do just that.

No More Copycat

In our world, most people are trying so desperately to be like someone else. They look to models, actors, and actresses and want to be like them, act like them, look like them, and dress like them. But if you have the power to create anything you like, why on earth would you want to copy someone else instead of dancing to the beat of your own drum?

You've been given the ability to creatively express yourself in an infinite number of ways. Dare to be an original! Dare to have the courage to be yourself and to become the very best version of yourself you can possibly be.

Before we dig down and get busy creating, let's spend a moment talking about the one thing we need to pull our energy away from so that we can banish it for good.

FEAR: SEPARATING FACT FROM FICTION

Fear comes in many forms, and physical fears are much more obvious to us than nonphysical fears. We can be afraid of a spider or a snake or a scorpion or of flying ... these are easy fears to pinpoint. Other fears aren't so easy to recognize, such as fear of change, fear of rejection, fear of failure, or fear of disappointing yourself or others. These are the fears that can seriously debilitate us and prevent us from achieving our goals.

Fear is the result of buying into the illusion that we're powerless, that we don't have the ability to create the life we want.

Fear-based emotions have no real foundation. They're simply a creative expression, albeit an unpleasant one, that we've given energy to. They stem from buying into the illusion we're powerless, and they're the result of the restrictions and limitations we've imposed on ourselves. The more we believe in them, the more we fuel them with energy and the stronger they get until they become a form of self-induced slavery. Very quickly, fear becomes a tyrannical master if we decide to put it in charge.

If you believed in your power to create the type of life you want to live, then you wouldn't have any reason to worry or doubt or feel fear about your finances, your health, or challenging relationships. Why? Because they wouldn't exist.

What Are You Afraid Of?

You always carry with you the power to overcome your fears.

Similar to limiting beliefs, you don't need to figure out why you have an unconscious fear. It's important instead to focus on its opposite. For example, if you're afraid of rejection or failure but your goal is to open a business, then the answer is to get busy focusing all your efforts on your inevitable success, on taking all the steps necessary to make that goal a success, including using special tools that we'll discuss a little later. The more time, energy, and attention you spend believing in and focusing on the success of your business, the less time can be spent devoted to the fear of rejection or failure.

When you feel fear, or limiting or judgmental thoughts, acknowledge them, thank them for showing up and being your teacher, then dismiss them. Every single time they show up, dismiss them repeatedly. Dismiss, dismiss, dismiss—as many times as it takes. And *every* time you dismiss them, *immediately* replace those fearful thoughts with energy devoted to the exact opposite.

Let's take a look at a healthy, self-empowering response to 3 different situations that cause you fear or stress:

1. **A Bill Shows up in the Mail That Causes You Emotional Distress**
   "Thank goodness I won't be dealing with this much longer. I'm so relieved. My finances are now drastically improving, and more than enough money is coming to pay these pesky bills. What a HUGE relief not to have to stress about future bills anymore! I'm so excited!"

2. **You're Very Distressed about a Serious Health Condition**
   "I fully recognize that the way I think and the way I eat dramatically affect my ability to heal my body from this disease. I have far more power and control over this disease than I ever imagined possible, and worrying is a waste of my time. More importantly, it's a waste of my health. I care far too much about my body to squander it with the damaging energy of worry—I'm too busy healing!

3. **You're Driving to Work for a Job You No Longer Enjoy**
   "Thank goodness this will be over very soon! I'm far too busy launching all my energies into something new and exciting to waste my energy feeling down. Best to shrug this off my shoulders and enjoy it while it lasts because it won't last much longer. I'm so excited for the changes coming—I can hardly sit still!"

Every time you feel the fear or anxiety, it's important to *immediately* diffuse it by taking away its energy (your thoughts and emotional reactions toward it), and instead, devoting energy to what will *replace* it. Always replace it with a reminder of what's coming and feel excited and expectant about the change. You may find yourself spending all day "replacing" negative thoughts with positive ones, and that's okay—that's exactly what you need to be doing!

It all comes down to recognizing and accepting you have the power to create the change you want in your life. After all, if you can change your circumstances and create anything you like, what is there to fear?

The 4 Big Fears

We give energy to four very popular fear-based emotions:

1. **Depression**
   Feelings of depression stem from the belief that we're a victim of our circumstances and that we're not the ones in control of those circumstances. In short, we feel powerless.

2. **Anger**
   Again, anger stems from feeling powerless. We're angry at others or at the world in general for our lot in life. We haven't yet realized that we have—in some way, shape, or form—energetically attracted the very situations that cause us anger.

3. **Failure**
   With the fear of failure, we give up before we even try. It comes from the fear that we don't have what it takes to accomplish our goals. We're afraid of losing our savings, of being ridiculed, of making mistakes, or of not having what it takes.

4. **Change**
   When we fear change, we often desperately cling to something that no longer serves us because it offers us comfort and familiarity. When we work with energy, we must completely trust that, despite our fear, it's the act of letting go of what no longer serves us that clears the path for the new.

Each of these fear-based emotions is a reflection of our state of mind. Because we don't yet understand this, we continue to attract more of the same in a cycle that continuously re-creates itself until we change it. A person who's distraught and who frets will always attract situations that cause them to feel distraught or anxious. A person who's angry toward others or the world will always attract situations that make them feel angry. A person afraid of change will always avoid anything that involves change, and when it's forced upon them, they'll feel unstable and insecure.

Most people who are successful have experienced the fear of failure, of rejection, of wasting their time, of going broke, and of outgrowing friends. Conquering these feelings is a completely natural growth experience. You're challenging yourself out of your comfort zone so that you can accomplish what was not in your current comfort zone. But once you embrace your ability to be a powerful creator, there will be no such thing as being "out of your comfort zone."

Getting rid of your fears may give you a few bumps and bruises, but you're now a part of the "I'm a powerful creator" camp. When the ride gets bumpy, strap on your bouncing suit and enjoy the ride!

TIME & SPACE

Time is a relative term. When it comes to using energy to create the things we want, the subject of time and space takes on new meaning. We're working with something that isn't bound by either time or space, but what exactly does this mean? Let's take a look.

Pure energy exists beyond the limits of time and space. Such limits only exist in what we call the "third-dimensional space" in which our body exists, but in reality, there are no "dimensions." This is just a helpful term we use to talk about the different densities of energy frequencies.

Just as there are types of light we can see (such as the visible spectrum of colors) and ones that we can't (such as ultraviolet and infrared), there are other things that exist that we can or can't see. For example, physical objects exist within a range of frequencies that we're physically aware of; we can see and feel them with our physical senses. But what about thoughts, feelings, and energies that we sense but that aren't physically tangible?

We live our lives within the constraints of our very limited awareness of energy frequencies. There are rules that govern how things exist for objects we're physically familiar with, just as there are rules that govern how other nonphysical things exist.

Back to Quantum Physics

When we talk about the concept that our thoughts and the thoughts of others affect both our body and our surroundings, it may sound somewhat mystical and "otherworldly," but it isn't. In fact, it's just science of the quantum-physics kind.

QUANTUM THEORY

Derived from the Latin word meaning "unit of quantity," quantum physics is a branch of physics that studies the behavior of energy as individual units rather than continuous electromagnetic waves. The existence of these tiny units (far smaller than protons and neutrons) became the first assumption of quantum theory.

In quantum physics, the outcomes of experiments have been shown to be directly affected by "thoughts" and "expectations." These findings confirm that the world interrelates by using an intelligent source of light energy, and have led quantum scientists to consider that our thoughts have a direct impact on not only our bodies, but also the world around us and in the creation of life itself. In short, everything's connected.

Plain-old science can't help us here because the limitations of science are pretty substantial and leave us with countless questions left unanswered. Science itself is a continually evolving process of discovery, and it doesn't have all the answers—it doesn't even come close. But quantum physics is a part of the evolution of science, and old-school scientists are struggling to accept that change.

When we walk into a room where an argument has occurred, we feel "tension" in the air. What we actually feel is a form of friction in the energy that's been created by the argument. It's not physical, but we can definitely sense it—it may as well be physical because we can feel it very clearly. How do we simply "know" or "sense" something without any idea how we came to this knowing? When we have a sense of foreboding shortly before an upsetting event occurs, what we're feeling is the energy of that event beginning to coalesce into form. We're tuning into the mass sea of energy and feeling the energy behind the actual event itself before it physically happens.

Why is it that dogs may howl mournfully the moment their owner passes away, even though they weren't in the same room? How do the psychics that are used by various police agencies around the world successfully locate missing people and help solve crimes? And why are some people so much more able to connect to these abilities than others? It isn't because they're better or smarter, and it isn't because they're different. Just as learning to ride a bike or learning a new language or learning to fly a plane or helicopter comes easier to some people than others, so to do these abilities. Some people may have a leg up on mastering abilities we all have, but we're not the beginners we may think we are either.

When we begin changing our perception and expanding our awareness of what we can do, we start tuning into different abilities. It start believing we have these abilities. We then begin to experience things that exist outside our current awareness (frequency range). This is slowly and naturally occurring as we all evolve. But now, more and more people are beginning to learn about and develop abilities and levels of awareness that were previously inaccessible to them.

The Limitless Nature of Existence

The knowledge we've learned up to this point, the dreams we dream, the memories we hold—these aren't physical objects, and they're not stored in any "physical" location. Yet they exist. But where exactly do they exist, and if we don't know where they exist, then how do we instinctively know how to access them? What else can we access that we don't even know about? Let's take that one step farther ... if everything and everyone that exists is pure energy—be it a table, a food item, a human, a plant, an animal, a thought, a dream, a feeling—and if we're all connected, then are we really limited to accessing knowledge based on just our *own* experiences? Or can we also access a limitless supply of collective knowledge that's the result of the experiences of all life on earth?

We haven't been taught to think this way. Most of us haven't even considered such thoughts, and if we have, we quickly dismissed these things as silly or impossible. We don't even give them another "thought."

Are you beginning to think more expansively? Great! Let's move on.

Can I Have It Now?

We experience the limited constraints of what we're consciously and physically aware of via time and space. When it comes to working with energy and manifesting specific things, there are no such constraints. Energy isn't limited by these things.

When we direct the energy of our thoughts to complete specific tasks, this energy rearranges the physical display that is the world we experience. The speed at which the results happen is determined by how skilled we are at directing and intensifying the energy of those thoughts. The better we get, the more quickly things are orchestrated.

The more adept we become at working with energy, the more we experience what I call a "quickening," which is when things begin to happen very quickly. You put out energy for something specific that would normally take weeks or months to come to you, and it happens in a matter of hours or days—so quickly that even you are shocked. As we adapt to this "quickening," our energy naturally manifests faster and faster. We become masters of time and space.

The more you practice, and the better you get, you'll quickly discover that when it comes to creating what you want, it doesn't have to come "later" because "later" is a limitation that you impose on yourself. There is only the present. There is only the *now*. When we break free from the concept of "it must take time for great things to happen," then what we want begins to appear much quicker in our lives.

We haven't yet reached the point in our growth where we can visualize an object and it instantly manifests right in front of us. Our thoughts *do* become things, but within the constraints of the physical world in which we live there is a process, and that process requires a series of physical events to occur. These steps almost always require some physical action on our part. As the saying goes, if you want to win the lottery, you do have to at least buy a ticket. If someone happens to buy that winning ticket for you, even though you didn't ask them to, well then, you can truly call yourself a master!

Now that we know the basics, let's take a look at a few final things before we begin.

GETTING STARTED

It's now time to roll up our sleeves and get busy putting what we've learned into action—action of the powerful kind!

What Are Your Goals?

When it comes to creation, we're all artists. Our thoughts are creative, making us all natural-born artists. We exist in a study lab, a magical playground where we get to play witches and wizards. We design our lives by how we think, and we get to be as creative as we like.

You have a blank canvas with the title of "My life" written at the top. You can either consciously choose what to write, or you can be at the whim of surrounding energies and let it be written for you, "hoping" for the best. Now is the moment we're going to pick up the pen, but this is no ordinary pen because this pen is fueled by energy, not ink. It doesn't matter what was on yesterday's page. What matters is the page you create today, in the "now." You can't change the past (time-traveling aside), and the past should never be your focus.

Before we can get what we want, we first have to figure out *what* we want. If we haven't given it much thought, then we may have some general ideas, but we're not talking "general" here. We're talking specifics. Sometimes, knowing exactly what we want isn't as obvious as we may think, and it requires a little soul-searching.

HOMEWORK

Take a blank piece of paper and a pen. We're going to spend 30 minutes first clarifying (and getting intimate with) what we've created, and then exploring what it is we'd like to create.

The Old
Rate, in detail, how you feel about the following 6 categories:

1. Your career
2. Your finances
3. Your body
4. Your relationships
5. Your health
6. Your state of mind

Be as specific as possible for every category. For example: Do you enjoy your job? Does it make you feel fulfilled? In what way? If your job is a source of stress, what exactly causes that stress—a coworker, your boss? Is the workload stressful? Is it unchallenging or boring? Or do you simply not enjoy what you do?

The New
On a fresh page and using the same 6 categories, rewrite your descriptions as you'd like them to read, as they would read in the ideal world you're about to create. If you had the ability to direct and control energy to change the circumstances of these categories (which you do), how would you change each of them?

Begin Small While Thinking Big

Now that you've taken a good look at your life, let's begin to formalize some goals.

When it comes to your goals, always shoot for the stars and beyond, and don't hold back. If they seem far out of your reach right now, it may take you a little while to get them, but always know that all the necessary stepping-stones will be created that will take you there.

> "Where you are is never who you are."
>
> Mike Dooley
> Notes from the Universe

It's very important to get a few small wins under your belt at the beginning. The more wins you get, the more confidence you'll have in your capacity to create, and the more comfortable you'll feel about creating loftier goals. Begin with short-term goals (such as the successful completion of a project at work that brings you accolades or unexpected recognition). When you see the results of just how powerful you are on a small scale, it'll soon become clear that the scale doesn't really matter.

Creating Fun & Easy Stuff

Include fun, small goals each day—perhaps a compliment you'd like to receive or a small success you'd like to accomplish that day. Keep a "Daily Fun Goals" list. As each one is fulfilled, cross it off that list. Make the goals simple, small, and easy for you to believe in, things that are absolutely possible but have a 50/50 chance or less of happening. The more they occur, the more your confidence will grow.

Every time you cross something off the list, *always* give yourself credit. When you give yourself credit, you consciously acknowledge the part you played in the success of completing that goal. If something didn't happen, use that as an opportunity to be clearer and more focused in your request next time.

The more you create goals, believe in those goals, and manifest them, the better you'll become. It's just like learning a new skill—the more you practice, the more inevitable the results, and the quicker they'll happen.

With this in mind, take stock of your starting point.

- If you live in a 1-bedroom apartment and you'd like to live in a 7-bedroom manor with a big swimming pool, a live-in maid, and a masseuse who stops by four times a week, you may have a little dilemma. Is it possible for you to make such a drastic change in your life within a short period of time? Yes, it's absolutely possible. Is it probable? No, it's not. That's a drastic change in mind-set—a drastic change in what you believe you can and can't have, and it may take you a while to make that change. But don't even think of changing that goal because we have some special tools to significantly reduce the time frame.
- If you're suffering from a stage 3 cancer and your goal is to be in complete remission in 2 weeks, this may be challenging. If you've always subscribed to the belief that you're limited to the success, failures, and statistics of traditional medicine, and you're new to the belief that *you* are in the driver's seat when it comes to your health, you have a little work ahead of you to change this mind-set. Again, is it possible? Absolutely. Is it probable? It may be difficult in such a short time frame.

In both examples, you must change your current reality by first moving into a different energy space.

Coming up, we'll talk about the "tools of the trade," which will help to quickly move you into that different energy space. The more you practice using these tools, the quicker you'll embrace and move into that much more expansive mind-set. If that 7-bedroom manor "feels" a little out of your reach at this moment, soon enough, it won't. If that stage 3 cancer seems hopelessly beyond your control, trust that you'll conquer that hopelessness.

It's very important to keep focusing all your attention on the end result you want and to be on the lookout for a stepping-stone or two that will take you there.

There's Nothing Wrong with Wanting Too Much

Our natural expression is to be abundantly happy, fulfilled, content, and healthy. It's the basis for the human blueprint. The experiences we attract to us exist to help us achieve this natural state of being. Any type of lack or denial or misery isn't our natural state; they exist as by-products of our fears or low vibrational thoughts. They're learning experiences to help us evolve beyond them.

There's nothing spiritual about denying ourselves, limiting ourselves, or believing that we should detach ourselves from having things in the physical world that bring us pleasure and happiness. We're no more spiritual because we deny ourselves than we're less spiritual if we choose to create money and other material possessions. Everything we experience stems from energy. Lack and poverty consciousness are simply two manifestations that we can choose to—or choose not to—experience.

Never confuse poverty and lack with being spiritual. Part of recognizing our spiritual heritage is to claim our ability to create—to create a life that's happy and fulfilling and beautiful for ourselves, and one that also benefits those around us. Not only can we have our cake and eat it, we can have as many cakes as we like, in as many different flavors as we choose.

Can we become codependent on other people, or over-identify with material objects and place too much importance on them? Yes, we can. When we begin to develop unhealthy attachments and a reliance on other people or our external surroundings, instead of the power always within us to create all that we want and need, we often attract a rude awakening to us in the form of a wake-up call. The things we're attached to may be taken away from us, or events will take place that force us to revisit our true priorities.

It's All Relative

Our perception of "ordinary" is what we're comfortable with. Take a moment to consider what "ordinary" means to you. Your perception and definition of "ordinary" can be very different from someone else's. To a person who lives in a palatial mansion and has several homes around the world that they visit, depending on the weather and the seasons, their 4-bedroom manor in Hawaii priced at $4 million may seem quite ordinary, and certainly not exceptional.

While a 2-bedroom, 2-bathroom house in a lovely area with a front and back garden may seem pretty ordinary for some, I promise you that for others, it seems like a dream home.

When you consider the infinite supply of energy that's available to mold into anything you want, you're free to create whatever version of "ordinary" or "extraordinary" you like. But whatever events you want to experience and whatever physical objects you want to have, their foundation should always be infused with the energy of bringing you health, happiness, contentment, and fulfillment. If not, you'll find that they leave you feeling empty and unfulfilled.

Becoming Close Friends with Our Goals

Once you've decided on the goals you want to accomplish, you need to become very close friends with them. These goals are about to become an intimate part of your life, so let's spend some time getting comfy with how they feel.

Time for more homework. (Don't even THINK about letting a groan slip from your mouth!)

HOMEWORK

Take a blank piece of paper and a pen. Getting to know your goals involves transporting yourself to the place where they've already been created and seeing how it feels to mentally, emotionally, and physically achieve those goals.

How Have Things Changed?
For each of your goals, spend 5-10 minutes detailing:

1. How different your life feels a result of achieving the goal
2. Others' reactions and comments about your achievement
3. How you feel about yourself now that you've achieved the goal
4. What you've purchased (if anything) associated with your goal

For a new house, examples would be how the house has changed your day-to-day life, the experience of living in a different area, the things you'll purchase for your home, the sense of pride and accomplishment you feel, the happiness others share with you about your accomplishment, etc. For improving your health, examples would be doing different physical activities that had become difficult or impossible and how it feels to have that freedom.

Get Scenic
Visualize and then write down a detailed description of 5 different scenes where you're enjoying the experience of what accomplishing your goals has brought to you. If it's a skill set, detail 5 different scenes where you use this skill.

Never Lose Sight of the Real Goal

With each goal fulfilled, we learn more about ourselves, and the more we learn about ourselves, the more expansive we become and the more we grow and evolve.

In the beginning, we may not know what we really want. We ask for various things, and we indeed get them. We then reach for different things. Sometimes, we realize that what we asked for didn't bring us the sense of happiness or gratification we thought it would. We may waste our time asking for things we really don't want or need, but at the time we created them, we thought differently. We realize that we shortchanged ourselves.

When we get what we ask for and then change our mind when we receive it, we may spend some time chasing our tails as our goals come to fruition (believe me, I've done it many times). But we can save ourselves a lot of time by understanding that what we really want, in the end, is to be happy. Instead of hoping and assuming our goals will bring us happiness, let's instead make it a habit to *always* make being happy the number-one goal above all others.

Doing what you love and what brings you happiness is the important key to living the life of your dreams. It's also the key to raising your body's energy frequency.

Did you place happiness as your number-one goal?

True Wealth

As we become more and more adept at creating what we want and collecting the stuff of our dreams, we inevitably reach an interesting destination. We begin to realize that "more" is no longer a physical thing, and we begin to look beyond our physical belongings. When we realize we're limitless human beings, we begin to turn inward and look at ways we can improve upon ourselves and what we can personally accomplish to make the world a better place. It's an urge to become something greater. Some call it a spiritual awakening. It's simply called evolving.

A by-product of evolving means that we always know we'll be taken care of and that we'll always have the things we need. We no longer have to focus our energy on these "things" because they automatically come to us even before we ask for them. The energy of having what makes us happy has become the predominant energy that shines from us at all times, and it becomes our natural state. This is the definition of true wealth.

Making Adjustments

Now that you've had some time to think about your goals and how it feels to accomplish them, do you need to tweak them? You may discover you've changed your mind about one or two of them. Perhaps you've realized that a goal is limiting you and decide to expand on it. Or it may not reflect what you really want to experience, after all.

As time goes by, you may decide to make some adjustments along the way, and occasionally, you may decide to change directions completely. You'll likely raise the bar as you become more confident in your ability, and that's perfectly okay. There's nothing wrong with changing your mind; it's a natural by-product of self-realization, not a sign of failure—you're just getting smarter.

Just make sure you think carefully when you make your changes and adjustments, and make as few as possible so that your energy isn't spliced and diced in different directions. After you make your adjustments, always keep your focus steady and your mind on the new end result.

3 Reality Checks

When you've fine-tuned your goals, make sure you avoid these 3 common pitfalls:

1. **Approval of Others**
   Is your goal based upon gaining the approval or acceptance of others around you? These are very disempowering goals; they signify that you need to work on your sense of self-worth and self-esteem. True happiness and fulfillment are not about needing someone else's acceptance or approval. If we believe that, then we put conditions and limits on our happiness. Do you really want your happiness to be conditional on the approval of others? Of course not! Your mission in life is to always simply be yourself, to recognize your place as a creator, and to create the life that you would like to experience based only on *your* approval.

2. **Being Perceived as Better Than Others**
   Nobody is better than you, and you're no better than anyone else. By now, the truth should be obvious that we're all created equal, and that as individualized expressions, we each uniquely express ourselves based on how we use the energy that fuels us. Your goals should never focus on being "better" than someone else because there's no such thing. If you believe that, then you've bought into an illusion, and it's important to reevaluate your thinking. Your goals should always be focused on being the "best" version of "yourself" that you can be.

"Resentment is like drinking poison & waiting for the other person to die."

Carrie Fisher
Actress, Author

3. **Envy, Jealousy, & Resentment**
Being jealous or envious of someone is a very destructive emotion that significantly lowers your energy frequency. When you're envious of someone else for something you don't have, you must first realize that the reason you don't have it is because you didn't choose to create it and take the necessary steps to get it. You either didn't believe you deserved it, or you believed you weren't good enough to have it, or you simply didn't understand how to use your inborn ability to create the things you want.

If you can create anything you like, what reason do you have to be resentful of someone else for their accomplishments? Comparing ourselves to others is one of the biggest forms of misery in the world today. If you feel resentment or envy toward someone else, immediately stop and recognize that any lack you're experiencing in your life is only because on some level you've chosen to experience that lack. Nobody else has denied you your ability to have what you have not yet created.

Focus on the person toward whom you feel jealousy, anger, or resentment, and silently thank them for bringing to light this important lesson. Thank them for helping set you on the path of recognition that you, too, can create things that are similar to (or even better!) than what they have. Feel a sense of gratefulness that their presence has helped you experience this awakening. Does that seem like a difficult thing to do? No, it really isn't. You can do it ... I know you can. Way to go to raise that energy frequency!

Now that we have a firm grasp on our goals, let's talk about how we're going to energize them and bring them to life ... your life!

TOOLS OF THE TRADE

The way we energize our goals is simple: We spend our time and energy focusing on them, and we become emotionally excited and expectant about getting them. There are 3 different but very important tools, each of which we can use to do just that. The tools you prefer will depend on what works best for you, but I strongly recommend you use all 3.

When it comes to using our tools, there's no right or wrong way to wield them. However, we can be either more or less effective at accomplishing our goals, depending on how actively we put them to use.

As you become more and more proficient in achieving your goals in shorter and shorter time frames, you'll find your need to use these tools will lessen. But while you do use them, keep this in mind: All your tools should be powered by fun and excitement! *Never* look at using these tools as a chore. We're talking about the stuff of your dreams here ... which means it's time to have a blast!

TOOL #1: Living As If

This is a *very* important tool of the trade. When you "live as if," this means you're acting as if what you want is already here (or is arriving). The more you begin to generate the energy that you've already received what you want, or that it's on its way, the stronger your energy becomes, and the sooner your goal will arrive. This is because you're no longer directing energy to what currently exists, but rather toward what's coming.

"Living as if" doesn't mean that you deny your current circumstances or pretend they don't exist. It means that you see these circumstances as temporary, as on their way out, while you begin to actively prepare for the exciting arrival of new things.

LIVING AS IF is the single-fastest and most powerful way to generate the energy necessary to quickly accomplish what you want.

Whether it's a job, a relationship, travel, a new car, a new skill, or regaining our health, we always begin by:

1. Physically thinking and acting as if we know the goal is either here (or about to arrive), and
2. Doing things involving "living as if" we'd already accomplished the goal.

This takes us *out of* our current energy space, and puts us *into* the new one we're replacing it with.

Let's take a look at 5 practical examples of putting this tool in action.

Healing from Heart Disease

If you'd suffered from heart disease and fully recovered, having regained your strength, how would your life have changed? In what way would your days be different? What physical activities could you do that your heart disease prevented you from doing before? You'd better start looking into taking them up again, or exploring new ones. Were you a runner who can no longer run? Then see yourself running even longer distances than you were ever able to previous to your condition, and actively plan new routes in preparation for when you have healed. Perhaps buy yourself new running gear.

How much worry and stress do you feel over your condition? How has your illness affected your energy level? What symptoms do you have? Focus on the exact opposite, and know these symptoms are on their way out. Begin regaining your peace of mind, being confident and powerful in your ability to be the master of your health and to attract whatever you need to heal your body. See yourself as fully energized, pain-free, and feeling better than you felt in your twenties.

Even though your health may be suffering at this moment and you are currently limited in your activities, the key is to move the energy of your thoughts away from the disease and into the new energy state of being where that illness doesn't exist. This is how we move from "here" to "there." This is how we create great change. You're not denying where you are, but instead, you're focusing all your energy on where you'll soon be.

A New House

Want that new house? Then ask yourself this question: If the money you wanted for the type of house you specified in your goal would be wired to your account within the next few weeks, what would you be doing? You'd most likely begin by finding a realtor. So do just that. Interview several different ones, and discuss what you're looking for. Let the realtor know that you're expecting the funds soon and need to begin your search. Visit open houses and check out online realtor websites such as Zillow, Redfin, and Realtor.com. Subscribe to alerts that notify you when houses come on the market that fit your criteria. Begin to devote as much time as possible to anything associated with what you'd be doing if you had the means to accomplish this goal.

At the same time, spend time picturing actually owning the home. How would you be spending your time then? Well, you'd be looking for furniture! What kind of furniture would that be? Begin looking online and get yourself down to the furniture store to plan what pieces will be in your new home. Subscribe to home-furnishing magazines in the mail. Check out **Houzz.com** for some home design ideas. Does your home have a large garden? If so, you may want to consider a weekly gardening service. Start looking into them, and interview prospective companies. Are you planning to move to a new location? Then start exploring that location, and if it's not within driving distance, then begin exploring different neighborhoods online and put your intent on taking a trip out there to look around.

A Big Vacation

Want to go on an exciting vacation to Tahiti (or wherever prefer)? Then ask yourself this question: If the money for the trip was sitting in your hands right now, what would you be doing? How about beginning to plan the trip, fully expectant that you'll soon be on your way? What's the best time of year to visit in terms of weather? That's something to look into (monsoon season in Thailand may not be up your alley). What hotel will you stay in? Better start exploring different choices. How about the airline? See what airline works best for the flight route, and join their frequent-flyer program (it's free). Does the hotel you like offer a points program? Explore the activities offered by the hotel by speaking to the concierge at the hotel desk about fun things to do once you get there (if the calls are expensive, contact them via email). What about other activities in the area? Who'll be taking care of the pets or babysitting the children?

How would you be spending your time on your vacation? Would you be swimming? If so, make sure you have a bathing suit, and if you don't have one, head to the store to find one or order one online. Would it be a relaxing vacation where you'd be reading? Better buy the books you'll be taking with you, or download them to your smartphone or e-reader.

Financial Independence

If you had all the money specified in your goal, think how much fun you'd have when it came to buying the things you like! What would you be doing? Again, if the money would be in your bank account in 3 or 6 weeks, what would you be doing differently? Would you quit your job? How different would your shopping experiences be? What about buying brands of clothes or appliances that you used to avoid because they were too expensive?

Let's also get practical: How would you be managing your money? Would you hire a financial planner? If so, then start making appointments and interviewing which one feels best for you. Let them know the amount of money you'll be receiving and discuss how they can help you manage it.

Losing Weight

If you're overweight and your goal is a slim, toned body, prepare for its inevitability. Even though you may have to buy clothes that are large at the moment, do so knowing that it's only temporary, and begin thinking about who you can give them to or what organizations you can donate them to when they become too big. Plan how your closet will change when you have different types of clothes that you'd never have worn when overweight. Begin looking at clothing in the size you want to wear, and perhaps buy an outfit or two in eager anticipation of when you'll be wearing them. When I was 210 pounds, I bought some beautiful size 4 dresses and hung them in my bedroom. I was so excited to wear them during the next summer! Not only did I wear them, but two of them were a little too loose on me.

Even though you're living in your present state of being overweight, do you see that you're no longer giving it any power? Instead, your energy and focus are on what you want and what's on its way. The more you redirect your energy like this, the faster your new circumstances will arrive.

Now that you no longer have to ever worry about being overweight again, what then? If weight's been a big part of your life, as it was for me, suddenly being slim and no longer being embarrassed by how I looked, being able to wear the clothes I'd always wanted to wear, and never having to think about diets ever again was a big shock to my system. I didn't realize how much of my time and effort and energy was focused on weight loss and diets. Suddenly, I felt lost. I literally didn't know what to do with myself when I no longer had to obsess about my weight! How would losing all your excess weight change your life?

The important lesson here is to *not* focus your thoughts and energy on what you're moving away from or you'll only create more of the same. You must not get lost in the difficulty or frustration of your present circumstances. If you do, they'll always be your present circumstances because your energy and focus will continually recreate them. You have to begin behaving and thinking *as if* what you want is on its way ... because it is!

The interesting thing about "as if" exercises is that they train you to become more and more expansive in your thinking. The more expansive your thinking, the farther away from your current state of mind you'll get, until your present circumstances begin to feel "off" and "unnatural"—like they should've been long gone. Bingo! Get ready for a quickening!

Make It Fun!

"Living as if" should be a very fun, uplifting experience! Make it creative. Enjoy the activities it involves because that's what life is really about—enjoyment and happiness and adventure! And don't do just one or two things and call it done. "Living as if" is a continual process until your goal arrives, so repeat! repeat! repeat! Always be on the lookout for new, exciting ways to prematurely experience the outcome of your goals.

Consistency is the key to how quickly you'll see results.

Engage Your Spouse or Significant Other

If they're on board, don't hesitate to ask your significant other to join you in "as if" scenarios. The more energy directed toward the goal, the merrier (and more powerful!). For example, over dinner begin chatting about that trip to Greece you'll be taking in the fall. Talk about who's responsible for planning the day trips and who's responsible for booking the hotel. Talk about the things you'd both like to do on that trip—perhaps relax on the beach or visit remote villages in the mountains. Will you be staying on the mainland, or on one of the islands? How about a cruise to explore several different islands? Do you need a camera? Swimsuit? Who'll be taking take care of your pets?

Beyond "As If"

Okay, so you've been practicing how it feels to physically experience having your goal. As you become more adept at acting "as if," you'll begin to look beyond that accomplishment and look toward your next steps. Now that you no longer have that health condition, now that you've lost all your weight and are in great shape, or have lived in that beautiful house for a few months, or a year, or traveled to the countries you've always wanted to visit, what then? If you think these things will be enough for you, you'll likely be disappointed.

Now that you no longer have to worry about your living conditions or your finances or your body, where will you focus your energy? You'll soon find that working on yourself, discovering your talents, and spending time on personal accomplishments become your primary focus. Exploring ways you can help others and make the world a better place may also take center stage.

TOOL #2: See It & Say It

When it comes to getting what we want—and getting it quickly—we have to infuse our entire being with the thought of it. Visualizations and affirmations are two of the most powerful tools we have to do just that. The key to visualizing and/or affirming is *not* to do it just once a day for 5 minutes. Instead, create specific pictures and phrases (or key words), and sprinkle them throughout your entire day.

When we saturate our mind with words and pictures, they have a very powerful effect on the deeper levels of our consciousness. Remember, our unconscious doesn't reason or judge what it receives; it simply accepts or rejects based on our current beliefs. But the more we saturate our mind with new thoughts (which we can do with words and pictures), the quicker these new thoughts will become strong enough to overpower old, worn-out beliefs.

Visualizations

In the beginning, making a collage of the things you want and looking at it often can be invaluable. Use pictures, or write poems or phrases or quotes about what's coming to you. Add to the collage whatever you like that reflects the end result of your goal. Put a photo of your smiling self slap-bang in the center of it! Be creative—print a copy of your bank statement and change the numbers to reflect your goal. Keep it updated and refreshed. Get pictures of that perfect body you want, make 50 copies, and paste them all over your house.

Surround yourself with constant reminders.

The purpose of these tools is to keep your attention and your energy focused on one thing: the end result. You can't effectively focus on two different things at the same time, and if you're focused on the goals that are coming to you, this prevents you from focusing on your current circumstances and from feelings that detract from that goal.

When I was just over 200 pounds and my goal was to be under 140 pounds, I made 200 photocopies of the body I wanted and laminated several of them at Office Depot. It was a fantasy art picture by illustrator Boris Vallejo, and it was beautiful! It was the body of my dreams! I pasted this picture everywhere—in the bathroom, the bedroom, on the ceiling, in the refrigerator, on the refrigerator, in the closet, the shower, the car. I carried it in my bag and made miniatures for my wallet. I kept a copy in the drawer of my office at work and continually took sneak peeks at it.

I made sure this image saturated my entire life. I was hungry for that body, and I claimed it as MINE. The first 50 pounds dropped off in just under 4 months as I ate massive quantities of high vibrational foods such as fresh, ripe fruits and vegetables. The rest slowly dissolved at a steady pace.

Affirmations

When we use an affirmation, we repeat specific words that represent what we want to achieve. We also visualize the end result along with our affirmation, which gives it so much more power.

Developing empowering affirmations to repeat on a regular basis is extremely effective. French physician Dr. Emile Coué developed the following affirmation for his patients and achieved significant success with the power of autosuggestion. Coined the "Coué method," it involves repeating an affirmation throughout the day of the goal you want to achieve.

For example, the general affirmation Coué used was:

"Every day, in every way, I am getting better and better."

By consciously using autosuggestion, Coué observed that his patients could cure themselves more efficiently by replacing thoughts of their illness with thoughts of being cured.

According to Coué, repeating words or visualizing images enough times caused the unconscious mind to absorb them, and the cured condition was the result. When you continually saturate your mind with an idea—a specific goal—instead of thinking and stressing about what you no longer want, the mind will always work toward turning that goal into a reality.

The words in this affirmation can be changed to suit your individual needs and to be much more personalized for you, for example:

"Every day, in every way, I am getting healthier and stronger."
"Every day, in every way, I am calmer and more relaxed."
"Every day, in every way, my mind grows sharper and more focused."
"Every day, the mirror displays my body is slimmer and slimmer."

Understanding How Affirmations Work

Affirmations work by impressing specific words and their associated images into our unconscious. It's very important that we *not* use words in our affirmations associated with what we're moving away from. For example, "I now give up my addiction to caffeine." Do you see why? Take a look at the words used to create this affirmation. Do you see the words "addiction" and "caffeine"?

When you state, "I now give up my addiction to caffeine," images of caffeine and the thought of addiction become imprinted in your mind, and the unconscious mind responds to these images. The unconscious doesn't rationalize the meaning of the entire statement; it simply focuses on the energy behind individual words and their meanings. It'll zone in on the words "addiction" and "caffeine" and create more of these things for you, or make it difficult for you to give up the caffeine addiction.

Always use positive statements that reflect the successful goal you want to achieve, and use them in the present tense so that you don't keep them in the future. For example:

"I AM powerful, confident, and in control of my actions."
"I NOW reclaim my power."
"I NOW fully restore myself to vibrant health."
"I AM healthy and full of energy."
"I eat only when my body needs nutrition."
"I AM the creator of my own reality."
"My body IS NOW firm, toned, and in fantastic shape."
"I ALWAYS have everything I need to be successful."
"I AM always in the right place at the right time."

When working with affirmations to overcome addictions, these addictions are related to our response to stress, making anti-stress affirmations a very good idea. For example:

"I AM calm, confident, and relaxed."
"I FEEL relaxed, content, and fulfilled."
"I AM powerful."

Repeat, Repeat, Repeat ... and Repeat Again!

Repeat your affirmations often throughout the day—when you're in the bathroom, making lunch, going for a walk, as you wake up, as you fall asleep ... Create a simple rhyme so that you'll remember the words. The more you say them, the more you generate energy that builds upon itself, and the quicker they'll produce change. Look for every excuse you can to fully saturate your mind with these important words.

Feel free to print copies of the affirmation (or related pictures) and paste them all around your home, as I did with the picture of the body I wanted.

Do What Works for You

Throw out your concept of sitting in the cross-legged yogic mantra position and chanting, or visualizing only when sitting in silence. That may work for some people but not for everyone, and it definitely doesn't work for me.

I have favorite, fun rhyme I created that I use every time I want a great parking spot. My husband knows how powerful this rhyme is because we always get a great spot, and he never fails to remind me when we get close to our destination, "don't forget to send out energy for the parking spot!"

Parking spot now come to me
come to me ***immediately***
right up close now come to me
near the door, ***immediately***

My mind is at its most powerful when I'm doing a background activity such as driving or cleaning or walking the dog or working out. That's just the way I work, and it's the best method for me. I can't visualize with my eyes closed—not at all. It's much easier for me when my eyes are open. In the beginning, I'd try simple visualizations to quiet my mind, but no matter what I tried, it was like swimming against the tide. I also prefer "feeling" the emotion of what I wanted to create, rather than "seeing" it. That, along with a few key words and simply "knowing" I can accomplish what I ask for is more than enough for me.

When it comes to visualizations and affirmations, it's not about following only one method. It's about finding what method(s) work for you and using them to your advantage.

Who said your method has to be orthodox or the norm anyway? Trailblazers don't DO norm!

TOOL #3: Taking Action

Above all, you must take action. The mind is an incredibly powerful thing, and when you give it a directive, it'll start to focus its attention on that directive.

When you release energy for specific goals, that energy immediately begins rearranging itself to present you with all the things necessary to achieve your goal. It brings new people into your life and causes you to think things that urge you to take action you wouldn't normally take. If you don't act on these impulses, you make it much more difficult to achieve these goals. New energy always propels us into some form of action, and this requires us to follow through.

Because we've fallen out of touch with our bodies and our intuition, in the beginning it can be easy to miss the subtle signals we receive to help us fulfill our goal, but trust me when I say they'll be there, and they will continue to nudge us. We just need to stop and listen. Perhaps you'll suddenly feel the urge to take a new driving route to work, or you'll feel like shopping in a store you've never been in before. You may strike up a conversation with a person in the grocery store or at the gym, or take up a new hobby. If your goal is focused on your health or weight loss, you may develop strange cravings for tomatoes or oranges or other healthy foods in mass quantities.

The key is that the body will begin to call out for what it needs to get it from point A (where you are) to point B (where you're going). Your body will always naturally gravitate toward where you direct it. Part of getting the job done is receiving signals to take action when you need to. You must then take action on these signals.

The single-best thing you can do at this time is listen to your inner voice and pay attention to little urges. If you suddenly feel like doing something unusual or atypical, go with the flow and see what happens. Trust you'll know what to do and when to do it.

Intent Isn't Enough

Intent isn't enough and never will be. Taking physical action to support your goals is almost always necessary. Physical action is a natural extension of our beliefs. For example, if we perceive we're in danger, we take action to protect ourselves. If we think we'll be late for work, we take action to try to be on time. If we want to host a successful dinner party, we must purchase food and drinks and send out invitations. If we want to go to a concert, we need to buy a ticket and get ourselves to the concert. How can you have a successful novel if you never write the book? How can you become a successful artist if you don't create the piece of art?

To achieve the goal, you must take some sort of physical action. The more adept we become at creating, the more efficiently we wield our ability to work with energy, the faster these things occur. But we're still limited by the physical constraints of the world in which we live, which means we must take action.

THE 7 GOLDEN RULES

As we work on accomplishing our goals, there are 7 golden rules to follow that will not only prevent us from needlessly worrying about how and when we'll achieve our goals, but they'll also help us enjoy the journey so much more. Let's explore these rules in detail.

RULE #1: Expect Synchronicities

When energy becomes stronger and denser and begins to manifest itself, it has an interesting property. It creates all sorts of synchronicities to let us know we're on the right track. If you've ever focused your attention on wanting something specific, you'll likely have experienced this interplay of energy.

Here are a couple examples:

- Let's say you're considering selling your home, or your lease is up and you're thinking of moving out of your apartment. Suddenly, you begin receiving things in the mail associated with these changes. It may be an introductory pamphlet from a realtor, or you may begin seeing random signs of move-in specials for an apartment. Things will begin happening out of the blue (or so you think) that have something to do with the move you're considering.
- Let's say you focus your energy on a new relationship. You may suddenly receive pieces of mail related to meeting new people, or you may have the urge to go to new places or do things you've never done before where you meet new people. You may stumble upon a Meetup group and make a new friend. There may be a roadblock preventing you from driving to your normal grocery store, and you end up at a different store, where you slap-bang into a relationship opportunity.

These are synchronicities that happen while we journey toward our goal, and they're a sure sign we're on the right track, exactly where we need to be. Now, not all of these synchronicities have anything to do directly with the end result of our goal. They're signposts, and they may or may not lead to the end result. But they do let us know we're headed in the right direction. Don't get too distracted, thinking that every single experience or dream or event is profound and prophetic. Many times, they mean very little, and we shouldn't attach great meaning to them or overreact to them. They're just a collection of experiences to enjoy on the way to our goal.

Definitely check them out, but don't be concerned if they never pan out, and don't assume they mean more than they really do. If you continue to provide enough energy, the perfect outcome for you will make itself known.

Always Acknowledge Synchronicities

Each time a synchronicity takes you by surprise with events associated with your goal, *immediately* recognize and affirm it. The more you give credibility to these events, the more they'll happen.

A natural by-product of being open to and acknowledging these synchronicities is that you'll become much more intuitive. Each time you experience a flash of intuition, always acknowledge and embrace it. This is the best way to sharpen your intuition and make it a more conscious, consistent part of your life.

Examples of intuition:

- You stopped by a grocery store you never normally stop at, and the very thing you want to buy is on sale.
- In a packed parking lot, you suddenly turn the corner and get a spot right near the door.
- A Groupon comes out that offers a deal specific to what you were about to buy at full price.
- A flash of inspiration pops up from nowhere and helps you solve a difficult, troubling problem.

The higher you raise your vibrational frequency (through taking action on what you've learned in the protocol), the more intuitive you naturally become. Each time you experience the power of your intuition, stop, smile, and get excited—that intuition is only going to get clearer and stronger.

Begin to ask yourself for advice, and over the course of the next few hours or days, EXPECT the answer to become clear. As your intuition sharpens, you'll be shocked by how accurate it becomes. Answers to your questions will not only become instinctive, but you'll realize you already know the answers before you've even asked the question. New, wonderful experiences you desire will begin entering your life before you've even asked for them.

RULE #2: Don't Indulge in Negative Thoughts

The more your pay attention to your everyday thoughts (as you did in your homework), the more you'll catch limiting thoughts sneaking into your head. Get into the habit of watching what you think. Every time you catch yourself thinking something that's negative or in direct opposition to your goal, immediately turn it around and diffuse its energy.

Turning It Around

The best way to sap the strength and energy from a negative thought is to:

1. Laugh at it, and think just how silly and limiting that thought is, and then
2. Turn it around and spend a few moments putting energy into its exact opposite.

We talked about this earlier, but let's talk about it a little more with an example:

An Unexpected Bill Shows up That Causes You Some Stress

You have a choice. You can sit and worry about it, and continue to stress about how you'll pay it. Or you can choose to use your tools to free yourself of financial worry, feeling a sense of relief that soon these and other bills will be easily taken care of. Smile at yourself and say, "Geez, do I *still* worry about these things? How quaint!" Look at the stress with humor, and then quickly focus on the emotions surrounding how you'll feel receiving bills you can easily pay, or better still, bills that your bookkeeper will be taking care of for you.

ALWAYS REMEMBER: Indulging in stress (anxiety and worry) does you no good. Whether the bill gets paid now, or whether it gets paid later, stressing about it doesn't change or help the situation at all. What it does do is create more of the same. It also negatively affects the biological processes of your body, causing premature aging and triggering the release of stress hormones.

By taking this approach, you're not avoiding the here and now, nor are you in denial. You're simply not engaging in stress or worry. You're no longer fueling your *current* circumstances with any emotional energy that will effectively create *more* of the same. Instead, you're acknowledging the present, trusting that this bill will be taken care of, and choosing to focus your energy on its exact opposite.

Now is the time to make limits no longer part of your reality. Put your back against the wall and say, "Absolutely not!" to any limiting thoughts. It's not just about trusting in your ability to create what you want, it's a flat-out refusal to even entertain the reality of anything else.

Where the Mind Goes, Energy Flows

Recognize that thoughts will always attract similar thoughts. The more you think thoughts of what you want, the more the energy will be directed toward those thoughts, and the more you automatically think other thoughts related to the accomplishment of that goal. This is why what you spend your day thinking about is important. In the beginning, you *must* spend time consciously controlling your thoughts, taking them by the hand and guiding them in the direction they should be pointing. They may fight you in the beginning, but soon they'll surrender as you conquer them. Soon, you'll wear them down. At the moment, their negative chitchat may make it seem like they're the ones in control, but that won't last long once you show them who's boss.

Watch out for runaway trains. For good or bad, some thoughts often generate situations that very quickly build up more and more energy, building momentum like a runaway train and creating more of the same types of situations. We call these "streaks of bad luck" (or streaks of good luck!). We become so lost in the experience and in the emotions generated from these experiences, that we rapidly create more and more of the same thing. The only way to screech a "bad-luck train" to a halt is to stop feeding fuel to that train by taking away its energy. We do that by simply focusing on where that train should be headed instead.

REMEMBER: When you think negative thoughts, or thoughts that are in opposition to your goal, you unwittingly provide them with the energy they need to strengthen and reproduce.

Falling Short

Suppose that the business you launched isn't what you'd hoped it would be, or that it's not as successful as you'd like. You may need to tweak your belief in yourself just a little more so that the next one will be a skyrocketing success. You may have needed the setback and the experience it taught you to lay the foundation for what will soon be coming, or to put you into a different and necessary frame of mind for upcoming success. Perhaps it orchestrated new people into your life that will become key players in your current business or a new one.

The fact that you went all the way means you had the courage to do what many others don't because of their fear. Successful people rarely get it right the first time. It often takes several "practice" rounds.

RULE #3: No More Procrastination or Excuses

We can rationalize why we avoid taking action toward our goals all we want. Whether it's laziness, doubt, or inactivity due to our fears, the end result is the same: nothing gets done. The best, most powerful way to deal with procrastination is to hit it head-on, and as the Nike tagline says: Just Do It!

> "If youth only knew; if age only could."
>
> Henri Estienne
> French Painter, Scholar

If a project seems overwhelming, instead of looking at the entire project as a whole, begin by looking at the first step, and take it. Separate the things that must be done into bite-size pieces, tackling them one at a time. If you begin today, then by this time next month, you'll have taken a giant stride and will be well on your way. Conversely, this time next month, you can be making the same excuses (or different ones) that forever put your goals out of reach.

When I feel like I have the weight of the world on my shoulders with my goals, I sometimes play a little trick on myself. I say, "I'm going to get started now, and I'm going to give it absolutely all I've got, but I'm only going to do this for 1 week and then I'll see what happens." Because my commitment is for only 1 week, it's not so bad! Well, invariably, a week goes by, and I get totally psyched about my progress. I'm already caught up in the momentum, and I'm now moving at breakneck pace. At the end of the week, I may say, "Ahhh ... just a few more days, then maybe I'll walk away." But in a few more days, I know in my heart of hearts that I've come too far down the path and I'm now fully and energetically committed to the inevitability of my goal. My trick was just enough to get me started ... to help me take those first few important steps and set me on the path to being well on my way.

As the sobering quote goes, "If youth only knew, if age only could." When you put things off until later (when you get your education, when you have more money, when you feel less stressed, when you've lost weight, when you're older, when the kids have finished school, after you've moved), you lose out big time. If you want something, you *must* actively take steps to get it and remove the limitations of procrastination, excuses, and justifications.

It's very presumptuous for us to think we all have the rest of our lives to do whatever we want. We never know when we'll be hit by a curve ball, or when something may happen to permanently prevent us from doing something specific we want to do. We never know when loved ones will be taken from us. This is why we must *always* live in the present and not put off our plans and dreams until "later" in our lives, assuming that we'll always have the "later" we want. The energy of "later" always keeps your dreams just out of arms' reach.

Necessity Is the Mother of Invention

When it comes to committing to your goals, put yourself in a position where you have no choice in the matter. Look for things you can do or say that give yourself no way out. By not only making promises to yourself, but also making promises to others that depend on your commitment, you back yourself into a corner.

Years ago, I landed a job in Southern California running the web technologies department of a large company. I got the job based on an interview and making an outrageous promise that I had no idea if I could fulfill. I blatantly claimed I could easily redesign, build, and launch their corporate website in a week. A week! 10 years ago, that was a much more difficult feat than it would be today, and even today, it's not that simple in a large corporation.

Not only did I have no idea what budget was available, how easy it would be to work with the art department (the people who must approve the design) and editorial department (the people who must approve the text), and how long the approval process normally takes, I also had no idea what resources they would provide me. I had also been told the current website redesign had been in the works for 11 months and had gone nowhere. All I knew was that I wanted the job, and there was absolutely no way I was going to let it slip through my fingers.

Not only did I get that job, but sure enough, I somehow launched that website in one week, and it was a success. I had backed myself into a corner where I was *forced* to scramble to accomplish what I'd promised.

The "It's Too Late" Excuse

It's never too late to experience success or happiness. The many years of study required to become a vet or a doctor or an astronaut may not be on the horizon, but there are countless other avenues. Every problem contains its own solution, and at every point in your life there are always new dreams to follow, creative outlets to be explored, and experiences to have.

If you're not quite sure what those avenues are, trust that you'll figure it out if you put out the energy to do so. If you need guidance, trust that you'll have the help you need in the form of strength, courage, hunches, intuition, and synchronicities.

If you're expecting to simply sit there, do nothing, and be told what to do and how to do it, then don't hold your breath because that's for you to figure out. Sometimes, when you have a crossroads before you and you're unsure whether to go left or right, have the courage to take the plunge and trust that whatever decision you make is the best choice for you at this moment in your growth, because your focused energy has already dictated your success. Sitting around doing nothing simply because you haven't received any clear "signs" or been "struck by lightning" (proverbially speaking) will get you nowhere fast.

RULE #4: Lighten (& Brighten) Up!

Enjoy the journey because that's what life is all about! The adventure of achieving your goals isn't just about reaching your destination; it's about the journey of getting there. If a goal is going to take a month or two (or longer) to manifest itself, you have the choice of enjoying the ride ... or not. Why choose not to have fun on the journey? Or let me put it another way: If you knew—positively knew, 100 percent—that your goal was coming to fruition very quickly, how would you be feeling? You'd be ECSTATIC! You'd definitely not be miserable because you'd be too busy being on cloud 9! You would also be far too busy living "as if" to be miserable.

It's never just about reaching the destination and getting what you wanted, because the destination is only a very small part of a much bigger experience. Achieving your goals is only possible as a result of the journey it took to get there.

Make Time for the Things You Enjoy

This is one of the best ways to fast-track not only the successful completion of your goals, but to also move your body into a higher vibrational space. The happier you feel, the lighter and brighter your energy becomes. When we do things we enjoy, things that give us a sense of accomplishment and fulfillment and that bring smiles and laughter to our faces and the faces of others, we feel the sparks of happiness that literally cause us to sparkle.

Start finding ways to incorporate into your life the things that you enjoy doing. Never underestimate the joy you can feel from simple things, things such as curling up to read a good book, or listening to music you enjoy, or playing roly-poly with your pup or kitty, or cuddling and smooching with your loved one. Carve out that time, no matter what excuses you try to come up with. Give yourself no choice in the matter because making time for yourself is essential, just as breathing air and eating food are essential.

If there's a hobby or sport you'd like to take up, then swing into action. Begin pricing it out and talking to the instructor. If the cost seems currently out of reach, you now know that it doesn't matter. Do the legwork and begin planning for it because as soon as you put out energy for it, the cost won't matter.

Old mind-set: "I'd love to take up that hobby, but I'm just too busy. It's too expensive, and I don't have the budget for it. Maybe I'll look into it in the future when I have more time and money." (Notice that this mind-set keeps your goal in the "future" and doesn't energetically bring it into the "present.")

New mind-set: "Although I understand and respect that old mind-set, I now see that it's the reason I can't afford the time (or money) to take up the hobby I'd like to. The way to create the energy of what I want is to begin the process of "living as if" I can do what I want and using the tools I've learned. Instead of focusing on what I don't have, I'm going to focus my attention on what I want. I deserve it! It's high time I said goodbye to what I don't have and prepare for what's now coming."

See the difference? You've fully accepted responsibility for creating your present circumstance and have now made a conscious decision to create something new instead. It doesn't matter that today you're short of time or short of funds for that class or course. That's not the problem. By researching your new hobby, meeting the teacher (or researching an online course), and reading up on the curriculum and any supplies required, you're putting the energy in motion that's needed to bring it into your space. By actively focusing on having it and expectantly waiting for it, you begin to create its existence.

There will always be that awkward transition period where even though your thoughts and attention are on what you're creating, you still have to live with the "old" circumstances that are on their way out. Just accept them, ride through them, and see them as a temporary inconvenience while saying your silent goodbyes.

RULE #5: Forget about How, When, & Where

This is one of the biggest pitfalls people fall into. When we begin to put energy in motion, we get busy thinking of all the hard work we have to do to achieve the goal, and for the loftier ones, we quickly begin to fret and feel overwhelmed, wondering how on earth we're going to make them happen! And if it takes longer than we'd hoped, we start to doubt ourselves and assume something is wrong.

When it comes to your goals, always keep the following three things in mind:

FORGET THE HOW
FORGET THE WHEN
FORGET THE WHERE

For Heaven's Sake, Forget the "How!"

It's not our job to figure out how. It's our job to come up with the goal, focus our attention on the end result, and have absolutely no doubt that we'll achieve it. Then, we live in a state of expectancy for its arrival.

There's no way that we can fathom the infinite number of ways that energy can manifest itself. If we limit ourselves to focusing on the few avenues that may come to mind, we then cut ourselves off from all the other possibilities. We never have to worry about how the energy will orchestrate the events and situations necessary for our goals. The biggest limit we can place on ourselves is to get hung up on how it will happen. This will only cause us to worry and stress and to doubt our abilities. It's also the quickest way to unravel all our hard work.

When we worry about "how," we're trying to take on a much bigger responsibility than we should. We're not meant to figure out the how. That's not our job. We're meant to use the resources provided to us, namely the energy. All we need to do is direct it. When we take a flight to another city or country, do we busy ourselves with understanding the inner mechanisms of the airplane? Do we expect to fly the plane ourselves? Of course not! It's not our job to worry about how the transport works or what's involved in getting us to our destination safe and sound. When we go to a fancy restaurant and order the culinary specialty of the day, do we head back into the kitchen to worry about how the ingredients are being prepared and how our dish will be cooked? Nope! Our job is simply to place our order and expectantly wait for it to appear.

Forget about the Details

Forget about the details of the journey. They'll be as they should be to get you to your goal. Just focus, focus, focus on the end result. Feel it, live it, breathe it, and bask in its inevitability. Feel the sensations of achievement in your body. Hear the people around you excitedly congratulating you. You must trust that your energy will create the necessary circumstances around you. You'll feel the urges and hunches that you need to feel. Ideas will suddenly pop into your head. Unexpected events will occur. People will show up. Strange coincidences will happen. It's inevitable!

ALWAYS REMEMBER: The energy of creation, which is the essence of all life, isn't a visible thing; therefore, you can't judge your progress by external appearances. If you feel distressed that something is taking too long to show up, or feel impatient or concerned or worried, simply continue to focus on your goal. If a goal seems thwarted at every turn, or if it seems like you're actively being blocked from receiving this goal, then you may need to get busy making some adjustments or approach it from a different angle and learn from the experience (more on this later).

Our job is to trust in the process. We can't control the details, or the hows, whens, or wheres. It's our job to focus only on the destination and to enjoy the ride.

RULE #6: Resist the Urge to Control & Manipulate

When it comes to goals involving people and relationships, we need to take a slightly different approach. We don't focus our intention on manipulating people, nor do we waste our energy with the intent to make others do what we want them to do. Instead, we always focus on the benefits we'll experience from what we want to achieve.

Are you looking for a promotion within your company? You may feel like you want to focus your energy on causing your boss to choose you. Or if there are other people also in line for that promotion, you may want to prevent others from achieving the same goal. Manipulation is never the right course of action, and it's also completely unnecessary.

Instead, focus your energy on the benefits you'll gain from the end result, on what the promotion will bring you. What does the promotion offer that makes it so appealing to you? Why do you want it so badly? Dedicate 100 percent of your energy to what you'll gain from the promotion. When you focus on that essence of success, then whether you get that promotion or not is irrelevant because instead of the promotion, you may end up getting something so much better. It may be within the same company, or it may just be in the shape of an entirely new job opportunity.

If we're powerful creators, then we don't need to achieve success at the cost of someone else's failure; there's more than enough for everyone. You should also consider that the promotion may not be in your best interest, and it may not bring you the happiness you want or be in line with other goals you have. In fact, it may do just the opposite and cause you stress and much longer work hours. This is another important reason to focus on the essence of the end result and the ultimate benefits and sense of happiness the goal will bring to you. Focusing on happiness in all your goals is a fail-safe.

Relationships

Are you looking for a relationship, and do you have someone specific in mind? Be careful here. Rather than focusing your energy on that person, instead, focus on the type of relationship you'd like to experience and how incredible you'd feel if you were a part of that relationship. Focus on the feeling of being loved and nurtured and of loving and nurturing someone else, on the fun and

> "With great power comes great responsibility."
>
> Voltaire
> French Writer, Philosopher

exciting experiences you'll both share, and on how your weekends and evenings will change once you're a part of that relationship.

By attaching names and faces to the outcome, you not only limit what you can receive and experience, but you also indirectly manipulate the energy of the other person. You may get what you want, but it may not be in your best interest, nor in the best interest of the other person who was swayed by the strong power of your intention and energy. If that's the case, at some point in the relationship, both of you will feel a sense of imbalance and resistance. As Voltaire warned us: "With great power comes great responsibility."

If you're trying to prevent a relationship from ending, again, rather than focusing on saving it, focus instead on the qualities of the relationship you're looking for. If this relationship is in both of your best interests, it'll work out. But sometimes, a relationship may be drifting out of your life because it's time for someone new to arrive. By limiting your expectations to only one relationship, you may be waving off any chance of their arrival.

Can you free yourself from the urge to focus on that one specific person? Can you trust in yourself and take a leap of faith that, regardless of whether your current relationship continues or ends, the end result will be a happy, fulfilling relationship that's in your best interest?

RULE #7: Time Frames & Details

As we now know, energy isn't bound by the limitations of time or space as it orchestrates reality. The more practice you have, the more adept you become at making changes in your life. Then, these changes will naturally happen quicker and quicker, and the time frame of "as quickly as possible" becomes very quick.

When you place exact time frames on a very lofty goal, you can create problems because the time frame can short-circuit the possibility of achieving a goal. If a house matching the one of your dreams goes on the market in 8 months, but you've asked for it in 4, you may end up having to settle for something less. If you're looking for a job and the ideal position is set to come to you 2 months down the line, yet you want it in 3 weeks, you may end up getting less than you hoped for. Not only do you not get what you want, it's also a blow to your self-confidence as a creator because you'll feel that you've failed.

We're used to functioning in linear time (one thing happening after another on a timeline), and this is how we experience our lives. As a result, we tend to tag deadlines and time frames onto everything. But when it comes to working with energy, time frames force energy to constrain itself to our time and space. In some situations, time frames may be necessary, but wherever possible, focus on the success of your end result with the words "now" or "is now coming" or "quickly." If you have a driving test in a week, instead of setting a goal to pass your test in a week, simply focus on successfully passing the test, having your license, driving alone in your car, etc.

The same concept holds true for monetary sums. If you feel stressed about your mortgage payment coming due in 3 weeks, instead of asking for a specific amount of money in 3 weeks, focus on all your mortgage payments being paid easily and without any stress. You're limiting yourself to receiving only the amount of money for your one mortgage payment by specifying an amount, and you're also negating the possibility of the payment being made in other ways that you may not have thought of.

Time frames for the larger goals should be loose and light—6 months, 1 year, 3 years, 5 years—because this gives your energy lots of wiggle room. I guarantee that with practice, you'll naturally manifest these goals quicker and quicker to the point that they take your breath away. You may set time frames, but you'll instinctively know that what you want is coming and move beyond the need to specify something exact.

Nothing Is Happening!

HELP! I'm waiting ... I'm still waiting ... and ...

NOTHING IS HAPPENING!

When we begin to work directly with energy, it's a big adjustment to how we normally look at our daily lives and our goals. One of the most common things I hear is "HELP! Nothing is happening!"

Invariably, this is due to one of three things:

1. Not using your tools
2. Impatience
3. The need to make adjustments

Use Your Tools

Your tools must be used on a continual basis for them to be effective, and that takes discipline. If you use them halfheartedly, your success will be fleeting.

Many people aren't successful at the game of creation because they don't use their tools effectively. In the beginning, you must use your tools, or you'll achieve very little success.

You must also be crystal-clear about your goals and make sure they're "goal-oriented" as opposed to "wishful-thinking" oriented. Wishy-washy goals equal wishy-washy results. It's also important to change your mind as little as possible, or the energy never has time to strengthen and build upon itself.

The biggest issue by far is not devoting enough time to living "as if" and relegating positive thinking to a few minutes each day. Some people focus solely on affirmations, dutifully repeating them on a regular basis. You can think all the positive thoughts and repeat all the positive affirmations you want, thinking those thoughts and saying those words until you're blue in the face, but if you spend most of your day not focused on your goal, or engaged in thoughts that are in opposition to your goal, they'll be a big waste of your time.

Compare this: Let's assume you suffer from a chronic disease, and you spend 15 minutes each morning and each evening visualizing perfect health. The visualizations are very clear. You see yourself fully recovered and doing the things you'd be doing if you were healthy.

You feel confident and excited that you'll fully heal from your condition, but then you go about your day. You feel the pain or discomfort from your condition and generally worry and stress and fret out of habit. You feel depressed about your health and worry about medical bills. The things that you do, the actions that you take, and the thoughts you think throughout your day back up the reality of your health condition ... except for those 15 minutes in the morning and 15 minutes in the evening.

To this: You spend 15 minutes each morning and each evening visualizing a state of perfect health, of your heart beating strong, and of your body regenerating only healthy cells and tissues. Not only is every piece of food you eat full of radiant, living energy, but you also begin the process of integrating things into your life that you'd be doing if you were healthy. How about looking into local 5K runs that are coming up, and checking what the training schedule would be? What about looking into how you'd create a Meetup group to share with others your success of healing from disease? Begin typing a letter to a friend you haven't seen in years, sharing your journey and how relieved you are that you've experienced a full recovery.

Every single time you feel physical discomfort, pain, tiredness, or limitation from your condition, you never feel disheartened or distressed because you know that it's just temporary. It's transient, and you look forward with excitement and expectancy to your full recovery. You live this excitement. You feel it infusing your entire being throughout the course of your day.

What a big difference! Note that you're not physically "doing" the 5K run, but you begin to prepare for the fact that you could do it as soon as you're healed. Nor do you need to start any groups or mail the letter. But you're living *as if* your health situation has resolved—and there lies the real power. Not only are you generating the energy associated with a healthy body 15 minutes twice a day, but you're also living and breathing that energy in everything you do and every thought you think. How can you not succeed?

It's not the thoughts we think for a few minutes each day that are the creators of our reality. It's the thoughts we think on a habitual basis that control the reality we experience and the body we produce.

Consider this saying: You can take a rich man and strip him of all his wealth, and within 1 year he'll be back to where he was before his wealth was stripped from him. Conversely, you can take a poor man and give him $5 million in lottery winnings, and within 1 year he'll be back to where he was before his wealth was given to him. Both individuals are bound vibrationally to a state of being that cannot be denied because it's intrinsically who they are.

Be Patient

In the physical world, change usually doesn't happen instantaneously. With practice, it happens faster and faster, but time frames are still involved. When we begin to put out energy for our goals, we may be tempted to wait a few days and then exclaim, "Nothing is happening!" Really? Are you able to physically see the interplay of the energy you're directing? Nope. Just as you can't "see" your thoughts, you also can't "see" them at work and "see" the changes taking place behind the scenes.

In reality, a mass orchestration is going on with billions of molecules rearranging themselves. Just because you can't see them doesn't mean they aren't very busy in action. With practice and experience, you'll actually begin to "feel" and "gauge" your progress.

In our impatience, because we see no "physical" results immediately, we assume we did something wrong and feel disheartened and full of self-doubt. We very quickly begin to unravel all the hard work we've done. In frustration, we end up calling it quits.

Spending quality time focusing on what you want, only to intermittently doubt you're going to get it, is like planting a seed and then continually digging it up, or drawing a picture and midway scribbling it out, beginning to draw it again. The end result can never come to fruition.

Never underestimate the destructive power of impatience when it comes to your goals.

When impatience and worry begin to create storm clouds, using the following tactics to chase them away:

- Keep yourself busy.
- Keep affirming your goals and focusing on the end result.
- Turn the energy of your impatience around and use it to your advantage. Channel it into phrases of excitement, such as, "I'm so excited I can barely wait! The anticipation of how incredible it will be is driving me crazy!"
- Chill out. Stop beating yourself up, and allow yourself to laugh at how silly you're being.

Do *not* judge the progress of energy by trying to use your physical senses.

Know When to Make Adjustments

Let's say you've dutifully created your goal and have saturated your days with thoughts and visualizations of that goal. Every day, you're living and breathing it and are doing things that are "as if" it's already been accomplished. You've been very patient, and despite waiting, weeks are going by and nothing seems to be happening. There aren't even any signs to show you that you're on the right track—no cool synchronicities, absolutely nothing. What gives?

Sometimes, the exact opposite of synchronicities begins to happen. We may experience unpleasant circumstances. We seem thwarted at every turn. There's simply a silence. It's almost as if there are invisible rocks that cause us to stumble. Unexpected events that are the opposite of what we're trying to accomplish occur.

If, no matter how much time and effort and energy you put into a goal, nothing happens (or it feels like you're continually fighting against the current), then it's likely that what you're asking for isn't in your best interest or that it conflicts with other goals. Take a step back, reassess your goal, and make some changes. Have you limited your goal? Have you tied it to a specific event or person or place or time frame, instead of expanding the possibilities of how this goal can express itself? If you always ensure that happiness is your primary goal, you'll always be actively prevented from receiving a goal that's not in your best interest.

Years ago, I sent out energy for a specific position at a company based in Colorado. I was fully qualified for the position, and this was a company I very much wanted to work for. As usual, I took for granted that I'd soon be working there and prepared myself for my new job. I went all out. I did everything you could imagine in terms of energy work and taking physical action.

The days and weeks went by, and absolutely nothing happened. I was very used to getting "synchronicities," but none appeared. I quickly became irritated and confused because I was also used to things happening quickly. In fact, at the 1-month mark, I was downright indignant! How DARE my energy not work! Sheesh ... this was ridiculous!

I kept striking out. I tried harder, I took more action, but all I received was silence. I visited in person; I even had references from two officers of other Fortune 100 companies vouch for me. All I did was continually strike out, no matter what angle I hit it from. Not only did none of those angles pan out, I didn't even receive so much as a phone call or e-mail. How on earth could it be possible?

I finally had enough. I threw up my hands in despair and shouted, "What am I MISSING here?!" In my pigheadedness, it turns out I'd been missing a lot. I'd developed such tunnel vision with this specific goal that I hadn't noticed the Universe had been coordinating some interesting experiences, experiences that would soon lay down the path of an entirely new—and ultimately much, much more fulfilling—career. But I was just too busy fueling the energy to the wrong opportunity to notice.

Looking back, I experienced a very important realization. I made sure that my main driving force was my desire to be happy and very fulfilled by my career. Back then, I didn't particularly like what I did. My career was successful, I earned a great salary, and I had an impressive title and the respect of my peers, but when it came to a sense of accomplishment and fulfillment, I was pretty miserable. I often found myself wishing I was doing something else or had chosen a different career.

I'd used my power to direct energy and manifest many, many goals in my life, and I'd always wanted to teach others to do the same thing. I loved helping friends and coworkers and strangers move beyond their limitations. I'd also always wanted to fly a helicopter and become a pilot, and yet, there I was, in a career that I didn't enjoy. Because my job paid me so well, I was afraid to walk away from it. Somewhere along the line, I'd fallen into the trap of thinking that choosing the career of my dreams meant that I'd have to do without money and all the things I wanted.

But the power of my energy won out. It was so powerful that it would absolutely not let me choose an opportunity that would *not* fulfill my goal of being happy. I'd effectively blocked myself from *any* job that would continue taking me down this path of remaining unfulfilled and buying into the illusion that I had to stay in that career to be financially successful.

I was left suspended in time until I finally let go, threw up my arms, and simply focused on the end result of being fulfilled and happy. Today, I can't express how relieved I am that I was never given the job I wanted at that company.

In hindsight, I now realize this was a fantastic learning experience in teaching me the important lesson of always keeping my eye on the true goal of happiness, instead of rigidly constraining my options.

When life seems "stuck," you can be sure it's a sign you're going against the flow and need to make some adjustments. Focus on the feelings of happiness and freedom your goal will bring you and how it will change your life for the better. Learn from my mistake (which I made sure to never repeat!). If you've focused your attention on something specific, then instead, focus your attention on the reasons you've asked for the goal (what it will bring you, how it will change your life, and how you'll feel once your life is changed). This is a more expansive way of thinking. There may be something about the "specifics" you're requesting that aren't in your best interest or that are in conflict with other goals you have.

Roller-Coaster Events

Don't confuse the need to modify your goals with unexpected (and sometimes quite unpleasant) events that can occur in your path from point A to point B, which in reality, propel you closer to your goal. These circumstances may need to happen to pave the path for necessary change.

> **Example**
> You've been stuck in a job for years that's just a daily 9-5 grind. There's nothing about it you particularly enjoy except that it brings you a paycheck. In fact, it saps your spirit. You focus your energy on a happier, more fulfilled life, and BAM! You're suddenly laid off, or perhaps you were even fired. You've lost your job! Well, of course you did! How can we lay down a new foundation if we don't blow up the old one?

If you fully trust in the process and in your ability to create what you need, you'll recognize that the job loss was necessary to propel you into a new space and new growth experiences. It forced you out of your comfort zone and put you into an alert state where you now have no choice but to take action toward something new. Instead of panicking, be positive and expectant that what you want is on the approach.

Roller-coaster events are very different from multiple events that are consistently in opposition to what you want to accomplish, the ones that make you feel like you're headed in the wrong direction.

Speaking of roller-coaster events, let's spend a few minutes talking about how to troubleshoot some of the tougher situations we may encounter, situations such as dealing with difficult people, or when emotionally challenging things happen in our lives.

WORKING THROUGH TOUGH TIMES

Once we get busy changing our lives, we can sometimes get blindsided by unexpected things that happen along the way. It may be a situation that causes us severe distress, or we may struggle with a very traumatic experience.

Let's take a look at how to deal with the most common scenarios:

1. Dealing with difficult people
2. When bad things happen
3. Grief
4. Guilt

Dealing with Difficult People

Instead of Turning Them into a Frog ...

When dealing with difficult people or people we just can't stand, let's face it: we can quickly reach the end of our rope. Whether it's someone at work that really gets our hackles up, or a family member that drives us to distraction, we've all wished they'd disappear off the face of this earth (or worse, turn into a frog!). But there's always a solution that involves the absolute best outcome for us and the other person.

Let's take a look at a practical example.

A Coworker You Absolutely Can't Stand

You dread having to interact with them. Not only that, you feel emotionally traumatized to the point you begin to dread your job.

Instead of focusing on how much this person's presence is traumatizing you, focus instead on the end result: you being very happy at work and having no interaction with *any* person that causes you distress. Begin by focusing on your work environment being happy and stress-free. Don't limit it to "this specific work environment," but rather the essence of working in a position (and with a company) that brings you happiness and is free of stress, with coworkers you very much enjoy being around and interacting with.

How about also throwing in a few images of the person you dislike celebrating the success and achievement of a new job offer or promotion that brings them great happiness, as well as putting space between you both? Make sure you leave yourself open for all possibilities, including a promotion or new job situation for yourself, too.

Always Look at the Reflection

Remember something very important: the reason the person (or situation) in question exists in your life in the first place is that on some level your state of mind and the energy that radiated from you has brought them close to you. Look at the reflection and consider why their presence has arrived and what there is to learn from it.

Changing your energy state will always alter the players in your life.

When you live in the lower energy frequencies, what then gets reflected back to you is the energy of difficult times (and irritating people!).

Throughout our lifetime, people will flow into and out of our lives as necessary. Our presence in their life and their presence in ours is not accidental or random; we're all willing participants in the game of life, helping and guiding each other. The more a person emotionally impacts us, the more they have to teach us about ourselves and our state of mind, and the more profound the growth lesson we need to experience. How do we begin to understand the lesson? By recognizing this person as a reflection of our current energy state, of the energy of the environment with which we have chosen to surround ourselves.

As difficult as it may be, silently thank the person for their presence in your life, and use this experience to gauge your state of mind and how you can change it.

When Bad Things Happen

If we're the creators of our reality, then a very big question comes to mind. It can seem unfathomable that we'd ever have a hand in generating energy that brings a horrible situation into our lives. Would we ever consciously choose to experience a devastating event? No, of course we wouldn't. We can all agree on that.

When we experience a traumatic event, it's transformational by its very nature. We may not realize it at the time, but in hindsight, it can create great change in our lives. We may experience levels of empathy, compassion, and understanding that we couldn't before the event. Such experiences can teach us important lessons about how we view ourselves and others; they can cause us to reexamine the way we think and to make some very drastic, necessary changes in our lives, changes that take us to new frontiers.

Every challenge is a growth opportunity.

I hear you cry: "Are you saying that every terrible thing that's happened in my life is all my fault? Does that mean my husband beating me up is my fault? Are you saying my autoimmune condition is my fault? I refuse to accept that!"

"Fault" isn't the right word here. When it comes to horrible situations we experience in our life, let me offer you 4 reasons they've appeared on our doorstep:

1. We're unaware that our energy creates our daily lives, and so we haven't engaged in "consciously" creating what we want. Instead, we do it unconsciously, fueled by the stress, limiting beliefs, and generally negative thoughts that are often the backbone of our daily lives. This reflects back chaotic energy that draws to it more of the same. We feel the effects of this chaotic energy in the form of unwanted experiences, and from the environment we choose to live and/or work in.
2. There's an important lesson to learn from the experience, a lesson that will propel us into a new stage of growth.
3. We've consistently engaged in diet and lifestyle habits that lower the overall frequency of our body. We now know that when we lower our vibrational frequency, we open ourselves up to diseases that resonate at these lower frequencies.
4. If it involves the passing of a loved one, then we aren't able to see the greater picture of the growth path another person is on, and why they've experienced the events they have. We may feel deeply the pain of loss, but we have no control over the life path of another.

There are times when events happen around us that are so despicable, so shocking, and impact us so intensely that we feel completely numb. We're unable to comprehend how such things could possibly be part of the "big picture." How can it ever make sense that a young child should die of a terminal disease, or a loved one suffer an unspeakable act of violence? Because we're at the disadvantage of not being able to see the bigger picture, we're unable to rationalize that any possible benefit or good could ever come from such a tragedy.

We can only ever gain an understanding of our own journey, and we may never understand why these unspeakable experiences happen to others, and what it means in the grand scheme of their own entire existence.

We'll always attract to us challenging circumstances that help us grow beyond where we are now. It's our nature to continually evolve. The impact of a devastating experience is far-reaching and deeply transformational. It rips away our foundation, shredding it to pieces. It may be years down the line, looking at the experience in hindsight, before we recognize how we're better people for the experience.

I say "years down the line" because in the moment that our house has been foreclosed on, or cancer has taken away our loved one, or we suffer a heart attack, we simply can't see or understand the greater picture. We're too immersed in shock or grief, and it's very difficult to step out of the pain and see the situation with any objectivity. The passage of time is what helps us look at the event with a deeper understanding and a different perspective.

Grief & Death

Grief is a very difficult emotion. When we experience true grief, such as the loss of someone we love deeply, or the loss of a pet, it can feel like we've literally had our heart ripped apart. Energetically speaking, it's a devastating experience, and no matter how calm or well-equipped we are to handle stress, some curve balls hit us very hard.

When we experience the death of a loved one, we fight to come to terms with that loss. Because death is beyond our control, it makes us feel powerless. In that powerlessness, in that stripping of all control, we're forced to give in to something higher than ourselves.

The passage of time and the support of others are our two biggest healers. Draw on the support of family and friends, of support groups and those who love you, to help you work through this difficult period. Do not go it alone and alienate yourself because the healing process will be much more difficult to work through, and you are far likelier to suffer from depression.

There's a direct correlation between happy people and societies that have a strong support structure. The Greeks, for example, talk about their issues openly. Family members, neighbors, and communities are much more close-knit, and when somebody is angry or upset or needs emotional support, it's always available to them. They "have it out," and there may be yelling and screaming and tears, but antidepressants and other prescription pills aren't part of the equation. Gaining strength from family and friends and neighbors is all the "drugs" they need. Two of the healthiest states within the US are Vermont and Utah, both of which have inhabitants that developed a much stronger support structure than their neighboring states.

No matter how it may seem from your current perspective, the Universe is always perfectly balanced. When upsetting things happen to those we love, and we can't understand why, it's because we're limited in our capacity to see the greater picture for both ourselves and our loved one; however, we can always count on the fact that their presence in our life and ours in theirs provided us each with important lessons to help us grow and evolve. It's fruitless to try to judge those lessons. As hard as it is, focus your thoughts on the happy times together, the joy and the love and light you experienced together, and how much more enriched your life became as a result of this loved one being in your life. It's not our time to go, yet it may be someone else's, and we have to accept this. Just as one day those who love you must let you go, so too must you move on, knowing that even though your loved one may no longer be on this earth, they're always in your heart and will forever be a part of the beautiful person you are.

The pain of emotional loss lessens when we begin to understand the true, timeless nature of reality. On a higher level, each of us moves through many cycles of growth and many lives on this earth. We grieve the death of a loved one because we feel that the loss is forever, but it isn't. It's a loss here in the physical world, but we're all eternal beings, infinitely connected, that are continually evolving toward higher forms of existence. Accepting this truth helps us gain a deeper understanding and helps us heal the pain.

Guilt

Guilt is a very damaging emotion that can seriously debilitate us if we allow it. When we feel guilty, we're in a self-punishment mode. We've done something terrible and have decided we need to make ourselves suffer.

When you experience guilt, there's only one way out of this emotion, and that is to recognize that the entire purpose of your existence, and every experience that you have, is to help yourself and those around you grow and evolve.

You would never, ever have attracted circumstances to you that bring you guilt if there wasn't an important lesson to learn from that guilt. Now that the guilt is here, it's serving a purpose. It's your teacher. You can choose to learn from it, or you can fail the course and take it again, and again, and again, in the form of bringing to you more reasons to feel guilty. At some point, you'll finally stop and realize that until you move past your need for self-punishment, you'll be stuck in the cycle, and that cycle isn't where you should be.

If you're experiencing chronic guilt over something in your past, ask yourself the following two questions:

1. If you've hurt someone or done something bad that's caused someone else pain, then don't you owe it to yourself as well as to them to learn from that experience and become a better person because of it?
2. Everything and everyone exist in a vast sea of interconnected energy. The energy you radiate out not only significantly affects those around you, but on a subtler level, has a much more far-reaching impact. Don't you have a responsibility to forgive yourself, release the guilt, and radiate a higher vibrational energy toward those around you?

It's important to accept yourself for who you are—the sum total of all the experiences you've had in your life up until today. No matter how much you beat yourself up for what's happened in the past, the future is unwritten. You can choose right now to move forward and do amazing and beautiful things, to help make the world around you a better place ... or not.

If you've hurt another person and feel guilty for it, you must use this experience to become a better person, realize your mistake, and not repeat it. You've brought this experience into your life to learn from it. The person is here to provide you with a lesson to learn from your interaction with them. Don't make that sacrifice a waste.

You're not here to be perfect and never make mistakes, and to then judge yourself and punish yourself for those mistakes. You're here to experience the growth lessons you need to propel yourself into higher levels of being. We all make mistakes—every single one of us—and we've all done things we wish we hadn't. That's life, and it's how we learn and grow and evolve. Forgiving yourself is an important part of that life. The ultimate mistake is to not learn from guilt, and instead choose to wallow in misery.

Release the Past

Whether we're dealing with grief, guilt, or regret, time is the biggest healer, but the passage of time can't heal us if we're continually reliving moments that have caused us pain. When we do this, we keep those events close to us and never give time the chance to become a healer.

Time can only be a healer if we don't dwell on or live in the past.

For those who dwell on the past and live in perpetual sadness and regret, moving forward becomes impossible because they've tied themselves to the energy of past event(s).

Getting "High" on Life

This is an unprecedented time, a time of great change, and a time when the mass consciousness of our species is making a quantum leap and taking control of their lives and their destinies. We can go with the flow and take that leap, which many are now doing, or we can root ourselves firmly in the old paradigm, resist the changes, and stay exactly where we are. But now that we've woken up, we know that it's our destiny to go with the flow.

The blueprint of each and every one of us has always been to claim our stake as powerful creators and move onward and upward.

Let's move on to the last section of the protocol and talk about how to cultivate a high vibrational state in the realm of infinite possibilities.

PART III

LIVE, THRIVE, EVOLVE!

CULTIVATING A HIGH VIBRATIONAL STATE

For many on this earth, life is simply about surviving, about getting through the daily grind. It's about spending 8 hours or more at a job we don't particularly enjoy, fighting traffic we'd rather avoid, and living from paycheck to paycheck to pay bills that bring us stress. It's about suffering from diseased states, challenging relationships, and weight-control issues. As time goes by, the pressures of life become overwhelming, and feeling depressed is par for the course. Millions are addicted to sleeping pills, antidepressants, stimulants, and highly processed and refined food, with rates of chronic disease skyrocketing.

For some of us, life is less of a struggle. We're basically healthy, we live in a nice home, and we aren't short of money. Whether we're happily married, single, or in a relationship, we feel content. But many of us can't say that we feel "exceptional," or that life is an incredible experience, or that we feel fulfilled beyond our wildest dreams. Life still feels pretty good, but in the quiet moments, we find ourselves wondering whether there's something more, and if so, why it eludes us. We feel wanting, yet we don't quite know for what. We cannot help but feel we have settled for less.

Surviving vs. Thriving

Surviving means just that: whether we're healthy or sick, happy or depressed, skinny or fat, we're still surviving. But we now know that this isn't what life's about. It was never meant to be constrained within the scope of simply surviving. Ultimately, that isn't what we're here for.

We aren't here to merely survive. Surviving is only part of the equation when it comes to life, an equation that only becomes balanced when we take the quantum leap forward and begin to evolve.

When we begin to raise the vibration of our body by eating high vibrational foods and cultivating high vibrational thoughts and habits, subtle yet profound changes begin to happen. Light begins to infuse our entire body at a cellular level. It happens automatically; we don't have to do anything else. This infusion of light affects our body in three ways:

1. The very substance of which our body is made will experience an "upgrade." Degraded tissue and diseased cells will shed, while healthier cells of a higher vibration will take their place as our body not only rebuilds itself, but recalibrates to a higher state.
2. We'll begin to attract situations, people, and circumstances into our life of a higher vibrational pattern. Like a fine-tuned antenna, we'll automatically tune into and find them, and they'll find us.
3. Our state of mind will experience a dramatic change. We'll feel much calmer, centered, and in tune with our physical, emotional, and spiritual needs.

On the flip side, we'll begin to feel friction with the things in our life with which we no longer resonate. This can be a career, relationships, food choices, a bad habit, a state of mind, or where we live. In short, we need to prepare to make some very drastic, positive changes in our life! They'll happen naturally and for the best, and it's very important to embrace each and every one of these changes without fear.

You Can't Buy Your Way to a Healthy or Evolved State

No matter what anybody or any website tells you, when it comes to getting healthy, leaving behind what no longer serves you, and evolving beyond it, there are no shortcuts. That would deprive you of experiencing the growth that's part of the process, and from experiencing the greatest discovery of your life ... the discovery of the powerful, limitless nature of your existence.

Everything that occurs in your life reflects who you are at any given moment in time. If you're experiencing difficult situations or are in an abusive relationship, you exist in an energy state that's in "harmony" with those types of situations. As you learn and grow from experiencing these situations, you raise your vibrational frequency and attract different and better things to you that reflect your new vibration. And so the cycle continues. The higher your energy frequency, the healthier the cells and tissues that are constantly recreating your body, and the more different (and pleasant) the experiences, circumstances, and people in your life become. You begin to evolve.

Ditch the Detoxes & Cleanses

By now, you'll have come to the realization that you no longer have to pay hundreds of dollars for a cleanse or detox program, course, or seminar. You now have all the knowledge you need, and likely far more than most who teach these courses. There are many nutritionists, dietitians, and authors charging $200 to $500 or more to teach you far less than the principles you've learned in this protocol. There are detox nutritionists who even charge in excess of $1,000 to teach you only a fraction of the basic principles you now know.

I wasn't kidding when I said this protocol would be the most important (and financially sound) investment you'd ever make. You now have everything you need to, as Dr. Spock would say, "Go forth and prosper."

Don't be fooled by any program or seminar that claims they can "make you enlightened" or perform energy work on you that "transforms you" or assures you "a higher energy state" when you pay a fee for their course. Not only are these false promises, they can also be a very big drain on your wallet. Never buy into the illusion that you're less than capable of achieving all you ever dreamed without a "guru" or "expert" draining your funds. You have all you need. It's now up to you. You'll always attract help when you need it, and the more committed you are, the quicker the changes you want in your life will occur.

From limited to limitless ... the possibilities are infinite.

INFINITE POSSIBILITIES

As we bring the protocol to a close, we walk away with an entirely different and exciting understanding of life.

Life-force energy animates all life on earth. Every one of the trillions of cells in our bodies are born with this life-force energy that animates our entire physical body and rearranges itself to create every single event we experience, from the minute we are born until the minute we pass from this earth. The more life-force energy we have, the healthier, more vibrant, and more evolved we become. The less we have, the sooner we begin to suffer from premature aging, degenerative diseases, and lower states of mind, such as depression and sadness.

Magical You

By eating high vibrational foods and incorporating high vibrational lifestyle habits and thoughts that raise your energy, you're rebuilding and transforming your body from the ground up, and from the inside out. The reward is a level of health, vibrancy, extrasensory abilities, and an evolving state of mind that is your birthright. It's also the ability to direct energy to create anything in life you choose.

Whether you accept this or deny it doesn't change the fact that it's true.

Does that sound like magic? Yes, it does—and that's because it is! We're incredibly powerful human beings, and the higher our vibrational state, the more magical we become. Then, the possibilities become truly limitless.

What you decide to do from this moment forward is up to you. When it comes to playing with energy, you have nothing to lose and everything to gain. Thousands of people practice these principles and reap the enormous physical, emotional, and spiritual benefits, with more discovering their ability to do the same with every day that goes by.

When you realize that the possibilities are infinite, your life will never be the same.

Always Remember ...

You're supposed to succeed. Remember that at every moment in time, you always have everything you need to change your circumstances. As long as you're alive and conscious, you're a powerful creator. You simply need to become aware of this truth and embrace it.

You were born with all the answers.

It was always in your nature to succeed.

YOU ARE limitless potential.

ENDNOTES

FOUNDATION

The Root Cause of Disease

1. Essential Oils Integrative Medical Guide, by author Dr. D. Gary Young.
2. Hippocrates Life Force, by author Dr. Brian Clement.

How We Get Sick, How We Heal

1. MD Anderson Cancer Center.
2. Cancer Is a Preventable Disease That Requires Major Lifestyle Changes. Pharm Res. Sep 2008. 25(9): 2097–2116.
3. Genes & Human Disease. World Health Organization.
4. Intelligence & How to Get It: Why Schools & Cultures Count, by author Richard E. Nisbett.

The Dependent Gene: The Fallacy of "Nature vs. Nurture" by author David S. Moore.

Why Drugs Don't Cure

1. How to Stop Hospitals from Killing Us. Wall Street Journal. Sept. 21, 2012.
2. A New, Evidence-Based Estimate of Patient Harms Associated with Hospital Care. J Patient Saf. 2013 Sep;9(3):122-8.
3. Is US Health Really the Best in the World? JAMA. Jul 26, 2000. Vol 284, No. 4 p485.

All-Important Enzymes

1. For the Love of Enzymes: The Odyssey of a Biochemist, by Nobel Prize Winner Dr. Arthur Kornberg.
2. Enzyme Nutrition, by author Dr. Edward Howell.
3. The Enzyme Cure, by author Lita Lee.

How Enzyme Depletion Affects Health

1. Enzyme Nutrition, by author Dr. Edward Howell.
2. The Rat: Reference Tables & Data for the Albino Rat, by author Dr. H. H. Donaldson.
3. Enzyme Nutrition, by author Dr. Edward Howell. pp.104.
4. Enzyme Nutrition, by author Dr. Edward Howell. pp.114.
5. Enzyme Nutrition, by author Dr. Edward Howell. pp.29.
6. Enzyme Nutrition, by author Dr. Edward Howell. pp.27.
7. The Effect of Repeated Stimulation of the Pancreas on the Pancreatic Secretion in Young & Aged Men. Gerontol Clin 11:56–62, 1969.
8. Some Factors Influencing the Catalase Content of Organisms. Jour. Exp. Zool. 1921. Vol 32.
9. Lipase Actions of Extracts of the Whole Rate at Different Ages. J Gen Physiol. 1925 Sep 18;8(2):75-88.
10. Enzyme Nutrition, by author Dr. Edward Howell. pp.29.

For the Love of Enzymes: The Odyssey of a Biochemist, by Nobel Prize Winner Dr. Arthur Kornberg.

How We Depelete & Destroy Enzymes

1. Enzyme Nutrition, by author Dr. Edward Howell. pp.113.

Understanding Chronic Inflammation

1. Macrophage Content in Subcutaneous Adipose Tissue. Diabetes. Feb 2009; 58(2): 385–393.
2. Chronic Insomnia & Stress System. Sleep Med Clin. Jun 2007. 2(2): 279–291.
3. Obstructive Sleep Apnea, Inflammation, & Metabolic Sndrome. Metab Syndr Relat Disord. Aug 2009. 7(4): 271–277.
4. Neuroinflammation in Alzheimer's Disease. J Alzheimers Dis. 2010. 21(1): 1–14.
5. Inflammation & Alzheimer's Disease. Neurobiol Aging. May-Jun 21, 2000. (3):383-421.
6. Small-Bowel Side-Effects of Non-Steroidal Anti-inflammatory Drugs. Eur J Gastroenterol Hepatol. Apr 11, 1999. (4):383-8.
7. Determining Small Bowel Integrity Following Drug Treatment. Br J Clin Pharmacol Sep 2003. 56(3): 284–291.

Life Extension Foundation.

THE PROTOCOL

The Vibration of Foods

1. The Whole Soy Story: The Dark Side of Soy, by author Kaayla Daniel, PhD, CCN.
2. National Association for Child Development.
3. Pediatric Group Position Statement on the Use of Soya Protein for Infants. J Fam Health Care. 2003, 13, 4, 93.
4. Health Committee Warns of Potential Dangers of Soya. BMJ. 2005, July 30, 331, 7511, 254.
5. Soy Formulas & the Effects of Isoflavones on the Thyroid. New Zealand Medical Journal. Feb 2000.
6. Brain Aging & Mid-Life Tofu Consumption. J Am Coll Nutr. 2000 Apr;19(2):242-55.
7. Serum Estrogen Levels, Cognitive Performance, & Risk of Cognitive Decline in Older Community Women. J Am Geriatr Soc. 1998 Jul;46(7):816-21.

How We Damage Food

1. Low-Dose Effects of Bisphenol A. Environ Health Perspect. Aug 2005. 113(8): 926-933.
2. Principles of Orthomolecularism, by author R. A. S. Hemat.
3. Effects of Microwave Cooking on Bioactive Compounds in Broccoli. J. Agric. Food Chem. 2007. 55 (24), pp 10001–10007.
4. Effects of Microwave Radiation on Anti-Infective Factors in Human Milk. Pediatrics. Apr 1992. 89(4 Pt 1):667-9.
5. Chemist, author, lecturer, and nutritionist Dr. Lita Lee, Ph.D.

6. Breast & Artificial Feeding. JAMA. 1934. 103(10): 735-739.
7. Intolerance of Cow's Milk & Chronic Constipation in Children. N Engl J Med. 1998. 339(16):1100-4.
8. Randomised Controlled Trial of Effect of Raw & Holder Pasteurized Human Milk & of Formula Supplements on Incidence of Neonatal Infection. Lancet. Nov 17, 1984. 2(8412):1111-3.
9. Unpasteurized Milk: Health or Hazard. Clinical & Experimental Allergy. May 2007. 35(5) 627-630.
10. Cross-Cultural Association Between Dietary Animal Protein & Hip Fracture: A Hypothesis. Calcif Tissue Int. Jan 1992. 50(1):14-8.
11. Milk, Dietary Calcium, & Bone Fractures in Women. Am J Public Health. June 1997. (87):992-997.
12. Calcium Intake & Fracture Risk: Results from the Study of Osteoporotic Fractures. Am J Epidemiol. 1997. (145): 926-934.
13. Dietary Factors & Fracture in Post-menopausal Women: A Case-control Study. Int J Epidemiol. 1992. (21):953-8.
14. The Wulzen Calcium Dystrophy Syndrome in Guinea Pigs. Am J Physiology. 1955. Vol 43(1):185-209.
15. Natural Milk Proves Best & Erf. Jersey Bull. 50:210-211; 224-226, 237.
16. Childhood Leukemia & Parents' Occupational & Home Exposures. J Natl Cancer Inst. Jul 1987. 79(1):39-46.
17. Residential Pesticide Exposure & Neuroblastoma. Epidemiology. Jan 2001. 12(1):20-7.
18. Canine Malignant Lymphoma & Dog Owner's Use of 2,4-D. J Natl Cancer Inst. Sep 1991. 4;83(17):1226-31.
19. Case-control Study of Pesticides & Fetal Death Due to Congenital Anomalies. Epidemiology. 2001 Sep;12(5): 595-6.
20. Pesticide Applications & Autism among Children in the California Central Valley. Environ Health Perspect. 2007 Oct;115(10):1482-9.
21. High Pesticide Exposure Associated with Cognitive Decline. NIIEHS. Nov 2011.
22. Two Pesticides Associated with Parkinson's Disease. NIH. Feb 11, 2011.

Real Milk.

Farm to Consumer.

Mix 'n Match Foods

1. The Stomach & the Duodenum, by authors GB Eusterman & DC Balfour.
2. Guyton & Hall Textbook of Medical Physiology, by authors AC Guyton & JE Hall.

The Question of Organics

1. Proportionate Mortality Study of Golf Course Superintendents, Am J Ind Med. 1996 May;29(5):501-6.
2. Agricultural Herbicide Use & a Risk of Lymphoma & Soft-Tissue Sarcoma, JAMA. 1986 Sep 5;256(9):1141-7.

   Mortality Study of Canadian Farm Operators, Med Lav. 1990 Nov-Dec;81(6):499-505.

   Non-Hodgkin's Lymphoma among Phenoxy Herbicide-Exposed Farm Forkers, Chemosphere. 18(1-6):401-406, 1989.

   A Case Control Study of non-Hodgkin's Lymphoma on the Herbicide 2,4-D, Epidemiology. 1990 Sep;1(5): 349-56.
3. High Pesticide Exposure Associated with Cognitive Decline. NIIEHS, 2011.
4. Study Finds Two Pesticides Associated with Parkinson's Disease. NIH, 2011.
5. Child Development & Environmental Toxins. NIIEHS.
6. Home Pesticide Use & Childhood Cancer. Am. J. Public Health. 1995;85:249-252.
7. Canine Malignant Lymphoma & Dog Owner's Use of 2,4-D, J Natl Cancer Inst. 1991 Sep 4;83(17):1226-31.
8. Case-Control Study of Pesticides & Fetal Death Due to Congenital Anomalies. Epidemiology. 2001 Sep;12(5): 595-6.
9. Residential Pesticide Exposure & Neuroblastoma. Epidemiology. 2001 Jan;12(1):20-7.
10. Childhood Leukemia & Parents' Occupational & Home Exposures. J Natl Cancer Inst; 1987 Jul;79(1):39-46.
11. Pesticide Applications & Autism among Children in the California Central Valley. Environ Health Perspect. 2007 Oct;115(10):1482-9.
12. Organophosphate & Carbamate Pesticides. Medical Disability Advisor.
13. 7-Year Neurodevelopmental Scores & Prenatal Exposure to Chlorpyrifos. Environ Health Perspect. 2011 Aug; 119(8): 1196–1201.
14. Organically Grown Foods Higher in Cancer-fighting Chemicals Than Conventionally Grown Foods. Science Daily. Mar 4, 2003.
15. 10-Year Comparison of the Influence of Organic & Conventional Crop Management Practices on the Content of Flavonoids in Tomatoes. J. Agric. Food Chem. 2007. 55 (15), pp 6154–6159.
16. Determination & Comparison of Vitamin C, Calcium & Potassium in Four Selected Conventionally & Organically Grown fruits & Vegetables. African Journal of Biotechnology. Aug 18, 2008. Vol. 7 (16), pp. 2915-2919.
17. Antioxidant Activity & Phenolic Content in Organic & Conventional Vegetables. Food Sci. Technol. Apr/Jun 2010. Vol.30, No.2.

The Last Detox You Will Ever Do

1. There Is a Cure for Diabetes, by author Gabriel Cousens.

Omega 3 Fatty Acids

1. The Franklin Resources Institute for Science Learning.
2. The Slow Discovery of the Importance of Omega-3 Essential Fatty Acids. J Nutr. Feb 1998. 128(2 Suppl): 427S-433S.
3. Dietary Linoleic Acid Influences Desaturation. Biochim Biophys Acta. Aug 4, 1994; 1213(3):277-88.
4. Weston A. Price Foundation.

5. Supplementation with an Algae Source of Docosahexaenoic Acid. J Nutr. 1996. 126:3032-3039.
6. Microalgal Docosahexaenoic Acid Decreases Plasma. Br J Nutr. Apr 2006. 95(4):779-86.
7. Fish Consumption, Fish Oil, Omega-3 Fatty Acids, & Cardiovascular Disease. Arterioscler Thromb Vasc Biol. 2003. 23:e20-30.
8. Docosahexaenoic Acid Supplementation & Cognitive Decline in Alzheimer Disease. JAMA. 2010.304: 1903-1911.
9. Beneficial Effects of Dietary Omega-3 Polyunsaturated Fatty Acid. FASEB J. 2008. 22:1213-1225.
10. Neuroprotective Action of Omega-3 PFAs against Neurodegenerative Diseases. Prostaglandins Leukot EFA. Nov/Dec 2007. 77(5-6):287-93.
11. Plasma Fatty Acid Levels in Autistic Children. Prostaglandins, Leukotrienes & Essential Fatty Acids. 2001. Vol. 65, pp.1-7.
12. Essential Fatty Acids & Phospholipase A2 in Autistic Spectrum Disorders. Prostaglandins Leukot Essent. Fatty Acids. Oct 2004. 71(4):201-4.
13. Omega-3 Fatty Acids Supplementation in Children with Autism. Biol Psychiatry. Feb 2007. 61(4):551-3.
14. Evaluation on the Effects of Neptune Krill Oil on Chronic Inflammation & Arthritis. J Gastroenterol. Dec 2005. 100(12):2674-80. PMID: 17353582.
15. Cognitive & Cardiovascular Benefits of Docosahexaenoic Acid in Aging & Cognitive Decline. Curr Alzheimer Res. May 2010. 7(3):190-6.
16. Extremely Limited Synthesis of Long Chain Polyunsaturates in Adults. Appl Physiol Nutr Metab. Aug 2007. 32(4):619-34.
17. Maternal Supplementation with Very Long-Chain n-3 Fatty Acids. Pediatrics. Jan 2003. 111(1):e39-44.

Antioxidants

1. Effects of Microwave Cooking on Bioactive Compounds in Broccoli. J. Agric. Food Chem. 2007. 55 (24), pp 10001–10007.
2. Exogenous Antioxidants: A Double-Edged Sword in Cellular Redox State. Oxid Med Cell Longev. Jul-Aug 2010. 3(4): 228–237.
3. Sickle Cell Anemia: A Potential Nutritional Approach for a Molecular Disease. Nutrition. 2000. 16:330-8.
4. Role of Antioxidants in the Skin: Anti-aging Effects. J Dermatol Sci. May 2010. 58(2):85-90.
5. Prevention of Cervical Cancer. Crit Rev Oncol Hematol. Mar 2000. 33(3):169-85.
6. Meta-Analysis of Studies on Breast Cancer Risk & Diet. Eur J Cancer. Mar 2000. 36(5):636-46.
7. Reevaluation of Ascorbate in Cancer Treatment. J Am Coll Nutr. Aug 2000. 19(4):423-5.
8. A Randomized Factorial Trial of Vitamins C, E, & Beta Carotene. Arch Intern Med. 2007. 167(15):1610-8.
9. Progression of Early Atherosclerosis & Intake of Vitamin C & Vitamin E from Supplements & Food. Circulation. 2001. 103:1365d.
10. Serum Vitamin C Concentration was Inversely Associated with Stroke. 2000. 31(10):2287-2294.
11. Serum Vitamin C Concentration is Low in Peripheral Arterial Disease. Circulation. 2001. 103(14):1863-1868.
12. Vitamin C for Asthma & Exercise-Induced Bronchoconstriction. Cochrane Database Syst Rev. Jun 17, 2014. (6):CD010749.
13. Enzyme vs. Diclofenac in the Treatment of Osteoarthritis. Clin Rheumatol. Oct 2004. 23(5):410-5.
14. Bromelain Reduces Mild Acute Knee Pain & Improves Well-being. Phytomedicine. Dec 2002. 9(8):681-6.
15. Curcumin & Age-Related Macular Degeneration. Front Aging Neurosci. 2014. 6: 191.

CANDIDIASIS, DIABETES & CANCER

For Candidiasis

1. Effects of Garlic Extract Treatment in Normal & Streptozotocin Diabetic Rats Infected with Candida Albicans. Indian J Clin Biochem. Apr 2010. 25(2):182-7.

For Cancer

1. The Risk of Developing Uterine Sarcoma after Tamoxifen Use. Int'l J Gynecol Cancer. 2008 Mar-Apr;18(2):352-6.
2. Long-term Risk of Cardiovascular Disease in 10-year Survivors of Breast Cancer. J Natl Cancer Inst. Mar 2007. 7;99(5):365-75.
3. What If the Cure Is Also a Cause? Washington Post, Jan 15th, 2005.
4. McGill Cancer Center.
5. Dr. Charles F. Schnabel, Scientist, Agricultural Chemist.
6. Wheatgrass Juice May Improve Hematological Toxicity Related to Chemotherapy in Breast Cancer. Nutr Cancer. 2007. 58(1):43-8.
7. Effect of Wheat Grass Juice in Supportive Care of Terminally Ill Solid Organ Cancer Patients. Cancer Prev Res. Nov 2008. 1; B139.
8. Inhibition of in vitro Metabolic Activation of Carcinogens by Wheat Sprout Extracts. Nutrition & Cancer. Aug 4, 2009.
9. Chlorophyll: The Active Factor in Wheat Sprout Extract Inhibiting the Metabolic Activation of Carcinogens in vitro. Nutrition & Cancer. Aug 4, 2009.
10. Wheat Grass Juice in the Treatment of Active Distal Ulcerative Colitis. Scand J Gastroenterol. Apr 2002. 37(4):444-9.
11. Chlorophyll, Chlorophyllin & Related Tetrapyrroles Are Significant Inducers of Mammalian Phase 2 Cytoprotective Genes. Carcinogenesis. 2005. 26 (7): 1247-1255.
12. Antiproliferative Effects of Carotenoids Extracted from Chlorella Ellipsoidea T Chlorella Vulgaris on Human Colon Cancer Cells. J. Agric. Food Chem. 2008. 56 (22), pp 10521–10526.
13. Evaluation of Chemoprevention of Oral Cancer with Spirulina Fusiformis. Nutr Cancer. 1995. 24(2):197-202.

14. Anticancer Effect of Spinach Glycoglycerolipids as Angiogenesis Inhibitors Based on the Selective Inhibition of DNA Polymerase Activity. Mini Rev Med Chem. Jan 2011. 11(1):32-8.

15. Digestion, Absorption, & Cancer Preventative Activity of Dietary Chlorophyll Derivatives. J Nut Res. Dec 2006.12.003.

16. Effect of Dietary Chlorophyll Derivatives on Mutagenesis & Tumor Cell Growth. Teratog Carcinog Mutagen. 1999. 19(5):313-22.

17. Superoxide Dismutase as a Target for the Selective Killing of Cancer Cells. Nature. Sep 2000.21;407(6802): 390-5.

18. Marine Algal Natural Products with Anti-Oxidative, Anti-Inflammatory, & Anticancer Properties. Cancer Cell Int. 2013. 13: 55.

19. Anticancer Effects of Blue-Green Alga Spirulina Platensis. Ann Hepatol. 2014 Mar-Apr;13(2):273-83.

20. Resveratrol Inhibits the Proliferation of Human Melanoma Cells. Mol Med Rep. Jan 2015. 11(1):400-4.

21. The Combination of Rapamycin & Resveratrol Blocks Autophagy & Induces Apoptosis in Breast Cancer Cells. J Cell Biochem. Mar 2015. 116(3):450-7.

22. Cancer Chemopreventive Activity of Resveratrol, a Natural Product Derived from Grapes. Science. Jan 1997. 10;275(5297):218-20.

23. Resveratrol & Curcumin Enhance Pancreatic ß-cell Function by Inhibiting Phosphodiesterase Activity. J Endocrinol. Nov 2014. 223(2):107-17.

24. Nutritional Composition & Antioxidant Activity of Four Tomato Varieties. Food Chem Toxicol. Mar 2012. 50(3-4):829-34.

25. Protection against Esophageal Cancer in Rodents with Lyophilized Berries. Nutr Cancer. 2006. 54(1):33-46.

26. Cancer Chemoprevention by Carotenoids. Molecules. Mar 14, 2012. 17(3):3202-42.

    Carotenoids in Cancer. Chemoprevention. Cancer Metastasis Rev. 2002. 21(3-4):257-64.

27. Inhibitory Effects of Feeding with Carrots or (-)-Falcarinol on Development of Azoxymethane-Induced Preneoplastic Lesions in the Rat Colon. J Agric Food Chem. Mar 2005. 9;53(5):1823-7.

28. Inhibitory Effect of Caffeic Acid on Cancer Cell Proliferation by Oxidative Mechanism in Human HT-1080 Fibrosarcoma Cell Line. Mol Cell Biochem. Mar 2011. 349(1-2):11-9.

29. Onion & Garlic Use & Human Cancer. Am J Clin Nutr. 2006 Nov;84(5):1027-32.

30. Fresh Garlic Extract Induces Growth Arrest of MCF7 Breast Cancer Cells. Genes Cancer. Feb 2012. 3(2): 177-86.

31. Anticancer Effects of Garlic & Garlic-Derived Compounds for Breast Cancer Control. Anticancer Agents Med Chem. Mar 2011. 11(3):249-53.

32. Vegetables, Fruit, & Colon Cancer in the Iowa Women's Health Study. Am J Epidemiol. Jan 1994. 1;139(1):1-15.

33. Garlic & Its Significance for the Prevention of Cancer in Humans. Br J Cancer. Mar 1993. 67(3): 424–429.

34. Mechanisms of Inhibition of Chemical Toxicity & Carcinogenesis by Diallyl Sulfide (DAS) & Related Compounds from Garlic. J Nutr. Mar 2001. 131(3s): 1041S-5S.

35. I3C Inhibits the Expression of Cyclin-Dependent Kinase-6 & Induces a G1 Cell Cycle Arrest of Human Breast Cancer Cells. J Biol Chem. 1998 Feb 13;273(7): 3838-47.

36. I3C & Diindolylmethane as Aryl Hydrocarbon (Ah) Receptor Agonists & Antagonists in T47D Human Breast Cancer Cells. Biochem Pharmacol. Apr 1996. 26;51(8):1069-76.

37. Reduction of Oxidative DNA-Damage in Humans by Brussels Sprouts. Carcinogenesis. Apr 1995. 16(4):969-70.

38. Epidemiological Studies on Brassica Vegetables & Cancer Risk. Cancer Epidemiol Biomarkers Prev. Sept 1996. 5(9):733-48.

39. Discovery May Help Scientists Boost Broccoli's Cancer-Fghting Power. Univ. of Illinois. Food & Function (Vol. 1, pp. 162-167).

40. What's in Your green tea? NY Times. May 23, 2013.

41. Green Tea Extract Appears to Keep Cancer in Check in Majority of CLL Blood Cancer Patients. Mayo Clinic. Jun 4, 2010.

42. Green Tea Compounds in Breast Cancer Prevention & Treatment in Humans & Animal Cancers. World J Clin Oncol. Aug 10, 2014; 5(3): 520–528.

43. Chemoprevention of Oral Cancers by Green Tea. Gen Dent. Mar/Apr 2002. 50(2):140-6.

44. Green Tea Inhibits Vascular Endothelial Growth Factor (VEGF) Induction in Human Breast Cancer Cells. J Nutr. Aug 2002. 132(8):2307-11.

45. Urinary Tea Polyphenols in Relation to Gastric & Esophageal Cancers. Carcinogenesis. Sep 2002. 23(9):1497-503.

46. Improved Prognosis of Postoperative Hepatocellular Carcinoma Patients when Treated with Functional Foods. J Hepatol. 2002 Jul;37(1):78-86.

47. An Evidence-Based Review of a Lentinula Edodes Mushroom Extract as Complementary Therapy in the Surgical Oncology Patient. JPEN J Parenter Enteral Nutr. Jul 2011. 35(4):449-58.

48. Immunomodulatory & Anticancer Effects of Active HemiCellulose Compound (AHCC). Int'l Journal of Immunotherapy XI. (1) 23-28. 1995.

49. In vitro Cytostatic & Immunomodulatory Properties of the Medicinal Mushroom Lentinula edodes. Phytomedicine. Jun 2008. 15(6-7):512-9.

50. Induction of Apoptosis in Human Prostatic Cancer Cells with Beta-glucan (Maitake Mushroom Polysaccharide). Mol Urol. Spring 2000. 4(1):7-13.

51. Ganoderma Lucidum (Reishi) in Cancer Treatment. Integr Cancer Ther. Dec 2003. 2(4):358-64.

52. Medicinal Uses of the Mushroom Cordyceps Militaris. Fitoterapia. Dec 2010. 81(8):961-8.

53. Anti-Aromatase Activity of Phytochemicals in White Button Mushrooms. Cancer Res. Dec 15, 2006;66(24): 12026-34.

54. Oral Ingestion of Shiitake Mushroom Extract Inhibits B16 Melanoma Growth via Mitigation of Regulatory T Cell-Mediated Immunosuppression. Cancer Sci. Mar 2011. 102(3):516-21.

55. Enhancement of in vitro / in vivo Anticancer Activities of Polysaccharide Peptide from Grifola Frondosa by Chemical Modifications. Pharm Biol. Nov 2011. 49(11):1114-20.

56. Immunization of Fucose-Containing Polysaccharides from Reishi mushroom Induces Antibodies to Tumor-associated Globo H-series Epitopes. Proc Natl Acad Sci USA. Aug 20, 2013. 10(34):13809-14.

57. A Phase I/II Trial of a Polysaccharide Extract from Grifola Frondosa (Maitake Mushroom) in Breast Cancer Patients: Immunological Effects. J Cancer Res Clin Oncol. Sep 2009. 135(9):1215-21.

58. Effect of Various Natural Products on Growth of Bladder Cancer Cells: Two Promising Mushroom Extracts. Altern Med Rev. Mar 2007. 12(1):63-8.

59. Clinical Application of a Combination Therapy of Lentinan, Multi-electrode RFA & TACE in HCC. Adv Ther. Aug 2008. 25(8):787-94.

60. Targeting Cancer Stem Cells by Curcumin & Cinical Applications. Cancer Lett. May 1, 2014. 346(2):197-205.

61. Curcumin Inhibits Prostate Cancer Metastasis in vivo by Targeting the Inflammatory Cytokines CXCL1 & -2. Carcinogenesis. Dec 2012. 33(12):2507-19.

62. Curcumin Inhibits Breast Cancer Stem Cell Migration by Amplifying the E-cadherin/ß-catenin Negative Feedback Loop. Stem Cell Res Ther. Oct 14, 2014. 5(5):116.

63. The Role of Cancer Stem Cells in the Anti-Carcinogenicity of Curcumin. Mol Nutr Food Res. Sep 2013. 57(9):1630-7.

64. Anti-Carcinogenic Properties of Curcumin on Colorectal Cancer. World J Gastrointest Oncol. Apr 15, 2010. 2(4): 169–176.

65. Curcumin Down-Regulates Ets-1 & Bcl-2 Expression in Human Endometrial Carcinoma HEC-1-A Cells. Gynecol Oncol. Sep 2007. 106(3):541-8. Epub 2007 Jun 27.

66. Aromatase Inhibitor Letrozole in Synergy with Curcumin in the Inhibition of Xenografted Endometrial Carcinoma Growth. Int J Gynecol Cancer. Oct 2009. 19(7):1248-52.

67. Inhibitory Effect of Curcumin on Uterine Leiomyoma Cell Proliferation. Gynecol Endocrinol. Jul 2011. 27(7): 512-7.

68. Origanum Vulgare Induces Apoptosis in Human Colon Cancer Caco2 Cells. Nutr Cancer. 2009. 61(3):381-9.

69. Anti-Proliferative Effects of Carvacrol on Human Prostate Cancer Cell Line, LNCaP. The FASEB Journal. 2012. 26:1037.5.

70. Carnasol in Oregano: A Promising Anticancer & Anti-Inflammatory Agent. Cancer Lett. Jun 1, 2011. 305(1):1-7.

71. Effects of Ginger Supplementation on Cell-Cycle Biomarkers in the Normal-Appearing Colonic Mucosa of Patients at Increased Risk for Colorectal Cancer. Cancer Prev Res (Phila). Apr 2013. 6(4):271-81.

72. Protein & Ginger for the Treatment of Chemotherapy-Induced Delayed Nausea. J Altern Complement Med. Jun 2008. 14(5):545-51.

73. Anti-Emetic Effect of Ginger Powder as an Add-on Therapy in Those Receiving High Emetogenic Chemotherapy. Pediatr Blood Cancer. Feb 2011. 56(2): 234-8.

74. Ginger Reduces Acute Chemotherapy-Induced Nausea. Support Care Cancer. Jul 2012. 20(7):1479-89.

75. Ginger (Zingiber Officinale) & Chemotherapy-Induced Nausea & Vomiting: A Systematic Literature Review. Nutr Rev. Apr 2013. 71(4):245-54.

76. Cancer Preventive Properties of Ginger: A Brief Review. Food Chem Toxicol. May 2007. 45(5):683-90.

77. Chemopreventive Efficacy of Ginger, a Naturally Occurring Anticarcinogen during the Initiation, Post-Initiation Stages of 1,2 Dimethylhydrazine-Induced Colon Cancer. Clin Chim Acta. Aug 2005. 358(1-2):60-7.

78. Benefits of Whole Ginger Extract in Prostate Cancer. Br J Nutr. Feb 2012. 107(4):473-84.

79. Antimicrobial Activity of Essential Oils from Plants against Selected Pathogenic & Saprophytic Microorganisms. J Food Prot. Jul 2001. Vol. 64, No. 7, pp. 1019-1024.

80. Anti-Proliferative Effects of Carvacrol on a Human Metastatic Breast Cancer Cell Line, MDA-MB 231. Phytomedicine. 2010 Jul;17(8-9):581-8.

81. Antimicrobial Agents from Plants: Antibacterial Activity of Plant Volatile Oils. J Appl Microbiol. 2000 Feb;88(2):308-16.

82. Oregano Oil May Protect against Drug-Resistant Bacteria. Science Daily. Oct 11, 2001.

83. Glutathione & Morbidity in a Community-Based Sample of Elderly. J Clin Epidemiol. Sep 1994. 47(9):1021-6.

Nature's Healing Grasses, by author H. E. Kirschner, M.D.

SUPPLEMENTS

Using Supplements

1. Lead Content of Calcium Supplements. JAMA. 2000. 284(11):1425-1429.

2. Lead Content in 70 Brands of Dietary Calcium Supplements. Am J Public Health. Aug 1993. 83(8):1155-60.

3. Lead, Mercury, & Arsenic in US & Indian Manufactured Ayurvedic Medicines Sold on the Internet. JAMA. 2008. 300(8):915-923.

Danger of Synthetic Supplements

1. Folate Intake, Alcohol Use, & Postmenopausal Breast Cancer Risk in Cancer Screening Trial. Am J Clin Nutr. Apr 2006. Vol. 83, No. 4:895-904.

2. Folic Acid & Risk of Prostate Cancer. J Natl Cancer Inst. Mar 18, 2009. 101(6):432-5.

3. Effect of Supplemental Folic Acid in Pregnancy on Childhood Asthma. Am J Epidemiol. Dec 15, 2009. 170(12):1486-93.

4. Folic Acid Supplements in Pregnancy & Early Childhood Respiratory Health. Arch Dis Child. Mar 2009. 94(3): 180-4.

5. Excessive Dietary Intake of Vitamin A Associated with Reduced Bone Mineral Density & Increased Risk of Hip Fracture. Ann Intern Med. Nov 15, 1998. 129(10):770-8.

6. Beta-Carotene, Carotenoids, & Disease Prevention in Humans. FASEB. 1996. 10(7):690-701.

   Prevention of Lung Cancer. Current Opinion in Oncology. 1998;10(2):122-126.

7. Studies Find Beta-Carotene Cannot Forestall Cancer or Heart Disease. New York Times, Jan 19, 1996.

8. Effects of a Combination of Beta-carotene & Vitamin A on Lung Cancer & Heart Disease. N Engl J Med. May 2, 1996. 334:1150-1155.

9. Antioxidant Supplements for Prevention of Mortality in Healthy Participants & Patients with Various Diseases. Cochrane Database Syst Rev. Apr 16, 2008. (2): CD007176.

10. National Cancer Institute.

11. Unpasteurized Milk: Health or Hazard. Clinical & Experimental Allergy. May 2007. 35(5) 627-630.

12. Breast & Artificial Feeding: Influence on Morbidity & Mortality of 20,000 Infants. JAMA. 1934. 02750360011006.

13. Nutrition & Sports Supplements: Fact or Fiction. J Clin Gastroenterol. Oct 2002. 35(4):299-306.

14. Cooking-Induced Protein Modifications in Meat. Comprehensive Reviews in Food Science and Food Safety. Nov 24, 2016. Vol 16, Issue 1.

15. Effect of Cooking on Meat Proteins. J. Agric. Food Chem. 2014, 62 (32), pp 8187–8196.

Vitamin D

1. Importance of Vitamin D in Preventing Cancer, Type 1 Diabetes, Heart Disease, & Osteoporosis. Am J Clin Nutr. May 2004. 79(5):890.

2. Melanoma Epidemic: A Midsummer Night's Dream? Br J Dermatol. Sep 2009. 161(3):630-4.

3. Is There More Than One Road to Melanoma? Lancet. Feb 8, 2004. 363(9410):728-30.

4. Vaccines for Preventing Influenza in the Elderly. Cochrane Database of Systematic Reviews, 2006.

5. Vaccines for Preventing Influenza in Healthy Adults. Cochrane Database of Systematic Reviews, 2010.

6. Vaccines for Preventing Influenza in Healthy Children. Cochrane Database of Systematic Reviews, 2008.

7. American Thoracic Society's 105th Int'l Conference. May 2009. San Diego, CA.

8. Vitamin D Supplementation to Prevent Type A Influenza. Am J Clin Nutr. May 2010. 91(5):1255-60.

9. The Trouble with Chemical Sunscreens, Environmental Working Group.

10. The case against Vitamin D_2 as a supplement. Am J Clin Nutr. 2006 Oct;84(4):694-7.

11. Effect of Calcium Supplements on Risk of Myocardial Infarction & Cardiovascular Events. BMJ 2010; 341: c3691.

12. Randomised Controlled Trial of Effect of Raw & Holder Pasteurized Human Milk & of Formula Supplements on Incidence of Neonatal Infection. Lancet. Nov 17, 1984. 2(8412):1111-3.

Vitamin B_{12}

1. The 80-10-10 Diet, by author Douglas Graham, MD.

2. Vitamin B_{12} Studies in Total Vegetarians (Vegans). J Nutr Environ Med. 4(4):419-430. Jan 1994. Vol. 4, No. 4:419-430.

3. Conscious Eating, by author Gabriel Cousens, MD.

4. Guyton's & Hall's Textbook of Medical Physiology, by authors AC Guyton & JE Hall.

5. Vitamin B_{12} Synthesis by Human Small Intestinal Bacteria. Nature. Feb 21, 1980. 283:781-2.

6. Vitamin B_{12}: Are You Getting It? by author Jack Norris.

7. Neuroenhancement with Vitamin B_{12} - Underestimated Neurological Significance. Nutrients. Dec 2013. 5(12): 5031–5045.

Dr. Joel Fuhrman, MD.

Vitamin B_{12} warning: Avoid Cyanocobalamin, Take Only Methylcobalamin. Mike Adams, Natural News.

Probiotics

1. Anaphylaxis from Inulin in Vegetables & Processed Food. N Engl J Med. May 4, 2000. 342:1372.

2. Live & Ultraviolet-Inactivated Lactobacillus Rhamnosus GG Decrease Flagellin-Induced Interleukin-8 Production in Caco-2 Cells J. Nutr. Nov 2008. Vol. 138 no. 11 2264-2268.

3. Probiotics Grow in Popularity but Don't Always Deliver on Promises. ConsumerLab.com.

Essential Oils

1. 6th Edition Essential Oils Desk Reference, Life Science Publishing.

2. Essential Oils Integrative Medicine Guide, by author D. Gary Young, ND.

3. Antimicrobial Activity of Essential Oils Against Helicobacter Pylori. Helicobacter. Jun 200. 8(3):207-15.

4. Inhalation of Odorants for Weight Reduction. Int J Obes. 1994. pg. 306.

5. Dr. Hirsch's Guide to Scensational Sex, by author Dr. Alan R. Hirsch, MD, FACP.

Anticancer Activities of Essential Oils Constituents & Synergy with Conventional Therapies. Phytother. Res. 05/2014; DOI: 10.1002/ptr.5165.

Inhibition of Rat Mammary Carcinogenesis by Monoterpenoids. Carcinogenesis. 1989 Nov;10(11):2161-4.

Essential Oils in Cancer Research. Nicole Stevens, UNLV Cancer Research Institute.

MOVEMENT

Getting a Move on

1. Implications for the Role of Acid-Base Imbalance in the Genesis of Osteoporosis. J Bone Miner Res. 1995 Oct;10(10):1431-6.
2. Intake of Fruit and Vegetables: Implications for Bone Health. Proc Nutr Soc. 2003 Nov;62(4):889-99.
3. The Effects of Metabolic Acidosis on Bone Formation & Bone Resorption in the Rat. Kidney Int. 1986 Nov; 30(5):694-700.
4. Worldwide Incidence of Hip Fracture in Elderly Women: Relation to Consumption of Animal & Vegetable Foods. J Gerontol A Biol Sci Med Sci. 2000 Oct;55(10):M585-92.

HEALTHY HOME

Cookware & Food Prep Utensils

1. Melamine in Tableware, Q&A: Federal Drug Administration (FDA). Jun 20, 2014.
2. Environmental Working Group (EWG).
3. Environmental Working Group (EWG).

Danger of Household Chemicals

1. The Best Way to Sanitize Kitchen Sponges. EMSL Analytical Testing Lab / Good Housekeeping.
2. Environmental Working Group (EWG).

Germs: An Unhealthy Phobia

1. Consumer Antibacterial Soaps: Effective or Just Risky? Clin Infect Dis. Sep 1, 2007. 45 Suppl 2:S137-47.

Allergies & Childhood Illnesses - An Epidemic

1. Genetically Modified & Wild Soybeans: An Immunologic Comparison.
2. Vaccine Injury.
3. A Look Inside the Immmunization Dilemma. Long Island Press.
4. Cancer, Simian Virus 40 (SV40) & Polio Vaccine. CDC Factsheet.
5. Influenza Vaccine Effectiveness: How Well Does the Flu Vaccine Work? CDC. Dec 21, 2015.

VacTruth.com.

National Vaccine Information Center.

The Natural, Non-Toxic Cleaning Cabinet

1. The Best Way to Sanitize Kitchen Sponges. EMSL Analytical Testing Lab / Good Housekeeping.

Freshen Up the Air

1. Health Risks of Second Hand Smoke. American Cancer Society. Nov 13, 2015.

Health Benefits of Houseplants

1. Antioxidant Activity & Phenolic Compounds in Selected Herbs. J. Agric. Food Chem. 2001. 49 (11): 5165–5170.
2. Antimicrobial Activities of Commercial Essential Oils & Their Components against Food-Borne Pathogens & Food Spoilage Bacteria. Food Sci Nutr. Jul 2014; 2(4): 403–416.

The Secret Life of Plants, by authors Peter Tompkins & Christopher Bird.

Healing with Whole Foods, by author Dr. Paul Pitchford.

Plant Intelligence & the Imaginal Realm, by author Stephen Harrod Buhner.

Making Natural & Safe Choices

1. Cosmetic testing fact sheet. The Humane Society.

Made in the USA
San Bernardino, CA
17 April 2018